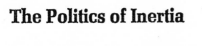

The Politics of Inertia

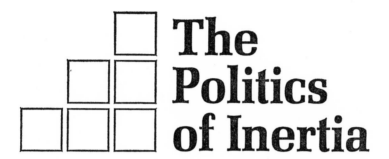

The Politics of Inertia

The Election of 1876 and the End of Reconstruction

KEITH IAN POLAKOFF

Louisiana State University Press
BATON ROUGE

ISBN 0–8071–0210–5
Library of Congress Catalog Card Number 72–96400
Copyright © 1973 by Louisiana State University Press
All rights reserved
Manufactured in the United States of America
Printed by The TJM Corporation, Baton Rouge, Louisiana
Designed by Dwight Agner

For
CAROL

Contents

Preface

WHEN I first read C. Vann Woodward's fascinating account of the disputed presidential election of 1876, *Reunion and Reaction*, I remember wondering what Samuel J. Tilden and his fellow northern Democrats were doing while their erstwhile southern allies were helping the Republicans steal the election. That was during my undergraduate days, more than a decade ago. I never imagined at the time that I might someday try to answer that question myself.

Woodward, of course, had no reason to answer it. He was principally interested in the origins of the "New South" and in the political policies adopted by that section's leaders in pursuit of the goal of economic development after Reconstruction. When he unearthed evidence of previously undisclosed negotiations between certain southern Democrats and sundry friends of Hayes, and discovered, moreover, that such clearly economic objectives as a federal subsidy for the Texas and Pacific Railroad were involved in the bargaining, he was in no way surprised. These discoveries fitted in perfectly with his larger theme, and they explained the peaceful resolution of the electoral crisis quite persuasively.[1] Woodward's narrative in *Re-*

1. For Woodward's explanation of how he came across this material, see his note on sources in *Reunion and Reaction: The Compromise of 1877 and the End of Reconstruction* (Boston: Little, Brown and Company, 1951), 247. His principal acknowledgment (p. v) is to Charles A. Beard for developing the concept of the Civil War and Reconstruction as a "Second American Revolution."

union and Reaction, accordingly, revolves almost exclusively around the secret deal by which southern Democrats of "Old Whig" antecedents assented to the seating of Rutherford B. Hayes in return for various political and economic concessions to be granted their section by the new administration.

Writing in 1950, Woodward assumed a degree of central direction in the national political parties that subsequent scholarship has shown to have been largely nonexistent. Thus, Woodward took for granted the Republican view that Tilden controlled the actions of most Democrats, accepted the statements of H. V. Boynton that Tom Scott of the Texas and Pacific could deliver innumerable congressional votes, and never doubted that the abandonment of the House filibuster was the product of a secret transaction.

It is the thesis of this book that, quite the contrary, the very inability of party leaders to control their own organizations, even in a crisis demanding centralized direction, assured a pacific, if blundering, solution to the electoral dispute. The extraordinarily decentralized structure of both major parties must be shown, of course. The initial five chapters of the narrative to follow are devoted, first, to a careful unraveling of the events leading to the nominations of Hayes and Tilden, and then to an equally detailed re-creation of the presidential campaigns.

Strictly speaking, the major parties in the nineteenth century had no national leaders. There were Democratic and Republican mayors, state legislators, congressmen, governors, and senators. Some of these men were well known to voters beyond their immediate constituencies, but public office and a degree of popularity rarely translated into effective power. The president exercised a certain limited authority over the administration of the federal government, but only at the price of losing most of his former influence in his home state. Leaders of both parties worked diligently to remain abreast of the slightest shifts in the public mood, especially in their own states and districts; yet seldom did they try to alter that mood. In fact, the small degree of political security that they possessed derived from the certainty that their opponents would be equally cautious.

Eventually, an ambitious and popular state politician inevitably became interested in national office; but the road to that goal was incredibly tortuous. The selection of delegates to the national nominating conventions began with primary elections and district meetings at the township or ward level. And there were literally thousands of townships. Moreover, "bosses" were generally unable to influence this process except at the most parochial level. The greatest strength of the party system was its ability to represent accurately the remarkable diversity and diffuseness of the American electorate. In a country so large, finding an issue which would appeal to a broad cross section of the party's voters or officeholders was a formidable task, one rarely undertaken successfully. As a result, nominations did not seem to be planned; rather they just happened. The eventual winner was generally noted more for his lack of enemies than for his possession of friends. His stature as a leader of men had yet to be established.

Likewise, the work of campaign management was prosaic in nature, haphazardly conducted, and best performed at the local level: the canvassing of voters, the scheduling of speakers, the distribution of literature. Funds came principally from the candidates and their personal friends.[2] Against such a background, it would be unrealistic to expect effective or decisive leadership in the electoral crisis.

In truth, the electoral dispute was a story of confusion and inefficiency, in which the leaders of the two parties were about equally unable to control the activities of lesser politicians in their own ranks. Paradoxically, Hayes's willingness to delegate to friends power he really did not possess worked to his benefit, for it reflected the actual fragmentation of power in his party and thereby helped to hold it together. The failure of the more able but uncommunicative Tilden to share authority in the same way proved to be a handicap, for it made other Democratic leaders aware of the existing power vacuum.

2. This analysis of party organization is confirmed by Robert D. Marcus, *Grand Old Party: Political Structure in the Gilded Age, 1880–1896* (New York: Oxford University Press, 1971).

Tilden was warned early in December that he might be betrayed by disgruntled southern members of his own party; yet he made no effort to strengthen his ties with these important leaders or even to inform them of his plans for guiding the Democratic party to victory in the electoral dispute. Moreover, this strangely reticent man seemed to treat even his personal advisers in the same abrupt manner. Knowing that most Democrats considered him the president-elect, he apparently expected them to follow his lead unhesitatingly. There was no need for time-consuming consultations, which might well lead to damaging misunderstandings or leaks of information. Little wonder that the management of the party failed pathetically in moments of crisis.

Equally important, on the day the electoral commission, which had been created to arbitrate the dispute, rendered its decision in the Florida case, thus giving the first positive indication of how the electoral crisis would be resolved, Tilden and John Bigelow, his closest friend, began planning a lengthy tour of Europe for 1877. Privately at least, they accepted the imminence of defeat and were plotting no extra-legal remedies—Republican assertions to the contrary notwithstanding.

Under these conditions, Scott, Boynton, Kellar, Matthews, and the other figures in Woodward's "Compromise of 1877" appeared to determine the outcome of the dispute because the objectives of their devious negotiations largely coincided with the results the blind force of inertia was already bringing about in the absence of effective leadership.

It should be emphasized at the outset that the main purpose of this book is not to refute Professor Woodward's work. After all, the negotiations he described did take place. The principal question at issue is whether those negotiations settled the electoral dispute. Our differences in interpreting the political events of the tense winter of 1876–1877 should serve as an interesting example of the fundamental way in which perspective sometimes influences historical perception. Woodward was concerned with the economic policies of the South's political leaders.

I am interested in the configuration of power in nineteenth-century political parties.

Historians generally work alone, but that does not mean they work unassisted. I owe a particular debt of gratitude to Grady McWhiney of Wayne State University and Robert H. Wiebe of Northwestern University. It was in Professor McWhiney's seminar, when he was at Northwestern, that I first began investigating Tilden's role in the electoral dispute. Professor Wiebe supervised my doctoral dissertation on Democratic party organization in the 1870s. He also read the first draft of the present manuscript in its entirety and provided counsel, both copious and wise, for its improvement. His professional judgment is rarely off the mark. In addition, my colleague, Professor Albie Burke, not only helped shape my thinking about Reconstruction, but permitted me to borrow extensively from his recently completed study of the remarkable John I. Davenport and the Federal Elections Law of 1871. Professors Jaime E. Rodríguez O., William F. Sater, and Irving F. Ahlquist of California State University, Long Beach, Professor Robert D. Marcus of the State University of New York, Stony Brook, and Linda Alexander Rodríguez all read the manuscript in whole or in part and offered many valuable suggestions. Professor Marcus deserves credit for the title. William V. Miller, a graduate student at California State University, Long Beach, typed the first draft of the manuscript with a critical eye for minor flaws I would never have noticed. I gladly accept sole responsibility for whatever inadequacies or inconsistencies remain.

Historical research is fascinating work under any circumstances. It is even more enjoyable when assisted by capable and cooperative librarians. I must include a special word of thanks, therefore, to Watt P. Marchman, director, Ruth E. Ballenger, manuscripts librarian, and Rose N. Sberna, assistant librarian, of the Rutherford B. Hayes Library in Fremont, Ohio; and to the staffs of the Manuscript Division, Library of Congress, and the Henry E. Huntington Library and Art Gallery, San Marino,

California. Work on this project was aided materially by grants from the Inland Steel-Ryerson Foundation and the Long Beach California State University Foundation.

Finally, my wife Carol was my frequent traveling companion through many eastern and midwestern states, reading dusty books and letters, taking notes, and buoying my spirits when the going occasionally got rough. Without her help this book would never have come about.

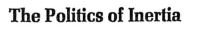

The Politics of Inertia

Chapter I □ The Shrine of Party

I NOW DECLARE the International Exhibition of 1876 closed." With this nine-word speech, delivered on a rainy afternoon in Philadelphia, President Grant brought the official celebration of the first century of American self-government to an end. The date was November 10.[1] An election had been held three days before to select Grant's successor. Though the president appeared unperturbed, the results of that contest were not yet certain, nor would they be for many weeks to come. On the centennial of the nation's independence, the excessive partisanship of the Reconstruction era threatened to destroy the democratic political system that had been for so long the basis of the average American's sense of his country's historic purpose in the world.

The politics of the Republic had always been characterized by a degree of personal invective which would be unthinkable in the twentieth century. The intensity of traditional party rivalries became still more bitter as a result of the Civil War. For years thereafter, Republicans experienced the greatest difficulty in overcoming their suspicion that every Democrat was tainted with treason at worst, Copperheadism at best. Why else would a man oppose the party of Lincoln and the Union? In the Democratic party, by contrast, there was growing fear that the at-

1. Dee Brown, *The Year of the Century: 1876* (New York: Charles Scribner's Sons, 1966), 288–90.

tempt to remake the Confederacy in what Republicans believed to be the image of the North, however laudable in principle, was in practice a scheme designed to keep the party of Lincoln and the Union in power forever. How else should one explain the impeachment of Andrew Johnson only a few months before the end of his term of office, or the stationing of federal troops at the polls in the South? One symptom of this heightened distrust was the frequency with which the leaders of each party referred to their opponents as "the enemy" in their correspondence. Actually, both parties were essentially backward-looking. Republicans continued to glory in the triumphant battles against slavery and disunion, while Democrats yearned nostalgically for the days of Andrew Jackson and the Bank War.

The intemperateness of American politics was even more consequential because electoral activity was an important part of the very social fabric of the nation. Most people lived on farms or in smaller or larger towns. Even the rapidly growing cities tended to break down into distinct neighborhoods, loosely tied together by a few rail or trolley lines. In the words of Robert Wiebe, the urban dweller, like his small-town counterpart, lived in an "island community"; [2] he worked, shopped, went to church, educated his children, and found recreation within walking distance of home. Life was simpler than in our own day, more isolated and less comfortable materially. Membership in a national political party was one way of transcending the seeming insignificance of routine existence in a confining locality. By the same token, to the average voter, casting a ballot, especially in a presidential election, meant more than expressing one's opinion as to which party should run the government; here was a simple act through which one participated in the distinctive greatness of the country. To farmer and urbanite alike, a trip to the polls was a serious and exciting occasion.

Politics, of course, could also be great fun. The forms of recreation available in 1876 were limited. The motion picture,

2. Robert H. Wiebe, *The Search for Order, 1877–1920* (New York: Hill and Wang, 1967), 2–4.

radio and television, and the automobile had not yet been invented, and the telephone, developed in that centennial year, remained a costly urban luxury; so it is not surprising that the political mass meeting was one of the important features in the social life of many people. Mass meetings were more than mere campaign rallies. They were occasions when the rank-and-file members of a political party renewed their sense of solidarity. Men brought their families and relaxed in the company of hundreds or thousands of other men who shared the right principles. The magnitude of these meetings was impressive: "On Thursday, October 26th, 1876, the Democracy of Berks county will have a grand parade in the morning, and after that, a Barbecue of two Buffaloes on the Fair Grounds, in the city of Reading. One hundred young ladies will sing patriotic airs from the Grand Stand." Honored guests from outside the community were met at the railroad depot or their hotel and were accompanied to the banner-bedecked courthouse square or other suitable location. Several hours of flamboyant speechmaking followed. Competition for outstanding speakers was fierce. The reputation of the party dignitaries present at a mass meeting was often instrumental in bolstering the sense of importance a voter felt in himself and his community: "Berks county is the Gibralter [*sic*] of Democracy, in Pennsylvania, and her influence, particularly throughout this section, is potent"—so one invitation assured former presidential candidate Horatio Seymour.[3] After the last address was completed, the typical meeting, which had become an all-day affair, was perhaps closed with a fireworks display. A torchlit procession then conveyed the speakers back to the depot or to their hotel.

Political campaigning in most of the Union was a year-round activity. Nominations for high office were often made several months in advance of the day of election—a heritage of the time when the information took that long to disseminate. Moreover, elections for different offices might occur at widely diverse times.

3. Printed invitation, Henry M. Keim to Horatio Seymour, October 14, 1876, in Horatio Seymour Papers, New York State Library.

County, township, and municipal canvasses were most frequently held in the spring or early summer. Texas chose its
governor in February, New Hampshire in March, Rhode Island
in April, Oregon in June, Kentucky in August, Maine and California in September, Ohio, Indiana, Iowa, Georgia, and West
Virginia in October. The United States Constitution was silent
on the timing of elections, save for its requirement that presidential electors be chosen everywhere on the same day. Congress
had designated the first Tuesday after the first Monday in November. United States senators were not elected popularly, but
by a joint ballot of the two houses of their respective state legislatures. These often exciting contests were generally staged
during the otherwise dreary winter months. Finally, terms of
office tended to be short. New Jersey elected one third of her
senate and her entire house of representatives annually. Several
New England states passed judgment on their gubernatorial
candidates with the same frequency. If, perchance, the people of
one state were momentarily deprived of the spectacle of somebody campaigning for office at home, there was bound to be an
exhilarating struggle in a neighboring state that could be followed closely.

That the public was intensely interested in all this political
activity is indicated by the extent of the newspaper coverage
devoted to mass meetings, conventions, and local elections occurring even in distant parts of the country. The vast majority
of ninetenth-century newspapers, whether daily or weekly, were
bitterly partisan. The New York *Times* and New York *Tribune*,
Cincinnati *Commercial*, *Ohio State Journal*, and Chicago *Tribune* made no pretense of appealing to men of other than Republican sympathies; whereas the New York *World* and Chicago
Times were just as unabashedly Democratic. It was not that
these papers were directly dependent on a political organization
for financial support. Most urban dailies were not. They merely
shared the profound partisanship characteristic of the times,
a partisanship shared, too, by their readers. When, in the wake
of the Grant administration scandals, William Cullen Bryant,

editor of the New York *Evening Post,* inclined to support Democrat Samuel J. Tilden for the presidency, his partner and business manager, Isaac Henderson, firmly overruled him. Four fifths of the paper's advertising revenue came from Republicans.[4] Henderson's concern may not have been misplaced. When the supposedly independent *Nation* objected to the manner in which Rutherford B. Hayes was ultimately declared elected, it lost nearly three thousand subscribers.[5] Most newspapers devoted several full columns of every issue to coverage of routine political affairs, particularly of their own party. The few independent journals differed only in making a somewhat more honest attempt to provide balanced treatment of both parties. These political columns were printed separately from the routine reporting of congressional or state legislative developments and were the more remarkable for appearing in papers totaling only four to eight pages.

The literal nature of the coverage was as striking as the quantity of political news. When a newspaper reported on a nominating convention, it might begin with a few brief paragraphs describing the scene and summarizing the results, but it then inevitably printed a detailed step-by-step account of the proceedings. This "journal" of the day's activity included every parliamentary motion, excerpts from important speeches, and each name proposed for party or state office. The story had the appearance of formal minutes. Dramatic speeches by statesmen of outstanding oratorical ability or national reputation were handled in an equivalent manner—party journals reprinted them in their entirety, often filling all eight columns on a page, occasionally more. Letters to the editor dealt almost exclusively with the relative merits of rival politicians or the dishonesty of the leaders of the other party. During state and national

4. Allan Nevins, *The Evening Post: A Century of Journalism* (New York: Boni and Liveright, 1922), 401–405; A. G. Browne, Jr., to James M. Comly, July 13, 1876, in James M. Comly Papers, Ohio Historical Society Library.

5. George S. Merriam, *The Life and Times of Samuel Bowles* (2 vols.; New York: The Century Company, 1885), II, 303.

campaigns, the more avowedly partisan papers published detailed lists of the forthcoming speaking appointments of the party's notables throughout the local area or perhaps the state.[6] Newspapers had adopted such forms of coverage specifically because they best satisfied their readers' wish to feel closer to the processes of American democracy, the source of the nation's greatness.

Political party organization was itself designed to encourage a high degree of popular participation. Everything was radically decentralized. When the national chairmen issued the official calls for the Democratic and Republican national conventions, they set into motion extraordinarily cumbersome procedures. Theoretically, every voter could take part. Augustus Schell specified in 1876: "Democratic, Conservative and other citizens of the United States, irrespective of past political associations, desiring to co-operate with the Democratic party in its present efforts and objects, are cordially invited to join in sending delegates to the National Convention." [7] Edwin D. Morgan's announcement recommended that "the committees of the several states . . . invite all Republican electors, and all other voters, without regard to past political differences or previous party affiliations," who supported the principles of the Republican party, to join in the election of delegates.[8] The state central committees then issued their convention calls. In New York the Republicans simply adopted Morgan's language: "All Republican electors and all other voters, without regard to past political differences or previous party difficulties," who believed in the

6. See, for example, the New York *Times*, September and October, 1876.

7. *Official Proceedings of the National Democratic Convention, Held in St. Louis, Mo., June 27th, 28th and 29th, 1876. With an Appendix Containing the Letters of Acceptance of Gov. Tilden and Gov. Hendricks* (St. Louis: Woodward, Tiernan and Hale, 1876), 15; New York *World*, February 24, 1876.

8. *Proceedings of the Republican National Convention, Held at Cincinnati, Ohio, Wednesday, Thursday, and Friday, June 14, 15, and 16, 1876, Resulting in the Nomination for President and Vice-President of Rutherford B. Hayes and William A. Wheeler* (Concord, N.H.: Republican Press Association, 1876), 3.

principles of the Republican party, were "cordially invited to meet in their respective localities at the call of the appropriate local committees, and participate in the election of delegates to the said State Convention." [9] When the necessary invitations had all been published, the flow reversed and the machinery worked from the lowest levels back toward the top. Primary meetings were held in townships in the countryside, in wards, or occasionally even in election districts in the cities, where the voters of each party gathered to elect delegates to county conventions. Each political subdivision was commonly entitled to one delegate for each twenty-five party votes at the last general election. The county conventions chose delegates to the state conventions, and the state conventions—remarkable assemblages of three hundred to a thousand men, which might be equivalent to one representative for every one hundred or so party voters—selected the delegates to the national conventions. The same machinery, it should be noted, was used to nominate congressional, gubernatorial, state legislative, and local candidates.

The system itself was completely democratic, or, to be perfectly precise, republican. How well it worked in practice, of course, depended on the degree of popular participation achieved. In many urban areas, crowded with tens of thousands of immigrants unfamiliar with American political procedures, unable to converse in English, or too poor to take time to attend the primaries, these processes were breaking down under the strain of the wide variety of abuses associated with machine rule. In the towns and rural areas, however, and in the wealthier areas of the cities, the convention system was a vital part of political life. In most states elaborate precautions were taken to keep the exercise of power as close to the people as possible. In both parties, for example, each state was entitled to two national convention delegates for each senator and representative in Congress, yet the full state convention generally balloted for

9. New York *World*, February 23, 1876.

only four delegates at large—two for each senator. The convention then resolved itself into a series of congressional district caucuses, with each caucus to select two delegates. The caucuses also designated the members of the next state central committee. In this way every voter was guaranteed a theoretically equal voice in the management of the party. The system did not always work well, but at its best it was as democratic as anything that has been devised since.[10] It was also practical, for at each level on which a nomination for office was made, the appropriate committee to supervise the campaign was simultaneously created.[11]

The decentralized system for selecting political candidates reflected a widespread enthusiasm for participating directly in the governance of the country. As such, it was a sign of health; but it was a creation of the parties themselves and not of national, state, or local laws. The next step in the political process, the holding of elections, was also governed far more by custom than by law. In an era of intense partisanship that situation was most unhealthy, as the fateful year 1876 clearly demonstrated.

Local agencies of government provided only the barest essentials for the conduct of elections: ballot boxes, designated polling places, and officials to keep an eye on voters and tally results. The election officials were generally appointees of the sheriff—a local party leader who might himself be a candidate for another term or office. Requiring the presence of bipartisan election judges was not a common practice until the mid-eighties. Registration laws, seemingly an obvious necessity for a fair vote, were also not widely adopted until after the Civil War. Small-town and rural voters knew each other by sight and were certain they needed no such contrivances, although they displayed no comparable aversion when it came to imposing such

10. Frederick W. Dallinger, *Nominations for Elective Office in the United States*, Harvard Historical Studies, IV (Cambridge: Harvard University Press, 1897), 51–126.

11. James Staton Chase, "Jacksonian Democracy and the Rise of the Nominating Convention," *Mid-America*, VL (October, 1963), 236–37.

safeguards on the anonymous masses of the great cities. Thus, the registration law in Pennsylvania originated as a gift bestowed on Philadelphia by the rurally dominated state legislature.[12] In 1876 Indiana still lacked any provision for the registration of voters prior to an election. Proof of residence alone was required.[13]

State laws invariably specified that votes be written out on paper, but invariably that was all they specified. A voter, if he chose to do so, could record, in the comfort and leisure of his own home, a complete list of candidates he preferred and then merely walk to his polling place to deposit the list in the box. The political parties, of course, were prepared to save the public from such laborious procedures. Several days before the election they printed and began distributing in each election district tickets with the names of all their candidates. The vast majority of all voters cast these printed tickets, designed to facilitate straight party voting. To split his ballot, a voter had to "scratch" the objectionable candidates off the printed slip and write or paste in the names he preferred. Few people were so inclined, however. In Indiana and Ohio, for example, the shift in party strength from an October state election to a November presidential contest was seldom more than 1 or 2 percent. The party emblems prominently displayed on printed tickets provided convenient assistance to illiterate voters in making the "correct" choice. Party ballots also came in a wide variety of sizes and colors, but these distinctions were designed to aid precinct captains rather than the electorate. The preferences of most voters, as a result, were no more secret than in the early days of the Republic when elections were conducted *viva voce*.[14] The state of Massachusetts and the city of Louisville, Kentucky, first intro-

12. Albie Burke, "Federal Regulation of Congressional Elections in Northern Cities, 1871–1894" (Ph.D. dissertation, University of Chicago, 1968), 31–32.

13. O. P. Morton to R. B. Hayes, October 17, 1876, in Rutherford B. Hayes Papers, Rutherford B. Hayes Library, Fremont, Ohio.

14. Frank B. Evans, *Pennsylvania Politics, 1872–1877: A Study in Political Leadership* (Harrisburg: Pennsylvania Historical and Museum Commission, 1966), 6–7.

duced the Australian ballot to America in 1889. This device was nothing more than a uniform ticket, listing the candidates of every party, supplied to each voter at the polling place directly by the government.[15] Only then did voting become a truly private affair.

Intense partisanship was a key ingredient in adding vitality to American life in the nineteenth century. In 1876, the centennial year, it was also the impulse which very nearly destroyed the fragile machinery of the country's democratic political system. But that is a story for the succeeding chapters to tell.

15. Burke, "Federal Regulation of Congressional Elections," 26–28.

Chapter II □ The Republican Party, 1876: Rutherford B. Hayes and the Scramble to Succeed

THE REPUBLICAN party is the most successful political organization ever built around a single compelling issue. It was established in the summer of 1854, part of the angry northern reaction to the Kansas-Nebraska Act. That unhappy legislation had been designed by Illinois Democrat Stephen A. Douglas to encourage more rapid settlement of the lands west of Iowa and thus enhance the economic feasibility of Douglas' dream—a transcontinental railroad from Chicago to California. To get his bill through Congress Douglas had to overcome southern opposition; so he agreed to incorporate a provision repealing the old Missouri Compromise line (36° 30'), north of which slavery had been prohibited in the Louisiana Territory, purchased from France in 1803. In Douglas' mind the harsh winds, short growing season, and sparse rainfall of Kansas and Nebraska made the South's peculiar institution impossible there. A vast and growing number of northern voters, however, were unwilling to take that chance.

Uncompromising opposition to the extension of slavery into any lands where it did not already exist was the sentiment that animated the first Republicans. It was an extraordinary issue, capable of bringing together men who disagreed on all other questions and, indeed, men whose views on slavery itself were diametrically opposed. Political abolitionists like Salmon P. Chase resisted the extension of slavery because they considered the institution an unmitigated moral evil and believed that, deprived of the opportunity to expand, it would die everywhere. In other words, containment was the first step toward extinction. On the other hand, western farmers were prepared to countenance reasonable measures to protect slavery in the southern states. But they opposed extension of the institution because they coveted the western territories for themselves and their children and were determined to avoid competition from black labor—slave or free. Similarly, because slavery seemed to pose a direct challenge to the whole northern ideology of free labor, self-help, and social mobility, men who had clashed violently over the advisability of protective tariffs, internal improvements, government subsidies, and banking legislation agreed to submerge those differences in the face of this more immediate threat. The Kansas-Nebraska Act created an atmosphere of impending crisis in the North, an atmosphere which became still more charged with tension as a result of civil war in Kansas and the Dred Scott decision. Within six and a half years of its founding, the Republican party elected its first president.[1]

Thereafter, secession, the Civil War, and Lincoln's assassination necessitated continued unity. Immediately after the war there was a brief period of uncertainty about the course to follow in reconstructing the Union. However, when several of the lately seceded states refused to accept in complete good faith Andrew Johnson's lenient plan of restoration, the Republicans were all but unanimous in imposing a much more stringent set of terms designed to remake the entire electoral system of the South. Purely political considerations were undoubtedly a factor. The three-fifths clause of the Constitution having become a dead letter with the abolition of slavery, the southern states stood to gain thirteen seats in the House of Representatives and thirteen votes in the electoral college. Were the "solid South"

1. Eric Foner, *Free Soil, Free Labor, Free Men: The Ideology of the Republican Party before the Civil War* (New York: Oxford University Press, 1970), *passim.*

to join just two northern states—New York and Indiana—in voting Democratic, the party of Douglas, Buchanan, and Jefferson Davis would recapture the presidency and resume control of the nation's destiny. It was an appalling prospect for any sincere Republican to contemplate; so the party had no choice but to follow the lead of Charles Sumner and Thaddeus Stevens on the questions of Reconstruction.

Yet throughout these years the Republican party concealed a striking diversity behind its apparent unity. Many New England members were horrified at the increased tariffs and cheapened money rammed through Congress in 1862 and 1863, but they grudgingly acquiesced because those measures were vital to the war effort. Similarly, conservatives within the party, who in no way shared the Radicals' concern with equal political rights for Negroes, accepted black suffrage in 1867 and 1869 because the exigencies of the situation seemed to demand it.

Inevitably, the sense of urgency that had so long sustained the party had to subside with the passage of time. By 1876 the divisions within the organization were beginning to show—in fact, they were obvious to everyone. Most Republicans no longer supported Radical Reconstruction. The Republican governments in the South had been weak and sometimes corrupt. Many of them had already passed into history. The wartime tariff and the greenback currency, on the other hand, were still very much in evidence and still a source of extreme discomfort to many eastern Republicans. The Grant administration itself, repeatedly rocked by revelations of corruption in high official places, had become a subject of enduring controversy. All of these tensions within the party were aggravated when a severe economic recession in 1873 brought in its wake a dramatic Democratic victory in the congressional elections a year later. The organization's ability to preserve its ascendancy within the national government was suddenly at stake. The factions that emerged under these unaccustomed circumstances can be traced in the rival candidacies for the party's presidential nomination.

1

The ablest and most popular Republican politician in America was James G. Blaine. At the age of forty-six, Blaine was already a veteran of fourteen years in Congress; during six of these he had served as Speaker of the House. Well-proportioned physically, with a dignified beard and attractive voice, he poured all his strength into powerful and dramatic orations. Though he permitted himself few close friends, he had great charm and can fairly be said to have possessed the closest thing to a charismatic personality in his time. He diligently cultivated an excellent memory for names and faces. His expertise in interpreting election returns was widely recognized. Blaine, who very much wanted to be president, could usually be relied on to steer a middle course in the Republican party on any important issue— the tariff, the currency, civil service reform. He supported black suffrage in 1867 but insisted on the political reconstruction of the southern states rather than their indefinite military occupation. When the popularity of Radical Reconstruction declined, Blaine, as Speaker, helped defeat bills intended to increase federal supervision of congressional elections.

If Blaine had a weakness in early 1876, it was among the southern Radicals who found his moderation on the reconstruction issue unpalatable. He was struggling with this problem when Democrat Samuel J. Randall's Amnesty bill came before the House in January. Randall sought to restore full political rights to those southerners still barred from holding public office by the third section of the Fourteenth Amendment. Blaine, as a member of the Rules Committee, had voted for the identical proposal in 1873. This time, however, he proposed an amendment to exclude Jefferson Davis from the provisions of the bill "on this ground, that he was the author, knowingly, deliberately, guiltily and wilfully, of the gigantic murders and crimes at Andersonville." [2] The long exercise in "waving the bloody shirt" that followed was designed to reassure distrustful southern

2. Quoted in David Saville Muzzey, *James G. Blaine: A Political Idol of Other Days* (New York: Dodd, Mead and Company, 1934), 78.

Radicals, give Blaine center stage in the political arena, and perhaps provoke a thoughtless response from angry southern Democrats, thereby furnishing valuable campaign material. The speech was successful on all counts.[3] Even the militantly Democratic New York *World* was astonished enough to carry the oration in full, spread across five of the six columns on its front page.[4]

Although Blaine was clearly the leading candidate, he was certain to have numerous opponents. As national committee Chairman Edwin D. Morgan pointed out, it was something of a novel situation. The last three national conventions had been "really nothing but ratification meetings of action already determined upon by the people. I refer to Mr. Lincoln's second nomination and to Gen'l Grant's first and second nominations. The people had decided upon the nomination of these gentlemen previous to the assembling of the National Convention in 1864, 1868, & 1872. Now, precisely *that* state of things is to exist no longer." [5]

The Republican organizations in the two most populous states of the Union had favorite sons to offer. Neither man possessed a large popular following, but to their supporters that weakness was a minor concern. Senator Roscoe Conkling of New York and Governor John F. Hartranft of Pennsylvania were products of machine politics, of the spoils system. In the decade and a half following the Civil War, the federal bureaucracy doubled in size, growing from about fifty thousand employees to a hundred thousand. More than half of these civil servants worked for the Post Office Department. All were political appointees.[6] During the years of unbroken Republican ascendancy since 1860, this army of government workers had become practically an integral

3. Robert Granville Caldwell, *James A. Garfield, Party Chieftain* (New York: Dodd, Mead and Company, 1931), 247–49.
4. New York *World*, January 11, 1876.
5. Letterpress copy, E. D. Morgan to T. C. Jones, January 15, 1876, in Edwin D. Morgan Papers, New York State Library.
6. Ari Hoogenboom, *Outlawing the Spoils: A History of the Civil Service Reform Movement, 1865–1883* (Urbana: University of Illinois Press, 1961), 1, 279.

feature of the party. In a few large eastern states they formed virtually a second constituency. In the cities, especially, where attendance at primary meetings had long since drastically declined, and where the municipal officeholders who might otherwise have challenged them were usually Democrats, the sheer weight of their numbers was often sufficient to control the local party machinery. Accordingly, one of the cornerstones of the Conkling machine was laid in overwhelmingly Democratic New York City. The oil that lubricated the machine was the federal patronage. Civil servants who owed their jobs to a state party leader could be relied on to labor diligently when called on to keep that leader in power. And the state politician's influence, in turn, might well depend as much on his ability to command a large share of the intermediate federal appointments in his state as on his success in winning elections.[7] The principal difference between Conkling's candidacy in 1876 and that of Hartranft was that whereas one reflected general satisfaction with Grant's dispensation of jobs, the other was the product of disappointment.

Senator Simon Cameron, the veteran boss of the Republican party in Pennsylvania and the man who had failed so pitifully as Lincoln's first secretary of war, wanted his son appointed to a cabinet position as a reward for his own services in securing Grant's reelection. No Pennsylvanian then served in the cabinet, yet the Camerons were repeatedly snubbed. When the Treasury secretaryship was available in early 1874, the president offered the position first to a Philadelphia banker, Anthony J. Drexel, and then to a Philadelphia industrialist, Joseph Patterson, who was a Democrat, of all things. Drexel and Patterson declined, whereupon the post was given to Benjamin H. Bristow of

---

7. James G. Blaine was not a machine politician in this sense, although he had the support of many federal officeholders outside Pennsylvania and New York. Maine was blessed with no large navy yard, custom house, or post office, and Blaine's influence had more often been used to obtain patronage appointments in the distant western territories and in the District of Columbia than in his home state. These men were in a poor position to aid Blaine in a primary or election campaign. Besides, with his wide popular following, he had little need for the methods of a Conkling or a Simon Cameron.

Kentucky. A month later the postmaster general resigned, and Pennsylvania was bypassed again for Marshall Jewell of Connecticut. Perhaps J. Donald Cameron was a victim of his father's unhappy performance in office. In any event, when the Pennsylvania Republican convention assembled a few weeks later, a resolution endorsing Grant for a third term was overwhelmingly rejected. The convention proposed Governor Hartranft, a loyal member of the Cameron organization, but hardly a figure of commanding national stature, for the presidential nomination— more than two years before the election.

After a couple of additional cabinet changes had once more ignored Don Cameron's claims, the state convention in May, 1875, reiterated that the party was "unalterably opposed to the election to the presidency of any person for a third term." Grant, obviously annoyed, responded with a public letter explaining: "I am not, nor have been, a candidate for a renomination. I would not accept a nomination if it were tendered unless it should come under such circumstances as to make it an imperative duty, circumstances not likely to arise." [8] Grant's language was frustratingly evasive for some people. Even so, the possibility of a third term was remote once the great Whiskey Ring conspiracy was exposed that same month. At the end of the year the House of Representatives laid the question to rest, adopting 233 to 18 a resolution declaring a third term for any president "unwise, unpatriotic and fraught with peril to our free institutions." [9] Even most Republicans preferred not to contemplate such a prospect. Thereafter, the Hartranft candidacy was regarded by most politicians as a device to obtain bargaining leverage for Simon Cameron and his friends.[10]

Roscoe Conkling, in contrast to Cameron and Hartranft, had

8. Frank B. Evans, *Pennsylvania Politics, 1872–1877: A Study in Political Leadership* (Harrisburg: Pennsylvania Historical and Museum Commission, 1966), 247–51.

9. Muzzey, *James G. Blaine*, 75.

10. James G. Blaine, *Twenty Years of Congress: From Lincoln to Garfield. With a Review of the Events Which Led to the Political Revolution of 1860* (2 vols.; Norwich, Conn.: Henry Bill Publishing Company, 1893), II, 568. But see Edw. McP[herson] to Blaine, April 6, 1876, in James G. Blaine Papers, Manuscript Division, Library of Congress.

no objection to Grant as president. Indeed, Conkling became a candidate only when Grant was unavailable for another term. Control of New York's huge block of delegates and the president's personal blessing were expected to be Conkling's sources of strength. The arrogant and ostentatious senator could expect little public support, for he was uncomfortable speaking before large audiences of common men and had never cultivated a wide following. Conkling was a gifted lawyer, yet his contribution to the legislative process was slight. He was best known, and widely feared, as a master of personal invective. Cartoonists delighted in caricaturing his splendid physique, curly red hair, and elegant dress (he often wore white flannel trousers and florid waistcoats). Conkling sometimes gave the impression of being more interested in the operations of his machine than in the affairs of the nation. It is conceivable that his principal motive in seeking the presidency was to stop Blaine, for whom he cherished an abiding hatred. A decade before, during consideration of an army bill of modest importance, a debate on the floor of the House unexpectedly developed into a bitter exchange of personal insults, in the course of which Blaine referred to Conkling's "haughty disdain, his grandiloquent swell, his majestic, supereminent, turkey-gobbler strut." To the end of his life the hypersensitive Conkling neither forgot nor forgave the remark. In 1884, when Blaine finally garnered the Republican presidential nomination, Conkling coldly sat out the campaign. A group of anxious Blaine workers appealed to him, but he replied, "No, thank you, I don't engage in criminal practice." [11]

Also bidding for Grant's support was Senator Oliver P. Morton of Indiana. Morton was the ruthlessly dedicated wartime governor who had responded to Lincoln's call for volunteers in 1861 by supplying more than twice the number of troops Secretary of War Cameron was prepared to accept. When pacifist

---

11. Muzzey, *James G. Blaine*, 60–61; David M. Jordan, *Roscoe Conkling of New York: Voice in the Senate* (Ithaca: Cornell University Press, 1971), 421.

Democrats gained control of the state legislature in 1863 and tried to curtail his powers, the Republican members withdrew in order to prevent a quorum. Unable to transact business, the Democrats adjourned. Since the annual appropriation bills had not yet been passed, the Democrats fully expected Morton to call a special session. Instead the governor met the costs of the state government partly from his own pocket, partly with funds supplied by loyal county officials, and party with money borrowed from wealthy private citizens and the Lincoln administration. After the war he inclined at first toward Andrew Johnson's plan of restoration, but on viewing the resistance that developed in the southern states he became a thoroughgoing Radical, one of the key figures in the adoption of the Fifteenth Amendment, and a master in the art of waving the bloody shirt. Morton was popular with the Republicans of Indiana and was the favorite of the southern Radicals. To eastern liberals, however, his name was anathema because of his views on Reconstruction and his sympathy for western inflationists. His health was also a handicap. During the summer of 1865 Morton had suffered a paralytic stroke which left him permanently crippled, barely able to hobble about with the aid of heavy crutches. Yet his enthusiasm for the rough and tumble of politics remained undiminished.

Undoubtedly, the strangest candidacy in 1876 was that of the secretary of the treasury, Benjamin H. Bristow, who found himself supported by the men least likely to remain loyal to the party. The Republican organization was built, it must be recalled, as an instrument of change. Its leaders presided over the war for the Union, the destruction of slavery, and the reconstruction of the southern states. They had adopted a wide range of economic policies calculated to foster more rapid industrialization. Many of them had exploited to the full the possibility inherent in the rapidly growing federal patronage of building organizations designed to preserve personal place and power. Every Republican had supported the party's initial objectives— the restriction of slavery and the preservation of the Union; but once these crises had been successfully resolved, many dedicated

Republicans became restive as their party pursued on other issues a course for which they had little sympathy.

Indignation over Grant's performance as president surfaced briefly, but spectacularly, in 1872 in the Liberal Republican movement. Led by Senator Carl Schurz of Missouri, and supported by several other senators and a coterie of influential newspaper editors, the Liberal Republicans determined to place their own presidential ticket in the field and thus force Grant's withdrawal. They hoped thereby to modify substantially the party's southern and tariff policies and to achieve needed reforms in the civil service system. But they were faced by the problem that they were wholly in agreement only on the desirability of "universal suffrage and universal amnesty" for the South. When their presidential nominating convention met in Cincinnati, Horace Greeley, long-time editor of the New York *Tribune*, somewhat surprisingly emerged the winner, largely because of his identification with the proposed change in Reconstruction.

The regular Republicans unanimously renominated Ulysses S. Grant. The Democratic convention "endorsed" the Greeley candidacy, but many Democratic voters could not forget the years of verbal abuse suffered at the *Tribune*'s hands. Grant gained his second term in office by a far larger majority than he had won his first. The Liberal movement was crushed out of existence—temporarily.

The Liberals themselves were still around and by no means reconciled to Grantism. A few drifted over to the Democratic party, but most regarded themselves as the best of Republicans. Indeed, they were convinced they wanted nothing more than to restore their party to its original principles. By 1876, with most of the southern states reclaimed from Radical control, southern policy was no longer their chief concern; they were preoccupied instead with the immediate necessity of rescuing the government from the hands of the spoilsmen who were corrupting it. Civil service reform was their new slogan and Benjamin H. Bristow became their new hero. After all, when the gigantic

Whiskey Ring conspiracy was exposed by the St. Louis *Democrat* in May, 1875, the secretary of the treasury moved against the perpetrators of the fraud with such vigor that 238 men were indicted, including President Grant's private secretary, General Orville E. Babcock. What further proof was needed that Bristow was not only personally honest, but dedicated to a thorough reformation of the federal bureaucracy?

John Hay, who personally preferred Blaine, thought this a strange reason to make Bristow president: "His one sole public act is the prosecution of the Whiskey Ring. It is enough to make him a Governor, if he could carry his own State, and might honestly win him the Vice-Presidency. But twenty men are ready to work for Blaine to one for Bristow. Blaine has shown positive capacity for government and Bristow has not." [12] Perhaps "positive capacity for government" was not all that the Liberals (or Independents, as some of them called themselves) sought. The Liberals constituted something of a displaced class in American society. Most of them were professional men—lawyers, journalists, professors, college presidents, clergymen—or businessmen (merchants and financiers rather than industrialists). Many had inherited the basis for a comfortable living, most were highly educated, and all believed themselves firmly committed to a tradition of public service. In short, they were members of a self-conscious elite.[13] These "reformers" sensed with growing resentment that they no longer possessed the influence that they had before the war. Political bosses, exploiting the spoils system and the ignorance of the immigrant masses, had taken over the government and were operating it solely for their own personal gain. The remedy was civil service reform—appointment to office based solely on competitive, written examinations. The fact that the Liberals were the men best qualified to succeed on such tests was *prima facie* evidence

12. Quoted in Royal Cortissoz, *The Life of Whitelaw Reid* (2 vols.; New York: Charles Scribner's Sons, 1921), I, 335.
13. Hoogenboom, *Outlawing the Spoils*, 21–22; John G. Sproat, *"The Best Men": Liberal Reformers in the Gilded Age* (New York: Oxford University Press, 1968), chaps. 1–4 and 10.

of the proposal's soundness. Employing like reasoning, the Liberals did not merely want Bristow nominated for the presidency; they wanted him nominated under circumstances that would indicate unmistakably that the action was taken specifically because the Liberals demanded it. No other course would satisfy their craving for power, or at least their deeply felt need for the appearance of great influence.

The circumstances surrounding such support created an almost impossible situation for Bristow. For one thing, the Liberals wanted him to signify his willingness to accept an Independent nomination, possibly in the manner of the Greeley candidacy four years before. Bristow and his canny Kentucky friend, John Marshall Harlan, fully recognized that such a step would be an act of political suicide so far as the Republican party was concerned. The secretary was himself enough of a partisan (a Kentuckian had to have strong feelings to become a Republican), and had just enough support from the more reform-minded regulars within the organization, to assure that he would not seriously contemplate such a course. On the other hand, Grant's resentment was aroused by the fact that Bristow, while a member of the cabinet, had appeared so clearly the beneficiary of the administration's embarrassment. The president wanted his treasury secretary's resignation in February, but Secretary of State Hamilton Fish and other party leaders warned that firing Bristow would strengthen his support among the administration's enemies by making him a martyr.[14] Grant's displeasure, nevertheless, was soon public information. Bristow, previously a reluctant candidate, decided to enter the presidential race actively. He warned Morton's friends not to seek delegates in Kentucky and, after several newspapers attempted unjustly to besmirch his reputation for honesty, he told Harlan:

14. Ross A. Webb, *Benjamin Helm Bristow: Border State Politician* (Lexington: University Press of Kentucky, 1969), 219–23; J. C. Burrows to Z. Chandler, February 21, 1876, in Zachariah Chandler Papers, Manuscript Division, Library of Congress.

"I will make the best fight I can, and, if I must go down will at least fall with my face to the foe." [15]

2

The scramble for delegates to the national convention began officially (and the eventual result of the contest may well have been foreshadowed) when the members of the Republican National Committee met in Washington on January 13 to decide on when and where to hold the party's quadrennial conclave. Several cities had representatives present to explain their respective advantages. Supporters of Morton and Bristow were reported to prefer Cincinnati as the location closest to their home states. Blaine, who was born and raised in Pennsylvania and who once taught for two years at the state Institute for the Blind, evidently did not regard Hartranft as a serious contender, for he preferred Philadelphia as the site least likely to benefit any of his adversaries. Proximity to the Centennial Exhibition would also add a patriotic note to the Republican campaign. After a dozen ballots, formal and informal, Cincinnati was chosen by a majority of one vote.[16] The decisive factor was the desire of some committee members to enhance the party's prospects in Ohio, which conducted its state election in October, four weeks before the presidential balloting.[17] The result in October was universally assumed to herald the outcome in November. The date for the convention was then designated as June 14.

Clumsily, the state party machinery lumbered into motion. In Illinois the State Central Committee met on Washington's Birthday. Republican headquarters in Chicago had been specially festooned for the occasion with red, white, and blue bunting. A platform had been constructed beneath the banner inscribed "Illinois, the Home of Lincoln and Grant." Large por-

15. Webb, *Benjamin Helm Bristow*, 217–19, 226–31.
16. New York *World*, January 12, 14, 1876; Chicago *Daily Tribune*, January 14, 1876.
17. Letterpress copy, Morgan to Jones, January 15, 1876, in Morgan Papers.

traits of both presidents were prominently displayed. The seating in the room had been rearranged to accommodate the several hundred guests who had been invited, as well as a limited number of spectators. Shortly before noon, State Chairman C. B. Farwell called the gathering to order and introduced "the Hon. N. W. Branston, of Petersburg, Menard County," whom he asked to preside. Branston's remarks set the tone for the afternoon:

As a Republican . . . addressing an intelligent audience of Republicans,—and all audiences of Republicans are necessarily intelligent,—it is not necessary to refer to what are the political tenets of the party. But this I can say negatively, that in our ranks are not found numbered those who seek to extenuate the horrors of Libby Prison, or to apologize for the unknown and untold miseries of Andersonville. [Cheers.] In our party are found none who apologize for treason, or seek to make friends with traitors, except as traitors renounce their sins and become politically regenerated.

What followed was a campaign rally for party officials. Hours passed as prominent Republicans from each congressional district reported in detail on their local prospects. Finally, at the end of the day, immediately after this larger meeting had adjourned, the members of the committee assembled in a small adjoining room to select May 24 in Springfield as the occasion for their state convention. A gubernatorial nominee and other state candidates, presidential electors, and delegates to the Cincinnati convention would all be chosen the same day. The convention would consist of "one delegate for each 400 Republican voters, and one for every fraction over 150, the vote of 1872 being taken as the basis." [18]

More than two months elapsed before the various county conventions were held. Invariably the contests for state office overshadowed the matter of the presidency. The individual stature of a prospective delegate and whether he favored Shelby M. Cullom, John L. Beveridge, Thomas Ridgway, or Elihu B. Washburne for governor were the most important consider-

18. Chicago *Daily Tribune*, February 22, 23, 1876.

ations. Counties frequently instructed their delegates to the state convention to vote for one or another of these candidates. The action of the DeKalb County Convention in conducting an informal poll of the participants' presidential preferences was unusual. (The poll showed: "Blaine, 34; Morton, 11; Bristow, 6; and Conkling and Grant, 1 each.") [19]

The radically decentralized structure of this convention system, in contrast to the methods prevalent in New York and Pennsylvania, was best revealed in Cook County. In the eighteen wards of Chicago and the more than thirty suburban towns, five day's notice was given to the Republican electorate to choose county delegates on May 18. The basis for representation was one delegate for each 150 Republican votes in 1872. Actual participation in these primary meetings was very light. The First Ward, entitled to ten delegates, presumably had about 1,500 party voters, but only 125 participated. In most instances the local Republican Club nominated a slate of delegates in advance—designed to reflect more or less equitably the sentiment for Cullom and Beveridge—and aided this ticket by distributing printed ballots. Wherever such a "convenience" was provided the voters, suspense was notable only for its absence. The county convention met two days later in McCormick Hall. After the customary rules for formal organization had been observed, a resolution was adopted to apportion the eighty state delegates, to which the county was entitled, among the various wards and county commissioners' districts on the same basis as that which governed the present convention. The gentlemen from each ward and district then caucused and reported back their choices, and the convention adjourned. [20]

The state convention on May 24 was conducted essentially according to the same procedures. Two hours before the call to order, the delegates from each congressional district caucused and selected two delegates to the national convention, one presidential elector, and a member of every state convention com-

19. *Ibid.*, May 17, 1876.
20. *Ibid.*, May 13, 19, 20, 21, 1876.

mittee (there were five: permanent organization, credentials, resolutions or platform, nomination of a state central committee, and nomination of delegates and electors at large). The full convention of more than six hundred men merely ratified the delegates and electors chosen by the congressional districts and the "at large" committee, before turning to the business of nominating a state ticket.

Even before the convention opened, the Chicago *Tribune* found it an easy matter to predict a sweeping victory for Blaine; and, indeed, the state's forty-two delegates proved to be nearly unanimous for him. This result may not have been a perfect reflection of Republican sentiment in Illinois, but it was a reasonably accurate expression of the views of those voters who cared enough to participate in the primaries. Some party leaders—notably Chairman C. B. Farwell—worked diligently in Blaine's interest; yet the outcome could hardly be regarded as a product of bossism. The absence of centralized party machinery made this all but impossible. The crucial fact was that there were only a hundred Bristow delegates in the entire convention, and they were so spread out among the congressional districts that they were entirely powerless. The other candidates had no visible support at all. By contrast, the Blaine men discovered their strength so overwhelming that their earlier plan to instruct the delegation to Cincinnati on how to vote could be abandoned as superfluous. There was no need to risk antagonizing their opponents within the party.[21]

In late winter and throughout the spring every state and territory held its Republican convention. As the results were telegraphed across the country, two things became clear: Blaine was definitely the frontrunner for the nomination; and, on the other hand, the combined opposition might be able to stop him. The Wisconsin convention in February was a Blaine affair.[22] Maine, Maryland, California, and Oregon were for him.[23] Vir-

21. *Ibid.*, May 24, 25, 1876.
22. *Ibid.*, February 23, 1876.
23. New York *World*, May 1, 5, 1876.

ginia Republicans adopted a resolution expressing a "preference" for Blaine, then hedged their bets, voting another "complimentary" to Morton.[24] As expected, Morton was endorsed by Indiana, Mississippi, South Carolina, and Arkansas.[25] In New York and Pennsylvania, the two most populous states in the Union and the two states where the Republican nominating procedures were least responsive to the wishes of the electorate, the conventions performed as they were told. The highlight of the New York convention was the introduction of a platform that "presented" Roscoe Conkling "as our choice for the nomination for President" and gave "especial assurance" that he would carry the state's thirty-five electoral votes. Reformer George William Curtis objected strenuously, but the machine prevailed on a formal ballot, 250 to 113.[26] At least the New York Republicans followed the customary procedures. In Pennsylvania all pretense was discarded. The Cameron machine permitted a Blaine adherent, Edward McPherson, to be elected permanent chairman of the convention. Then the entire fifty-eight member delegation to Cincinnati, including the two delegates from each district, was carefully screened by a special nine-man committee. The state platform instructed the delegation to present Governor Hartranft's name for the presidency, to vote for him, and always "to cast the vote of Pennsylvania as a unit, as the majority of the delegation shall direct." [27] Insubordination, it was evident, would not be tolerated.

3

Meanwhile, two more favorite sons appeared. The Connecticut convention debated the advisability of placing Marshall Jewell's

24. *Ibid.*, April 14, 1876.

25. *Ibid.*, February 23, April 2, May 1, 1876.

26. *Ibid.*, March 23, 1876; printed circular, "State of New York Republican State Convention, Held at Syracuse, March 22, 1876, for the Election of Delegates to the Republican National Convention, to be Held at Cincinnati, June 14, 1876," in Rutherford B. Hayes Papers, Rutherford B. Hayes Library, Fremont, Ohio.

27. New York *World*, March 29, 30, 1876; Evans, *Pennsylvania Politics, 1872–1877*, 251–55; McPherson to Blaine, April 6, 1876, and G. W. Scofield to Blaine, April 6, 1876, both in Blaine Papers.

name in nomination at Cincinnati; then, overcome by indecision, it took no action. A few weeks later, however, a majority of the state delegation met in New Haven and decided formally to propose him for the presidency. Jewell was a successful leather-goods manufacturer who had served three terms as governor and a year as minister to Russia. Currently he was Grant's post-master general, with a reputation for operating his department on sound, honest business principles. Obviously some Connecti-cut Republicans hoped those qualifications might lead to the White House. Joseph R. Hawley, president of the United States Centennial Commission, which was responsible for the huge exposition of 1876 in Philadelphia, and a man whose own name was very nearly used in place of Jewell's, believed that his state's politicians were probably seeking a basis for trading votes for the presidency in return for the vice-presidency.[28]

Both more formidable and more interesting was Ohio's con-tribution, Rutherford B. Hayes—the very model of a Victorian gentleman in politics. He had been a lawyer, a Union general wounded while leading his troops into battle, and a member of the early Reconstruction congresses, where he was noted chiefly for his quiet party loyalty and meticulous attention to the affairs of Ohio's war veterans.[29] In 1867 he was elevated to the gover-norship, defeating one of the state's most popular Democrats, Allen G. Thurman. Two years later he was reelected over another Democrat of national stature, George H. Pendleton, who advocated expansion of the nation's money supply. Hayes will-ingly returned to private life after his second term; shortly thereafter the Democrats, capitalizing on the "hard times" of 1873, captured control of the state. The new governor, ancient William Allen, was another inflationist. Proper Republicans everywhere were scandalized, although it is hard to see what

28. J. R. Hawley to Samuel Bowles, April 24, 1876, in Samuel Bowles Papers, Yale University Library.

29. The best biographies are Harry Barnard, *Rutherford B. Hayes and His America* (Indianapolis: Bobbs-Merrill Company, Inc., 1954) and T. Harry Williams, *Hayes of the Twenty-Third: The Civil War Volunteer Officer* (New York: Alfred A. Knopf, 1965).

harm a state executive could do to the currency. What the Republicans of Ohio needed was a winning candidate. As late as April, 1875, Democrats scored heavily in a series of municipal elections.[30]

In desperation, therefore, Ohio Republicans turned back to Hayes. One of them explained:

> I have lately been talking a good deal with sundry people about the prospects of the Republican party in the coming gubernatorial campaign, and so far as my observation extends the opinion is pretty nearly unanimous, that if we succeed at all, it will be very much as the Dutchman got into Heaven [,] viz by a 'damn tight squeeze [.]'
>
> There is no use trying to disguise the fact that the party is badly demoralized, and to make a successful campaign next Fall we must have a candidate, who can impart some life to it, unite the discordant and wavering elements of the party, and impress people with the idea that there is something at stake beyond a mere struggle for place.
>
> There is no one who can do this so well as yourself, and when I say this I am not merely expressing my own opinion but that of every man with whom I have talked.[31]

There can be no doubt that the vain and sensitive Hayes was flattered. He promptly noted in his diary: "The Republican Caucus at Columbus last Thursday [March 25] according to report was unanimously for me for Governor. A third term would be a distinction—a feather I would like to wear. No man ever had it in Ohio." [32] And yet he hesitated, writing a series of letters stating that his personal financial situation would not permit a return to political life. James M. Comly, editor of the *Ohio State Journal*, replied, "The office of Governor requires none of your time—your private business can go on all the same precisely." Comly continued:

30. Forrest William Clonts, "The Political Campaign of 1875 in Ohio," *Ohio Archaeological and Historical Publications*, XXXI (1922), 66.
31. W. A. Knapp to Hayes, April 9, 1875, in Hayes Papers.
32. Entry for March 28, 1875, in T. Harry Williams (ed.), *Hayes: The Diary of a President, 1875–1881, Covering the Disputed Election, the End of Reconstruction, and the Beginning of Civil Service* (New York: David McKay Company, Inc., 1964), 2.

I have thoroughly tested the matter—more thoroughly than in any previous canvass, and the result is, an absolute conviction—

1. That everybody wants you, and in all the talk there is not one breath of objection to you or your record.

2. You can make a brilliant canvass, and be elected by a sweeping majority; *ergo,*

3. You will be the most prominent and unexceptionable candidate for President in 1876. . . . And I tell you with more earnestness than I am accustomed to use in any such matter, this is the opportunity that comes to no man twice in a life time.[33]

Hayes was "astonished, but flattered greatly." [34] He duly informed his diary: "Several suggest that if elected Governor now, I will stand well for the Presidency next year. How wild! What a queer lot we are becoming. No body is out of the reach of that mania." [35] No, indeed!

What made Hayes unsure of himself was a conflict between his ambition and his Victorian morality, which told him that a man might welcome high office but must not seek it. In addition, he may have been afraid of losing something he very much wanted, for in the privacy of his precious diary he remarked, "The prospect of an election seems to me to be not good." [36] To Comly, however, he explained: "If there was an issue that I felt interested in, I might be led to reconsider. But the Catholic question is not yet up; it may never be." [37]

Hayes did not actually refuse to be a candidate, although he did tell Comly, "I now authorize you, (and request), to withdraw my name, if when in your judgment it is proper or necessary." [38] As the impression spread that the former governor was unavailable for a third term, men who would otherwise have supported him turned instead to Judge Alphonso Taft of Cincinnati as the

33. James M. Comly to Hayes, April 4, 1875, in Hayes Papers.
34. Hayes to Comly, April 7, 1875, in James M. Comly Papers, Ohio Historical Society Library.
35. Entry for April 14, 1875, in Williams (ed.), *Hayes: The Diary of a President*, 3.
36. Entry for April 18, 1875, *ibid.,* 3.
37. Hayes to Comly, April 18, 1875, in Comly Papers.
38. Hayes to Comly, April 17, 1875, *ibid.*

next strongest candidate.[39] Taft himself entered the race only because he thought that Hayes had retired from it. Taft's opponents, unfortunately, as well as those Republicans who considered him too weak a candidate, continued to speak of Hayes. The latter was thus placed in a thoroughly embarrassing position and had no choice but to state unequivocally: "In no conceivable circumstances will I be a candidate, directly or indirectly, against Judge Taft." Hayes even wrote a letter defending the judge's record on the "Catholic question." Five years earlier Taft had written a decision supporting the right of a school board to ban the Bible—meaning in practice the King James Bible—from the classroom; the opinion pleased Catholics, but offended many Protestant Republicans. Hayes said he was as "confident" of Taft's soundness on the issue "as I want to be." [40]

On May 31 Hayes summarized his intentions for the benefit of his diary: "If notwithstanding my declination and known preference the members of the Convention with substantial unanimity insist on . . . the use of my name, I shall regard this wish as a command, and obey it. If the friends of Judge Taft or of other candidates still present their names, I will under no circumstances be a candidate against them. In that event my name must be unqualifiedly withdrawn." [41] Two days later Hayes was nominated over Taft, 396 to 151. When Charles P. Taft, the judge's son, moved that the nomination be made unanimous, Hayes seized the moment and accepted the honor. He also assured himself that Taft "had such a record on the Bible question in the Schools, that his nomination was impossible." [42] Hayes's entire performance in 1875 was but a dress rehearsal for the following year.

But first there was a gubernatorial campaign to be fought.

39. Thos. F. Wildes to Hayes, June 4, 1875, and W. D. Bickham to Hayes, June 14, 1875, both in Hayes Papers.
40. Hayes to Clark Waggoner, May 17, 1875, *ibid.*
41. Entry for May 31, 1875, in Williams (ed.), *Hayes: The Diary of a President*, 3–4.
42. Entry for June 3, 1875, *ibid.*, 4–5.

Eastern Liberals were capable of viewing the contest in one light only: the Democratic candidate stood for inflation, which they interpreted as a direct threat to the institution of private property. Charles Francis Adams, Jr., shrilled: "Allen's election will be our destruction; his renomination on the rag-money issue was a defiance and insult to us, and his success would render us contemptible. If we don't kill him, he will kill us." [43] Accordingly, the Adamses, Murat Halstead, Charles Nordhoff, Whitelaw Reid, and Henry Cabot Lodge joined in an effort to bring Carl Schurz back from a vacation in Germany to preach hard money to his countrymen in Ohio. Schurz returned in time to make several dramatic speeches that were probably publicized as much in New York and Boston as in Cleveland and Cincinnati.[44] Schurz was given much of the credit for the Republican victory and the legend was thereby created that the currency question was the principal issue of the campaign.

Rutherford B. Hayes saw the situation differently. The day after his nomination he wrote of the approaching contest: "The interesting point is *to rebuke the Democracy by a defeat for subserviency to Roman Catholic demands.*" [45] It need not be thought that Hayes himself was necessarily a bigot; but he certainly intended to exploit the bigotry of others. Earlier in the year the Democratic legislature had adopted the so-called Geghan bill to permit Catholic priests to minister the spiritual needs of inmates of the Ohio Penitentiary and other state institutions, whereas previously only the officially appointed chaplains, Protestants always, had possessed this privilege. The new law immediately became a subject of controversy and excited genuine fear in some people. Hayes proposed to capitalize on the situation by refocusing that fear onto an institution much

43. Charles Francis Adams, Jr., to Carl Schurz, July 16, 1875, in Frederic Bancroft (ed.), *Speeches, Correspondence and Political Papers of Carl Schurz* (6 vols.; New York: G. P. Putnam's Sons, 1913), III, 156–57.
44. Claude Moore Fuess, *Carl Schurz, Reformer (1829–1906)* (New York: Dodd, Mead and Company, 1932), 217–18.
45. Entry for June 3, 1875, in Williams (ed.), *Hayes: The Diary of a President,* 5.

closer to home than the state prison. "The Bible in the Public Schools—" he scrawled in his diary; " 'A division of the school fund is agitated and demanded' by the same power and upon the same grounds, by which and on which the passage of the Geghan Bill was demanded." [46] The strategy of the campaign was really quite simple. An ambitious young lawyer in Canton, Ohio, named William McKinley, explained it best: "We have here a large catholic population which is thoroughly democratic, a large protestant German element that hitherto have been mainly democratic, they hate the Catholics—their votes we must get." [47]

Throughout the campaign Hayes adjured his supporters: "We must not let the Catholic question drop out of sight. If they do not speak of it, we must attack them for their silence. If they discuss it, or refer to it, they can't help getting into trouble." [48] Hayes personally supervised the preparation of leaflets on the subject.[49] When Alphonso Taft discussed the issue in an address in Cleveland, the candidate thanked him effusively: "It is *the* speech of the Canvass. It is of far more importance than any other speech, in my judgment, that has been, or will be made. Your careful and sound statement of our position in favor of the complete secularization of the schools, puts us first where we ought to stand. The tracing of the whole difficulty back to Rome, & to the recent extraordinary assumptions of authority made on the Church by the Ultra-Montanes is masterly, and will command attention throughout the country." [50]

As the campaign progressed Hayes summarized the outlook: "The vote will be out in larger force than for many years at a State election. Our losses are in the mining districts & the manu-

46. Entry for June 4, 1875, *ibid.*, 5.
47. Wm. McKinley, Jr., to Hayes, June 8, 1875, in Hayes Papers.
48. Hayes to Bickham, July 10, 1875, in Charles Richard Williams (ed.), *Diary and Letters of Rutherford Birchard Hayes* (5 vols.; Columbus: Ohio State Archaeological and Historical Society, 1922–26), III, 284.
49. Hayes to [A. T. Wikoff], July 18, 19, 1875, in Hayes Papers.
50. Typescript copy, Hayes to Alphonso Taft, August 27, 1875, in Hayes Papers. The original is in the William Howard Taft Memorial, Cincinnati.

facturing people. We lose also by emigration to the West & by immigration on new R.R.s, to the Towns, of Irish. We gain mainly by returning Germans & Liberals, by the waking up of lazy Republicans, & somewhat by anti Catholic Democrats. On the whole I feel encouraged." [51] Hayes was elected by a plurality of about five thousand votes out of half a million cast. The professional politicians of the Republican party promptly discovered the "Catholic question" in Pennsylvania and other northern states.[52]

Just as his friends had prophesied, the new governor of Ohio was immediately spoken of as a presidential candidate. Republican newspapers all over the state expressed their support, and Hayes carefully listed them in his diary.[53] Hayes was strictly a dark horse, popular in his own state, but otherwise merely "available" as a neutral alternative to whom the friends of other candidates might turn. His friend Manning F. Force told him: "The rule is almost without exception that a [man] who seeks the presidency never gets it. And Morton, Conkling, [and] Blaine, who might as a means of defeating each other, in the end unite on you, would fight against you, if you should become too prominent before the convention meets." [54] The governor had another advantage. Ohio and Indiana would hold state elections on October 10, four weeks before the presidential balloting. It was an all but universal belief that the October results in those two states not only foretold their November choices but also influenced the outcome in such other closely contested states as New York and Pennsylvania. Hayes had established himself as the man best able to carry Ohio. As early as January,

51. Hayes to Horace Austin, August 22, 1875, in Horace Austin Papers, Minnesota Historical Society.
52. Evans, *Pennsylvania Politics, 1872–1877*, 196; Vincent P. De Santis, "Catholicism and Presidential Elections, 1865–1900," *Mid-America*, XLII (April, 1960), 69–70.
53. Entry for October 17, 1875, in Williams (ed.), *Hayes: The Diary of a President*, 10–11.
54. M. F. Force to Hayes, October 18, 1875, in Hayes Papers. Blaine analyzed Hayes's position in the same terms some years later. See Blaine, *Twenty Years of Congress*, II, 568.

1876, William Henry Smith, a close friend who was general manager of the Western Associated Press, and General Philip Sheridan, who had been the governor's commanding officer in 1864, suggested a ticket of Hayes and Wheeler.[55] Hayes responded: "I am ashamed to say, Who is Wheeler?" [56] Perhaps the question was facetious. Congressman William A. Wheeler of New York had recently attracted attention as the author of the "compromise" which settled the disputed gubernatorial and legislative elections of 1872 in Louisiana.

Hayes's candidacy received a boost of incalculable value from a public letter written by Senator John Sherman on January 21. Sherman reviewed the outlook for the campaign and concluded: "The Republican party in Ohio, ought in their State Convention to give Gov. Hayes a united delegation instructed to support him in the National Convention; not that we have any special claim to have the candidate taken from Ohio, but that in Genl. Hayes we honestly believe the Republican party of the United States will have a candidate for President who can combine greater popular strength and greater assurance of success than other candidates, and with equal ability to discharge the duties of Presd't of the U.S. in case of election." Incredibly, Hayes was offended by some of Sherman's remarks. The senator, reviewing the governor's strength in Ohio, noted: "He was a good soldier, and though not greatly distinguished as such he performed his full duty, and I noticed when travelling with him in Ohio that the soldiers who served under him loved and respected him." [57] Hayes complained of the reference to his not being "greatly distinguished in the Army" and detailed his military accomplishments at length in his diary.[58]

55. Wm. Henry Smith to Hayes, January 26, 1876, in Hayes Papers.
56. Hayes to Mrs. Hayes, January 30, 1876, in C. R. Williams (ed.), *Diary and Letters of Hayes*, III, 301.
57. John Sherman to A. M. Burns, January 21, 1876, in Hayes Papers. The letter was widely published in the newspapers and Sherman reprinted it in his memoirs. See John Sherman, *Recollections of Forty Years in the House, Senate and Cabinet: An Autobiography* (2 vols.; Chicago: Werner Company, 1895), I, 522–23.
58. Entry for February 1, 1876, in Williams (ed.), *Hayes: The Diary of a President*, 14–15.

Meanwhile, signs of acute presidential fever were appearing: "It seems to me that good purposes, and the judgment [,] experience and firmness I possess would enable me to execute the duties of the office well. I do not feel the least fear that I should fail! This all looks egotistical, but it is sincere." [59] The Ohio Republican Convention, with 750 members present, met on March 29 and unanimously instructed the four delegates at large and requested the forty delegates chosen by districts to work for Hayes's nomination for the presidency. The governor thereupon returned to his act of the previous year, feigning utter indifference: "I would be glad if now I could in some satisfactory way drop out of the candidacy. I do not at present see what I can do to relieve myself from the embarrassment of the position I am in. It does not greatly disturb me. My usual serenity carries me along. But I would like to be out of it. I will think of it." [60]

Thereafter, Hayes insisted, both to himself and to others, that he would do nothing to further his own political prospects: "Very few Republicans in Ohio are so completely out of the Hayes movement as I am." [61] Yet, when Edwin Cowles, editor of the Cleveland *Leader* and a district delegate, indicated he would vote for Blaine should it become certain Hayes could not win, the governor admonished him: "Being now in the field without any act of my own, I have no uneasy ambition to remain a candidate. I think I have a right, however, to considerate treatment at the hands of the Ohio delegation. If I am to be voted for at all, and as long as I am to be voted for at all, may I not reasonably expect the solid vote of Ohio?" [62] Nor was he above relaying the information from William M. Grosvenor to W. D. Bickham that "the Central Com[mittee] of

59. Entry for March 21, 1876, *ibid.*, 17.
60. Cincinnati *Daily Gazette*, March 30, 1876; entry for April 2, 1876, in Williams (ed.), *Hayes: The Diary of a President*, 18.
61. Typescript copy, Hayes to Guy M. Bryan, April 23, 1876, in Hayes Papers.
62. Edwin Cowles to Hayes, April 3, 1876, *ibid.*; Hayes to Cowles, April 6, 1876, in Williams (ed.), *Hayes: The Diary of a President*, 19–20.

West Va could be seen to advantage." But he qualified it with the remark, "You know I am leaving all of those matters well alone." [63] Hayes was more consistent in his refusal to be quoted on any of the probable issues of the campaign. When the Republican Reform Club of New York asked his views on various questions, he declined to give them: "You are aware that my name has been mentioned in connection with the nominations to be made next month at Cincinnati. Having thus far done nothing with the purpose of promoting my own nomination by that Convention I prefer not to change my course of conduct either by the publication of letters on political questions, or otherwise. I must therefore respectfully decline to write to you anything for publication as requested in your esteemed favor of the 22d instant." [64] The Reform Club then gave its support to Bristow.[65]

4

Most other Liberals were preparing to do the same. The question was how to proceed. Their attempt to hold a full-fledged nominating convention in 1872 had failed; it was so large that it got out of control and chose the "wrong" candidate—Horace Greeley instead of Charles Francis Adams. Thereafter the Liberals restricted their activities largely to their own kind. As early as the summer of 1875 Carl Schurz was contemplating "a meeting of notables—men whose names will be of weight with the country and who can be depended upon to agree to an independent course." Schurz thought that the meeting should be

63. Hayes to [W. D. Bickham], April 18, 1876, in Hayes Papers.
64. Gouverneur Carr to Hayes, May 22, 1876, *ibid.*; Hayes to Carr, May 25, 1876, in entry for May 26, 1876, in Williams (ed.), *Hayes: The Diary of a President,* 24–25. (The original letter is in Miscellaneous Manuscripts, Princeton University Library.) "I do not write letters to be shown or used in any way, on political questions. . . . Do not quote me." See letterpress copy, Hayes to J. A. Garfield, March 4, 1876, in Hayes Papers.
65. Printed Circular, "To the Republican National Convention of 1876," dated June 6, 1876, in Hayes Papers. The club's membership included John Jacob Astor, J. Pierpont Morgan, Theodore Roosevelt, Sr., and William E. Dodge.

held the following January or February and believed that it might "do the whole work usually done by conventions. This, however, will depend upon circumstances. At any rate, the meeting should be of the *best* sort of respectability in point of character, and not altogether composed of politicians." [66] Both then and later, Schurz's first choice for the presidency remained Charles Francis Adams.[67] However, even Henry Adams recognized that his father was "the candidate of a hopeless minority." Fortunately, the rise in Bristow's popularity solved that problem.[68]

The "meeting of notables" was delayed somewhat; but in March, Schurz, struggling to recover from the death of his wife, drafted an invitation and applied himself to the task of obtaining qualified signatures on it. His original plan was to hold the conference in Cincinnati, deliberately anticipating the Republican convention, but New York was more convenient to the "notables." [69] Schurz's letter, also signed by William Cullen Bryant of the New York *Evening Post,* President Theodore Dwight Woolsey of Yale, former governor Alexander H. Bullock of Massachusetts, and Horace White of the Chicago *Tribune,* was ready on April 6. It began by reviewing the nation's many crises—political corruption, uncertainty about the currency, machine domination—and concluded by calling "a free conference" on May 15 "to consider what may be done to prevent the National Election of the Centennial year from becoming a mere choice of evils." [70] Henry Cabot Lodge, just completing his doctorate in history under Henry Adams at Harvard, assisted in

66. Schurz to W. M. Grosvenor, July 16, 1875, in Bancroft (ed.), *Political Papers of Carl Schurz,* III, 155–56.

67. Schurz to Bowles, January 16, March 7, 1876, in Bowles Papers.

68. Henry Adams to Schurz, February 14, 1876, in Worthington Chauncey Ford (ed.), *Letters of Henry Adams (1858–1891)* (Boston: Houghton Mifflin Company, 1930), 274.

69. Schurz to Bowles, March 27, 1876, in Bowles Papers.

70. William Cullen Bryant, Theodore D. Woolsey, Alexander H. Bullock, Horace White, and Carl Schurz to Francis A. Walker, April 6, 1876, in Bancroft (ed.), *Political Papers of Carl Schurz,* III, 228–29.

compiling the list of dignitaries to whom invitations were sent, and he was designated to receive the replies.[71]

The next job was to make certain that Bristow would cooperate with his Liberal supporters. Henry Adams was pessimistic. Despite the fact that the regular Republicans were sure to overwhelm him in the convention ("the chances are a thousand to one against the nomination of any man who has made so many enemies as he"), Bristow would not bolt. Adams explained: "Bristow is a Kentucky Republican and has all the old traditions of party fealty." [72] In February, Schurz asked Lodge to visit the secretary of the treasury in Washington. Lodge went, spoke to Bristow several times, met two of his closest advisers, the brothers Bluford and James H. Wilson, but learned little besides the extent of the secretary's difficulties with Grant.[73] Before sending his conference invitations, Schurz himself tried to reassure Bristow. He warned that "the party machine men would surely prevent the nomination of a true reformer for the Presidency, unless they were made very clearly to understand that they cannot do so with impunity. That class of politicians will control the Republican Convention, and they will do the worst they dare. All indications on the political field point that way. Nothing but the alternative of the nomination of a true reformer, or defeat, will induce them to permit the former." Schurz wrote that the demonstration of that alternative to the party leaders in the most forceful manner was his sole concern and added: "I write these lines mainly to remove a misapprehension from your mind. You may rest assured that your name will not be trifled or made free with, and that you will in no manner be compromised or embarrassed by me and those under

71. H. C. Lodge to Bowles, May 4, 1876, in Bowles Papers.

72. Henry Adams to Lodge, February 15, 1876, in Ford (ed.), *Letters of Henry Adams*, 277–78.

73. Lodge to Schurz, February 24, 1876, in Carl Schurz Papers, Manuscript Division, Library of Congress; John A. Garraty, *Henry Cabot Lodge: A Biography* (New York: Alfred A. Knopf, 1953), 43; Webb, *Benjamin Helm Bristow*, 220–21.

my influence." [74] Bristow's friends remained uneasy. James H. Wilson wanted Walter Q. Gresham and John Marshall Harlan to attend the New York conference to "moderate and direct" its proceedings. Wilson warned that professional politicians "don't like to be dictated to." [75]

The Liberals planning to attend Schurz's "meeting of notables" may have been encouraged by a similar gathering of reformers in Worcester in early April. That session concluded by issuing an address, signed by such luminaries as James Russell Lowell, James Freeman Clarke, Edward Atkinson, and Alexander H. Bullock, cautioning the people of Massachusetts against leaving the Republican primaries "in the hands of those who make politics a business." [76] Three weeks later the state convention named an uncommonly distinguished delegation to Cincinnati: E. Rockwood Hoar, who had been dismissed as attorney general in part for opposing Grant's scheme to annex Santo Domingo; Richard Henry Dana, author of *Two Years Before the Mast*; John Murray Forbes, merchant and railroad builder; and Paul A. Chadborne, president of Williams College, were the delegates at large. George F. Hoar, Richard M. Dana, Henry L. Pierce, as well as Lowell and Clarke, were chosen by districts. Here, surely, were the "best men" in the party. Most were for Bristow. They were also Republicans, and most were prepared, if necessary, to accept Blaine.[77]

The larger "free conference" assembled in New York's Fifth Avenue Hotel on the afternoon of May 15. The roster of reformers in attendance was genuinely impressive, including Schurz, Bryant, Woolsey, Bullock, Grosvenor, Professor Julius H. Seelye of Amherst, then serving a term in Congress, David A. Wells, Dorman B. Eaton, Parke Godwin, Thomas Wentworth Higgin-

74. Schurz to Benjamin Helm Bristow, March 31, 1876, in Bancroft (ed.), *Political Papers of Carl Schurz*, III, 226–27.
75. E. Bruce Thompson, "The Bristow Presidential Boom of 1876," *Mississippi Valley Historical Review*, XXXII (June, 1945), 12.
76. George S. Merriam, *The Life and Times of Samuel Bowles* (2 vols.; New York: The Century Company, 1885), II, 274–75.
77. Garraty, *Henry Cabot Lodge*, 45. See also Birchard A. Hayes to R. B. Hayes, April 30, 1876, in Hayes Papers.

son, Anson Phelps Dodge, John Jay, Oswald Ottendorfer, Jacob D. Cox, Francis A. Walker, and Theodore Roosevelt, Sr. Lodge acted as convening chairman. With 150 men present, there was a limit to how much work could be accomplished without resort to committees. Even so, it is astonishing that such a distinguished group should consent to serve merely as a rubber stamp for the plans of Carl Schurz and as a receptive audience for innumerable, uninspiring, impromptu speeches. The sole accomplishment of the day was the appointment of a five-member committee, headed by Schurz, to determine a course of action and "to take charge of all resolutions that might be offered to the conference." The committee soon announced that its work would require several hours, and so the meeting adjourned to the next morning. When the notables reassembled, Schurz read the long address he had prepared, tracing the sorry record of recent defalcations in government and of machine domination of politics, stating the need for reform, and asserting that "at the coming Presidential election we shall support no candidate who in public position ever countenanced corrupt practices or combinations, or impeded their exposure and punishment, or opposed necessary measures of reform." The address, of course, was approved, along with resolutions supporting civil service reform and declaring, "It is not expedient for this conference to recommend anybody for the office of President." This last statement was a concession to those few Liberals who were predisposed toward Democrat Samuel J. Tilden. Lest the "machine politicians" mistake the determination of the reformers, an executive committee was created "to reconvene this conference, or a larger meeting of a similar character if circumstances require it." Then everybody went home.[78] The entire affair proved to be little more than a vehicle for Carl Schurz, allowing him to dispense his own advice to the Republican party, cloaked in the prestige conferred by the entire congregation of famous men. The hostile New York *Commercial Advertiser*

78. New York *World*, May 16, 17, 1876.

understood perfectly: "Business yesterday at the Fifth Avenue Conference was 'cut and dried,' just as at any other political gathering." [79]

5

The Liberal reformers were endeavoring to prevent Blaine's nomination, without mentioning him and without dirtying their hands in the normal routine of politics. Other members of the party were pursuing the same objective in an entirely different manner. Henry Van Ness Boynton was the Washington correspondent for the Cincinnati *Gazette*. As early as January he began attacking in his dispatches the methods Blaine was using to obtain delegates. He explained to his editor, Richard Smith, that he had no strong personal objection to Blaine. He had in his possession, however, evidence concerning the ex-Speaker's railroad dealings, which, if revealed in the course of the fall campaign, would defeat the party should Blaine be its standard-bearer. And he added that "prominent democrats know enough of this record to make it certain that it will become widely known, the moment his name is placed on the ticket." What Boynton proposed was to use the same information within the party to force Blaine's withdrawal. In the meantime he would keep the story secret.[80]

Boynton's disclosure about the Republican front-runner was not his first exposé. In the summer of 1867 a bitter dispute erupted between General O. O. Howard, head of the Freedman's Bureau as well as president of the recently established First Congregational Church in Washington, and the Reverend Charles Boynton, the pastor of the church, over the latter's reluctance to admit black members to the congregation. The quarrel dragged on for two years, culminating at last in the Reverend Boynton's resignation. The pastor's son Henry then undertook a personal vendetta against Howard in his letters to the *Gazette*,

79. New York *Commercial Advertiser*, May 17, 1876, quoted in Garraty, *Henry Cabot Lodge*, 47.
80. H. V. Boynton to [Richard] Smith, February 6, 1876, in William Henry Smith Papers, Ohio Historical Society Library.

assailing the general's actions in the church dispute, calling him an amalgamationist, and questioning his performance as commissioner of the Freedman's Bureau and as president of Howard University. The younger Boynton, an intensely partisan Republican, even went so far as to supply material for Fernando Wood, an intensely partisan Democrat and former Copperhead, to use in a House speech attacking Howard. The result was a congressional investigation and a permanent loss of reputation for the Freedman's Bureau.[81] Boynton charged into action again in 1875. William Tecumseh Sherman's *Memoirs* of the Civil War were published that year, and some people said the book exaggerated the role of the Army of the Tennessee. Boynton, who had served in the Army of the Cumberland, rushed into print with a book-length review, *Sherman's Historical Raid.* Sherman, who freely admitted he wrote solely from memory and gave only his own impressions, never denied his volume might contain some errors in judgment. So he could only account for Boynton's animus by concluding that the reporter had been prompted by old antagonists in the War Department. Perhaps money had something to do with it. Sherman opined publicly a few years later that Boynton would "slander his own mother for a thousand dollars" and refused to retract the remark when threatened with a libel suit.[82]

Whatever his motivation—and it is more than likely that he simply relished intrigue—Boynton brought experience to his offensive on Blaine. At the beginning of February he confidentially revealed his charge:

At the time that the Pacific railroads [the Union Pacific and Central Pacific] were buying through Congress the additional legislation by which the government first mortgage was made a second mortgage Blaine received from Stewart, the man who managed the

---

81. John A. Carpenter, *Sword and Olive Branch: Oliver Otis Howard* (Pittsburgh: University of Pittsburgh Press, 1964), 194–208.
82. H. V. Boynton, *Sherman's Historical Raid: The Memoirs in the Light of the Record. A Review Based upon Compilations from the Files of the War Office* (Cincinnati: Wilstach, Baldwin and Company, 1875); Lloyd Lewis, *Sherman: Fighting Prophet* (New York: Harcourt, Brace and Company, 1932), 616–17.

corruption fund here about 25 one thousand dollar construction bonds of the Kansas branch. This disposition of bonds appears among the papers, & on the books of the company. He has been in mortal dread of this record for two years, & has taken all means in his power to manufacture a defense, but no defense can be made to hold in a campaign. . . . When I tell you that I will not shrink from facing him if it becomes necessary [,] with all the immense efforts he would bring to bear, knowing that if he failed to crush me he would be politically ruined,—you can understand how strong I regard the case against him.[83]

This bribe had allegedly been accepted in 1863, during Blaine's first session in Congress. Richard Smith wrote to the ex-Speaker about it and received an evasive reply: Blaine said he had not known Stewart at that time and suggested vaguely that the same unsubstantiated accusation had appeared in the New York *Sun* two years before. Boynton disagreed with both statements.[84] Richard Smith then informed William Henry Smith (no relation) in Chicago of what was happening, and William Henry Smith told Joseph Medill, editor and publisher of the Chicago *Tribune* and an avid Blaine adherent. Medill, understandably, demanded proof. Boynton replied that he would certainly provide conclusive documentary evidence, but would need a little time. He agreed to meet with Medill and the two Smiths in Cincinnati as soon as the necessary affidavits were ready.[85]

Immediately after these arrangements were made, William Henry Smith went to Indianapolis on Associated Press business.

83. Boynton to [Richard] Smith, February 6, 1876, in Smith Papers.

84. Copy (in William Henry Smith's hand), Boynton to [Richard] Smith, February 17, 1876, *ibid.* The second statement, however, was true. A. M. Gibson, the reporter who filed the story in February, 1873, retracted his charge within twenty-four hours when his source disclaimed any knowledge of it. See Gibson to Blaine, March 17, 1876, in Blaine Papers.

85. Boynton to [William Henry] Smith, February 18, 1876, Boynton to [Richard] Smith, February 25, 1876, and Richd. Smith to [W. H.] Smith, February 28, 1876, all in William Henry Smith Collection, Indiana Historical Society Library, not to be confused with the Smith Papers; copy, J. Medill to Wm. Henry Smith, February 21, 1876, and letterpress copy, Wm. Henry Smith to Richard Smith, February 22, 1876, both in Smith Papers. On Medill's support for Blaine, see Medill to Blaine, February 23, 1876, in Blaine Papers.

Waiting for him at the depot was W. R. Holloway, postmaster at Indianapolis and brother-in-law of Senator Oliver P. Morton. Holloway imparted to Smith the information that, three years before, J. S. C. Harrison, a government director of the Union Pacific Railroad, had told him of some Little Rock and Fort Smith Railroad bonds in the possession of the company and known as "The Blaine bonds." These certificates, with a face value of $75,000 but actually worthless, had been accepted as collateral for a loan of $64,000 that Blaine had never been asked to repay. Orders for the transaction had come directly from the president of the road, Thomas A. Scott. William Henry Smith quickly relayed the second story of corruption to Richard Smith and Medill. Holloway himself ran up to Chicago for a fast visit with the *Tribune* editor, who in turn decided to write Blaine about the matter, alarming Holloway lest the Maine congressman hold Morton responsible for the attempt to smear him. Medill concealed Holloway's involvement, however, and Blaine explicitly denied the entire affair.[86]

Boynton, Medill, and Richard and William Henry Smith met as planned on March 18. Boynton was armed with court transcripts that seemed to sustain his indictment of Blaine in every respect. Richard Smith and Medill again wrote to the ex-Speaker, who this time was slower to respond.[87] Meanwhile, word of the discoveries spread. The conspirators themselves told Murat Halstead, editor of the Cincinnati *Commercial*, and he shortly received a second account of the parley of journalists in his city from an express company agent who should have known nothing about it. Horace White, Medill's associate on the *Tribune*, passed his information along to both Carl Schurz and Samuel Bowles, editor of the Springfield *Republican*. James H.

---

86. Wm. Henry Smith to Boynton, April 30, 1876, in Smith Collection; W. R. H[olloway] to W. H. S[mith], February 26, 28, March 1, 13, 1876, *ibid.*; Horace White to Schurz, February 25, 1876, in Schurz Papers. James F. Wilson, another government director of the Union Pacific, confirmed this story for White. See White to Schurz, March 11, 1876, in Schurz Papers.
87. Wm. Henry Smith to Hayes, April 18, 1876, in Hayes Papers.

Wilson and Walter Q. Gresham, Bristow's friends, also learned of the Little Rock and Fort Smith bonds Morton's brother-in-law had spoken of.[88]

The conflicting objectives of the participants in this involved tale are important. William Henry Smith was one of Rutherford B. Hayes's closest personal friends. Holloway was working in the interest of Morton. Boynton, Halstead, White, Schurz, and Bowles favored Bristow. Medill alone cared to defend Blaine. The principal concern of each of Blaine's antagonists was that the story should not be revealed under circumstances that would cause their candidate to be held accountable. At the same time, Boynton and Holloway were determined to have the scandal disclosed in some way if the disclosure was needed to prevent the ex-Speaker's nomination. Since that was the case, the results of the investigation had to come out.

The honor of first publishing an account of the $64,000 "loan" went to the Indianapolis *Sentinel*, a Democratic paper, on April 11. The source of its information is unknown, but Medill and William Henry Smith blamed Morton and his friends, thereby infuriating Holloway.[89] Blaine himself planted an article in the Chicago *Inter-Ocean*, attributing the effort to slander him to the cabal of newsmen in Cincinnati and noting that most of them were for Bristow.[90] Blaine's version was more plausible: Morton would probably not have divulged what he knew so close to home. With rumors of the entire affair becoming commonplace in Washington, the *Sentinel* may also have obtained the story through its regular channels. A few particulars about Boynton's

88. M. Halstead to W. Henry Smith, March 29, 1876, in Smith Collection; Thompson, "The Bristow Presidential Boom of 1876," 19. See also E. B. Wight to W. W. Clapp, February 28, 29, 1876, in William Warland Clapp Papers, Manuscript Division, Library of Congress. Wight was Washington correspondent of the Boston *Journal* and apparently gained his information directly from Boynton.

89. W. R. H[olloway] to W. H. S[mith], April 14, 1876, in Smith Collection.

90. Letterpress copy, Wm. Henry Smith to Boynton, April 21, 1876, in Smith Papers; Wm. Henry Smith to Boynton, April 30, 1876, in Smith Collection. Richard Smith denied that he or his friends were responsible. See Cincinnati *Daily Gazette*, May 3, 1876.

original discovery of the Kansas Pacific construction bonds were printed a couple of weeks later in Bowles's Springfield *Republican*, only to be completely overshadowed by the uproar created by the earlier revelation.

Blaine's response to these disclosures was a performance of consummate audacity, played with such skill that what should have been outrageous appeared sincere. On April 24, on the floor of the House, the congressman from Maine rose to a point of personal privilege. He read a series of letters, one from E. H. Rollins, treasurer of the Union Pacific, two more from the banking house that handled the company's affairs, one from Tom Scott, and another from Sidney Dillon, Scott's successor as president of the road, all denying there had ever been a transaction between the railroad and Blaine involving $64,000 or Little Rock and Fort Smith bonds. Blaine went further. He denied that he had ever owned a Little Rock and Fort Smith bond, "except at the market price, and instead of making a large fortune out of that company, I have incurred a severe pecuniary loss from my investment in its securities, which I still retain." [91] Blaine's denials were so thorough and explicit that his adversaries were completely taken aback, whereas his supporters were jubilant. During May the Kentucky Republican Convention voted to present Bristow for the nomination, while the Tennessee delegation leaned heavily toward Morton. Elsewhere, however, a veritable Blaine tide seemed to have set in. Maryland, Delaware, and Nebraska adopted resolutions instructing their delegates to vote for Blaine; Oregon, West Virginia, Minnesota, Kansas, and Iowa all "preferred" him; and New Jersey, New Hampshire, and Illinois, though adopting no resolutions, obviously favored him.[92]

All during this time a subcommittee of the House of Representatives continued to probe the former Speaker's past relations with the Union Pacific Railroad. In mid-May, J. S. C. Harrison, the original source of this story, testified that at a

91. Muzzey, *James G. Blaine*, 83–86.
92. New York *World*, May 5, 12, 18, 19, 25, 26, June 1, 1876.

meeting of the road's board of directors in 1872 he had moved the appointment of a committee to determine how the company had acquired the Little Rock and Fort Smith bonds. Then, said Harrison, "E. H. Rollins the Secretary took me to one side and told me that I must withdraw the motion . . . as it would involve James G. Blaine. He said the fall elections were at hand, and Blaine was a candidate for reelection to congress in Maine. An exposure of the transaction just at that time would be sure to defeat him. With that I withdrew the motion." Rollins explained: "As near as I can recollect, prior to this meeting of the board, I had heard a report—I cannot now recollect the source from which I heard it—that these bonds in question were the bonds of Mr. Blaine." But Rollins added that he was sure a thorough investigation would reveal that his earlier opinion had been based on hearsay and was incorrect. On the last day of the month, two weeks before the Republican National Convention, another witness, James Mulligan, formerly the bookkeeper for Warren Fisher, Jr., one of the men who built the Little Rock and Fort Smith Railroad, was sworn in. He testified that Blaine had been the agent in the sale of $130,000 of Little Rock and Fort Smith bonds to friends in Maine. Blaine had received additional bonds of his own as a commission. What about the bonds now held by the Union Pacific? Mulligan said that he had been told by Elisha Atkins, another Union Pacific director, "that Mr. Blaine gave the bonds to Tom Scott and that Tom Scott made the Union Pacific take them" for $64,000. Almost inadvertently, Mulligan mentioned that he possessed some letters from Blaine to Fisher which related to these transactions. The candidate, who was present, immediately became quite agitated and prevailed upon the one Republican member of the subcommittee to seek an adjournment.

Mulligan's testimony was correct. Apparently, when the Little Rock and Fort Smith bonds rapidly became worthless, Blaine tried to recover the investment of some of his friends who could ill afford to stand the loss. His intentions had been honorable, he had broken no law, yet he found himself cornered. While a member of Congress, he had maintained a privileged relationship with railroads dependent on government land-grant subsidies. Contrary to his earlier statement, he had received Little Rock and Fort Smith bonds at other than the market price. The funds to repay his Maine acquaintances came directly from the president of the Union Pacific. If he still wanted the presidential nomination, it was a little late to make a clean breast of things; so once more Blaine decided to brazen his way through.

He went to Mulligan's hotel and demanded that the letters be turned over either to Fisher or himself. They were private correspondence and rightfully the property only of the sender or recipient. Mulligan refused. Blaine then asked to see the letters and Mulligan complied. The congressman examined the letters, proclaimed that with one exception they had no relevance to the subject of the inquiry, and refused to return them. Before the subcommittee the next day Blaine again refused to produce them as evidence. The astonished committee members, unsure of what course to pursue, adjourned for the weekend. Blaine climaxed his performance on June 5, during the regular Monday hour for questions of personal privilege. Before the full membership of the House of Representatives and an overflowing gallery, he insisted again that the Mulligan letters had no bearing whatever on the current investigation. Then he dramatically slammed the package of correspondence down on his desk and declared: "I am not afraid to show the letters. Thank God Almighty! I am not afraid to show them. There they are. There is the very original package. And with some sense of humiliation, with a mortification which I do not pretend to conceal, with a sense of outrage which I trust any man in my position would feel, I invite the confidence of 44,000,000 of my fellow countrymen while I read those letters from this desk." What Blaine proceeded to read were excerpts from the letters, carefully removed from their context and from their proper chronological order, but handled in such a manner that their selection seemed entirely at random. The audience must have been somewhat confused, but certainly gained the impression that the letters dealt only with personal business affairs. Blaine's supporters rejoiced anew, in the belief that he had fully exonerated himself.[93] The highly partisan reporter of the Democratic New York *World* agreed that Blaine had materially improved his chances for success.[94]

The subcommittee examining the congressman met several additional times during the week, hearing the first testimony about the Kansas Pacific bonds Boynton had unearthed, but making little progress. On Saturday, June 10, at Blaine's request, an adjournment was taken until Monday. Richard Smith thought "altogether the worst thing yet revealed concerning Blaine" would come out at that time.[95]

The intervening Sunday was hot and humid in Washington. Nevertheless, Blaine decided to walk the mile to services. He never quite made it. Mounting the front steps of the church, he felt a sharp pain in his head and fell to the ground unconscious. He was carried back to his home and did not revive until Tuesday. The nature of his ailment remains a mystery. It may have been heat prostration, although the seizure occurred in the morning, well before the warmest part of the day. Possibly it was a product of exhaustion—Blaine had been sick during the early spring and had been under constant strain for many weeks. A. M. Gibson, Washington correspondent of the Democratic New York *Sun*, sent his version of the story to his editor, Charles A. Dana, under the caption "Blaine Feigns a Faint." [96] Certainly any further investigation of the candidate would have to be postponed beyond the meeting of the Republican National Convention.

On the other hand, Blaine's sudden illness produced consternation among the delegates to the convention, most of whom were already assembling in Cincinnati. Would the name of the

93. Muzzey, *James G. Blaine*, 87–99.
94. New York *World*, June 7, 1876.
95. A. E. Lee to Hayes, June 11, 1876, in Hayes Papers.
96. Muzzey, *James G. Blaine*, 99–100. For Blaine's earlier illness, see McPherson to Blaine, May 24, 1876, in Blaine Papers.

leading candidate for the presidency have to be withheld? [97] Hayes wrote the former Speaker a letter that only he would have sent: "I have just read with deepest emotions of sorrow the account of your illness. My eyes are almost blinded with tears as I write. All good men among your Countrymen will pray as I do for your immediate and complete recovery. This affects me as I was affected by the death of Lincoln. God bless you and restore you." [98] Secretary Bristow had visited Blaine only the day before his attack. An obscure newspaper in Kentucky had printed a story intimating that Blaine's marriage many years before had been arranged most hastily as a result of the condition in which his wife suddenly found herself. Bristow learned from James H. Wilson and from Congressman William Dennison of Ohio that Mrs. Blaine held him responsible for this unwarranted aspersion on her reputation; so, accompanied by Dennison, Bristow went to see his rival for the nomination. Blaine was effusive in his expressions of friendship, denying he had ever heard Bristow's name mentioned in connection with the story about his wife, and reassuring the secretary that he believed him in no way responsible for the accusations against himself. The next day Bristow was at home writing Wilson an account of this meeting when he received word of Blaine's seizure. "Without a moment's reflection," he hurried back to the ex-Speaker's house, just a short walk's distance, only to be met at the door by an angry Mrs. Blaine: "Mr. Bristow you have got your will now; don't come in here." The secretary told Wilson, "My God, what mortification I felt." The whole episode was soon public information and did nothing to enhance Blaine's prospects for obtaining some of Bristow's delegates. [99]

Blaine finally recovered on Tuesday, barely twenty-four hours

---

97. New York *World*, June 12, 1876.
98. Hayes to Blaine, June 12, 1876, in Blaine Papers.
99. Webb, *Benjamin Helm Bristow*, 239–41; Josiah C. Reiff to William E. Chandler, June 9, 12, 1876, in William E. Chandler Papers, Manuscript Division, Library of Congress; statement of William Dennison in Cincinnati *Daily Gazette*, June 13, 1876.

before the national convention would be called to order. His first task was to demonstrate that his supporters were in no danger of nominating a corpse. Shortly after half past five Blaine's son Walker called on Secretary of State Hamilton Fish and asked that gentleman if he would mind calling on his father with a carriage. Fish explained that he had a dinner engagement later in the evening, but Walker insisted. Fish reluctantly agreed and the younger Blaine thanked him, remarking somewhat indiscreetly, "That will have a right good effect in Cincinnati." The congressman and the secretary rode for half an hour, with Blaine carefully indicating each street through which the carriage should pass. Later that night, while returning from dinner, Fish encountered Blaine's physician and inquired whether the candidate had suffered any ill consequences from his drive. The physician replied: "Oh, no. He went to bed soon after, and is sleeping as quietly as a child. But the news has been telegraphed to Cincinnati, and has produced great enthusiasm among his friends." [100] Blaine had used the secretary of state both to advertise his return to health and to suggest a degree of administration support for his candidacy which did not in fact exist. It was another worthy performance by one of the most accomplished actors of his time.

In Cincinnati "the Blaine men recovered their spirits, and professed to be *sure* of nominating their candidate." Yet one close adviser of Hayes thought "his recovery is not helping him much, as it has a tendency to diminish sympathy for him, and to turn public attention again to his letters." Although most Republicans had been exhilarated by Blaine's dramatic rebuttal, there seemed to be an undercurrent of uneasiness that his nomination might force upon the party a "defensive" campaign. With Blaine expected to come within one hundred votes of success on the first ballot, reports began to circulate of discussions between delegates from New York, Pennsylvania, and Indiana

100. Diary of Hamilton Fish, June 14, 1876, quoted in Allan Nevins, *Hamilton Fish: The Inner History of the Grant Administration* (rev. ed., 2 vols.; New York: Frederick Ungar Publishing Company, 1957), II, 828.

looking toward "a consolidation of all the anti-Blaine forces." [101] From the first this possibility, that the ex-Speaker's supporters and opponents might stalemate each other, had been the basis of the Hayes movement. As an entirely new personality in national politics, the governor of Ohio represented a neutral figure around whom the members of any faction could rally to prevent the triumph of their rivals.[102] Even before the convention opened, members of the New York delegation were hinting "as broadly as they could that they wanted" Ohio "to stand by" Hayes "to the last." [103]

6

The most important delegation was Pennsylvania's. Just two weeks before, the Cameron organization had achieved what appeared to be a complete reconciliation with Grant. A series of cabinet changes left the War Department open, and the president gave the post to J. Donald Cameron. Would Hartranft now be withdrawn in favor of Conkling, Grant's "residuary legatee"? Or would Cameron seek the role of kingmaker and switch to Blaine? Actually the delegation was divided almost evenly between Conkling and Blaine sympathizers. The most convenient course, therefore, was to keep Hartranft in the race on the chance that he might be a successful compromise candidate and as a means of avoiding a decision while awaiting further developments. The Pennsylvania delegates caucused several times and promised to stand by their governor as long as his vote increased on each ballot or until twenty delegates desired another consultation. They also agreed to cast their state's fifty-eight votes as a unit in accordance with the will of the majority, an arrangement designed to increase their weight in the convention. Finally, they announced that Hartranft would not be interested in the vice-presidency, since the duties of that

101. Lee to Hayes, June 14 [1876], in Hayes Papers.
102. Garfield to Hayes, March 2, 1876, Sherman to Hayes, May 22, 1876, and Wm. Henry Smith to Hayes, May 27, 1876, all *ibid*.
103. Lee to Hayes, June 12 [1876], *ibid*.

office were "not sufficient for him to leave the gubernatorial chair." Blaine's lieutenants were satisfied with these developments, but it seems that Don Cameron had already reached an understanding with Morton's friends to insure a small but steady improvement in Hartranft's position for at least several ballots. Blaine was unlikely to receive the full vote of Pennsylvania unless it appeared beforehand that he would win even without it.[104]

The Cameron organization's decision not to seek the vice-presidency was based strictly on the belief that they could not gain any advantage for themselves from that office. No one ever expected Blaine, Conkling, or Morton to accept the position either. Friends of Blaine, however, had approached both Bristow and Hayes about the possibility of becoming the former Speaker's running mate.[105] Bristow was definitely not interested and authorized Harlan, a member of the Kentucky delegation, to "say so distinctly and unequivocally at the proper moment." [106] Hayes, forty-eight hours after his gushing letter of sympathy to Blaine, wrote R. P. Buckland that Blaine's nomination would be fatal to the cause:

I do not see how we can get through in Ohio with him at the head of our ticket. It is proposed to put me in the second place. This will not help the cause. It is the man at the head who makes the canvass. I have the greatest aversion to being a candidate on the ticket with a man whose record as an upright public man is to be in question— to be defended from the beginning to the end. . . . I therefore have sent you a letter directed to the chairman of the delegation, Gov. Noyes, to be delivered to him in the event of the nomination of Blaine, authorizing and requesting him to withdraw my name, if it is proposed in connection with the Vice Presidency.[107]

The Ohio delegates caucused on June 10 and 12 and found three among their number who preferred Blaine, Morton, and

104. Evans, *Pennsylvania Politics, 1872–1877*, 259–60; Lee to Hayes, June 14 [1876], in Hayes Papers; James Joseph Flynn, "The Disputed Election of 1876" (Ph.D. dissertation, Fordham University, 1953), 63–64.
105. See, for example, F. Thorp to Hayes, May 30, 1876, in Hayes Papers.
106. Webb, *Benjamin Helm Bristow*, 237.
107. Hayes to R. P. Buckland, June 14, 1876, in Hayes Papers.

Bristow, respectively. The dissenters agreed, however, to support Hayes as long as there was a chance of his emerging victorious. To be certain the leaders of the delegation determined to keep a close watch on them. The Hayes men then "divided up into committees . . . to visit other delegates . . . for missionary purposes." Their candidate, waiting with his son, Rutherford, Jr., in the otherwise deserted gubernatorial offices in Columbus, was kept carefully informed of each development, though he did not personally interfere.[108] Manning F. Force, for example, reported having spoken to a number of Massachusetts people, including Forbes, Lowell, Richard Henry Dana, George F. Hoar, and E. L. Pierce. Forbes had dinner at Force's home and intimated that if Bristow could not be nominated, his Bay State supporters would probably look to Hayes. Force explained the line of argument he found effective:

The candidate nominated by the convention, cannot be elected unless he be a person who will draw at least a large part of what may be called the Bristow element. The very large number of men who have already shaken off their allegiance to the republican party from sincere disapproval of the administration, is reinforced by a great many still within the party lines, who will not vote for the nominee unless he is one whose character gives assurance of an administration strong enough in its own purity to insist on a correction of abuses.[109]

The southerners were another group of delegates the friends of Hayes sought to establish contacts with:

All the Southern delegates will be largely influenced by the drift of public sentiment as they catch it developed at Cincinnati. The Union men of the South feel personally very keenly the need of a Republican President. It means to them greater security to person and prosperity and they will feel disposed to forego personal preferences for the Candidate whose friends can guarantee the greatest strength. Feeling the need of success for their personal protection & peace they will look to availability of the candidate more than Northern delegates.[110]

108. Lee to Hayes, June 11, 12, 1876, and Hayes to [Birchard A. Hayes], June 15, 1876, both *ibid.*
109. Force to Hayes, June 12, 1876, *ibid.*
110. A. J. Ricks to (?), May 22, 1876, *ibid.*

7

The Republican National Convention was called to order by national committee Chairman Edwin D. Morgan of New York promptly at noon on Wednesday, June 14. The site was Exposition Hall, at Elm and Fourteenth streets—the same building which had been the scene of the Liberal Republican revolt against Grant in 1872. As always, the first day was occupied with procedural matters. Acting at the request of the national committee, Morgan proposed Theodore M. Pomeroy of New York as temporary president of the convention, and Pomeroy, having been confirmed by a voice vote of the delegates, was escorted to the stage to deliver a brief and undistinguished speech —what would today be called the keynote address. Then it was time to create the customary committees.[111] Two days earlier, the national committee had distributed printed circulars to the various delegations advising them to be prepared to designate the following: a vice-president of the convention; a member of the committees on credentials, permanent organization, resolutions, and rules and order of business; and a new national committeeman.[112] In the full convention, therefore, it was only necessary to call the roll of the states and have the chairman of each delegation send forward a brief list of names. Alabama, Florida, and the District of Columbia were denied the right to participate at this stage because each was represented by two rival delegations. When the composition of each committee was announced, committee members were asked to begin work at once in rooms provided for the purpose to the right of the stage. Addresses received from the National German Republican Convention and the Republican Reform Club of New York were read and referred to the committee on resolutions. After a half-

111. *Proceedings of the Republican National Convention, Held at Cincinnati, Ohio, Wednesday, Thursday, and Friday, June 14, 15, and 16, 1876, Resulting in the Nomination for President and Vice-President of Rutherford B. Hayes and William A. Wheeler* (Concord, N.H.: Republican Press Association, 1876), 3–10.

112. Printed circular, E. D. Morgan, Chairman, and Wm. E. Chandler, Secretary to [the several state delegations], June 12, 1876, in Hayes Papers.

hour recess none of the committees was prepared to report; so the assembled multitude devoted itself to listening to speakers called to the stage by popular demand: Senator John A. Logan of Illinois, former governor Joseph R. Hawley of Connecticut, former governor Edward F. Noyes of Ohio, the Reverend Henry Highland Garnet of New York, William A. Howard of Michigan, and Frederick Douglass. Finally, the committee on permanent organization announced that it was ready and reported Edward McPherson of Pennsylvania, a prominent Blaine adherent, as permanent president. The other committees were still at work, however, so the delegates gave up and adjourned until the next morning.[113]

The Thursday session opened with much the same routine. George F. Hoar obtained permission for Mrs. Sarah J. Spencer to deliver a short speech in behalf of the National Woman's Suffrage Association. The rules committee proposed adoption of the rules of the House of Representatives with a few modifications suitable for a nominating convention. Sharp opposition was expressed from the floor in respect to the requirement that the platform be adopted before nominations could begin, until McPherson announced that the resolutions committee was ready to report. The suggestion of a New York delegate that the convention take a half-hour recess after each presidential ballot was tabled. And the rules were then adopted.[114]

The credentials committee was the next to be heard from. There was little discussion of its recommendations concerning the Florida and District of Columbia delegations. The Alabama dispute, however, provoked an acrimonious debate. The committee voted twenty-six to thirteen to seat the delegation headed by Samuel F. Rice instead of the group led by carpetbag senator George E. Spencer. Most of the Rice delegates favored either Blaine or Bristow for the presidency, whereas Spencer's followers were strictly for Morton. As a result, the technical question

113. *Proceedings of the Republican National Convention . . . 1876,* 10–30.
114. *Ibid.,* 30–39.

of which Alabama faction had the stronger claim was over-shadowed by the struggle to obtain additional delegates for the various candidates. The floor vote on the question of substituting the minority report, favorable to Spencer's delegation, became a test of strength between Blaine and Bristow on the one hand and the opponents of Blaine on the other. Indiana and Pennsylvania were unanimously for Spencer, and New York nearly so; whereas Maine, Kentucky, Massachusetts, Wisconsin, and Illinois were all but unanimously for Rice. The Ohioans, consciously seeking to straddle the fence in behalf of Hayes, were divided. The substitute was defeated 375 to 354—the closeness of the decision providing the first conclusive indication that Blaine lacked the strength to control the convention. The substantial support he received from the friends of Bristow on this question was a product of circumstances that were not likely to recur once the presidential balloting began.[115]

Consideration of the platform was the next item on the agenda. The committee on resolutions, with about forty members, was too unwieldy a body to complete its task in the available time, so most of the work had been performed by a seven-member subcommittee.[116] The result was a tepid document that declared the United States "a nation, not a league," congratulated Republicans for saving the Union, promised "speedy, thorough, and unsparing" prosecution of corrupt public officials, opposed polygamy and sectarian interference with the public schools, and called for "respectful consideration" of demands for women's suffrage. One plank deprecated all appeals to sectional feeling and abominated Democratic hopes for a "solid South," whereas another pledged anew the party's sacred duty— eleven years after Appomattox—to achieve "permanent pacification of the Southern section of the Union," and a third charged the Democratic party with "being the same in character and spirit as when it sympathized with treason." The protective tariff was described as the best means "to promote the interests

115. *Ibid.*, 39–55.
116. Blaine, *Twenty Years of Congress*, II, 569–70.

of American labor and advance the prosperity of the whole country." The platform contained a firm endorsement of sound money and a wonderfully evasive stand on civil service reform: "The invariable rule for appointment should have reference to the honesty, fidelity, and capacity of appointees, giving to the party in power those places where harmony and vigor of administration require its policy to be represented, but permitting all others to be filled by persons selected with sole reference to the efficiency of the public service and the right of citizens to share in the honor of rendering faithful service to their country." The only plank that stirred controversy was the eleventh: "It is the immediate duty of congress fully to investigate the effect of the immigration and importation of Mongolians on the moral and material interests of the country." Edward L. Pierce of Massachusetts objected bitterly: "The Republican party this year, this centennial year, is twenty years old . . . and this is the first time in all that long period that any attempt has ever been made to put in its platform a discrimination of race." The eleventh section was retained, nevertheless, on a roll call vote of 532 to 215, and the entire platform was "unanimously adopted" on a voice vote.[117]

By the time nominations for the presidency were in order, it was midafternoon. Although a candidate did not have to be formally presented in order to receive votes during the balloting, it was customary for the serious contenders, and a variety of favorite sons as well, to be introduced in short speeches which were nominally supposed to total no more than ten minutes for each nominee, though they invariably lasted longer. Most of the nominating addresses were undistinguished and, by consuming time, served principally to heighten the tension. The only remarks of any note were Robert G. Ingersoll's in behalf of Blaine, in the course of which the Maine stateman was dubbed the "Plumed Knight." Ingersoll was repeatedly interrupted by applause, but it is doubtful whether he changed any votes. Conk-

117. *Proceedings of the Republican National Convention . . . 1876*, 55–65.

ling, Morton, Hartranft, Bristow, Hayes, and Marshall Jewell of Connecticut were also placed in nomination. When these formalities were complete, the time was past five, the hall was becoming dim, and Will Cumback of Indiana moved an adjournment to Friday morning. The anti-Blaine forces wanted another night to discuss the possibility of a union on one candidate. The Blaine managers preferred an immediate ballot; William P. Frye of Maine obtained the floor and, pointing to the gas fixtures, asked why darkness outside should pose a problem. McPherson, in the chair, replied: "I am informed that the gaslights of this hall are in such condition that they cannot safely be lighted"; and with that the convention adjourned.[118]

The third session on June 16 opened in an atmosphere of feverish expectation. The opening prayer was delivered, several routine announcements were read, and the clerk called the roll of the states in alphabetical order on the first ballot for the presidency. With 379 votes (a simple majority) required to win the nomination, James G. Blaine received 285. He had at least one vote from twenty-eight of the thirty-eight states and seven of the nine territories. No other candidate had such broad support. His total vote was slightly more than his opponents had conceded, but slightly less than his lieutenants had publicly claimed. His most embarrassing weakness was in his own section—he obtained only 30 of the 80 votes cast by New England. Morton was second with 124 votes, 30 of which were from his own state of Indiana, 2 from the District of Columbia, and the rest from the South. Bristow was third, with 113 votes drawn from nineteen states and Wyoming Territory. Conkling followed with 99 votes, 69 of which were from New York. The first jarring note of the balloting was struck when George William Curtis refused to cast even a complimentary ballot for Conkling and defiantly voted for Bristow. The remaining, in order of strength, were: Hayes, who drew a scattering of votes from eight states besides the 44 of Ohio and thus totaled 61; Hart-

118. *Ibid.*, 65–82.

ranft, who received only the 58 votes of Pennsylvania; Jewell, who secured but 10 of Connecticut's 12 votes, after obtaining 1 from Alabama; and Congressman William A. Wheeler of New York, who got 3 votes from Massachusetts.

No provision had been made for a recess after each ballot; so as soon as the results were announced the clerk was ordered to call the roll again. Any conferences on strategy would have to be held while the voting proceeded. The most dramatic development of the second ballot occurred when Pennsylvania was reached. The chairman of that delegation once more cast his state's 58 votes for Hartranft. Immediately four Pennsylvania delegates were on their feet demanding that their ballots be counted for Blaine. The governor of the Keystone State had already received 4 votes from Nevada that had previously been cast for Bristow and Hayes and 5 more from North Carolina that had formerly gone to Conkling and Blaine. The dissidents realized, perhaps for the first time, that arrangements might have been made to secure a steady increase in Hartranft's vote, thus under the caucus agreement making his candidacy more than temporary and preventing them from voting as they pleased. As president of the convention, Edward McPherson, a Blaine supporter, announced that the unit rule was out of order: Pennsylvania cast 54 votes for Hartranft and 4 for Blaine. This decision triggered an explosive debate on the floor; yet McPherson was sustained, 395 to 353, in another roll call conducted without recourse to the unit rule. Blaine's managers defended McPherson strenuously, but the breakdown of the vote revealed no clear pattern. Most people had strong feelings on the subject, with the result that almost every delegation was divided. On the presidential ballot itself there were few significant changes: Blaine gained 11 votes, reaching 296; Bristow also gained 1, Hayes 3, and Hartranft 5; while Morton lost 4 and Conkling 6. Wheeler kept his 3 votes; but Jewell, having received his complimentary ballot, was withdrawn. One Minnesota delegate voted for Elihu B. Washburne, whose principal attraction seems to have been that, after more than seven years outside the country as minister to France, he could not be charged with corruption.

The next two ballots followed a similar pattern. Blaine lost 4 votes, falling to 292; Morton's total declined by 12 and Conkling's by 9. Bristow showed the most significant improvement, picking up a dozen votes for a total of 126, second only to the "Plumed Knight." Hartranft gained 8 votes, Hayes 4, and Washburne 2. Wheeler lost one.[119]

The convention was beginning to look like the sort of deadlocked affair backers of dark horses always hope for. The fifth ballot began with a few more switches of little consequence; so the chairman of the Michigan delegation polled his colleagues:

On the 4th ballot 10 had voted for Bristow 5 for Hayes & 7 for Blaine. All were admirers of Blaine but believing his nomination would force upon the party a *defensive* campaign & perhaps defeat we felt bound to prevent his nomination [.] The 5th ballot commenced & 13 were for Bristow 5 for Hayes & 4 for Blaine [.] It was certain that Conklin [*sic*] & Morton must soon be withdrawn & if the Bristow and Hayes strength could be united & draw to itself the greater part of the Conklin & Morton vote it would defeat Blaine. So I told the delegation if they would unite & throw the vote solid & adhere firmly we could make a nomination & perhaps save the party from defeat. The Bristow men said unite on him, the minority ought to yield to majority &c. In the absence of facts we were obliged to rely on the supposed logic of the situation. I thought the two N. Y. delegates must have exasperated the other 68 by the persistency with which they had advocated the nomination of Bristow, even refusing to join in a harmless complimentary vote for Conklin. I said if we strike for Bristow we shall fail for want of New York votes. It is not in human nature while exasperated & heated that they, the 68, should take the candidate of the two. *"If we strike for Hayes we shall win."* They reluctantly yielded—the last man after I was on my crutches to announce the vote.[120]

The Michigan delegation cast 22 votes for Hayes, an increase of 17. Moments later nine delegates from North Carolina abandoned Blaine and two more switched from Hartranft to vote

119. *Ibid.*, 82–102.
120. Wm. A. Howard to Hayes, July 4, 1876, in Hayes Papers.

for Ohio's governor. Hayes gained 36 votes on this ballot, while all the other major candidates lost ground: Blaine slipped 6 more votes, Morton 13, Conkling 2, Hartranft 2, and Bristow 12. It was the first time either Hartranft or Bristow suffered a decline. When the result was announced, the clerk resumed the call of the states. Alabama did not respond. McPherson conceded that there might be a widespread desire for consultation and said he would entertain a motion for a recess. Will Cumback of Indiana at once objected, noting that another ballot had already begun and that any motion would be out of order. McPherson agreed and ordered the clerk to continue.

There were no startling developments on the sixth ballot until North Carolina was reached. The delegates from that state were working diligently at "making a nomination"—any nomination. All eleven of them who had switched to Hayes on the previous tally now voted for Blaine, who also gained 1 vote formerly cast for Hartranft. Nine more Pennsylvania men broke with their governor to vote for Blaine. And in South Carolina, also, five delegates gave up on Bristow and Morton and jumped aboard what they thought might prove to be a bandwagon for the "Plumed Knight." Blaine gained 22 votes, reaching 308, 71 less than he needed to win. Hayes also improved his position, picking up 9 votes despite his loss in North Carolina; moreover, nearly all his gains were in the South. The other candidates saw their support further eroded: Morton by 10 votes, Conkling by 1, Bristow by 3, and Hartranft by 19.

The showdown vote was obviously only minutes away. Several delegates again sought a recess, but they obtained the floor after Alabama had been called, and McPherson ruled them out of order. The seventh ballot proceeded. Alabama cast 17 of her 20 votes for Blaine, an increase of 2. Arkansas transferred 10 votes from Morton to Blaine. Florida changed 4 votes the same way. Georgia gave the former Speaker 5 votes more than previously, Illinois 3. Blaine was headed for victory if his opposition would just remain divided. When Indiana was called, Will Cumback walked to the stage and announced the withdrawal of Morton. Indiana cast 5 votes for Bristow and 25 for Hayes. The

Hoosiers wanted a western candidate. For Kentucky, John Marshall Harlan withdrew Bristow's name. Harlan had been surprised by the action of Michigan two ballots earlier and felt then that Bristow's cause was hopeless. Now, he told the secretary, he only wanted his state's influence to be used so "as to make it tell upon the rings, and secure a good nominee." [121] Kentucky cast 24 votes for Hayes. Cumback then tried to change the 5 votes Indiana had cast for Bristow to Hayes. Robert G. Ingersoll of Illinois complained that Cumback was out of order: the vote of a state could not be altered after it had been announced. McPherson agreed. The clerk continued to call the roll. Louisiana changed 8 of the 10 votes she had previously cast for Morton to Blaine and the other 2 to Hayes. Massachusetts transferred 21 votes from Bristow and Wheeler to Hayes. Mississippi, which up to that time had been divided among five candidates, consolidated on Hayes. New York then withdrew Conkling and cast 61 votes for the governor of Ohio and only 9 for the congressman from Maine. Conkling's friends would never consent to serve the interests of Blaine. North Carolina gave another demonstration of her peculiar consistency and jumped back to Hayes. Don Cameron withdrew Hartranft and Pennsylvania divided, 30 for Blaine and 28 for Hayes. Had the unit rule been preserved, Blaine would have gained this entire bloc of votes. Some of the ex-Speaker's friends said, therefore, that McPherson had made a mistake. McPherson, however, was acting as Blaine wanted him to, and the ex-Speaker had earlier gained votes as a result of the decision.

When all the votes were counted, Hayes had 384 votes—5 more than the simple majority he needed. Blaine had 351 and Bristow retained the 21 he had received before his name was withdrawn. McPherson proposed the formality of making the nomination unanimous, and Blaine's first lieutenant, William P. Frye, seconded the motion, which was carried *viva voce*.[122]

---

121. Webb, *Benjamin Helm Bristow*, 249.
122. *Proceedings of the Republican National Convention . . . 1876*, 103–10.

William Henry Smith wrote of Edward F. Noyes's leadership of the Ohio delegation: "Better management I never saw. It was able, judicious, untiring, unselfish, inspiring, adroit." [123] Actually Hayes's nomination required very little skill. It had been necessary only to keep Ohio united behind him while maintaining an utter neutrality, indeed almost a bored indifference toward all other candidates and delegations. Manning F. Force, a close friend of Hayes, was right when he stated: "The voting by being prolonged, had the effect of visibly separating the elements of the party." He misunderstood, however, when he told the governor: "The worse elements congregated about Blaine; the better elements about you and Bristow." [124] The treasury secretary's supporters turned to Hayes as a compromise candidate; but, strictly speaking, they were alone in doing so and they did not nominate him. Morton, Cameron, and Conkling were hardly among the "better elements" of the party. Their friends voted for Hayes not as a compromise, but from spite; they preferred to have an unknown quantity rather than a traditional rival in control of the government. The North Carolina delegates, likewise, were animated by no higher motive than that of fishing for the eventual winner in the hope that their votes would serve as bait to attract a rich catch of patronage jobs. Henry Adams interpreted the situation correctly when he sourly dismissed Hayes as "a third-rate nonentity whose only recommendation is that he is obnoxious to no one." [125]

The vice-presidency was disposed of more easily. Since Hayes was from Ohio, the ticket would have to be balanced with an eastern candidate. Five men were placed in nomination. The Bristow forces had two candidates: John Marshall Harlan proposed Joseph R. Hawley of Connecticut, and Luke P. Poland of Vermont suggested William A. Wheeler of New York. E. Rockwood Hoar presented the name of Marshall Jewell. New Jersey's

123. Wm. Henry Smith to Hayes, June 21, 1876, in Hayes Papers.
124. Force to Hayes, June 16, 1876, *ibid.*
125. Henry Adams to Carle [M. Gaskell], June 14, 1876, in Letters Received and Other Loose Papers, The Adams Papers, Massachusetts Historical Society.

favorite son was Frederick Theodore Frelinghuysen, and Thomas C. Platt, speaking for the Conkling machine, advocated Stewart L. Woodford of the Empire State. Wheeler, an obscure politician preoccupied with his failing health and noted chiefly for his role in settling a disputed election in Louisiana, was acceptable to almost everyone.[126] By the time New York was reached on the first ballot, it was apparent who would win. Woodford asked that his own name be withdrawn, and the huge New York delegation voted unanimously for Wheeler. Shortly thereafter a Connecticut delegate obtained the floor, withdrew Jewell from consideration, and moved that the rules be suspended so that Wheeler's nomination might be made by acclamation. The proposal was entirely irregular in the light of McPherson's earlier decisions, but the delegates were losing interest in these anticlimactic proceedings and McPherson allowed it. The Republican National Convention had completed its work.[127]

The man most deeply disappointed by the entire course of the scramble to succeed Grant was the most gracious in defeat. "It will be alike my highest pleasure as well as my first political duty to do the utmost in my power to promote your Election," Blaine telegraphed Hayes. "The Earliest moments of my returning & confirmed health will be devoted [to] securing you as large a vote in Maine [as] she would have given for myself [.] " [128] Hayes's reaction to the telegram was predictable: "It for a few moments quite unmanned me," he told his diary.[129] Blaine had some consolation. Shortly after the convention Bristow resigned as secretary of the treasury. Grant appointed Senator Lot M. Morrill as his successor and the governor of Maine named Blaine to the Senate seat Morrill left vacant. These

126. Blaine, *Twenty Years of Congress*, II, 572.
127. *Proceedings of the Republican National Convention . . . 1876*, 110–14.
128. Telegram, Blaine to Hayes, June 16, 1876, in Hayes Papers.
129. Entry for June 18, 1876, in Williams (ed.), *Hayes: The Diary of a President*, 26–27.

appointments promptly terminated the House investigation of the former Speaker's business affairs.[130]

Senator Justin S. Morrill of Vermont, who had remained in Washington during the convention, surveyed the Republican outlook:

We have a good platform and a fair ticket—not brilliant but safe. Of the four prominent candidates Blaine was the only one that could have been elected, I think, and he would have roused so much enthusiasm as to have crushed the hot personal drift of the campaign. I know of nothing against the character of Blaine but he would have pleased me better if he had had less to do with those Railroad men he would have pleased me vastly better. A public man ought not to [be] mixed up with desperate ventures.

There will be no vim in the campaign but I hope for enough hard work to make it successful.[131]

130. Webb, *Benjamin Helm Bristow*, 250–51; Muzzey, *James G. Blaine*, 115.

131. Justin S. Morrill to G. G. Benedict, June 17, 1876, in Justin S. Morrill Papers, Manuscript Division, Library of Congress.

Chapter III □ The Democratic Party, 1876: Samuel J. Tilden and the Effort to Control

THE DEMOCRATIC party was almost destroyed by the Civil War. The leading secessionists in the South and the principal advocates of peace in the North were Democrats; association with these men was nearly fatal. In the Thirty-ninth and Fortieth congresses, elected in 1864 and 1866, Republicans outnumbered Democrats by four to one in the Senate and roughly three to one in the House. The ticket of Horatio Seymour and Francis P. Blair achieved a hopeful showing in the presidential canvass of 1868, briefly throwing a mild scare into the Republicans; but the Democratic party made little progress in the congressional contests two years later. By the early weeks of 1872 the prospects for victory were so dim that national and state leaders across the country joined in a movement to postpone the party's national convention until after the Liberal Republicans had met in Cincinnati. Even endorsing Horace Greeley, who had spent half his life heaping ridicule upon Democrats throughout the pages of the New York *Tribune*, seemed preferable to going it alone. But Greeley, too, was soundly defeated at the polls.

The democratic party did not revive until a Wall Street panic in 1873 ushered in a severe economic crisis. In the congressional elections the next year the party secured ten new senators and gained a remarkable seventy-seven seats in the House of Representatives. The Republicans would still control the Senate, but in the lower house their former margin of better than two to one was converted overnight into a Democratic majority of sixty. This so-called "Tidal Wave" meant that, following the "lame duck" session of the Forty-third Congress, Reconstruction would be over as far as the legislative branch of the government was concerned. It meant also that the Democrats would enter the presidential campaign of 1876 with a real possibility of winning for the first time in twenty long years.

Sudden success brought with it some unexpected problems. After two decades of wandering rather aimlessly in the political wilderness, the Democratic party was noticeably lacking in experienced politicians of national reputation. The most important fresh personality to emerge from the "Tidal Wave" was Samuel J. Tilden, elected governor of New York by an impressive majority. By merely demonstrating that he could carry the Empire State with its huge bloc of electoral votes, Tilden became a formidable contender for the presidency. The new governor was talented, wealthy, and irrevocably committed to the respectable belief in sound money. The dramatic Democratic gains of 1874, however, were primarily the result of inflationist sentiment in depressed areas of western Pennsylvania, Ohio, Indiana, and Illinois. Increasing disagreement over the currency aggravated the traditional friction between eastern and western Democrats and threatened to prevent selection of a candidate acceptable to both sections.

1

Most of the story of the Democratic party in 1876 revolves about the enigmatic figure of Governor Tilden.

From a sickly youth in which he had no play group to the peak of his political power, Tilden moved through life a remote and lonely little man, erect and cold-mannered, largely friendless, admired but not liked.... Given the opportunity, he preferred to quantify human problems and relations; he enjoyed computing distances, populations, taxes, national income, and expenditures.

Similarly, he sought obsessively for precision and order in his personal life and in the world around him. Inflexible in his own life pattern, he found it hard to adjust to new conditions. Faced with facts in a jumble, he flung himself upon them consumedly until he could hammer them into tight, unbreakable patterns. This character made him a brilliant political administrator, for he loved working out the votes and factors in every precinct. His legal fortune came from this same inexhaustible talent for achieving understanding of complex situations.[1]

When faced with unforeseen developments, however, with the need to make difficult decisions on short notice, Tilden often failed as a political leader.

Tilden first entered New York politics during the presidency of Martin Van Buren, a close personal friend of his father, and he remained throughout his career essentially a Jacksonian Democrat. He believed in negative government honestly administered, reduced taxation, a sound currency, and home rule.[2] Tilden became prominent in New York in 1866 when he organized a Union state ticket in support of President Andrew Johnson. Two years later, as chairman of the state party organization, he would have liked to play the "kingmaker" at the Democratic National Convention in Tammany Hall's new "Wigwam." He was uncertain who would make the strongest candidate, however, and delayed so long in making his preference known to the delegates that on the twenty-first ballot they stampeded to a fellow New Yorker, Horatio Seymour, the Civil War governor. It was a development that pleased neither Seymour nor Tilden. Seymour tried to decline, then agreed to run, and Tilden served as his personal campaign manager.[3]

As chairman of his state central committee and a leading member of the New York bar, Tilden could hardly have been ignorant of the nature, if not the scope, of the depredations of the Tweed Ring in New York City, yet on his own initiative he did nothing. The crucial first steps against Tweed were taken

1. Robert Kelley, "The Thought and Character of Samuel J. Tilden: The Democrat as Inheritor," *Historian*, XXVI (February, 1964), 177.
2. *Ibid.*, 178–83, 203.
3. Alexander Clarence Flick, *Samuel Jones Tilden: A Study in Political Sagacity* (New York: Dodd, Mead and Company, 1939), 151–91.

by the Republican New York *Times*, which devoted its front page throughout most of the summer of 1871 to the publication of records that left no doubt about the ring's corruption.[4] When Tilden finally acted, it was to make certain that Tweed was overthrown by Democrats rather than Republicans, lest the party itself be smashed in the process. He explained, "We have to face the question whether we will fall with the wrong doers or whether we will separate from them and take our chances of possible defeat now, with resurrection hereafter." [5] After the *Times* exposé Tilden played a major role in prosecuting the ring.[6] In the campaign of 1871 he cooperated with a new organization called Apollo Hall, an uneasy coalition of reformers and anti-Tweed politicians that captured nearly all the city offices. Tilden himself was elected to the state legislature. Once Tweed's men had been swept from their official places, however, Tilden, recognizing the advantages of an established organization, returned to Tammany to work for reform from within. Apollo Hall was left to its own devices and soon disappeared.[7]

Organization was Tilden's forte. Although he shared the belief of most reformers in politics that a campaign ought properly to be directed toward the education of voters, he recognized that the party structure necessary for this task could not be created overnight merely by issuing a circular letter. A successful organization required dedicated and experienced workers. Since finding and training such men was a time-consuming process, it followed that the enterprise had to be permanent. As state chairman, Tilden concentrated on locating reliable canvassers in every election district—men who would confine their

4. *Ibid.*, 209–14; Alexander B. Callow, Jr., *The Tweed Ring* (New York: Oxford University Press, 1966), 238–39, 253–62; Mark D. Hirsch, "Samuel J. Tilden: The Story of a Lost Opportunity," *American Historical Review*, LVI (July, 1951), 790–96.

5. Draft, S. J. Tilden to Robert Minturn, August 12, 1871, in Samuel J. Tilden Papers, New York Public Library.

6. Seymour J. Mandelbaum, *Boss Tweed's New York* (New York: John Wiley and Sons, Inc., 1965), 84; Callow, *The Tweed Ring*, 271.

7. Flick, *Samuel Jones Tilden*, 216–30; Mark D. Hirsch, *William C. Whitney: Modern Warwick* (New York: Dodd, Mead and Company, 1948), 53–65.

activities to their own small areas of responsibility: "Remember,—that the effort you are asked to make in your town or election district is *part* of a *system*. You are acting *in concert*. Your associates depend on you to keep up your portion of the line." Morale, a prerequisite for success, required universal implementation of the system: "It is wrong that what our friends gain in several towns by extreme exertions and sacrifices should be lost by the inefficiency of some in *one* town or election-district [.] " [8] For Tilden, encouraging each worker to concentrate on his own assignment was the secret to making this method work. By 1871 he had developed poll books to standardize the gathering of information about both reliable and doubtful voters.[9] Soon he learned to use the canvass of voters as a guide for the effective distribution of campaign literature. In time he compiled a list of fifty thousand Democrats, more than 10 percent of the party's voters, consisting of all those men who could be relied on for various tasks in a campaign.[10] Roeliff Brinkerhoff visited Tilden in Albany during the canvass of 1876 and saw this system in operation: "He seemed to have made it his business . . . to deal with individual workers of his party in each locality, rather than with party committees. By this personal attention each man felt complimented, and would naturally be more interested in his welfare. Of course this method required a large correspondence, but it was a work his secretaries could do for the most part, and the results were a popularity for Mr. Tilden among the rank and file of his party, that few men have equaled." [11] The secret to maintaining so large a correspon-

8. Circular letter, Tilden and Allen C. Beach to [Democratic election district workers], October 26, 1870, in Daniel Scott Lamont Papers, Manuscript Division, Library of Congress. See also circular letter, William Cassidy and Tilden to [Democratic election district workers], October 28, 1871, in Tilden Papers.

9. Circular letter, Tilden to [Democratic election district workers], September 11, 1871, in Lamont Papers. Another copy is in the Tilden Papers.

10. William C. Hudson, *Random Recollections of an Old Political Reporter* (New York: Cupples and Leon Company, 1911), 45–46.

11. Roeliff Brinkerhoff, *Recollections of a Lifetime* (Cincinnati: Robert Clarke Company, 1900), 227.

dence was the use, as circulars, of lithograph copies of original letters in Tilden's own hand.

Despite Tilden's best efforts, the Democrats of New York were routed in the presidential election of 1872. Horace Greeley lost his home state decisively. Republican John A. Dix captured the governorship by a record plurality. No doubt, these results reflected at least in part the public reaction to the Tweed scandal, uncovered only the year before.

The obvious solution to Democratic woes was to nominate for high office the man who had made himself most conspicuous in finally ridding the party of Tweed and his associates. Accordingly, during the summer of 1874 Tilden's friends urged him to run for governor.[12] Tilden, as was his custom, hesitated for a time. Once he had decided to make the race, however, he and his associates worked diligently in every township of the state to round up the necessary delegates to assure success when the nominating convention met.[13] Tilden was aided by the seeming impossibility of defeating Governor Dix and by the open admission of such partisan Republican journals as the New York *Times* and New York *Tribune* that he would be a candidate of the highest caliber.[14] On September 16 he was nominated on the first ballot.[15]

Tilden supervised his own campaign, assisted by his successor as state chairman, Allen C. Beach. The network of district workers he had built was the foundation of the effort and functioned well. Newspapers were kept fully informed on favorable developments, and large quantities of literature were distributed. Horatio Seymour, Francis Kernan, Abram S. Hewitt,

12. R. Earl to Tilden, July 8, 1874, Francis Kernan to Tilden, July 21, 1874, and Daniel Magone, Jr., to Tilden, August 21, 1874, all in Tilden Papers.
13. John Bigelow, *The Life of Samuel J. Tilden* (2 vols.; New York: Harper and Brothers, 1895), I, 222–23; Kernan to Tilden, September 12, 1874, in John Bigelow (ed.), *Letters and Literary Memorials of Samuel J. Tilden* (2 vols.; New York: Harper and Brothers, 1908), I, 336; Tilden to Kernan, September 9, 1874, in Francis Kernan Correspondence, John M. Olin Research Library, Cornell University.
14. Bigelow, *The Life of Samuel J. Tilden*, I, 224–29.
15. Flick, *Samuel Jones Tilden*, 244–45.

and William Dorsheimer led an able corps of speakers.[16] Tilden confided to a friend a week after his nomination: "I do not see how with a good organization to get the voters out, we can fail. . . . In this city everything looks finely. There is no democratic defection worth speaking of. . . . We expect a large share of the German Republican vote; and a large share of the non partisan business & professional classes who went for Dix two years ago." [17] On election day Tilden told another friend that he would win by "a little in excess of fifty thousand." [18] The official margin was 50,317. In a vivid demonstration of the power of urban political machines, Tilden carried the cities of New York and Brooklyn by 55,526 votes, overwhelming the 5,209-vote edge Dix obtained in the state's fifty-eight other counties.[19]

Having achieved the governor's mansion, Tilden set out to further his political career by repeating the strategy that had already brought him so far. He employed at his own expense an engineer and an auditor to examine the operations of the Erie Canal. With the information thus obtained he prepared a message to the legislature detailing the machinations of the bipartisan Canal Ring, which annually defrauded the state of large sums of money through the use of inflated repair contracts.[20] During all this time Tilden missed few opportunities to review the various excesses of the Grant administration. In January, 1876, fully a third of his second Annual Message dealt with the need for a thorough house-cleaning in Washington.[21] The New York *World*, edited by Tilden's close friend, Manton Marble,

16. *Ibid.*, 249–50; circular letter, Tilden to [Democratic election district workers], August 29, 1874, and circular letter, Beach to [Democratic election district workers], October 9, 1874, both in Tilden Papers; circular letter, Tilden to election district captains, October 10, 1874, in Manton Malone Marble Papers, Manuscript Division, Library of Congress.
17. Tilden to Frank Abbott, September 23, 1874, in Tilden Papers.
18. Allan Nevins, *Abram S. Hewitt: With Some Account of Peter Cooper* (New York: Harper and Brothers, 1935), 297–98.
19. *The Tribune Almanac and Political Register for 1875* (New York: The Tribune Association, [1875]), 52.
20. Flick, *Samuel Jones Tilden*, 265–78.
21. John Bigelow (ed.), *The Writings and Speeches of Samuel J. Tilden* (2 vols.; New York: Harper and Brothers, 1885), II, 238–92.

headlined this event with the phrase that was to become the Democratic campaign slogan in 1876: "Tilden and Reform." [22] To become president, the governor of New York had to pull his party away from the issues of the Civil War, while avoiding the divisive question of the currency. A campaign for "reform" would be his means for doing so. The size of his victory over Dix and the publicity attending his attacks on the Tweed and Canal rings made Tilden the leading contender for the Democratic presidential nomination from the outset. [23]

2

Other candidates were not lacking, of course, but none possessed the stature of New York's governor at the start of the presidential year. Aristocratic Thomas F. Bayard was heir to a long family tradition of representing Delaware in the United States Senate—his grandfather, his uncle, and his father all having served there before him. Before being elected to the upper house, his grandfather, James A. Bayard, Sr., the leading Federalist in Delaware, had served in the House of Representatives and played a key role in arranging a settlement of the deadlocked presidential election of 1800 between Thomas Jefferson and Aaron Burr. James A. Bayard, Jr., was an ardent Unionist who briefly became a Republican to express his support for Abraham Lincoln. He opposed measures against slavery, however, and resigned his Senate seat in 1864 to protest the Test Oath for officeholders. Later reelected, he stepped down again in 1869 and was succeeded by his son. Thomas F. Bayard was a strict constructionist, an untiring opponent of militarism, socialism, and special interest legislation, who sought the backing of the same conservative, sound-money Democrats who formed the core of Tilden's support.

Thomas A. Hendricks, elected governor of Indiana in 1872

22. New York *World*, January 3, 1876.
23. E. Casserly to M. Marble, November 26, 1874, in Marble Papers; David A. Wells to Tilden, May 20, 1875, in Tilden Papers; Geo. L. Miller to Horatio Seymour, November 11, 1875, in Fairchild Collection of the Papers of Horatio Seymour, New York Historical Society.

in what was otherwise a Republican year, and former governor William Allen of Ohio, the man Hayes defeated for reelection in 1875, represented the western inflationist challenge. Allen's nephew, veteran Senator Allen G. Thurman, also of Ohio, appealed to the West's desire for recognition while shunning the financial heresies popular in the region. Supreme Court Justice David Davis had the support of several congressmen from his home state of Illinois and, briefly, of Senator David M. Key of Tennessee as well. Davis had been a close friend of Abraham Lincoln; indeed, he had been one of his managers at the national convention in Chicago in 1860. Thus, a Nashville friend promptly asked Key, "Is he a 'reliable Democrat' as you suggest, and where is the evidence of it?" [24]

General Winfield Scott Hancock was interested, as always, in becoming Pennsylvania's favorite son. He had some strength there and elsewhere among Democrats anxious to copy the Whig-Republican formula by nominating a military hero in their search for a winner.[25] Jeremiah S. Black, a prominent figure in the Buchanan administration, was also spoken of as a candidate in Pennsylvania, but on May 1 he asked that his name be withdrawn in favor of Hancock.[26]

Several candidacies on the Democratic side were truly ephemeral, existing principally in the minds of the aspirants involved. Journalist William Purcell told Senator Francis Kernan, with undisguised astonishment, that Chief Justice Sanford Church of the New York State Court of Appeals had written asking that quiet "inquiries" be made on his behalf. Purcell added: "As I do not regard his nomination as particularly im-

24. Lyman Trumbull to J. M. Palmer, March 2, 1876, in John M. Palmer Papers, Illinois State Historical Library; Jas. D. Porter to D. M. Key, February 28, 1876, in David M. Key Papers, Chattanooga Public Library.

25. Winfd. S. Hancock to J. S. Black, March 17, 1875, in Jeremiah S. Black Papers, Manuscript Division, Library of Congress; R. P. Spalding to James R. Doolittle, May 22, 1876, in James Rood Doolittle Papers, State Historical Society of Wisconsin; New York *World*, May 24, 1876.

26. Black to James P. Barr, May 1, 1876, in New York *World*, May 6, 1876.

minent, I think you might relieve his mind without injury to anyone." [27] At least one man, former abolitionist Cassius M. Clay of Kentucky, diligently solicited support during 1875 for the vice-presidential nomination, even writing to leading Republicans on the subject.[28]

Against these rivals Tilden waged a relentless and resourceful campaign, confident that against such weak and divided opposition he had only to educate the rank and file of the party concerning his own strengths as a candidate. His advisers were Abram S. Hewitt, Manton Marble, Montgomery Blair, Henry Watterson, David A. Wells, John Bigelow, and others. These men had reliable lieutenants in every state who kept the candidate informed of local developments and urged his cause before county and state conventions.[29] Tilden's supporters hammered away continuously at the theme that their candidate represented the new cause—reform—which would free the party of past issues without entangling it in new internal disputes.[30] Accurate information was vital to this effort. To obtain local news quickly, one of Tilden's assistants queried Marble concerning the expense of exchanging issues of the New York *World* for copies of 2,600 other papers in all parts of the country.[31] High costs may have necessitated a reduction in the number of newspapers traded,

27. Wm. Purcell to Kernan, April 11, 1876, in Kernan Correspondence.

28. Cassius M. Clay to Cyrus H. McCormick, September 18, 1875, in Cyrus Hall McCormick Papers, State Historical Society of Wisconsin; Clay to T. F. Bayard, October 8, 1875, in Thomas F. Bayard Papers, Manuscript Division, Library of Congress; Clay to Z. Chandler, November 20, 1875, in Zachariah Chandler Papers. Manuscript Division, Library of Congress.

29. Bushrod Morse to Kernan, May 18, 1876, in Kernan Correspondence; H. M. Doak to Marble, May 13, June 10, 1876, Geo. S. Miller to Marble, April 9, 1876, John P. Irish to Marble, May 19, 1876, and L. D. M. Sneed to Marble, June 15, 1876, all in Marble Papers; Wells to Tilden, May 5, 1876, and John T. Morgan to Montgomery Blair, June 3, 1876, both in Bigelow (ed.), *Letters and Literary Memorials of Samuel J. Tilden*, II, 403–404, 432–34.

30. Blair to Wm. H. Owens, May 10, 1875, in Montgomery Blair Papers, Manuscript Division, Library of Congress; Marble to Wm. H. English, May 8, 1876, in William H. English Collection, Indiana Historical Society Library.

31. W. T. Pelton to Marble, March 28, 1876, in Marble Papers.

and on May 1 financial difficulties forced Marble to sell the *World*; [32] but the plan nevertheless indicates the magnitude and meticulousness of the Tilden campaign. Tilden could rely on these methods to obtain adequate support in most parts of the country. The one exception—and Tilden's greatest problem— was the South.

As a new figure in national politics, Tilden was hardly known beyond Mason and Dixon's line. Accordingly, a southern bureau was established "to send out publications and missionaries in order to make his character and career known to the Democratic masses of the South, whose votes would necessarily be controlling in the coming Presidential convention." [33] At the same time, "a committee of Southerners residing in New York was formed. Never a leading Southern man came to town who was not seen. If of enough importance he was taken to No. 15 Gramercy Park [Tilden's fashionable residence]. Mr. Tilden measured to the Southern standard of the gentleman in politics." [34] Watterson, Blair, and General Richard C. Taylor,[35] son of President Zachary Taylor, led the campaign to enhance Tilden's reputation in the South.

The Tilden men were soon satisfied that, although the first choice of most southerners was Bayard, the southern delegates would cast their votes in a bloc for whichever candidate was strongest in the North. Southern Democrats were convinced that any candidate they appeared to be working for would be damned in the eyes of northern voters: "Bayard, as you may suppose, would be our first choice; infinitely first beyond all others. But would not his nomination 'fire the northern heart', and would not many who would vote for Tilden vote against Bayard as a Con-

32. Sister Mary Cortona Phelan, *Manton Marble of the New York World* (Washington: Catholic University of America Press, 1957), 92.

33. Abram S. Hewitt, "Secret History of the Disputed Election, 1876–77," in Allan Nevins (ed.), *Selected Writings of Abram S. Hewitt* (New York: Columbia University Press, 1937), 157.

34. Henry Watterson, *"Marse Henry": An Autobiography* (2 vols.; New York: George H. Doran Company, 1919), I, 288.

35. R. Taylor to Sam[uel L. M. Barlow], April 8, 1876, in Samuel Latham Mitchell Barlow Papers, Henry E. Huntington Library, San Marino, California.

federate candidate?"[36] This attitude crippled Bayard's hopes for the nomination, all the more so since Delaware, his home, was itself a former slave state. Tilden's friends worked to encourage southern "passivism," confident that their man would be the beneficiary of it by virtue of his strength in New York and Connecticut.[37] Bayard himself, perhaps unwittingly, aided this strategy. He advised at least one southern politician, "The man of our party who combines [the] most capacities for obtaining the confidence & support of the Northern & Western States should in my opinion be accepted by the South whether they would under other circumstances have preferred him or not."[38]

With Bayard's candidacy so effectively neutralized, Tilden's chief opposition came from the various western aspirants; and Senator Eugene Casserly had assured Marble in 1874 that these men "will chew up each other."[39] Two of them even hailed from the same state. William Allen had once represented Ohio for twelve years in the United States Senate, serving as chairman of the Foreign Relations Committee in the days of the Mexican War. Defeated for a third term by Salmon P. Chase in 1849, he retired to his 1,400-acre farm near Chillicothe and remained there contentedly for nearly a quarter of a century. In 1873 Allen G. Thurman was up for reelection to the Senate and wanted the strongest possible candidate for governor to help assure the Democrats control of the legislature. The political resurrection of his uncle was his idea. The strategy worked. Allen was elected governor, the Democrats captured the legislature, and Thurman won six more years in Washington. Only later, when Allen discovered the popularity of greenbacks in a depression and both

36. Wm. M. Browne to Barlow, April 29, 1876, *ibid.* See also John D. Tremain to H. D. Manly, April 16, 1876, and S. Bassett French to Tilden, June 2, 1876, both in Tilden Papers; N. H. Massie to Blair, April 17, 1876, N. H. R. Dawson to Blair, April 17, 1876, L. N. Whittle to Blair, April 18, 1876, and James L. Kemper to Blair, April 28, May 2, 1876, all in Blair Papers. Kemper was governor of Virginia.
37. August Belmont to Bayard, June 9, 1876, and Perry Belmont to Bayard, June 20, 1876, both in Bayard Papers.
38. Draft, Bayard to Eppa Hunton, June 20, 1875, *ibid.*
39. Casserly to Marble, November 26, 1874, in Marble Papers. Casserly told Bayard the same thing. See E. C[asserly] to Bayard, November 26, 1874, in Bayard Papers.

men developed symptoms of presidential fever, did complications arise.

Allen lost his bid for a second term in the statehouse in October, 1875. This damaging defeat dulled his appeal elsewhere, but did nothing to curtail the enthusiasm of many Ohio Democrats either for inflation or for the man who had bravely solicited votes on the issue. At the state convention in May, 1876, the Thurman forces at first appeared to have a narrow edge. They controlled the committee on resolutions, which adopted, by a vote of eleven to nine, a platform combining a demand for repeal of the Resumption Act with a pledge to return to specie payments as soon as that could be accomplished without disturbing the nation's business. On the floor of the convention, however, Thurman's supporters revealed a disastrous lack of leadership. A minority report, advocating currency inflation and instructing the state's delegates to the national convention to vote as a unit for Allen for president, was ably presented by George W. Morgan and Thomas Ewing. Caught off guard, the Thurman men lost control of the situation. The minority report was adopted, 368 to 300. The result was a delegation that probably favored Thurman, twenty-three to twenty-one, but which was required to vote for Allen so long as he chose to remain in the race.[40] The bitterness of the Thurman adherents was so great that Allen's lieutenants decided not to have their candidate address the convention that had just endorsed him.[41]

Just as Allen effectively nullified Thurman as a candidate, the rivalry of Hendricks and Allen reduced the chances of both. Hendricks had several advantages. He was still governor of Indiana. He was fifty-six years of age, whereas Allen was seventy-two. He also had the unanimous support of his state organization. Hendricks enjoyed particular success with the familiar argument that only Indiana, New York, and the "Solid

40. New York *World*, May 18, 1876; Durbin Ward to Allen G. Thurman, May 21, 1876, Llewellyn Baker to Thurman, May 26, 1876, and Ed. N. Bingham to Thurman, May 24, 1876, all in Allen G. Thurman Papers, Ohio Historical Society Library.
41. G. W. Morgan to Wm. Allen, May 19, 1876, in William Allen Papers, Manuscript Division, Library of Congress.

South" had to be carried for the Democratic party to capture the presidency. No one doubted that Hendricks was the most popular Democrat in Indiana. His supporters emphasized tirelessly that the result in the Hoosier State in October usually foretold the result in New York in November.[42] On the other hand, wise New Yorkers recognized that the Indianan's connections with some of the less savory elements of Tammany Hall would ultimately hurt the party in the Empire State. Samuel Barlow told Senator Bayard: "Schell and his friends are committed absolutely to Hendricks. He in turn is committed to the Canal Ring & to Tilden's enemies to such an extent as to render his nomination unwise, if not impossible and so as to render his final success, in my judgment, utterly out of the question." [43]

Hendricks and Allen both had appeal among the inflationists of the western and southern states. Thomas Ewing, for example, who became one of Allen's managers in Ohio, also spoke favorably of Hendricks as a candidate.[44] Throughout the spring it was clear that Hendricks would obtain enough delegates to stand second behind Tilden on the early ballots, but without the large Ohio vote it was doubtful whether he could successfully challenge the New Yorker. Nevertheless, Allen, even when informed that he was making little progress against the better-organized Hendricks forces,[45] refused to withdraw from the race.

3

The Democratic National Committee met on February 22 and designated June 27 as the date and St. Louis as the site for the party's national convention.[46] As the appointed time approached, Tilden's supporters, as they had before, moved with

42. Marvin H. Bovee to Dr. Wendell A. Anderson, April 26, 1876, in Wendell A. Anderson Papers, State Historical Society of Wisconsin.
43. B[arlow] to Bayard, March 25, 1876, in Bayard Papers. In June, 1875, Allen also had one of his supporters negotiating with the New York leaders whose toes had been stepped on when Tilden moved against the Canal Ring. See G. W. Morgan to Allen, June 25, 30, 1875, in Allen Papers.
44. Thomas Ewing to Doolittle, March 28, 1876, in Doolittle Papers.
45. G. W. Morgan to Allen, June 25, 1876, in Allen Papers.
46. New York *World*, February 23, 1876.

assurance. The most significant obstacle Tilden still had to overcome was the frequently voiced concern that the feuding within the New York party would jeopardize his chances for carrying that state.[47] These internal disputes had arisen partly from the battles against the Tweed and Canal rings and partly from a struggle for control of the party organization in New York City. Tilden attributed his difficulties with city boss John Kelly to the latter's desire to control the federal patronage in New York should Tilden achieve the presidency.[48] He questioned whether the leaders of the Canal Ring possessed any real strength and doubted that either Kelly or the ring could muster many votes against him; so his method of demonstrating his popularity at home was direct. The New York convention was called for April 26, before most of the states had chosen their delegates. When the other state conventions met, their members would have fresh in their minds another example of Tilden's ability to win.

Tilden's gamble may have paid off better than even he anticipated. On April 10 the New York *World* surveyed those counties that had already chosen delegates to the state convention and found ample indications that the governor's friends would have overwhelming control.[49] The *World*'s predictions were correct. When the convention met, a resolution instructing the delegation to St. Louis to present Tilden's name as the one best calculated to carry the Empire State in November encountered virtually no opposition. Francis Kernan, William Dorsheimer, and Abram S. Hewitt were selected delegates at large.[50] Tilden's closest friend and adviser, John Bigelow, was surprised to find that "the hostility of the Kelly or Tammany delegation seemed to disappear the moment they got into the Convention." Moreover, Bigelow welcomed the token opposition Kelly did offer Tilden: "It will give him the benefit of whatever prejudice there

47. J. B. Gordon to Barlow, June 7, 1876, in Barlow Papers; Miller to Kernan, May 20, 1876, and Pelton to Kernan, May 20, 1876, both in Kernan Correspondence.
48. John Bigelow Diary, April 19, 1876, in John Bigelow Papers, New York Public Library.
49. New York *World*, April 10, 1876.
50. *Ibid.*, April 27, 28, 1876.

is in the Country against Tammany." [51] Samuel Barlow, keeping Bayard abreast of developments, still thought Tilden had a precarious hold on the New York organization, but conceded that "he may be much stronger than I suppose him to be." [52] Richard Taylor, one of Tilden's southern lieutenants, was much more specific when he warned Barlow: "The New York opposition to Tilden is proving beneficial to Hendricks instead of to Bayard. John Kelly, Schell, S. S. Cox and the Church influence are for Hendricks. All the trading people take naturally the same direction—including those fragrant flowers—the Pennsylvanians. Bayard's name is used to break down Tilden, but all the rogues are for Hendricks. . . . Bayard's friends are gifted with a credulity surpassing that of Joseph if they believe the Tammany thieves or the Canal thieves are in favor of his nomination." [53] Barlow, at least, recognized this fact, for he had long believed that Bayard should be held in reserve as a compromise candidate, to be vigorously presented only if Tilden failed, and then only with the governor's support.

But it is likely that Tilden's opponents never understood the nature of the opposition to him in his own state. The fastidious Bayard wrote David A. Wells in May: "For a '*skillful* manager' he has succeeded in working up an antagonism to himself within the ranks of his own party which an open enemy could hardly have hoped to create. I have looked with a great deal of apprehension upon this wide and violent breach in the ranks of the Demo party in this state, which may result not in the defeat of *one* candidate but of *any* candidate." [54] A week before the national convention Barlow found himself compelled to explain to the senator from Delaware: "Tilden will win and he will carry this State, no matter what his opponents may say. There is no such feeling of hostility to him here as the various Ring men announce, and outside of these Rings his

51. Bigelow Diary, April 28, 1876, in Bigelow Papers.
52. Barlow to Bayard, May 11, 1876, in Bayard Papers.
53. Taylor to Barlow, May 18, 1876, in Barlow Papers.
54. Bayard to Wells, May 27, 1876, in David Ames Wells Papers, Manuscript Division, Library of Congress.

opponents are chiefly those who seek office and who fear that they will not succeed so well with him as with a stranger." [55] Barlow had already written a similar letter to John G. Priest of St. Louis, stressing that although he preferred Bayard he would gladly support Tilden as an unusually strong second choice: "At the election you may count all the democrats of the State, who do not support him earnestly, on your hand." Priest submitted Barlow's note to the St. Louis *Republican* (actually a Democratic paper), which published it. [56]

The Tilden strategy of impressing the delegates to St. Louis with his ability to win worked especially well in the South. At the Virginia convention on May 31, for example, Bayard and Hancock were reported to be the favorites. Yet that state's delegation was expected to vote for Tilden unless a last-minute canvass of northern Democrats indicated that his strength had faltered. [57] In the Democratic party a two-thirds majority was required to nominate a presidential candidate. Two weeks before the convention Tilden's lieutenants declared they would have 450 of the necessary 491 votes on the first ballot. Even the hostile Chicago *Times* conceded him 385 delegates. The friends of Governor Hendricks claimed only 200. [58] On the eve of the convention's first session most of the southern delegates caucused and reaffirmed their intention of casting their 254 votes as a bloc for the ticket most likely to carry the critical northern states. [59] That meant Tilden.

From St. Louis, J. S. Moore reported to Bayard on June 25:

Things look here only *one way*. Sam Tilden has nearly the only organized party machinery, all the other candidates look as primitive in organization. It does not follow that he will be nominated. But if hard work, influence, & strong & powerful uses can accomplish it, he will certainly carry his nomination. . . .

As for yourself, there is no actual organization. Men like Belmont, Travers, Hunter & a few others certainly urge you, but it is a sort of

55. B[arlow] to Bayard, June 21, 1876, in Bayard Papers.
56. Letterpress copy, Barlow to John G. Priest, June 12, 1876, and Priest to Barlow, June 15, 1876, both in Barlow Papers.
57. New York *World*, June 1, 1876.
58. *Ibid.*, June 11, 1876; Chicago *Times*, June 23, 1876.
59. New York *World*, June 27, 1876.

outside talk. I have failed to find any *"Southern"* outright honest expression for you, not even Maryland. . . . Of course they told *me* that you are their favorite, but they are going for Tilden.[60]

Without disguising his admiration, another Bayard supporter perceptively explained the Tilden strategy a few days after the convention:

The friends of Mr. Tilden were organized as one man. It was wonderful to see the operations of his friends. The whole situation had been overlooked. Every point had been examined. The popular sentiment began early to follow in the wake of the plan of attack, or of support of their candidate, and *before* the convention organized doubtful delegates, unfriendly delegates, delegates with first choices other than Tilden, began to say "well, it seems as if Tilden will be nominated on the second ballot [.]" This prepared the way for reaching the result, and *made it*. The states that were ready to vote for a compromise nomination, did not wish to be absent at the call that *made* the nomination, and others thought it best to be present at the *first* call. This is the exact state of the case. Mr. Tilden was nominated by those who did not wish a nomination to be made without *them*. Such was the wit and skill and the astute management of his friends. It was a result obtained as if it was the only one possible. Your position before the party is, from what I heard, a commanding one. But the most formidable and best position is only to be made effective by the troops that occupy it.[61]

The floor managers responsible for this effort were Henry Watterson, who won over the Kentucky delegation from Hancock; Montgomery Blair, who concentrated on the southern delegates; William L. Scott of Pennsylvania; and Abram S. Hewitt.[62] Even Samuel Barlow, though a warm friend of Bayard, worked hard in the end to counter any lingering influence John Kelly might have. During the convention he was in close communication with Tilden himself.[63]

60. J. S. Moore to Bayard, June 25, 1876, in Bayard Papers.
61. Richard Vaux to Bayard, July 4, 1876, *ibid.*
62. Joseph Frazier Wall, *Henry Watterson: Reconstructed Rebel* (New York: Oxford University Press, 1956), 129–31; Nevins, *Abram S. Hewitt*, 306–308.
63. Letterpress copy, Barlow to Gordon, June 26, 1876, and letterpress copy, Barlow to Tilden, June 26, 1876, both in Barlow Papers.

4

The convention opened on June 27. The selection of Watterson as temporary chairman, by a vote of twenty-five to seven in the national committee, revealed immediately the direction in which events were moving.[64] Later the same day, another Tilden supporter, John A. McClernand of Illinois, was named president of the convention by a similar vote in the committee on permanent organization.[65] A draft platform having been carefully prepared beforehand by Manton Marble, under Tilden's personal supervision,[66] only one problem remained to be solved by the committee on resolutions—how to obtain a majority for an acceptable financial plank. And Marble informed Tilden on the evening of the first day that their proposals could be "carried without alteration by tact and persistence." [67]

The committee on resolutions at first found the achievement of harmony on any currency plank a difficult matter. In a meeting which lasted into the early morning hours of June 28, a resolution calling for repeal of that clause of the Act of 1875 setting a specific date—January 1, 1879—for the resumption of specie payments was adopted, eighteen to sixteen. No agreement could be reached, however, on a substitute for the existing law. The committee reassembled an hour before the convention session of June 28. It promptly voted down the inflationist proposals of Thomas Ewing of Ohio and Daniel W. Voorhees of Indiana. Instead, an evasive compromise opposing both inflation and the "sham" or "forced" resumption of the 1875 act, was adopted by a very large majority.[68]

---

64. Wall, *Henry Watterson*, 131–32.
65. Telegram, Pelton to Geo. W. Smith, June 27, 1876, in Marble Papers.
66. See draft, M[anton] M[arble] to [Tilden, June 18, 1876], *ibid.*, in which Marble discusses some revisions he had made at Tilden's suggestion. Three drafts of the platform, two rough versions in Marble's hand, and a more polished one in the hand of an amanuensis, are also preserved in Volume 45 of the Marble Papers.
67. Telegram, M[anton] M[arble] to Geo. W. Smith, June 27, 1876, *ibid.*
68. New York *World*, June 29, 1876.

The convention debate on the platform took place that same afternoon. William Dorsheimer of New York read the majority report of the committee on resolutions. It was a lengthy document (James G. Blaine called it "the most elaborate paper of the kind ever put forth by a National Convention." [69]) that expounded two complementary themes. The Republican party was assailed for corruption, extravagance, and lack of leadership; reform was declared to be the order of the day in the civil service, taxation, government expenditures, and the currency.[70] Two minority reports were also introduced. The first, presenting the extreme hard-money position and signed by the committee members from Maine, Massachusetts, Connecticut, New York, and New Jersey, would merely strike out the line of the platform calling for repeal of the resumption clause. This proposal was never brought to a vote. Supported by the representatives of Pennsylvania, Ohio, Indiana, Iowa, Kansas, Missouri, Tennessee, and West Virginia, the second minority report expressed the inflationist position. It demanded repeal of the entire Resumption Act of 1875. General Ewing made a highly effective speech in behalf of this proposition, one which left the Tilden men distinctly uncomfortable, but the day was promptly saved by Dorsheimer. As the New York *World* described it, "Acknowledging that the majority report was a compromise, he then brought the convention direct to the issue in a clear, bold and forcible manner by declaring that the issue between the two reports was that of hard money and soft money." No Democrat could be elected, Dorsheimer maintained, without New York, and no one could carry New York on a soft money platform.

69. James G. Blaine, *Twenty Years of Congress: From Lincoln to Garfield. With a Review of the Events Which Led to the Political Revolution of 1860* (2 vols.; Norwich, Conn.: Henry Bill Publishing Company, 1893), II, 578.

70. *Official Proceedings of the National Democratic Convention, Held in St. Louis, Mo., June 27th, 28th and 29th, 1876. With an Appendix Containing the Letters of Acceptance of Gov. Tilden and Gov. Hendricks* (St. Louis: Woodward, Tiernan and Hale, 1876), 94–99. The full text of the platform is more conveniently available in Kirk H. Porter and Donald Bruce Johnson (eds.), *National Party Platforms, 1840–1960* (Urbana: University of Illinois Press, 1961), 49–51.

According to the *World*: "This announcement was like an electric shock to the convention and sent a thrill through the entire assemblage. It fixed the attention of the convention, and each sentence of his short speech made the issue more apparent. From that moment there was no doubt of the result." [71] Marble telegraphed Tilden, "Dorsheimer did magnificently today." [72] The inflationist plank was defeated, 515 to 219; the majority report was then quietly adopted, 651 to 83. [73]

The convention proceeded immediately to the selection of a presidential candidate. Six names were formally placed in nomination: Bayard, Hendricks, Governor Joel Parker of New Jersey, Tilden, Allen, and Hancock. The presentation of Hancock's name was the result of a prolonged struggle for power within the Pennsylvania delegation, which was irreparably split into two factions, one loyal to Senator William A. Wallace and the other to Congressman Samuel J. Randall. Wallace favored Hendricks and Randall supported Tilden. With the delegation required by its instructions to use the unit rule, a vote for either Tilden or Hendricks would necessarily entail the humiliation of one of the state's most prominent Democrats; so in St. Louis, Randall and Wallace compromised on Hancock. [74] By the time this decision was reached, the general's earlier appeal had substantially faded in the general disillusionment with Grant's performance. One eastern liberal who inclined toward the Democratic party noted that "our sort of folks, want *brains* not epaulets and feathers, for President." [75] Samuel Barlow agreed: "Our people and I believe the whole people are sick of military Presidents." [76] Some of the Illinois delegates had also planned

71. New York *World*, June 29, 1876. This episode is vividly remembered in Hudson, *Random Recollections*, 53–59.
72. Telegram, Marble to Tilden, June 28, 1876, in Marble Papers.
73. *Official Proceedings of the National Democratic Convention . . . 1876*, 99–117.
74. Evans, *Pennsylvania Politics, 1872–1877*, 264–69.
75. Jno. D. Defrees to Bowles, June 4, 1876, in Samuel Bowles Papers, Yale University Library.
76. Letterpress copy, Barlow to John Hunter, June 19, 1876, in Barlow Papers.

to present David Davis as a dark-horse candidate, but almost at the last minute they learned it was unlikely "that he would accept the nomination if tendered him. So *that* is ended." [77]

On the first ballot Tilden received at least some support from twenty-eight of the thirty-eight states and amassed 401½ votes; Hendricks was second with only 140½; Hancock obtained 75, 58 of which were from Pennsylvania; Allen got 54, all but 10 being from Ohio; Bayard secured a mere 33; and Joel Parker had New Jersey's 18. Missouri cast 16 complimentary votes for General James O. Broadhead, a favorite son, and then quickly transferred them to Tilden, giving the governor of New York 417½.[78] Tilden's managers were pleased. Only two states had failed to meet their expectations—Georgia, which gave most of its votes to Bayard, and Illinois, which at this point preferred Hendricks, 23 to 19.[79]

Tilden had a clear majority on the first call of the states. He was nominated on the second. Each of the first eight states— Alabama through Georgia—cast their ballots for the New Yorker unanimously, giving him 98 votes before any other candidate received one. Upon completion of the roll, he was only a dozen short of the two-thirds majority needed, and these votes were immediately obtained. Nevada, Iowa, and Illinois made minor switches in his favor, a practice permitted under the convention's rules; then Missouri put him over the top. When all the changes were complete, Tilden had 535, Hendricks 85, Hancock 58, Allen 54, Bayard 4, and Thurman 2. In the customary manner a resolution was adopted declaring the nomination

---

77. Chicago *Times*, June 23, 1876; Jno. D. Defrees to Bowles, June 21, 1876, in Bowles Papers.
78. *Official Proceedings of the National Democratic Convention . . . 1876*, 121–45.
79. Theodore P. Cook, *The Life and Public Services of Hon. Samuel J. Tilden, Democratic Nominee for President of the United States. To Which Is Added a Sketch of the Life of Hon. Thomas A. Hendricks, Democratic Nominee for Vice-President* (New York: D. Appleton and Company, 1876), 323. As Cook's work is an authorized campaign biography, it may be presumed that this information came either from Tilden or one of his close aides.

unanimous.[80] Tilden had passed the day in the Executive Mansion in Albany, occupied with his official duties and with the arrangement of some material in connection with a lawsuit to which he was a party. Late in the afternoon he ordered his carriage brought around. Asked whether the telegraph might not bring the results of the convention during his absence, he replied. "No, not until about half-past nine." [81] The governor received the Associated Press bulletin announcing his nomination later that evening in the presence of a handful of friends. " 'Is that so?' he inquired in the calmest tones, with not even a smile upon his countenance." Within minutes he was engaged in a conversation about campaign strategies.[82]

In St. Louis the convention adjourned for the night to permit canvassing of both the candidates and the delegates on the choice of a vice-presidential nominee. The New York *World* reported that the prevailing sentiment, as for some days past, was for a ticket of Tilden and Hendricks as the strongest the party could present.[83] A Louisianan expressed it best: "Cincinnati has played four aces on us, and if St. Louis don't draw to a royal flush and fill we shall all be invited to a big funeral in November—thats the way it looks to me now [.] " [84] Tilden accepted this judgment. The next day, Hendricks was nominated without opposition. Most Democratic leaders were well pleased with their ticket and exuberant over the prospects for a long-awaited victory. Precisely as Tilden and Samuel Barlow predicted, even John Kelly, who had earlier urged rejection of his fellow New Yorker's bid, mounted the platform in a mood of euphoria and made a conciliatory speech, pledging his active support in the forthcoming campaign.[85]

The national convention developed just as Tilden had planned.

80. *Official Proceedings of the National Democratic Convention . . . 1876*, 146–50.
81. Bigelow, *The Life of Samuel J. Tilden*, I, 307–308.
82. New York *World*, June 29, 1876.
83. *Ibid.*
84. F. H. Hatch to Barlow, June 18, 1876, in Barlow Papers.
85. *Official Proceedings of the National Democratic Convention . . . 1876*, 154–62.

It was not the first presidential nominating convention to be skillfully controlled in the interest of a particular candidate. Nor was Tilden the first politician to seek the presidency so actively. His unique achievement was the manner in which he asserted his control—in apparent conformity with the prevailing code of democratic political behavior. Great decisions were not made in smoke-filled rooms; the Democratic party in 1876 was not centralized enough to be susceptible to effective control by any group of political chieftains. Besides, such a procedure would have been repugnant to Democratic leaders and voters alike. Tilden's friends did their work well before the convention opened. They employed the same systematic organizational techniques Tilden had used to revitalize his state party. The difference was that whereas Tilden had worked with election district workers throughout New York, his friends were concerned with the delegates to county and state conventions throughout the country. Using this strategy Tilden could be assured of substantial convention strength without jeopardizing the necessary impression that the support was entirely spontaneous. It helped, of course, that the opposition was weak, divided, and poorly led. It helped, also, that after so many years out of power the Democrats possessed a natural unity—based on an overriding desire to return to office—which eluded the Republicans. The only potentially dangerous doctrinal dispute—that over the currency —was successfully straddled, at least for the time being. Thus, Tilden and his friends were able to control a traditionally open convention in such a manner that *it remained* an open convention. Unquestionably they were now in a favorable position to face the Republicans.

Chapter IV □ The Centennial Campaign

T HE DECENTRALIZATION of American political parties could be considered an advantage, at least when it came to nominating candidates, because it helped to make the system more democratic. But it was a constant headache for party leaders once the nominating process was completed; then it was a source of confusion and inefficiency, an obstacle to any party's attempt to take effective steps to improve its chances for winning an election. Virtually all organizational work, even in a presidential campaign, was performed by state party officials. The national committees largely confined themselves to raising funds and printing documents. The knowledge that some state leaders were less able or less dedicated than others was a source of continual anxiety to the candidates and national directors of each party, but they knew that little could be done to change the situation. Campaign committees were selected at the congressional district or county level, not imposed from above. Politicians of state or national importance occasionally developed elaborate schemes to restructure campaign organization along what the twentieth century would recognize as distinctly bureaucratic lines; but these hopeful proposals invariably fell victim to their alien formality, to the almost total absence of local workers capable of comprehending them, or to the charge that they were designed to centralize the party (as in fact they were). Furthermore, they were hindered by a pervasive lack of funds and the sluggish communications of the nineteenth century.

The election of 1876 was universally expected to be the most closely contested presidential election in more than a generation, even before the candidates were chosen. Republican and Democratic politicians alike were peculiarly alert to the importance that efficient organization would play in bringing out a full vote. Democratic leaders, especially, scenting victory after so many bitter defeats, made every effort to modernize their traditional canvassing techniques, only to be repeatedly frustrated by the complexity of the task. The Republicans, for their part, found that the large sums of money they were accustomed to spending in states of pivotal importance were unavailable in this depression year and soon fell to quarreling with one another in their uncertainty about what to do in such uncomfortable circumstances. In the end, the officials of both parties had to be content with performing as efficiently as possible the traditionally limited activities of the past. Indeed, it cannot be said that the efforts of either party organization clearly affected the outcome of the balloting.

1

One indication that the role of the national committees was narrowly circumscribed was the fact that they scarcely functioned except during presidential years and, accordingly, had to begin the work of preparing for a campaign anew each quadrennium. The Democratic National Executive Committee, for example, met in Washington on the evening of January 28 and "resolved to begin an early and active organization . . . for the campaign of 1876." The committee then chose several officers to assist Chairman Augustus Schell and within a few days opened a headquarters on F Street, two and a half blocks from the White House—the object of everyone's endeavors.[1] Otherwise, "the work of organization" consisted solely of compiling "large numbers of names of citizens, to whom Public Documents can

1. New York *World*, January 29, February 5, 1876.

usefully be sent," and obtaining the financial "assistance to en- able the Committee to proceed satisfactorily with this good work." [2] The committee could not be expected to do much else. After it issued the official call for the national convention and nominated a temporary chairman to preside over the conven- tion's first session, the committee itself would pass out of exis- tence; and the burden of conducting the campaign would fall upon the members of a new national committee chosen by the various state delegations at the convention.

The Republican and Democratic members of Congress had their own organizations, geared solely to the distribution of campaign literature and the accumulation of information about close congressional races. Not surprisingly, to congressmen documents usually meant reprints of their own best speeches. Representative L. Q. C. Lamar of Mississippi, as chairman of his party's House caucus, announced on February 1 the member- ship of what was variously called the Democratic Congressional Campaign Committee or National Resident Campaign Com- mittee. It consisted of twenty members of the House, three senators, and three well-endowed residents of the District of Columbia, including financier W. W. Corcoran. This committee elected officers, opened a headquarters on F Street, and by mid- March was ready for business, with a small staff of clerks.[3] The Republican Congressional Campaign Committee was even larger, with one member from each state and territory. The actual work would have to be done by a smaller executive com- mittee made up of five senators, four representatives, and two private citizens, and chaired by Simon Cameron of Pennsyl- vania.[4] As creations of the caucuses on Capitol Hill, these con- gressional committees were not really elements of party struc- ture and played a minimal role in the contest; but at least they had a constant membership for the entire campaign.

2. Copy, Augustus Schell to J. S. Black, March 8, 1876, in Jeremiah S. Black Papers, Manuscript Division, Library of Congress. See also Schell to C. H. McCormick, May 1, 1876, in Cyrus Hall McCormick Papers, State Historical Society of Wisconsin.
3. New York *World*, February 2, 29, March 10, 20, 1876.
4. *Ibid.*, January 24, February 4, 1876.

The national committees, by contrast, had to be completely reorganized once the conventions had done their work. After Tilden was nominated in St. Louis, the New York delegates named Abram S. Hewitt their new national committeeman, replacing Augustus Schell, who had supported Hendricks. There was speculation that the chairman of the committee would be Cyrus Hall McCormick of Illinois, the wealthy reaper manufacturer, who was known not to have a strong preference for the presidency.[5] Hewitt, however, had for some years been a very close business and political associate of Tilden, had played an important role in his nomination, was a member of the House, and served on the Democratic Congressional Campaign Committee. He was quickly chosen.[6]

In the Republican party, still badly divided, the basic task of preparing for the campaign was even more difficult. The incumbent chairman, Edwin D. Morgan of New York, had been denied reappointment to the committee by Conkling's friends, who regarded him as too friendly with the reform element.[7] In his place they selected Alonzo B. Cornell, naval officer of the New York customhouse, chairman of the state committee, and a possible gubernatorial candidate as well. Cornell was a principal cog in the Conkling machine. He apparently wanted to be chairman of the national committee, and he had the support of some members who believed his designation would appease Conkling and thus make New York a less doubtful state for the Republican party. On the other hand, Morgan and the New York reformers were unalterably opposed to Cornell, regarding him as "not in any sense the proper man"; so perhaps Cornell was not really much of a guarantee for carrying the Empire State.[8] Blaine's sympathizers in the party, of course, had their own candidate. Initially he was William E. Chandler of New Hampshire, for

5. *Ibid.*, June 29, 1876.
6. Allan Nevins, *Abram S. Hewitt: With Some Account of Peter Cooper* (New York: Harper and Brothers, 1935), 265–66, 293, 306.
7. Letterpress copy, E. D. Morgan to A. S. Divin, June 22, 1876, in Edwin D. Morgan Papers, New York State Library.
8. Morgan to Hayes, June 30, 1876, in Rutherford B. Hayes Papers, Rutherford B. Hayes Library, Fremont, Ohio.

the past eight years secretary of the committee. When Chandler found his support limited, however, he withdrew from the contest and was succeeded by Secretary of the Interior Zachariah Chandler of Michigan, who, though born in New Hampshire, was not related. The committeeman from Minnesota, John T. Averill, decided to vote for the Michigan Chandler because he was "a first class political organizer, possessing a liberal heart and abundant means." [9]

This protracted contest between the supporters of Blaine and Conkling, reflecting the unfortunate extent of divisions within the national convention, might have been avoided altogether had Hayes clearly expressed his own wishes on the subject. The candidate, however, was typically noncommittal. To William E. Chandler he wrote: "Without much acquaintance with the work of the National Committee, I appreciate its importance, and am particularly anxious that in this there shall be nothing to disturb the existing harmony. All interests should be fairly regarded, and an efficient committee organized." [10] Yet Hayes offered no useful advice. Edward F. Noyes of Cincinnati further confused matters by the way in which he sought to protect the candidate's interests in this touchy matter. Immediately after the convention, he strongly advocated to Hayes the choice of Cornell. But a week later he heard that Cornell and Morgan were "at the *outs*"; and, learning that Postmaster General Jewell and Interior Secretary Zach Chandler thought the chairman should come from Ohio, he rather tentatively suggested state chairman A. T. Wikoff. Noyes, rather than Wikoff, represented the state on the national committee, however; so one may reasonably conclude that Noyes was then bidding for his own advancement. Noyes consulted Hayes at length before leaving to attend the July 8 national committee meeting in Philadelphia, secure in the knowledge that he had won the candidate over to the idea of his own election. Once in Philadelphia, confronted by the scramble for votes between Cornell and

9. Fred. Driscoll to Wm. Henry Smith, June 27, 1876, in William Henry Smith Collection, Indiana Historical Society Library.
10. Hayes to Wm. E. Chandler, June 30, 1876, in Hayes Papers.

Zach Chandler, he became reluctant to alienate either, withdrew his name, then allowed it to be used, and finally watched timidly as Chandler was selected.[11] Richard C. McCormick, a former governor of the Arizona Territory, and the son-in-law of Democratic Senator Allen G. Thurman of Ohio, was chosen as the new secretary of the committee.[12]

Chandler's appointment as national chairman stirred immediate controversy. Cornell was reportedly angry because Noyes first indicated his support and then entered the race himself. Moreover, as one Hayes adviser noted the day before the committee met, Chandler, as secretary of the interior, "could not be in New York where the headquarters *must* be and more serious than that it [Chandler's election] would open the charge of Grantism." [13] The Washington correspondent of the Cincinnati *Commercial* agreed:

That Zachariah Chandler is personally honest nobody disputes, notwithstanding the fact that he began life as a post-trader or sutler at Fort Wayne, Detroit. There is nothing in his public life or his private life so far as known, to justify the assertion that he ever stole a cent to put into his private pocket. On the other hand there is nothing in his public career to justify the assumption that he would not steal any specified sum provided it could be safely done, for the use and benefit of his party. The fact that in 1872 while holding the position of Chairman of the National Republican Executive Committee he paid or consented to the payment of one of the Secretaries of the Committee out of the public funds, by having him carried on the role of the Pension Bureau where he rendered no services at all, may be accepted as evidence going to show his character and bent of inclination as a party man.[14]

Less than a month later McCormick wanted to resign as secretary of the committee because he disliked Chandler personally and felt that too much work was placed on his own shoulders

11. Edward F. Noyes to Hayes, June 18, 24, 25, 1876, *ibid.*; Noyes to Wm. Henry Smith, June 27, July 13, 1876, in William Henry Smith Papers, Ohio Historical Society Library. See also U. H. Painter to Hayes, July 10, 1876, in Hayes Papers.
12. Telegram, L. C. Weir to Hayes, July 8, 1876, in Hayes Papers.
13. Weir to Hayes, July 7, 1876, *ibid.*
14. Typescript copy, [Wilson J. Vance to Murat Halstead], July 11, 1876, *ibid.*

while the chairman remained in Washington. McCormick was only dissuaded by a personal appeal from Hayes.[15]

The naming of an executive committee to assist in supervising the Republican campaign was left to the discretion of the new chairman. It was largely a routine matter. William E. Chandler explained to Hayes the consensus of Republican leaders on campaign strategy:

Assuming, as I do, that your nomination makes Ohio sure and safe in October, the victory is to be accomplished, first, by concentration upon Indiana; and second, upon New York and New Jersey. With a Western Executive Committee composed of members from Ohio, Indiana, Illinois, and Iowa, Indiana can be looked after with what assistance we can render from the East. With an Eastern Committee composed of five or six members, say from Pennsylvania, New York, Massachusetts [,] from Connecticut and New Hampshire, we can do all that ought to be done for New York and New Jersey with something to spare for Indiana.[16]

Four days after his election as chairman Zach Chandler named a fourteen-member executive committee divided into two branches, with headquarters in New York and Chicago.[17] In early August a finance committee was created, composed of Zach Chandler, Richard McCormick, Marshall Jewell, Alonzo B. Cornell, and railroad entrepreneur John Murray Forbes.[18] The national committees were finally prepared for business.

2

The first critical problem that had to be met by both parties after their national conventions was the division within each organization on the important questions of government policy that were likely to be issues in the campaign. The presidential and vice-presidential candidates were expected to prepare public letters formally accepting their nominations. At the same time,

15. R. C. McCormick to Hayes, August 4, 1876, and Noyes to Hayes, August 5, 1876, both *ibid.*
16. Wm. E. Chandler to Hayes, June 27, 1876, *ibid.*
17. New York *World*, July 13, 1876.
18. Noyes to Hayes, August 5, 1876, in Hayes Papers.

they traditionally reviewed their own positions on national priorities. Since political custom dictated that the presidential nominees make no other overt display of interest in the office they were in fact anxiously seeking, their letters were awaited with great interest. But what stance should they take on topics of public discussion that their own supporters were debating, sometimes heatedly, among themselves?

Hayes was deluged with contradictory advice on the currency question. Edwin D. Morgan, speaking of the outlook in New York, thought, "It is evident there is disappointment as to the weakness of the financial resolution in our platform." The Republican financial plank had already pledged the party to a swift return to specie payments, but without mentioning a specific date. Morgan evidently wanted a public declaration that the greenbacks would be redeemed in coin on or before January 1, 1879, as required by the Resumption Act.[19] Indiana Republicans, by contrast, from State Chairman George W. Friedley and Indianapolis *Journal* associate editor Charles M. Walker on down, were unanimous in cautioning against such a course. F. M. Thayer of the Evansville *Daily Journal* assured James M. Comly of the *Ohio State Journal* that "if the Governor goes beyond the platform one iota he will greatly jeopardize his success in this State. We will have a desperate fight at best. I trust he will not unnecessarily make our load any heavier." [20] Hayes saw an obvious course to follow under the circumstances: "I am advised to harden by some, and to soften by others the money plank, and so on. Perhaps I would do well to approve it as it stands." John Sherman, the man who would one day be charged with implementing the policy of resumption, agreed.[21]

When Tilden was nominated by the Democrats, the Republi-

---

19. Morgan to Hayes, June 21, 1876, *ibid.* See also W. M. Grosvenor to A. T. Wikoff, June 20, 1876, *ibid.*

20. F. M. Thayer to Noyes, June 20, 1876, Charles M. Walker to Hayes, June 22, 1876, and J. M. Ridenour to Hayes, June 23, 1876, all *ibid.*; Thayer to Comley [*sic*], June 21, 1876, in James M. Comly Papers, Ohio Historical Society Library.

21. Typescript copy, Hayes to John Sherman, June 23, 1876, and Sherman to Hayes, June 26, 1876, both in Hayes Papers.

cans became aware, many of them for the first time, of the extent to which the Grant scandals might handicap their party in the campaign. Hayes was promptly swamped with warnings about the importance of civil service reform as an issue.[22] The counsel he relished most came from spokesmen of the "independent" movement, which had originally favored Bristow for president. "The best people," Hayes informed his diary, "many of them heretofore dissatisfied with the Republican party, are especially hearty in my support. I must make it my constant effort to deserve this confidence." [23] So Hayes heeded the words of George William Curtis:

In New York Mr. Tilden is strong as a party manager, as a hard money man and above all, as a ring smasher and reformer. This last consideration commends him most warmly to the great independent vote. Yesterday morning . . . I met one of the leading "Liberals" of 1872, who lives a few miles from town. "Well" said he "a good many Hayes men of last week are Tilden men today, for they had no hope that Tilden could be nominated. They go for the man who drove Tweed out of the country. For my part I am waiting for Hayes's letter, and so are a vast number of people. If he speaks plainly and boldly and shows that he will root out rings and rascals, and clean the civil service, we shall all go for him." [24]

The man who exercised the most influence on Hayes was Carl Schurz, who at the time was spending a much-needed vacation in Pennsylvania with his children, seeking to ease their adjustment to the recent death of their mother. Schurz did not know Hayes personally. He wrote the candidate for the first time on June 21, reviewing at length the ideas that he thought should find expression in the letter of acceptance. Schurz stressed that Hayes could not afford to rely on the Republican platform: "The

22. J. D. Cox to Hayes, June 20, 1876, Sherman to Hayes, June 26, 1876, George Walker to Hayes, July 3, 1876, and Joseph Medill to Hayes, July 6, 1876, all *ibid.*

23. Entry for June 23, 1876, in T. Harry Williams (ed.), *Hayes: The Diary of a President, 1875–1881, Covering the Disputed Election, the End of Reconstruction, and the Beginning of Civil Service* (New York: David McKay Company, Inc., 1964), 27. See also Grosvenor to Schurz, June 20, 1876, in Carl Schurz Papers, Manuscript Division, Library of Congress.

24. George William Curtis to Hayes, June 30, 1876, in Hayes Papers.

new Cincinnati platform promises civil service reform, but the platform of 1872 did the same, and it cannot be denied that public confidence in the mere paper promises of political parties is fatally shaken." [25] Instead, what the independents wanted from Hayes was "the strongest *personal* assurances of reform." [26] The distinction Schurz drew between a gentleman's personal pledge and a party's campaign promise seems strangely naive in retrospect, but it reflected an upper-class code of conduct to which the reformers attached great importance. Hayes expressed his gratitude for Schurz's guidance and declared in respect to civil service reform: "I want to make that *the* issue of the Canvass." He asked whether a declaration of determination not to seek a second term would be one way to do so. He also mentioned his reluctance to say anything about the currency.[27] Schurz responded favorably to Hayes's position on the civil service issue and especially to the question of a single-term vow: "It would be calculated to strengthen the earnestness of the reform pledge." But the German leader also argued that the candidate must say something about the currency; he must amplify the platform plank on that question even if he did not go beyond it. Schurz even drafted a paragraph on the subject which so impressed Hayes that he reversed his earlier decision to be silent and incorporated Schurz's language into his letter with only a few stylistic changes.[28]

There was another momentous issue that Hayes decided to discuss: the future of the South. Though he vigorously supported the Fifteenth Amendment extending the suffrage to black men and as governor had helped secure its ratification in Ohio, Hayes had never been wildly enthusiastic about his party's reconstruction program. He was a former Whig and by no means a believer in human equality. In January, 1875, he wrote a Texas friend from his college days, a former slaveholder and secessionist:

25. Schurz to Hayes, June 21, 1876, *ibid.*
26. Schurz to Hayes, June 23, 1876, *ibid.*
27. Hayes to Shurz [*sic*], June 27, 1876, in Schurz Papers.
28. Schurz to Hayes, July 5, 1876, in Hayes Papers.

It seems to me that the most important thing in Texas, as everywhere else, is *education for all.* I, of course, don't believe in forcing whites and blacks together. But both classes should be fully provided for. I recognize fully the evil of rule by ignorance. I see enough of it under my own eyes. You are not so much worse off in this respect than New York, Chicago, and other cities having a large uneducated population. But the remedy is not, I am sure, to be found in the abandonment of the American principle that all must share in government. The whites of the South must do as we do, *forget to drive and learn to lead* the ignorant masses around them. But I will not argue. You and I are now nearer together than we have been since our boyhood.[29]

Hayes was receptive, therefore, to the advice he received in a note from Charles Nordhoff, whose *Cotton States in the Spring and Summer of 1875,* an account of a tour undertaken for the New York *Herald,* had just been published: "The Southern troubles are substantially over; time and increasing prosperity have done & are doing their work. Events have justified the necessity & importance of the later Constitutional Amendments, as all wise & patriotic men in the South now acknowledge. There is reason to hope & believe that for the future Federal interference in the local affairs of the Southern states, always dangerous & to be deplored, will no longer be necessary; & I believe it shd. be avoided, except where the clearest & extremest necessity demands it." [30] Schurz also brought up this point. He insisted that "the equality of rights without distinction of color according to the constitutional amendments must be sacredly maintained by all the lawful power of the government; but that also the constitutional rights of local self-government must be respected." [31] Hayes did not appreciate the phrase " 'local self government,' in *that* connection. It seems to me to smack of the

---

29. Hayes to Guy M. Bryan, January 2, 1875, in Charles Richard Williams (ed.), *Diary and Letters of Rutherford Birchard Hayes,* (5 vols.; Columbus: Ohio State Archaeological and Historical Society, 1922–26), III, 262–63.

30. Charles Nordhoff to Hayes, June 28, 1876, in Hayes Papers; Charles Nordhoff, *The Cotton States in the Spring and Summer of 1875* (New York: D. Appleton and Company, 1876).

31. Schurz to Hayes, June 21, 1876, in Hayes Papers.

bowie knife and revolver. 'Local self government' has nullified the 15th amendment in several States, and is in a fair way to nullify the 14th & 13th." Still, he supposed that they were "substantially agreed on the topic." [32]

Hayes released his letter of acceptance on July 10. In addition to the passages discussing the currency, the civil service, and his "inflexible purpose, if elected," to serve but one term, it contained a brief dissertation on the "permanent pacification" of the country:

The condition of the Southern states attracts the attention and commands the sympathy of the people of the whole Union. In their progressive recovery from the effects of the war, their first necessity is an intelligent and honest administration of government, which will protect all classes of citizens in their official and private rights. What the South most needs is "peace" and peace depends upon the supremacy of the law. There can be no enduring peace if the constitutional rights of any portion of the people are habitually disregarded. . . . The welfare of the South, alike with that of every other part of this country, depends upon the attractions it can offer to labor and immigration, and to capital. But laborers will not go, and capital will not be ventured, where the constitution and the laws are set at defiance, and distraction, apprehension, and alarm take the place of peace-loving and law-abiding social life. . . . The moral and national prosperity of the Southern states can be most effectually advanced by a hearty and generous recognition of the rights of all by all,—a recognition without reserve or exception. With such a recognition fully accorded, it will be practicable to promote, by the influence of all legitimate agencies of the general government, the efforts of the people of those states to obtain for themselves the blessings of honest and capable local government. If elected, I shall consider it not only my duty, but it will be my ardent desire, to labor for the attainment of this end.[33]

Despite his carefully worded qualifications, the implication of Hayes's statement was clear. He was expressing the intense

32. Hayes to Shurz [*sic*], June 27, 1876, in Schurz Papers.
33. *Proceedings of the Republican National Convention, Held at Cincinnati, Ohio, Wednesday, Thursday, and Friday, June 14, 15, and 16, 1876, Resulting in the Nomination for President and Vice-President of Rutherford B. Hayes and William A. Wheeler* (Concord, N.H.: Republican Press Association, 1876), 116–18.

northern desire to be rid of the troublous issues left over from the Civil War. On the subject of reconstruction, as on the other topics he covered, Hayes sounded very much like one of the "best men." William A. Wheeler, in his own letter of acceptance, reiterated the same views, though much less ably.[34] The question was whether they also spoke for the rest of their party.

The more reform-minded among the regular Republicans were, of course, pleased. Whitelaw Reid, editor of the New York *Tribune*, serves as an example: "I want to thank you very heartily for your admirable letter of acceptance. If it had been specially designed to enable *The Tribune*, and those for whom it speaks, to make their support of you effective it could not have better accomplished the purpose." [35] On the other hand, Republicans accustomed to controlling a share of the federal patronage were not especially happy with the civil service paragraph. Senator John A. Logan of Illinois was reported to have called it "d——d stuff; Morton words to the same effect." [36] Conkling ominously said nothing at all. President Grant said nothing publicly, but he let his close associates know he was annoyed that so much of Hayes's letter seemed to reflect unfavorably upon his own performance in office. Grant was particularly irked by the one-term reference.[37] Before a week passed, Thomas C. Platt, an ally of both Conkling and Grant, traveled to Columbus to inform Hayes of the president's disaffection. The candidate prepared a hasty explanation:

The five leading candidates [that is, Hayes's opponents for the nomination] are all younger men than I am. Four years hence, I think, they will all be younger than I am now. At any rate they may all reasonably expect to be candidates in future if they desire to be. It seemed to me therefore that nominated as I was, it would tend to

34. *Ibid.*, 118–19.
35. Whitelaw Reid to Hayes, July 21, 1876, in Hayes Papers. See also Schurz to Hayes, July 15, 1876, Garfield to Hayes, July 11, 1876, and E. D. Morgan to Hayes, July 11, 1876, all *ibid.*
36. Nordhoff to Hayes, July 10 [1876], *ibid.*
37. Allan Nevins, *Hamilton Fish: The Inner History of the Grant Administration* (rev. ed., 2 vols.; New York: Frederick Ungar Publishing Company, 1957), II, 838–39.

unite and harmonize their friends if it were certainly known that I would not be in their way four years from now. If elected, it will surely strengthen my administration. I need hardly assure you that I would not say anything to reflect on you, but under the circumstances this much seems proper.[38]

Grant waited a month before he replied, finally professing, not altogether convincingly, to be satisfied.[39]

Meanwhile, Schurz was using his influence with the independent reformers in an effort to convert them to Hayes's support. He began by calling a meeting of the executive committee appointed by the Fifth Avenue Hotel Conference. The small group of independents present on June 30 agreed that with two reasonably acceptable candidates in the field there was no longer a need for a third-party movement. Instead, they resolved to organize a National Civil Service Reform League—though, in fact, such an organization was not created until five years later. Schurz then turned his attention to gentlemen like Henry Adams, who seemed to be inclining toward Tilden.[40] Adams was not much impressed with the German leader's arguments, as he told his former student, Henry Cabot Lodge:

I cannot help laughing to think how, after all our labor and after we had by main force created a party for Schurz to lead, he himself, without a word or a single effort to keep his party together, kicked us over in his haste to jump back to the Republicans. . . . Well! We knew what he was! I am not angry with him, but of course his leadership is at an end. The leader who treats his followers in that way, is a mere will-o'-the-wisp. I hope he will get his Cabinet office, and I hope he will forget that we ever worked to make him our leader, independent of party.[41]

Adams' father, Charles Francis, was not satisfied with Hayes either, feeling sure that Hayes would be subject to the same

38. Hayes to U. S. Grant, July 14, 1876, in Hayes Papers.
39. Grant to Hayes, August 16, 1876, *ibid.*
40. Schurz to [Henry] Adams, July 9, 1876, in Letters Received and Other Loose Papers, The Adams Papers, Massachusetts Historical Society.
41. Henry Adams to Henry Cabot Lodge, September 4, 1876, in Worthington Chauncey Ford (ed.), *Letters of Henry Adams (1858–1891)* (Boston: Houghton Mifflin Company, 1930), 299.

Conkling and Morton influences that helped nominate him. When Tilden emerged triumphant at St. Louis, the elder Adams made no secret of the fact that he preferred the Democrat candidate "over the Republican cipher." [42] Most of the men identified with the independent movement, being Republicans by tradition, went for Hayes; but exceptions like the Adamses were a source of concern; and Schurz was unable to prevent many German newspaper publishers and politicians from declaring for Tilden.[43]

The effectiveness of Hayes's letter was seriously reduced in the eyes of some of the more fastidious reformers because it followed by only two days the election of Zach Chandler as national chairman. E. L. Godkin, editor of *The Nation*, who eventually gave Hayes his reluctant support, expressed the bewilderment produced by this strange juxtaposition: "Just think of a Civil Service reform party making Zack [*sic*] Chandler chairman of the National Committee, and A. B. Cornell of New York chairman of the Executive Committee. It is impossible for the public to avoid the conclusion that these fellows regard the Civil service part of the Hayes letter as mere bunkum, and intend, after it has produced its proper effect in the popular mind, to play the game over again in the old way, as they did with Grant." [44] Schurz warned Hayes at length about this obvious contradiction, but not even Schurz could suggest a practical solution.[45]

The Republican party thus entered the campaign of 1876 somewhat frayed about the edges, yet closer to being united than it had been for the previous six years or more.

3

The leaders of the Democratic party were most concerned about their division over the currency question, a division per-

42. Charles Francis Adams Diary, June 16, 28, 1876, in Adams Papers.
43. Carl Wittke, "Carl Schurz and Rutherford B. Hayes," *Ohio Historical Quarterly*, LXV (October, 1956), 343.
44. E. L. Godkin to Charles Eliot Norton, July 14, 1876, in Rollo Ogden, *Life and Letters of Edwin Lawrence Godkin* (2 vols.; New York: Macmillan Company, 1907), II, 112–13.
45. Schurz to Hayes, July 15, 1876, in Hayes Papers.

fectly reflected in their presidential ticket. Congressman William R. Morrison of Illinois warned Manton Marble on Independence Day: "Attention is already being directed to the fact that our candidates are not in accord on the financial question. In view of this fact would it not be well to see to it that *the letters of acceptance* give the same interpretation to our platform purposes &c." Morrison was worried because the currency matter would certainly be taken up during the closing weeks of the congressional session, possibly in such a way as to damage the party's chances. The Democratic platform had coupled a call for repeal of the resumption clause with a demand that active steps be taken to prepare the country for a return to specie payments at an early date. After the convention the party's western inflationists wanted an immediate repeal measure; yet there was no possibility whatever of enacting a substitute for the resumption clause. Morrison was afraid that "naked repeal" would hurt the party, especially with German voters in the closely contested northwestern states.[46]

Hendricks wrote Tilden urging that the Democratic majority in the House of Representatives demonstrate the sincerity of the platform by approving a repeal measure. Success in Indiana would thereby be assured, and "a victory in Indiana in October would not leave a doubt of success in Nov."[47] Tilden and Hendricks met at Saratoga Springs on July 13 and 14 in an effort to find common ground on this issue. On the fourteenth, Tilden told E. L. Godkin, who was also vacationing at the posh resort, that "he had been laboring with him [Hendricks] all day yesterday about finance, and had, he thought, satisfied him that he must 'scramble up on the platform.' "[48] Actually, the candidates agreed only that they would meet again within two weeks to compare notes on their letters of acceptance.[49] The only cheerful

46. Wm. R. Morrison to Marble, July 4, 1876, in Manton Malone Marble Papers, Manuscript Division, Library of Congress.
47. T. A. Hendricks to Tilden, July 6, 1876, in Samuel J. Tilden Papers, New York Public Library.
48. Godkin to Norton, July 14, 1876, in Ogden, *Life and Letters of Edwin Lawrence Godkin*, II, 112.
49. New York *World*, July 16, 1876.

sign was that Hendricks, when interviewed upon returning home, denied the validity of published reports that the Democratic nominees were in less than perfect harmony on the issues of the campaign, including the currency.[50]

Meanwhile, with the congressional debate over repeal heating up, Hewitt asked Tilden for advice on how the New York members should vote. Hewitt wished he could persuade the inflationists "to do nothing, but that appears to be out of the question." [51] Tilden's reply provided little help. He reviewed his long discussion with Hendricks and noted that the Hoosier governor would be satisfied if repeal were accompanied by "substantial measures for preparation for resumption. Mr H asserts that whatever the House tenders should represent the *whole* platform; but he thinks that the repeal would largely help in Indiana." Tilden, however, preferred that Congress do nothing:

My opinion is that in a little time all the elements of disturbance in Indiana & Ohio will disappear, and then it [repeal] will be a barren policy if we have lost or weakened our position in the general public opinion of the country. . . .

We should exalt the reform issue on which we are united, and on which our antagonists can not resist us or defend themselves until it obtains the whole public attention. . . .

We are doing so well where the Convention left us that it is tempting fortune and fate for the House to temper [*sic*] with the situation [.]

At any rate, *our friends had better not commit themselves to details of a new proposition until after the letters of acceptance are out.*[52]

Tilden, rather than Hendricks, seemed to be the one who was reluctant to stand strictly on the language of the platform. Hewitt soon wrote back to Tilden to tell him of an Illinois congressman who failed to obtain renomination because he voted against repeal in the Banking and Currency Committee; and he

50. Cincinnati *Enquirer*, July 16, 1876, and Chicago *Times*, July 16, 1876, reprinted in New York *World*, July 19, 1876.
51. Abram S. Hewitt to Tilden, July 6, 1876, in Tilden Papers.
52. Copy, Tilden to Hewitt, July 15, 1876, *ibid.*

added, "I do not think you begin to appreciate the bitterness of these Western inflationists." [53] That was apparently true. The day after the meeting in Saratoga Springs, Hendricks, while changing trains, had a chance to speak to Democratic leaders in Cleveland. He reported to Tilden that "all say it is worth thousands of votes to repeal the resumption clause on some terms. I think you should urge a proper measure of repeal." [54]

The danger that the party would become irreparably divided over the currency question was finally averted, but not, however, as a result of firm leadership. When a month had passed after the convention without the issuance of formal acceptances, Samuel Barlow warned Tilden of the growing restiveness even among his own friends.[55] Tilden and Hendricks conferred again at Saratoga Springs on July 28. This time the Hoosier was persuaded or pressured into accepting most of the New Yorker's position on hard money.[56] Both candidates' letters of acceptance, which were released during the first week of August, stressed the necessity of ending corruption in government and of drastically reducing federal expenditures. In that way a sufficient reserve of coin could be amassed by the Treasury to prevent a scarcity of currency when specie payments were finally resumed. Tilden and Hendricks each attacked the resumption clause of 1875 as artificial because it designated the time when specie payments must begin but did not require any preparations. Only responsible and sensitive leadership could accomplish resumption without bringing about a damaging degree of contraction.[57]

53. Hewitt to Tilden, July 26, 1876, in John Bigelow (ed.), *Letters and Literary Memorials of Samuel J. Tilden* (2 vols.; New York: Harper and Brothers, 1908), II, 442–43.

54. Telegram, Hendricks to Tilden, July 15, 1876, *ibid.*, II, 442.

55. Barlow to Tilden, July 20, 1876, in Tilden Papers; letterpress copy, Barlow to Tilden, July 25, 1876, in Samuel Latham Mitchell Barlow Papers, Henry E. Huntington Library, San Marino, California.

56. New York *World*, July 29, 30, 1876; Chicago *Daily News*, July 29, 1876.

57. *Official Proceedings of the National Democratic Convention, Held in St. Louis, Mo., June 27th, 28th and 29th, 1876. With an Appendix Containing the Letters of Acceptance of Gov. Tilden and Gov. Hendricks* (St. Louis: Woodward, Tiernan and Hale, 1876), 170–99.

In the House events were allowed to take their own course. Hewitt proposed a study commission on the currency as an alternative to immediate repeal, but his motion was defeated by twelve votes. A bill repealing the Resumption Act was passed by twenty votes, and, on reconsideration, the House adopted the study commission also. Hewitt believed that "the matter has been managed as well as the difficulties of the situation would admit" and explained: "There was no hard feeling, and no bitterness remains. The hard-money men have made their record, and the soft-money men have got the repeal, and no longer any excuse for not carrying their States. I think that the matter is in the best possible shape. The party is committed to specie payments by the platform and your admirable letter, and by Hendricks' mushy acquiescence." [58] The House Democrats used a favorite device to dispose of this touchy problem. Each man simply voted the way he thought his constituents wanted him to, secure in the knowledge that the Republican Senate would never consider any repeal measure.

The House action established the rule for dealing with the currency problem during the campaign. In the Northwest, state and local Democratic candidates denounced contraction, while in the East they demanded hard money. The result was that the Democrats were not seriously hurt when western Greenbackers entered their own "Independent" candidate in the presidential race—ancient Peter Cooper, who was, interestingly, the father-in-law of Abram S. Hewitt.[59]

4

Sammy is worth $3,000,000. Everybody belonging to him is well off, so that he has no claims upon his fortune. He is a bachelor, you know. *He will not hesitate to spend $500,000 or if need be $1,000,000 to promote his election;* and I need not tell you what money can effect in the eastern cities. . . .

58. Hewitt to Tilden, August 6, 1876, in Bigelow (ed.), *Letters and Literary Memorials of Samuel J. Tilden,* II, 443–44.
59. Irwin Unger, *The Greenback Era: A Social and Political History of American Finance, 1865–1879* (Princeton: Princeton University Press, 1964), 293–321.

Besides, it is a mistake to underrate Sammy's own talents. He is one of the most expert organizers and adroit schemers I ever came into contact with.[60]

Such was the image most Republicans held of Samuel J. Tilden. William Henry Smith warned Hayes: "The enemy to be met is no common enemy. He is the embodiment of human craft and the experience in cunning of generations of Tammany." [61] Joseph Medill agreed: "We have a hard fight ahead of us. Your opponent is a tireless worker, a wonderful organizer, a shrewd, crafty, able man. . . . He makes no mistakes, although bold and aggressive." [62] Tilden was, of course, a talented and experienced politician, but it is doubtful whether anybody in the nineteenth century could have lived up to the extravagant descriptions given by Smith and Medill. The Republicans expected Tilden personally to supervise the entire Democratic campaign. Indeed, after the election both the New York *Sun*, which supported Tilden, and *The Nation*, which did not, stated that the Democratic candidate had in fact directed his party's canvass.[63] Perhaps this exaggerated notion of Tilden's role resulted in part from his secretive nature and from the fact that he seldom appeared in public.[64]

At any rate, American political tradition dictated that no man actively seek the presidency; and there is abundant evidence that Tilden took this injunction seriously, even more so than Hayes. As a result, the fears of Medill and Smith were wholly unwarranted.

As governors of their respective states, both Tilden and Hayes occupied much of their time with official duties. Tilden was forced to remain in Albany throughout the summer. Even when he returned to New York City in the fall, he devoted most of his

60. A. G. Browne, Jr., to Comly, June 28, 1876, in Comly Papers.
61. Wm. Henry Smith to Hayes, July 1, 1876, in Hayes Papers.
62. Medill to Hayes, July 6, 1876, *ibid.*
63. New York *Sun*, November 8, 1876; *The Nation*, XXIV (February 1, 1877), 69.
64. That is the explanation offered in Donald Barr Chidsey, *The Gentleman from New York: A Life of Roscoe Conkling* (New Haven: Yale University Press, 1935), 202.

attention to routine audiences with the innumerable visitors who came to see him. He gave little attention to the details of campaign organization, save occasionally "to counsel economy in the expenditures." Hewitt later wrote sarcastically that "the committee seemed to possess his confidence to such an extent that its members at times felt disposed to complain of Mr. Tilden's indifference." [65] Hewitt, as national chairman, was resentful that unofficial advisers such as Henry Watterson and Manton Marble suddenly seemed to have easier access to the candidate than he did.[66] Tilden's reluctance to become more involved in the canvass may have been inspired by the mild paralytic stroke he had suffered in February, 1875, shortly after assuming the burdens of the governorship. The break in his health was attributed to anxiety and overwork.[67] Whatever the reason, the Democratic nominee was more than content to have his friends seek the presidency for him.

Hayes, also, was not publicly active in the canvass. He did not even want to know the details of the national committee's actions in his behalf. Thus, when he received specific advice on the conduct of the campaign, such as a plan for appealing to the French vote in Maine, he forwarded the recommendations to R. C. McCormick in New York or asked his correspondents to contact the party headquarters directly.[68] On the other hand, he was not reluctant to make suggestions of a general nature on his own. As soon as his letter of acceptance was finished, he began prodding James A. Garfield to stir the congressional campaign committee into more vigorous activity, especially in aid of North Carolina Republicans.[69] Hayes also had some ideas on the principal issues of the contest. He reminded Garfield of the impor-

65. Abram S. Hewitt, "Secret History of the Disputed Election, 1876–77," in Allan Nevins (ed.), *Selected Writings of Abram S. Hewitt* (New York: Columbia University Press, 1937), 161.
66. Joseph Frazier Wall, *Henry Watterson: Reconstructed Rebel* (New York: Oxford University Press, 1956), 135.
67. Allan Nevins, *Abram S. Hewitt*, 312–13.
68. R. C. McCormick to Hayes, July 26, 1876, and Hayes to Wm. Henry Smith, August 10, 1876, both in Hayes Papers.
69. Typescript copy, Hayes to Garfield, July 8, 1876, *ibid.*

tance of "the School question"—hardly a new topic for Hayes—which "ought to be in every speech. Talk to our Southern friends about it." [70] During the closing days of the congressional session, Republicans in both houses, hoping to capitalize on anti-Catholic sentiment, pushed unsuccessfully for a constitutional amendment to prohibit the use of public funds by parochial schools. Hayes vigorously supported the proposal and counseled Senator John Sherman on ways to strengthen it.[71] Shortly thereafter Hayes discovered the "bloody shirt." He told Garfield, "Our main issue must be *It is not safe to allow the Rebellion to come into power*, and next that Tilden is not the man for President." [72] With Blaine he was even more emphatic: "Our strong ground is the dread of a solid South, rebel rule, etc., etc. I hope you will make these topics prominent in your speeches. It leads people away from 'hard times,' which is our deadliest foe." [73] What strange words to come from the man who had recently hinted in his letter of acceptance that he believed reconstruction should be ended!

Hayes further assisted with one of the most difficult tasks of the canvass—getting the party's prize speakers to appear where they could be employed to the best advantage. When James G. Blaine encountered difficulty obtaining prominent orators to stump Maine prior to the state election in September (the first important contest of the fall campaign), he turned to Hayes for help; and Hayes secured the services of Robert G. Ingersoll.[74] Hayes forwarded similar requests to those Republicans with whom he was in frequent correspondence during the summer (Carl Schurz, for example).[75] A few party dignitaries,

---

70. Typescript copies, Hayes to Garfield, July 8, August 4, 1876, *ibid.*
71. Typescript copies, Hayes to Garfield, August 5, 12, 1876, typescript copy, Hayes to Sherman, August 7, 1876, and Garfield to Hayes, August 5, 8, 1876, all *ibid.*
72. Typescript copy, Hayes to Garfield, August 5, 1876, *ibid.*
73. Quoted in Harry Barnard, *Rutherford B. Hayes and His America* (Indianapolis: Bobbs-Merrill Company, Inc., 1954), 311.
74. Telegram, Blaine to Hayes, August 5, 1876, and typescript copy, Hayes to Robert G. Ingersoll, August 8, 1876, both in Hayes Papers.
75. Hayes to Schurz, August 14, 1876, in Schurz Papers.

for various reasons, refused at first to do any speaking. Benjamin H. Bristow, after his resignation from the cabinet and a brief political tour of New England, returned to Kentucky and claimed to be in permanent retirement from public life. A personal letter from the candidate, however, was sufficiently compelling for the former secretary of the treasury to postpone his withdrawal from party affairs long enough to spend a month in West Virginia, Ohio, and Indiana prior to their October elections.[76] On the other hand, not even Hayes could get Roscoe Conkling to enter the battle. Conkling sat out the entire campaign at home, burdened, he said, with an array of business and personal concerns—a sufferer from "malarial fever" according to his lieutenant Tom Platt.[77]

The countless minor chores that Hayes performed did not add up to an unusually active role for a presidential candidate; yet they probably exceeded Tilden's total contribution to the Democratic effort. Actually, the primary function of each candidate was almost entirely negative: he must not present other than a spotless reputation to the public. This prescription seems simple at first glance, but it included the intensely disagreeable duty of responding to the assorted slanders that were a standard feature of nineteenth-century political life. Here, too, Hayes acted more decisively than Tilden.

In August the New York *Times*, after several months of investigation, charged the Democratic candidate with perjury for filing a false income tax return in 1863. John Bigelow, Tilden's closest friend, found the New York governor intensely "annoyed" by the accusation. He could not find the fourteen-year-old papers necessary to refute the charge, however, so he evidently planned to do nothing.[78] Meanwhile the *Times* story

76. B. H. Bristow to Murat Halstead, February 17, 1877, in Murat Halstead Collection, Historical and Philosophical Society of Ohio, Cincinnati; typescript copy, Hayes to Bristow, September 14, 1876, and Bristow to Hayes, September 15, 1876, both in Hayes Papers.
77. Draft, Hayes to Roscoe Conkling, August 15, 1876, Conkling to Hayes, August 23, 1876, and T. C. Platt to Hayes, September 23, 1876, all in Hayes Papers.
78. John Bigelow Diary, August 29, 1876, in John Bigelow Papers,

created a sensation. "Every one asks," Bigelow noted on September 4, "if Tilden does not intend to make a statement in regard to his income tax." [79] Before long, prominent Democrats everywhere were becoming alarmed. Samuel Barlow cautioned Hewitt: "I cannot express to you the anxiety that Gov Tildens friends feel about the charge of non-payment of his income [tax] and it is as certain as anything ever was, that the delay in answering these charges is doing great harm. The Govr. does not seem to understand how dangerous our position is. Some of his best & ablest friends begin to fear for the result." [80] In the middle of September, Bigelow spent an entire day "until after dinner with the Govr. reviewing and discussing his income tax return, which is supposed to be producing an unfavorable impression upon his party. I have recd many letters of that purport." [81]

Neither Bigelow nor Hewitt was able to prevail upon the governor to prepare a detailed refutation. Finally, Hewitt engaged Judge James P. Sinnott, Tilden's confidential law clerk during the Civil War, to do the job. Sinnott obtained Bigelow's help, and Bigelow forced the reluctant candidate to give the matter his attention.[82] Bigelow disgustedly confided to his diary on September 20: "Last night read proofs of Sinnotts letter which has occupied two or three men about three weeks of continuous work to do what should not have consumed more than a day. The matter has worried the Governor until he is scarcely fit or able to do any thing. He can't write or control himself. He finds fault with everyone about him & makes the most childish complaints of others for his own omissions & commissions. I

New York Public Library. For an indication that the *Times* exposé had been in the works for a while, see Wm. Henry Smith to Hayes, July 1, 1876, in Hayes Papers.

79. John Bigelow Diary, September 4, 1876, in Bigelow Papers.

80. Letterpress copy, Barlow to Hewett [*sic*], September 12, 1876, in Barlow Papers.

81. John Bigelow Diary, September 15, 1876, in Bigelow Papers.

82. Nevins, *Abram S. Hewitt*, 314; Margaret Clapp, *Forgotten First Citizen: John Bigelow* (Boston: Little, Brown and Company, 1947), 283–84.

begin to have some misgivings whether he will prove equal to the labors of the Presidency." [83] Sinnott's letter was published on September 21. It effectively answered the Republican charges. The highly skeptical Chicago *Daily News*, which had earlier found the case against Tilden "an exceedingly clear one," thought the Democratic reply generally "complete and satisfactory." [84] Even the fastidious E. L. Godkin of *The Nation* was convinced.[85]

Later in the campaign the Republicans, as a complement to the bloody shirt, raised the cry that a Democratic victory would result in federal payment of countless Confederate claims for wartime damages. Tilden again failed to make a public reply; so Hewitt resolved the problem by going to the candidate with "a letter calling attention to the subject, and a prepared answer; he obtained Tilden's approval of these documents, and Tilden added one sentence to the reply: 'Let the dead past bury its dead.' " The letters were then released to the press.[86] Once again the response was favorable, though belated.[87]

Several Democratic attacks on Hayes were as ill-founded as those leveled at Tilden. Hayes, like Tilden, was not inclined to dignify such malicious gossip with a formal reply; but he diligently compiled the pertinent information on which to base a response should one become necessary. The New York *Times* report on Tilden's taxes made Hayes almost as uncomfortable as it did Tilden. "What is there," he asked George William Curtis, "in the charge that Tilden by perjury swindled the Government of its income tax? If false it ought to be dropped. If true it ought to destroy all chance of his election." [88] Perhaps Hayes suspected that his opponent was not the only presidential

83. John Bigelow Diary, September 20, 1876, in Bigelow Papers.
84. Chicago *Daily News*, August 31, September 23, 1876.
85. *The Nation*, XXIII (October 5, 1876), 206–207.
86. Nevins, *Abram S. Hewitt*, 314; New York *World*, October 25, 1876.
87. See L. W. Walker to Tilden, October 27, 1876, in Bigelow (ed.), *Letters and Literary Memorials of Samuel J. Tilden*, II, 472; Marvin H. Bovee to Tilden, October 29, 1876, in Tilden Papers.
88. Hayes to Curtis, September 4, 1876, in Hayes Papers.

aspirant vulnerable on that score. He started checking his own papers and on September 14 confessed to his diary: "As an off-sett [sic] to what is said of Gov Tildens income returns mine have been examined. It appears that in 1868 & 1869 I made none at all." [89] Hayes considered issuing a public statement about his predicament, but was firmly restrained by his journalistic friends, Murat Halstead and James M. Comly.[90] As it happened, a correspondent for the Democratic Chicago *Times* did some probing in regard to Hayes's property tax payments and pub-lished some vague allegations on September 5, but the story had little effect.[91] The far more dangerous state of affairs concern-ing his income taxes remained the privileged intelligence of a handful of Republicans.

The Democrats did stage two major assaults on Hayes's repu-tation a short while later, carefully timing their offensives for maximum effect in the October states of Ohio and Indiana. On September 30 the Chicago *Times* denounced Hayes for pocket-ing $1,000 given him for safekeeping by a soldier in his Civil War regiment who was killed in the battle of Winchester in September, 1864. The *Times* backed up its story with a lengthy statement by the dead soldier's father, James LeRoy, and briefer affidavits signed by several gentlemen who claimed secondhand knowledge of the matter. For Hayes this particular source of harassment was nothing new. In 1869, and again in 1875, when he was running for governor, Hayes had been bombarded with threats from LeRoy that the whole affair would be made public if the money were not returned. LeRoy now combined judicious extracts from his previous correspondence with Hayes with

89. Entry for September 14, 1876, in Williams (ed.), *Hayes: The Diary of a President*, 35. Carl Schurz, too, discovered that, owing to a misunderstanding with his business partner in St. Louis, some of his income had not been properly reported while he was a member of the United States Senate from 1869 to 1875. See Schurz to Isaac Sturgeon, September 5, 1876, in Schurz Papers.
90. Halstead to Comley [sic], September 18, 1876, in Comly Papers.
91. Chicago *Times*, September 5, 1876; Hayes to Schurz, September 6, 1876, in Schurz Papers.

additional "letters" that were sheer fabrications, in an effort to strengthen his statement to the *Times*.[92] Hayes was lucky. Besides being a man of dubious reputation, LeRoy was also a windbag incapable of resisting the satisfaction of boasting to the local Republicans around Tomah, Wisconsin, of his intention to expose their presidential candidate. By the middle of August, therefore, Hayes had received advance warning of what might be coming. The governor of Ohio had also wisely preserved all his earlier papers relating to the LeRoy affair, and he ordered one of his sons to obtain them from the family home in Fremont.[93] In mid-September Hayes learned that a reporter from the *Times* was in consultation with LeRoy in Wisconsin. The candidate promptly began work on a careful memorandum, based on Treasury Department records as well as his own letterbooks, which demonstrated beyond cavil both that Nelson J. LeRoy had never possessed $1,000 at one time after he entered the army and that his father's purpose was nothing more lofty than extortion. A complete rebuttal was ready even before the journalist of the *Times* had finished his research.[94] When the story broke on the last day of September, William Henry Smith used his position as manager of the Western Associated Press to flood the northwestern states with his own immediate denial. Since the slander did not seem to produce too much harm, the Hayes memorandum was not used. The important thing, however, is that Hayes was fully prepared.[95]

92. Chicago *Times*, September 30, 1876. For proof that the LeRoy statement is gravely lacking in veracity, compare it to letterpress copy, Hayes to James LeRoy, December 11, 1869, in Hayes Papers.

93. J. O. Warriner and H. S. Beardsley to E. W. Keyes, August 4, 1876 (enclosed in Keyes to Wikoff, August 5, 1876), Beardsley to Hayes, August 14, 1876, and Hayes to Ruddy [Rutherford P. Hayes], August 20, 1876, all in Hayes Papers.

94. S. S. Fisher to Hayes, September 14, 1876, A. E. Bleekmen to Hayes, September 18, 1876, and letterpress copy, memorandum of R. B. Hayes, September 28, 1876, all *ibid.* Hayes was unable to locate the letters LeRoy had sent in 1869, but he had copies of his own replies and possessed the original of the highly incriminating epistle LeRoy fired off in 1875. See Hayes to Birch[ard A. Hayes], October 3, 1876, *ibid.*

95. Hayes to [Wm. Henry] S[mith], October 2, 1876, and letter and telegram, Wm. Henry Smith to Hayes, October 3, 1876, both *ibid.*

Four days passed, and the Democratic press struck again in a manner that provided a degree of poetic justice. For some time the Democrats had been seeking a way to counter Republican exploitation of anti-Catholicism. Somehow the rumor began to circulate that Hayes was a member of the American Alliance, a nativist organization dedicated to depriving foreign-born citizens of the right to vote or hold office; at the very least, it was said, Hayes had written a letter approving the Alliance's statement of principles. In truth, Hayes had never corresponded with the Alliance, but his private secretary had. When L. S. Tyler, secretary of the Alliance, notified Hayes that his candidacy had been endorsed by the organization in Philadelphia on July 4, Alfred E. Lee replied on behalf of his employer: "Governor Hayes desires me to acknowledge receipt of your valued favor of July 7, enclosing resolutions of the American Alliance, and to say in reply that he is deeply gratified by this expression of confidence. The importance of carrying the States of New York, New Jersey and Connecticut [where the Alliance claimed many members] in the approaching canvass is fully recognized, and at the proper time references will be given you to Committees for such aid and co-operation as seems to be advisable." [96] By the middle of September, Hayes and his advisers were plainly becoming nervous about the rumors they were hearing and quietly sought to retrieve Lee's note.[97] The officers of the Alliance may have been offended by this action, or maybe they simply wanted to call more attention to their order's existence; whatever the motive, someone passed Lee's acknowledgment to the New York *World* long enough for a lithograph copy to be made, and on October 4 a facsimile of the letter was reproduced in every Democratic paper in the Union. Some journals, including the *World*, padded their documentation by printing the text of a second letter to the Alliance, purportedly from Hayes,

96. Alfred E. Lee to L. S. Tyler, July 10, 1876, *ibid.*
97. Entry for September 14, 1876, in Williams (ed.), *Hayes: The Diary of a President*, 37. See also W. K. Rogers to Schurz, September 18, 1876, in Schurz Papers. Rogers was a member of Hayes's personal staff.

though actually a forgery.[98] Hayes hastened to explain this sensational development to William Henry Smith; but the authenticity of Lee's letter could not be disputed, and this made a contradiction of the forgery all but impossible.[99] Nor could the damage to the Republican cause be denied. From Chicago, Smith advised Hayes:

> I have a siege with our Republican friends here yesterday and today about Col. Lee's letter to the Amn. Alliance. A panic has prevailed, and there is a good deal of feeling. I had a talk over the wires with Col. L. yesterday, & thought we had the enemy again, but a private despatch from him to Mr. Medill [confirming the accuracy of the first letter] left us demoralized. Mr. M is quite put out—well downright mad, and so are Gens. Logan and Babcock. . . . I hope your wisdom will suggest some thing . . . to aid us, with the great foreign population of the N. W. It is absolutely necessary to offset the extensive & insidious work of the enemy in Wisconsin & Chicago especially. Of course it is too late to do any thing in Indiana.[100]

Hayes did have something to suggest: "The K. N. [Know Nothing] charges are more than met, (*not* by denial or explanation) but by charging Dems with their Catholic alliance." [101] At the same time, the national committee distributed a large number of leaflets, printed in German, demonstrating that the Republican candidate had no objection to naturalized Americans voting or holding office.[102] The Republicans were trying to make the best of a bad situation.

5

The strict sense of propriety that dictated a largely passive role for the presidential candidates did not as severely restrict the nominees for vice-president. They could take refuge behind the formality, which the presidential aspirants could not, that they sought their party's success rather than their own advancement. Accordingly, Thomas A. Hendricks agreed to address a limited

98. New York *World*, October 4, 1876; Chicago *Times*, October 4, 1876.
99. Hayes to [William Henry] S[mith], October 5, 1876, in Hayes Papers; Comly to W. H. Smith, October 18, 1876, in Smith Collection.
100. Wm. Henry Smith to Hayes, October 5, 1876, in Hayes Papers.
101. Hayes to Wm. H. Smith, October 20, 1876, *ibid*.
102. R. C. McCormick to Hayes, October 6, 1876, *ibid*.

number of campaign rallies, primarily in his own state, beginning with a speech at Shelbyville, Indiana, on September 2.[103] For the Republicans, however, William A. Wheeler refused to do even that much. To a request from Blaine that he speak before a series of mass meetings in Maine, Wheeler made this remarkable reply:

I greatly regret my physical inability to do little [*sic*] in the way of speaking in this canvass. But I have not reserve of strength to draw upon. I was driven from business in 1865, by broken health and have never been strong since. My work in the campaign of 1868, compelled me to spend the succeeding Winter in Florida. In the campaign of 1872, after making half a dozen speeches, I went to bed with the typhoid fever where I remained during the entire Autumn. My trouble for years has been wakefulness at night. No resident of the grave or a lunatic asylum has suffered more from this cause than I have. Speaking, and the presence of crowds, excite me and intensify my wakefulness. My family physician positively forbids my speaking in this canvass. Gov. Hayes wrote me, asking me to go to Indiana and Ohio, to which I answered as I write you. His reply was "You should do no work that will imperil your health. No friend of the cause will expect or desire it." . . . I trust you may see in what I have written sufficient reasons for my refusing to go to Maine. I regret that I was nominated. You know I did not want the place. I should have gone back to the House, and into a Republican majority. I should have almost to a certainty, been its Speaker, which I would greatly prefer to being *laid away*. . . .

I am thoroughly worn down, with calls, correspondence and the weather. I *must* break away somewhere, for a week of complete rest. I am delighted to see the evidence of your returning strength. Take the advice of one who has travelled the same road—*be exceedingly careful*. Your life is too valuable to be sacrificed to political demands.[104]

6

With all of the candidates playing limited roles, the direction of the Republican and Democratic canvasses became virtually the exclusive concern of the respective national committees.

103. Cincinnati *Daily Gazette*, September 4, 1876.
104. W. A. Wheeler to Blaine, August 11, 1876, in James G. Blaine Papers, Manuscript Division, Library of Congress. See also Wheeler to Hayes, July 25, 1876, in Hayes Papers.

E. L. Godkin was at Saratoga with Tilden in July and wrote Charles Eliot Norton that the Democratic candidate was "absolutely confident of his election." [105] A week later Whitelaw Reid warned Hayes that Tilden was "singularly confident," and, he noted, "my experience with him has led me to regard him as the most sagacious political calculator I have ever seen." [106] Tilden's optimism stemmed from the election strategy he had worked out with Abram S. Hewitt, probably well in advance of his nomination.

The Democratic National Committee headquarters was moved to New York and its organization was accomplished quickly despite serious inconveniences. Hewitt, an important member of the Banking and Currency Committee in the House, was forced by the debate on specie resumption to remain in Washington until the long congressional session's end in August. Since he was able to visit New York only on weekends, most campaign preparations had to be carried out through correspondence with Colonel William T. Pelton, nephew of Governor Tilden, who was temporarily placed in charge of the New York offices.[107] Pelton received assistance from various members of the national executive committee and from W. S. Andrews, the committee's secretary.[108]

The Democratic campaign structure was a remarkable achievement. The employees of the national committee were departmentalized in the pattern of Tilden's past campaigns. The staff which had distributed literature throughout the southern states prior to the St. Louis convention was enlarged and renamed the "literary bureau." Its principal task was the printing and distribution of documents—primarily leaflets recounting Tilden's reform career or speeches by Democratic congressional leaders. These documents were printed in a format resembling

105. Godkin to Norton, July 14, 1876, in Ogden, *Life and Letters of Edwin Lawrence Godkin*, II, 112.
106. Reid to Hayes, July 21, 1876, in Hayes Papers.
107. Hewitt, "Secret History of the Disputed Election, 1876–77," in Nevins (ed.), *Selected Writings of Abram S. Hewitt*, 159–60.
108. New York *World*, August 4, 1876.

pocket-sized railroad timetables.[109] The literary bureau even installed its own printing presses on Liberty Street to produce enormous quantities of material.[110] By mid-September more than five million pieces of literature had already been mailed.[111] Hewitt later estimated that "at least one copy was published for every inhabitant of the United States which would amount to about five for each voter." [112] Hewitt told George W. Julian that two million copies of one of his speeches alone had been distributed.[113] Nevertheless, the printing of speeches ran far behind the demand, provoking complaints that the New York headquarters was too slow.[114] Another important document, a feature of every presidential race, but one that the party committee did not have to worry about, was the campaign biography of Tilden and Hendricks, prepared with their cooperation by Theodore P. Cook and published commercially by D. Appleton and Company.[115]

Along a similar line Hewitt was responsible for a particularly valuable innovation in campaign planning. With the help of A. M. Gibson, Washington correspondent of the New York *Sun*, he prepared *The Campaign Text Book*. This massive volume, a 750-page catalog of every conceivable charge of Republican corruption that could be made in support of the campaign for re-

109. A number of these documents are preserved in the Samuel J. Tilden Papers, Columbia University Library, not to be confused with the Tilden Papers in the New York Public Library.

110. Alexander Clarence Flick, *Samuel Jones Tilden: A Study in Political Sagacity* (New York: Dodd, Mead and Company, 1939), 301–302.

111. Hewitt to Samuel J. Randall, September 14, 1876, in Samuel J. Randall Papers, University of Pennsylvania Library.

112. Hewitt, "Secret History of the Disputed Election, 1876–77," in Nevins (ed.), *Selected Writings of Abram S. Hewitt*, 160–61.

113. Geo. W. Julian to Laura G. Julian, November 3, 1876, in George W. Julian Papers, Indiana State Library.

114. Daniel Cameron to C. H. McCormick, August 26, 31, 1876, in McCormick Papers; James E. Harvey to Randall, September 7, 1876, in Randall Papers.

115. Theodore P. Cook, *The Life and Public Services of Hon. Samuel J. Tilden, Democratic Nominee for President of the United States. To Which Is Added a Sketch of the Life of Hon. Thomas A. Hendricks, Democratic Nominee for Vice-President* (New York: D. Appleton and Company, 1876), especially iii–vi.

form, was distributed to party workers in early September. Hewitt modestly thought that the book, unlike anything seen before in a political campaign, "determined the result of the struggle." [116]

An important part of any nineteenth-century campaign was the partisan press. The Democrats were able to use this venerable institution to excellent advantage in 1876. A "bureau of correspondence" was established to supply Democratic newspapers outside New York City with a weekly newsletter, carefully prepared editorial articles, extracts of speeches, and items from other papers. Democratic editors were told: "The purpose of the Committee is to secure to the press supporting the Democratic nominees, the advantages of organization during the campaign, giving you the benefit of the political information which the Committee has facilities for obtaining from all parts of the country. The material furnished will of course be used by you as your judgment may dictate, but care will be taken to adapt it to your requirements." One condition had to be met to receive this service—the bureau wanted to receive a copy of each issue published during the campaign in order to maintain one of its vital channels of information on local developments.[117] The bureau of correspondence was also charged with responsibility for answering the huge volume of mail that poured into party headquarters. Important communications were referred to Hewitt or to Tilden himself, who had a personal staff including Bigelow and Marble, with Charles A. Dana and Samuel J. Randall as advisers.[118]

In 1872 the Democratic-Liberal Republican campaign in be-

116. Hewitt, "Secret History of the Disputed Election, 1876–77," in Nevins (ed.), *Selected Writings of Abram S. Hewitt*, 160; [National Democratic Committee], *The Campaign Text Book. Why the People Want a Change. The Republican Party Reviewed: Its Sins of Commission and Omission. A Summary of the Leading Events in Our History under Republican Administration* (New York: [National Democratic Committee], 1876).

117. Printed circular, National Democratic Committee, Bureau of Correspondence to [Democratic newspaper editors], July, 1876, in Wendell A. Anderson Papers, State Historical Society of Wisconsin.

118. Flick, *Samuel Jones Tilden*, 302–303.

half of Greeley had become seriously demoralized by the frequent failure of speakers to appear at mass meetings as announced.[119] To avoid a recurrence of such chaos in 1876, a "speakers' bureau" was set up under Pelton's direction, with the duty of matching the available speakers to the requests of local and state committees for appearances by prominent men.[120] It was a difficult job, requiring a detailed knowledge of all the nation's railroad schedules. When occasional failures were reported, they brought a stern rebuke from Pelton.[121]

Thirty-five to forty men worked late each night during August at the national committee's Everett House and Liberty Street offices to meet the various demands of the campaign. More were expected to be hired when Hewitt returned to New York after the end of the congressional session.[122]

The campaign apparatus set up by Hewitt and Pelton was large and consequently expensive; but little success was achieved in developing adequate means for financing it. Obtaining funds was difficult because many of the party's normally reliable contributors believed Tilden wealthy enough to provide for his own campaign, while Tilden thought much of the cost should properly be met by numerous small donations. Hewitt and his brother-in-law Edward Cooper, acting treasurer of the national committee, worked diligently to raise $150,000, including their own large subscriptions. (In the past the national chairman had been expected to furnish $25,000. Hewitt and Cooper each seem to have contributed that much.) Of the amount thus raised, $60,000 went for printing costs and $17,500 for the bureau of correspondence. Payment of speakers and clerks, stationery, postage, and rent consumed the rest. Tilden himself disbursed $115,900 during 1876—much of it a gift from

119. Keith Ian Polakoff, "The Disorganized Democracy: An Institutional Study of the Democratic Party, 1872–1880" (Ph.D. dissertation, Northwestern University, 1968), 163–67.
120. Flick, *Samuel Jones Tilden*, 302.
121. W. T. Pelton to Kernan, September 23, 1876, in Francis Kernan Correspondence, John M. Olin Research Library, Cornell University.
122. New York *World*, August 16, 1876.

friends. Some of this money was used to obtain the presidential nomination; but Tilden also sent $60,000 to Indiana to assure success there in October. This last sum included twenty $500 bills from August Belmont.[123]

The scarcity of funds forced the national committee to concentrate on specific states—Indiana until October, then New York, New Jersey, and Connecticut.[124] Virtually no attention could be spared for such doubtful states as Ohio, Pennsylvania, Wisconsin, South Carolina, Florida, and Louisiana. The demand for money also forced Hewitt to advance $30,000 beyond his subscription by September 2. Hewitt instructed Pelton to speak to Tilden about the situation and wrote to the candidate himself: "I am now embarrassed beyond all endurance, & cannot answer the letters which come daily, because I do not know whence the means are to come. The danger is so great, that I am forced by every sense of duty to try to make you comprehend it." [125] Less than three weeks later Hewitt and Cooper were $70,000 beyond their subscriptions and refused to advance another cent. Blaming the defects of the campaign on the financial condition of the national committee, Hewitt wrote Senator Thomas F. Bayard: "To tell you the truth, I am so annoyed at the position in which I am placed, and the demands that are made upon me which I would be glad to meet but am utterly powerless to recognize, that I would be glad to be consigned for the next sixty days to any purgatory which I have ever heard described—so long as it would relieve me from this one." [126] On September 20 Bigelow, Hewitt, and Senator William H. Barnum of Connecticut each spoke to Tilden. Bigelow warned the candidate that "he at least must not have the responsibility of defeat for not supplying what he could perfectly well afford if the Chm who

123. Flick, *Samuel Jones Tilden*, 303–304; Nevins, *Abram S. Hewitt*, 312–13; Irving Katz, *August Belmont: A Political Biography* (New York: Columbia University Press, 1968), 223.

124. See Hewitt to Geo. B. Smith, October 12, 1876, in George B. Smith Papers, State Historical Society of Wisconsin.

125. Hewitt to Tilden, September 2, 1876, in Tilden Papers.

126. Hewitt to Bayard, September 20, 1876, in Thomas F. Bayard Papers, Manuscript Division, Library of Congress.

was his friend & a man of probity, said it was necessary." [127] Tilden assured Hewitt that neither he nor Cooper would be permitted to suffer any losses because of the advances they had made or would make; yet in January, 1878, Hewitt was still seeking reimbursement for more than $11,500 advanced after this September meeting.[128]

The cornerstone of Tilden's campaigns in New York had been, for several years, a careful canvass of the voters. Hewitt sought to institute Tilden's system on a national basis. The actual canvassing had to be supervised by the state organizations, however, and Hewitt encountered difficulty when he had to rely on circular letters to teach them the New York practices. W. S. Andrews, secretary of the national committee, first contacted the state chairmen in July: "It is proposed to make a thorough and immediate canvass of your State including the name of every voter of all parties, with the political complexion of each. In order that the business of the Campaign may be simplified, it is desirable that all of the States, so far as the National ticket is concerned at least, should be organized on a uniform system. Full sets of canvass books and blanks for the organization of clubs will be furnished by the National committee for each polling district." Andrews enclosed instructions and order blanks already addressed to each county. He asked that they be forwarded "immediately to the Chairman of each County Committee, or where no County Committee exists, to the proper person to take charge of the organization in that County." The national committee then wanted the names and addresses of the men to whom these materials were sent.[129] The instructions that Andrews referred to were from Hewitt, and they carried virtually the same message. The county chairman should appoint an organizer for each election district and have the organizers select an assistant for each subdivision of fifty voters. The

127. John Bigelow Diary, September 20, 1876, in Bigelow Papers.
128. Typescript copy, Hewitt to Tilden, January 9, 1878, in Abram Stevens Hewitt Papers, Cooper Union Library.
129. Printed circular, W. S. Andrews to (William Brown), July 26, 1876, in McCormick Papers.

county chairman should then tell Andrews how many canvass books and blanks he would need.

By using these books and blanks in accordance with the directions given, the whole country will be organized on a *uniform system*, and we shall have, in a few weeks, a complete record of every voter in the United States. By the use of this system we will, on ELECTION DAY, secure every vote to which we are entitled.

With such an organization of the Democratic party defeat will be impossible. . . .

The system of organization we propose to carry into effect has been tried in local elections with *absolute success*; it is *simple* and *practicable*. The National Committee can advise and suggest, and you will be furnished with blanks and documents to work with, *but the work must be done by you, and the success of the party depends upon your doing it thoroughly and faithfully.*[130]

A similar circular, containing further information on use of the canvass books and suggestions for the formation of Tilden reform clubs, was prepared for the election district organizers.[131]

Hewitt's only miscalculation lay in mistaking a "uniform system" for an established and experienced political organization. The sudden introduction of the one could not remedy the lack of the other. Tilden's organization in New York, after all, had required eight years to perfect. The shortage of experienced workers in particular hindered the operation of Hewitt's nicely ordered formations. For example, when Andrews received "only a small percentage" of the order blanks that had been distributed to county chairmen in Illinois, it was necessary to send fifteen hundred canvass books and eighteen thousand subdivision sheets to the state committee for distribution.[132] Unfortunately, the state committee encountered difficulty determining

130. Printed circular, Hewitt to Democratic county chairmen, 1876, in Tilden Papers, Columbia University Library. This collection contains several of the canvass books and blanks Hewitt spoke of.
131. Printed circular, Hewitt to [Democratic election district organizers], 1876, *ibid.* Copies may also be found in the Anderson Papers.
132. Andrews to C. H. McCormick, September 14, 1876, and G. Q. Leake to C. H. McCormick, September 16, 1876, both in McCormick Papers.

the needs of each county.[133] More serious than these bureaucratic problems was the inexperience of the canvassers. The final tabulation of the county canvass reports by the Illinois state central committee indicated a Democratic majority in the Prairie State, a majority which did not materialize on election day. Typically, returns from twenty-three counties were missing.[134]

Because it required the creation of an elaborate organization—reaching from the national committee down to thousands of localities—in the space of only a few weeks (an impossible task), the effectiveness of Hewitt's blueprint for the Democratic canvass fell far short of expectation. Nevertheless, it was a daring experiment that captured the imagination of many veteran party workers and convinced them that no stone would be left unturned in the struggle to elect Tilden and Hendricks. Moreover, the traditional tasks of a presidential campaign—distributing literature and speakers—were performed with unprecedented efficiency. Morale in the Democratic party remained uniformly high from June to November.

7

The Republican leadership, by contrast, envisioned no such ambitious schemes and was often beset by confusion even in the performance of routine work. Had the Republicans not been the party in power, with the resources of the federal government to fall back on, the Hayes and Wheeler campaign might well have been a disastrous affair from the outset.

After its organizational meeting on July 8, the national committee did not convene again until August 2 to plan the Republican canvass. By then John Sherman was reporting "much impatience at the long delay in opening." [135] Finally, regular correspondence was established with the state committees and a

---

133. See Rich. M. Atkinson to Cameron, September 23, 1876, *ibid.*

134. "County Report of Ballots for Democrats and Republicans, compiled by Democratic State Central Committee of Illinois, November 5, 1876," *ibid.*

135. Sherman to Hayes, August 1, 1876, in Hayes Papers.

list of speakers was prepared.[136] Zachariah Chandler returned to Washington, and dissatisfaction with the performance of the committee was soon apparent. Richard McCormick was left in complete charge of the operations in New York. According to his own assistant, he was "naturally an over-cautious and timid man, [who] often hesitates to act upon matters of vital importance, thus causing delay and a consequent loss of time." [137] However, McCormick worked hard, learned the everyday aspects of his job well, and was soon joining his aide in complaining about the chairman.

Zach Chandler was content to have the national committee play a very limited role in the campaign. He wanted the state organizations to arrange their own canvasses and pay their own bills. But, as McCormick soon discovered:

This would be very well if the Committees were composed of experienced and active men but in numerous instances this is not the case and the campaign cannot be properly and effectively conducted without the direct interference of the National Com[mitte]e. In some states it is useless to ask the Committees to provide for the expenses of speakers, or to select the men, and in others harmony in action can only be secured by the controlling influences of an outside and supreme Committee. It will not do, in my judgment, to think of working the Nat. Come upon a *negative* basis or to assign the many responsibilities belonging to it to the State Committees.[138]

In the matter of speakers McCormick would have been right even if the state committeemen had all been twenty-year veterans of political warfare. Every contested state, and many about which there was never a doubt, wanted appearances by the party's most illustrious orators—especially Schurz, Blaine, and Ingersoll. Knowing well the keen competition they faced, the state chairmen fired off dozens of form letters to prominent Republican politicians, pleading for permission to schedule three

136. New York *World*, August 4, 1876.
137. Wm. S. Dodge to W. E. Chandler, August 21, 1876, in William E. Chandler Papers, Manuscript Division, Library of Congress.
138. R. C. McCormick to Hayes, August 29, 1876, in Hayes Papers.

or five or an unspecified number of appointments.[139] Since speakers were presented with many more requests than they could possibly fulfill, each one was left to make his own assessment of priorities. No central direction was exerted. Zach Chandler occasionally suggested that a party dignitary visit a particular state from which complaints had been received, but his remarks were strictly advisory.[140] Adding to the difficulty was the fact that when local Republican clubs or county committees felt themselves neglected by their state leaders, they could usually be relied on to contact desired speakers directly.[141]

Chandler also wanted to abandon the responsibility for printing and mailing documents to the congressional campaign committee in Washington. McCormick, however, was not much impressed with the type of material favored by Senator George F. Edmunds, secretary of the congressional committee—campaign speeches delivered in the House and Senate: "Many of them are upon old issues and others are too long for popular use, and they have been distributed with no particular system, while Mr. Tilden's pamphlets are circulated with a most perfect system." McCormick, by his own admission, nagged Edmunds continuously until the latter agreed to revise his committee's literature and method of distribution: "We do not need a long list and great variety of documents but a few clear, concise

139. Noyes to Hayes, July 25, 1876, *ibid.*; Wikoff to D. D. Pratt, June 28, 1876, in Daniel D. Pratt Papers, Indiana State Library; Wikoff to A. D. White, July 18, 1876, in Andrew Dickson White Papers, Cornell University Library; Wikoff to Schurz, July 25, 1876, in Schurz Papers; G. W. Friedley to A. D. White, July 17, 1876, in White Papers; Friedley to Schurz, July 19, 1876, in Schurz Papers; Henry A. Glidden to Richd. Thompson, September 4, 1876, in Richard W. Thompson Papers, Indiana State Library; letterpress copy, E. D. Morgan to Richard J. Oglesby, September 12, 1876, in Morgan Papers.
140. Z. Chandler to Blaine, September 15, 1876, in Blaine Papers; Lew. Wallace to Z. Chandler, September 26, 1876, in Zachariah Chandler Papers, Manuscript Division, Library of Congress.
141. J. F. Oglevee to Robt. Ingersol [*sic*], September 25, 1876, H. C. Grant to Ingersoll, October 20, 1876, and Jas. Ferguson to Ingersoll, October 21, 1876, all in Robert G. Ingersoll Papers, Illinois State Historical Library.

and well printed tracts, devoted to an exposure of the false claims set up by Tilden & Hendricks and the dangers which must follow the success of the Democratic cause in the present important contest." [142] To make sure that this requirement was met, McCormick ordered the national committee in New York to prepare four leaflets and then described them for Hayes: "one contrasting your record with that of Mr. Tilden; one showing up Mr Tilden's war or anti-war record; another exposing his very slight claim to the title of 'reformer'; and a pamphet of 32 pages containing a brief sketch of your life and that of Hon W. A. Wheeler." [143]

Of course, there were commercially published campaign biographies of Hayes as well—two of them. The first, by journalist J. Q. Howard, appeared in August but had little influence.[144] The second, by William Dean Howells, the dynamic editor of the *Atlantic Monthly*, who had composed a similar work for Abraham Lincoln in 1860, was published in September. It had been completed in twenty-eight days.[145] Both books were prepared with their subject's cooperation. The candidate's son Webb and William K. Rogers, a long-time friend, spent a month advising Howells in Massachusetts. Howells also had access to Hayes's voluminous diaries; but the governor had not lost his customary caution when he made such a sensitive source available: "*No quoting* of anything on political or semi-political topics capable of being turned to account by the adversary." Hayes regretted that Howard had mentioned his membership in the Sons of Temperance: "That subject is not safe." [146]

Another vital matter on which the Republican campaign

142. R. C. McCormick to Hayes, August 29, 1876, in Hayes Papers.
143. R. C. McCormick to Hayes, August 25, 1876, *ibid.*
144. J. Q. Howard, *The Life, Public Services and Select Speeches of Rutherford B. Hayes* (Cincinnati: R. Clarke and Company, 1876); Lee to Schurz, August 7, 1876, in Schurz Papers.
145. Wm. D. Howells, *Sketch of the Life and Character of Rutherford B. Hayes. Also a Biographical Sketch of William A. Wheeler* (New York: Hurd and Houghton, 1876).
146. Typescript copy, W. D. Howells to Hayes, August 8, 1876, typescript copy, Hayes to Howells, August 24, 1876, and Howells to Hayes, September 7, 1876, all in Hayes Papers.

nearly foundered was the raising of funds. Chandler contributed $5,000, but was ineffective at encouraging others to do the same. His efforts in Washington and New York were disappointing, and a trip to Philadelphia accompanied by Secretary of War J. Donald Cameron proved little better. In late August former chairman Edwin D. Morgan of New York agreed to give his assistance.[147] Hayes, concerned about the reports of dissension in the national committee, sent Edward F. Noyes as a personal representative to investigate the situation. Noyes quickly discovered that "no doubt some other man than Chandler could have done better. There is a good deal of prejudice against him, especially in New York & Boston." On the other hand, Noyes thought Chandler was doing the best he could: "I think our friends hardly appreciate how hard it is to raise money this year. One half of all who contributed large sums four years ago are dead or broken up, and nobody has come up to take their places." [148] Noyes was not exaggerating. In Boston, where $83,000 had been collected to help reelect Grant in 1872, Republican leaders said they did not expect "to go beyond $25,000 now." [149]

With the situation becoming desperate, Republican fundraising efforts were reorganized at the end of August. Chandler, the coarse, self-made westerner, was relieved of responsibility for obtaining money from the more cultured easterners, whom he had difficulty approaching. The national and congressional committees united in circulating a joint appeal for means, signed by Chandler, McCormick, Simon Cameron, and George F. Edmunds, but with remittances payable to Jacob Tome, treasurer of the congressional committee.[150] At the same time, special finance committees, composed of "prominent citizens," were

147. R. C. McCormick to Hayes, August 25, 1876, *ibid.*
148. Noyes to Hayes, August 30, 1876, *ibid.*
149. W. K. R[ogers] to Hayes, August 16, 1876, *ibid.*
150. Handwritten copy of circular, Chm'n Republican Nat'l Committee, Sec'y Republican Nat'l Committee, Chm'n Republican Cong'l Committee, and Sec'y Republican Cong'l Committee to ———, 1876, in William E. Chandler Papers.

created in New York and Boston. Chaired by banker Levi P. Morton and industrialist John Murray Forbes, respectively, these seven-man task forces contacted wealthy Republicans in the two metropolitan areas that traditionally provided the bulk of party resources.[151] The methods used to obtain donations were not always such as would have borne public scrutiny. Shortly before the election the Treasury Department notified the National Bank Note Company that its lucrative contract with the government would not be renewed. Augustus D. Shepard, the treasurer of the company, appealed the decision to E. D. Morgan, who in turn spoke to the secretary of the treasury. When Morgan informed Shepard that the cancellation had been withdrawn, the latter gave the party $10,000.[152] That was probably the purpose behind announcing termination of the contract in the first place.

Freed from the onerous burden of dealing with the party's financial angels, Chandler devoted his attention to a type of work he understood more fully—levying assessments on the salaries of federal employees. This practice had been a standard feature of American politics for decades, a logical extension of the concept "To the victors belong the spoils." If an officeholder owed his job to the electoral triumph of his party, surely he had an obligation to help insure the continued success of that party in future campaigns. However, a growing number of articulate Americans objected to the entire concept of the spoils system. As early as January 1, 1872, one of the regulations recommended by the Civil Service Commission and promulgated by President Grant prohibited the levying or paying of assessments "under the form of voluntary contributions or otherwise." But Grant became disenchanted with the reformers—many of whom op-

---

151. Typescript circular, J. M. Forbes to ———, August 25, 1876, in Morgan Papers; printed circular, L. P. Morton, Legrand B. Cannon, Joseph Seligman, Waldo Hutchings, Marshall O. Roberts, C. L. Tiffany, and John W. Ellis to ———, September 13, 1876, and R. C. McCormick to Hayes, September 14, 1876, both in Hayes Papers.

152. James A. Rawley, *Edwin D. Morgan, 1811–1883: Merchant in Politics* (New York: Columbia University Press, 1955), 257–58.

posed his reelection—and the civil service rules were permitted to lapse.[153] In the fall of 1875 Chandler was appointed secretary of the interior and "a few weeks after taking office dismissed the experienced chief clerk of the Patent Office for refusing to pay an assessment."[154]

The Democratic majority in the House of Representatives sought to halt this practice before the presidential canvass would begin by attaching to an omnibus appropriation bill a clause prohibiting all assessments. The Republican Senate objected, however, and in the closing days of the session a conference committee of the two houses worked out an innocuous compromise. Under the law as finally adopted, only officers or employees of the federal government "not appointed by the President with the advice and consent of the Senate" were forbidden to collect "any money, property, or other thing of value, for political purposes."[155] Chandler, accordingly, did not face any legal obstacles that he could not easily circumvent. Soon newspapers were carrying stories describing the levy on government employees.

Carl Schurz, the most outspoken of the reformers supporting the Republican ticket, was furious. After questioning a friend in the Treasury Department about the matter and receiving the answer he frankly expected, Schurz repeated the key portion of his friend's letter in a vigorous protest to Hayes:

> In reply to your inquiry I beg leave to say that I have learned from my friends in the Interior and Post-office Departments, that they have paid an assessment "for political purposes" of 2 per cent. on their annual salaries, and that this assessment was collected from all of them. Genl. Rutherford, formerly 3d Auditor of the Treasury, has collected in some of the Bureau's [*sic*] of this Department the same amount for the same purpose and will visit the Bureau's in which the collection has not yet been made, about the end of this month. He goes from one Clerk to another with a list containing

153. Ari Hoogenboom, *Outlawing the Spoils: A History of the Civil Service Reform Movement, 1865–1883* (Urbana: University of Illinois Press, 1961), 96.
154. *Ibid.*, 136.
155. New York *World*, August 21, 1876.

the names of the clerks with the salaries they receive, for inst. "A. B. sal. p. a. $1,600; 2 per cent. $32," and so he collects on pay day the 2 per cent. from every one on the list. Excuses, as that the clerk has a large family, or that he wants to go home to vote at his own expense, are not accepted. Neither does he accept less than 2 per cent. We have, therefore, to pay the 2 per cent, or nothing, and in the latter case risk the consequences. . . . In my room Genl. Rutherford has not been yet, but I keep the money in my pocket ready to be handed over because I believe the "consequences" would this time be very disagreeable and certain.[156]

The Republican candidate had recently told William Henry Smith, "I hate assessments. They are all wrong, and are sure to do more harm than good." [157] Nevertheless, when Schurz reproached him for not speaking out publicly against this abuse and even threatened to "throw up" his appointments if nothing were done,[158] Hayes remained reticent. He told Schurz that he would stand by his letter of acceptance;[159] but he refused to take effective action to stop the levying of assessments in the current campaign. Instead, he wrote "a private note" to McCormick, specifying that "if assessments are made as charged, it is a plain departure from correct principles and ought not to be allowed. I trust the Committee will have nothing to do with it." [160] McCormick assured Hayes that the national committee as such had not made any assessments. It was perfectly understood, of course, that Chandler took care of the entire business on his own. McCormick also cautioned the candidate that "it is so difficult to raise money this year that I do not know how we can secure enough for perfectly legitimate campaign purposes unless the federal officers contribute." [161] Hayes sent Schurz a copy of his letter to McCormick, but restricted it to *"private use only*

156. Schurz to Hayes, September 5, 1876, in Hayes Papers.
157. Hayes to Wm. Henry Smith, August 10, 1876, *ibid.*
158. Schurz to Hayes, September 3, 1876, *ibid.*
159. Hayes to Schurz, September 6, 1876, in Schurz Papers.
160. Letterpress copy, Hayes to R. C. McCormick, September 8, 1876, in Hayes Papers.
161. R. C. McCormick to Hayes, October 13, 1876, *ibid.*

as matters now stand, and until I give consent to its publication." [162] Though disappointed in Hayes and frustrated at his own helplessness, Schurz was still too much of a partisan to withdraw from the contest and thus maintained his active role as a speaker.

The gathering of involuntary donations from civil servants continued. Edwin D. Morgan made the only attempt of even the least significance to curb Chandler, complaining merely that his successor as chairman had ranged too far afield:

It was a mistake on the part of the National Committee to assess office holders in Indiana, Ohio, or N York, the 3 States that are to decide this Election, and I earnestly request that you will immediately countermand the order and inform them that the regular Republican State Committees are the only ones to whom they will be expected to make any Contributions. Only $700 have thus far been collected in the *entire State of Ohio,* and our friends there will call on us for money, if you dont allow them to collect from the Federal officers in their own state.[163]

William E. Chandler stated many years later that Zach Chandler's "memorandum book" showed expenditures of the Republican National Committee in the campaign of 1876 to have been "only about $200,000." [164] Assuming that funds used to aid hard-pressed state committees were not included, Chandler's figure is probably correct. Certainly Republican spending was in line with the total disbursed by the Democrats. The vastly greater sums used during some later elections, in 1896 for example, were simply not available in the centennial year.

As John Murray Forbes noted in his memoirs, it was not hard to account, through "legitimate expenses," for the distribution of this money: "Public speakers sent over the country by the national committee are not often paid for their speeches, but

162. Hayes to Schurz, September 15, 1876, in Schurz Papers.
163. Letterpress copy, E. D. Morgan to Z. Chandler, September 1, 1876, in Morgan Papers.
164. Memorandum by W. E. Chandler, "The Hayes-Tilden canvass of 1876," in William E. Chandler Papers.

their expenses are usually paid out of the fund and are apt to be large,—traveling, as they do, in palace cars and living in first-class hotels; and they cannot well be scrutinized carefully, through vouchers or by auditors." Speakers of national reputation were reimbursed by state party officials only when they appeared in New York and perhaps in two or three other wealthy states. The expenses of printing documents were also very great. On occasion, full-page supplements or broadsides were ordered, to be distributed with newspapers "in the same wrappers without additional postage . . . a very valuable method, and in proportion to its value . . . not a costly one." [165] The partisan press itself was regarded as an indispensable element in the campaign. When a party organ was financially embarrassed, as happened often, the national committee was forced to consider, even if it could not always afford, some kind of subsidy. If the situation was not too critical, a printing contract might be sufficient to avert a paper's suspension in the midst of the canvass.[166] There were, as well, the bills of the national headquarters itself, traditionally located in the Fifth Avenue Hotel, and the wages of numerous employees. On September 18 William S. Dodge, McCormick's principal assistant, complained that he had not received his $100-a-month salary since May. The committee owed him nearly $500.[167]

Straining as he was to meet the imperative expenses of his own committee, Zach Chandler, a contentious man under the best of circumstances, became increasingly caustic when several state organizations began pleading for money to defray their costs. He scraped together $5,000 to send to Maine in two installments at the end of August and made plans to forward a similar amount to North Carolina in early September. He wanted it

165. Sarah Forbes Hughes (ed.), *Letters and Recollections of John Murray Forbes* (2 vols.; Boston: Houghton, Mifflin and Company, 1900), II, 199–202.
166. R. C. McCormick to Schurz, August 4, 9, 1876, in Schurz Papers; John A. Logan to Z. Chandler, October 19, 1876, in Zachariah Chandler Papers.
167. W. S. Dodge to W. E. Chandler, September 18, 1876, in William E. Chandler Papers.

understood, however, that nothing more could be spared for those states.[168]

Chandler lost all patience at the demands from Indiana and Ohio. Before the national committee had yet perfected its own organization, threatening sounds were emanating from the Hoosier State. Former Union general Judson Kilpatrick wrote Hayes to warn him of the Greenback menace in Indiana:

There is an independent party in this state—confined it is true mostly to a few counties—but formidable and it will defeat Gen. Harrison. There is but one way to overcome this movement. The leaders are poor, needy and in debt; they must be made to see their folly [.] A *bloody shirt* campaign, with *money* and Ind. is safe for us. A *financial* campaign and no money and we are beaten. The National Committee has done nothing for Ind.—alone they are fighting this battle—and bravely, but unless the National Committee does its duty now, at once to Gen. Hayes & the Republican party, defeat is certain in Oct.[169]

Kilpatrick's letter, it was soon learned, had been composed at the urging of the state committee, which was trying to pry more funds out of the national headquarters in New York. A more discreetly worded version was deliberately leaked to the press to embarrass Chandler and McCormick.[170] Kilpatrick mailed Chandler still a third variation, differing principally in that it specified the amount desired by Indiana Republicans—$800,000! Instead, the national chairman agreed to provide $40,000 in four installments between late August and the state election on October 10.[171] Chandler grumbled that "too much money has been wasted in Indiana in years past, and unless great care is

---

168. R. C. McCormick to W. E. Chandler, August 27, 1876, *ibid.*; Z. Chandler to Blaine, August 31, 1876, in Blaine Papers; letterpress copy, E. D. Morgan to Blaine, August 30, 1876, in Morgan Papers.
169. J. Kilpatrick to Hayes, August 21, 1876, in Hayes Papers.
170. R. C. McCormick to Hayes, August 28, 1876, *ibid.*
171. R. C. McCormick to Hayes, August 25, 1876, and Noyes to Hayes, August 30, 1876, both *ibid.* Contrast these figures with the statement of one popular historical writer of undoubted ability that both parties spent "several million dollars" in Indiana. See Dee Brown, *The Year of the Century: 1876* (New York: Charles Scribner's Sons, 1966), 245.

now taken, there will be the same result." [172] Officials in the western office of the national committee in Chicago also raised about $7,000 for Indiana, aided by an autograph letter from Hayes which urged "exceptionally liberal appropriations" for that state. But the man who collected the money cautioned Hayes not to tell Chandler, "*for if the national committee know it they may relax their efforts to raise money for Indiana.*" [173]

Chandler was even angrier when Hayes joined other Ohio leaders in asking that the Buckeye State be furnished $10,000. He agreed with Morgan, he said, that "Ohio, the third richest state in the Union should not call for outside assistance." Did Hayes not know "the names of wealthy and influential citizens in Cincinnati" who could form "a Committee to aid in raising means for Ohio and Indiana?" Chandler continued: "Maine has done wonderfully well and Indiana will do better. Even West Virginia can easily be carried with moderate means. Ohio alone exhibits no life." [174] The national committee supplied the amount requested, but Chandler, out of pique, made the drafts payable to the order of "R. B. Hayes." [175] Ten days before the November election an additional $5,000 was sent to Ohio, and twice that sum was sent to Indiana. Altogether, during the entire summer and fall the two branches of the national committee assisted six state organizations to the extent of $84,000.[176] For the Republicans it was not a lavish campaign.

Faced with this severe shortage of funds, the leaders of the Republican party felt themselves fortunate that they had a federal elections law to fall back on. It might not lead a supporter of Tilden to vote for Hayes, but the statute could be relied

172. R. C. McCormick to Hayes, August 25, 1876, in Hayes Papers.
173. Hayes to James P. Root, August 22, 1876, and Root to Hays [*sic*], September 20, 1876, both *ibid.*
174. Copy (in the hand of R. C. McCormick), Z. Chandler to Hayes, September 12, 1876, in Zachariah Chandler Papers.
175. R. C. McCormick to Hayes, September 14, 1876, in Hayes Papers.
176. Alphonso Taft to Hayes, October 26, 1876, *ibid.*; Jas. N. Tyner to Z. Chandler, November 1, 1876, in Zachariah Chandler Papers. West Virginia and Wisconsin each received $1000. H. C. Parsons to Hayes, September 9, 1876, and Wm. Henry Smith to Hayes, November 6, 1876, both in Hayes Papers.

on to make virtually impossible the kind of election frauds Republican rhetoricians habitually charged their opponents with plotting. Careful observance of the polls on election day, therefore, was not one of the "legitimate campaign purposes" on which Republicans had to expend much of their party's limited resources.

The federal elections law was, in a sense, a product of the Tweed Ring. In New York City in 1868 the naturalizing of an extraordinarily high number of foreign-born citizens in October was followed by an astonishing Democratic vote in November. Horatio Seymour outpolled Grant by sixty thousand votes in the city, and in doing so carried the state by ten thousand votes in what was almost everywhere else a Republican year. As many as forty thousand of the Democratic ballots may have been cast illegally. The gentlemen of the Union League Club were indignant. In retaliation they financed an investigation of the election and used the impressive evidence developed to support a petition to Congress demanding that such frauds be prevented in the future. Congress responded with an investigation of its own, which led in turn to the tightening of the naturalization laws in 1870 and the passage of a comprehensive elections law in 1871.[177]

Congress acted under the constitutional provision that gave it authority to alter or amend state laws governing the election of senators and representatives if the state statutes were found to be inadequate. Its action had little, if anything, to do with Reconstruction. Since it was applicable only to cities with a population of at least twenty thousand, it was aimed at the Democratic constituencies of the North. (In 1871 there were fifty-eight such cities in the North and only ten in the South.)

The legislation was carefully written to assure its utilization on the widest possible scale. Whenever two citizens from the same congressional district petitioned a United States circuit

177. Albie Burke, "Federal Regulation of Congressional Elections in Northern Cities, 1871–1894" (Ph.D. dissertation, University of Chicago, 1968), 37, 42–46, 71, 180.

court, stating their belief that frauds were about to be perpetrated either during registration or voting, the court was required to apply the law in its entirety. Two federal supervisors —a Democrat and a Republican—would be appointed for every polling place in the district to oversee both the registration of voters and the balloting. These supervisors had authority to examine registration lists, challenge the eligibility of voters, arrest citizens suspected of having balloted illegally, and participate in the tabulation of returns. To guarantee that the supervisors would not be impeded in the performance of their duties, the local United States marshal could deploy as many deputies as his professional judgment dictated. There was no restriction, incidentally, on the political affiliations of the marshals and deputies: they were all Republicans. Both supervisors and deputy marshals were paid by the Treasury at the rate of five dollars a day for a maximum of ten days. The coverage of the elections law was extended to rural districts in 1872. The broadening of the statute was misleading, however, because the supervisors in the countryside had substantially less authority than their counterparts in the cities, and they received no compensation for their services.[178]

Under these provisions the Grant administration spent more than $291,000 to hire 11,501 deputy marshals and 4,863 supervisors to police the elections of 1876 in the cities of the North and in selected rural districts of the South—the Democratic strongholds of the nation. The intent of this massive implementation should not be mistaken. In New York City deputy marshals were chosen and commanded by dedicated officials of the Republican party. In Philadelphia they wore party badges and distributed Republican ballots at the very polls they were supposed to guard.[179]

As summer passed into fall, and as the politicians touring the land encountered shorter days and chillier nights, the prospects for extending the long dominion of "the party that saved the

178. *Ibid.*, 3–6.
179. *Ibid.*, 112–13, 125–29, 171–72.

Union" were doubtful at best. George William Curtis suggested that perhaps not enough attention was being paid in the canvass to the importance of reform: "Your candidacy is not only that of the old times, but of the new. This fact your letter strongly emphasized, but the conduct of our campaign has not confirmed it and that has, I think, seriously injured us. Even here in the Republican heart of Massachusetts, people are waiting and watching. They see . . . Chandler's Chairmanship, and Blaine, Morton, Ingersoll, and the other brethren upon the stump, and, seeing these and similar things, they naturally ask where is the hope or promise of healthful and indispensable change." [180] Most Republicans looked in a different direction for a counter not only to the opposition's far more effective talk of "reform," but also to the depression and the undeniable popularity of the Democratic candidates in their home states. Hayes noted in his diary "A few watchwords" which "might be useful if well circulated":

Are you for a United South or are you against it?
Are you for the United South, or are you for the United States?
Are you for the Rebel South, or are you for the loyal North?
Who do you wish should rule—the South or the Nation? . . .
Rebel rule or Loyal rule? that is the question.
Are you for the Rebellion, or are you for the Union?
Are you for the United South, or are you for the United States?
   That is the question.
Are you for the men who wore the gray, or are you for the men who wore the blue? [181]

If the Republicans wanted the "bloody shirt," they had available in 1876 the one man best qualified to expound it: Robert G. Ingersoll.

I am opposed to the Democratic party, and I will tell you why. Every state that seceded from the United States was a Democratic State. Every ordinance of secession that was drawn was drawn by a Democrat. Every man that endeavored to tear the old flag from the

180. Curtis to Hayes, August 31, 1876, in Hayes Papers.
181. Entry for September 18, 1876, in Williams (ed.), *Hayes: The Diary of a President*, 37–38.

heaven that it enriches was a Democrat. [A voice—"Give it to them."] Every man that tried to destroy this nation was a Democrat. Every enemy this great republic has had for twenty years has been a Democrat. Every man that shot Union soldiers was a Democrat. [Cheers—"That's so."] Every man that starved Union soldiers and refused them in the extremity of death a crust was a Democrat. [Renewed cheering.] Every man that loved slavery better than liberty was a Democrat. The man that assassinated Abraham Lincoln was a Democrat. Every man that sympathized with the assassin— every man glad that the noblest President ever elected was assassinated, was a Democrat. Every man that wanted the privilege of whipping another man to make him work for him for nothing and pay him with lashes on his naked back, was a Democrat. [Cheers.] Every man that raised blood-hounds to pursue human beings was a Democrat. Every man that clutched from shrieking [,] shuddering, crouching mothers, babes from their breasts and sold them into slavery was a Democrat. [Cheers.] ... Soldiers, every scar you have got on your heroic bodies was given to you by a Democrat. [Cheers.] Every scar, every arm that is lacking, every limb that is gone, every scar is a souvenir of a Democrat. [Cheers.]

Ingersoll continued in this manner for more than two hours.[182] When Blaine, Morton, Garfield, and even Murat Halstead on one occasion, contributed speeches in the same vein, the "bloody shirt" set the tone for the closing weeks of the Republican campaign.

8

The most striking feature of the Democratic and Republican canvasses of 1876 was their essential similarity, which suggests that both campaigns were limited by the knowledge and technological level of the late nineteenth century. The Democratic candidate was distinctly more capable than his Republican opponent, but both men reacted with timidity and indecisiveness to the tremendous pressures brought to bear upon them by competing political interests in their own parties. That mattered little, of course, because custom decreed a passive role for presidential

182. Printed broadside, "FACTS FOR THE PEOPLE—NO. 7. The Greatest Speech of the Campaign.—Col. Ingersoll, of Illinois, at Indianapolis, Indiana [1876]," Broadside Collection, Illinois State Historical Library.

aspirants regardless of their ability. The national party organizations, which suddenly sprang into being for a few short months of frenzied activity, did not differ much either. They collected funds, printed documents, and ordered speakers onto the stump. Abram S. Hewitt attempted to systematize the Democratic effort, but his labors, though inspiring, were largely unsuccessful. The Republican committee ran a campaign that was frankly unambitious and unimaginative, relying on the partisan use of the machinery and personnel of the federal government to offset the more vigorous spirit of the Democrats.

In the end, if significant alteration of the electorate's thoughts was the purpose of all their work, the two parties must be said to have been about equally ineffective. The entire picture gains clarity when one examines the campaign at the state level— where most of the contest was fought.

Chapter V □ The Campaign in the States

THERE WERE in reality thirty-eight campaigns for the presidency in 1876, one in each of the states of the Union. Legally, voters cast their ballots for candidates to represent their state in the electoral college, rather than directly for president and vice-president. This constitutional arrangement was reflected in the structure of the Republican and Democratic parties. Every state organization was responsible for conducting its own canvass, aided to a limited extent by the national committees in New York and Washington.

Campaigning in many parts of the country was a comparatively simple matter because the outcome of the contests for state and national office was never in doubt. Vermont, Massachusetts, Kansas, and Nebraska had long been overwhelmingly Republican. In much of the South, on the other hand, savage factional feuds and sporadic violence against black voters had left the party of Lincoln a hopeless minority. In these states activity was concentrated in a doubtful congressional district or on a handful of the legislative seats held most precariously by the minority party.

National attention focused principally on the dozen or so states where Republicans and Democrats were approximately equal in strength. There the energy and resources of the state committees were taxed to the utmost, while the national organizations rendered whatever assistance they were able. The fact that several of these states held elections for state office a month or two before the presidential election in November added drama to the situation. In previous years these early elections had generally foreshadowed closely the results of the presidential contests in the same states. As a result the national campaign of 1876 quickly evolved into a bitter struggle to win state elections in September and October.

1

The first gubernatorial contest of interest occurred in Vermont on September 5 and produced a few rays of hope for both sides. In an unusually heavy turnout, the Republican margin of victory increased 3,400 votes over that of 1874, while the Democrats captured a slightly large share of the total cast (31.9 percent compared to 28.3 percent).[1] Each party claimed a victory. Six days later Maine elected its governor. This time there could be no quibbling about the result. In a record vote the Republicans won easily, erasing memories of the scare they had suffered a year earlier. The Democratic percentage dropped from forty-eight to forty-four.[2]

Then it was Colorado's turn. The admission of the Centennial State to the Union on August 1 was itself not unrelated to the election of 1876. Most of the western states and territories were strongly Republican, so the Democrats in Congress might have been expected to work hard to delay the admission of the new state. But Colorado had elected a Democratic delegate to Congress by a handsome majority in the "Tidal Wave" of 1874, and this delegate convinced his partisan fellows that the prospective state could be relied on to vote favorably in the future. Accordingly, the statehood bill was allowed to pass in 1875. Moreover, to save the expense of conducting two elections a month apart,

1. *The Tribune Almanac and Political Register for 1875* (New York: The Tribune Association, [1875]), 49; *The Tribune Almanac and Political Register for 1877* (New York: The Tribune Association [1877]), 122.
2. *The Tribune Almanac and Political Register for 1876* (New York: The Tribune Association, [1876]), 82; *The Tribune Almanac and Political Register for 1877*, 81.

the law specifically authorized the first legislature to choose the state's presidential electors in 1876. Nine weeks after Colorado entered the Union, the Republicans swept the elections of October 3, placing in office the first governor and obtaining a two-to-one majority in the first legislature. In a sense, therefore, Colorado was the first state to take its position in the Hayes and Wheeler column. The consternation of the former territorial delegate was readily understandable.[3]

These results were disappointing to the Democrats but not disheartening. If they could win, as they expected to, in all of the former slave states, thus creating a "solid South," they would obtain 138 electoral votes, with 185 necessary to elect a president. Then the additional combination of New York with either Indiana, Ohio, or Wisconsin, or with New Jersey and Connecticut, would make Tilden the nation's next chief executive. This arithmetic had influenced the presidential and vice-presidential nominations in both parties. It also explains the extraordinary importance attached to the state races in Indiana and Ohio.

The Indiana campaign illustrated dramatically the way in which the fortunes of the national tickets might turn upon the actions of state leaders. Benjamin Harrison was probably the most formidable gubernatorial candidate the Republicans could have presented in 1876. Early in the year, however, Harrison indicated that he preferred to devote himself to his law practice. His decision was accepted with alacrity by Oliver P. Morton, who was afraid that Harrison, if elected governor, might challenge his own reelection to the Senate in 1878. Morton and his allies settled on Godlove S. Orth, a former congressman who was then abroad as minister to Austria, and when Harrison remained steadfast in his refusal to run, Orth was nominated practically without opposition on February 22. Two weeks later Democratic newspapers in Indiana opened fire on Orth, accusing him of having used his position in Congress to obtain legislation

3. A. K. McClure, *Our Presidents and How We Make Them* (New York: Harper and Brothers, 1909), 261; *The Tribune Almanac and Political Register for 1877*, 66.

favorable to clients from whom he in turn received a large fee. It was a classic instance of a conflict of interest. The disreputability of the clients, men whose own conflicts of interest—they had speculated in the very claims against the Venezuelan government that they were supposed to be settling as diplomatic agents of the United States—had already been exposed, further damaged Orth. When the minister resigned and returned to Indiana in June to launch his campaign, he consistently declined to discuss the charges against him. After a while the reform-minded Indianapolis *Evening News*, a Republican paper, interpreted his silence as evidence of guilt and questioned his qualifications for the governorship. Clouded as it was, Orth's candidacy aroused little enthusiasm. On August 2 he consulted hastily with members of the state committee and announced his retirement from the race. In an emergency meeting two days later, the committee unanimously tendered the nomination to Harrison, who reluctantly accepted. The Republican campaign had suffered a devastating setback, and such petty considerations as Morton's jealousy could no longer be indulged.[4]

The Democratic candidate was more remarkable than either Orth or Harrison. After the state convention deadlocked between two more prominent aspirants, James D. Williams emerged the dark-horse winner. Williams was a veteran of more than thirty years in the legislature and of a single term in Congress. During his year in Washington he earned the nickname "Blue Jeans" by his practice of wearing neatly tailored suits of blue homespun produced from his own flock of sheep. Williams was a farmer and consciously made himself the representative of his state's multitude of disgruntled agriculturists. His campaign appearances, which resembled nothing so much as Grange meetings, were held almost exclusively in rural areas. In overwhelmingly agrarian Indiana, it seemed, one could still ignore the existence of cities. At any rate, Williams,

4. Harry J. Sievers, *Benjamin Harrison, Hoosier Statesman: From the Civil War to the White House, 1865–1888* (New York: University Publishers, Inc., 1959), 93–94, 98–102.

wearing his denim suits and telling bucolic stories, was obviously a popular figure in the countryside, and that fact spelled trouble for the Republicans.[5]

Another source of concern was the independent ticket placed in the field by Indiana Greenbackers. Senator Morton told Hayes in August that the Greenback candidates drew four fifths of their support from normally Republican voters. Asked how to deal with the situation, Morton replied, *"Money and speakers. Money to pay men to travel and organize—to print and circulate Documents—&c &c [.]* " Morton thought $100,000 would be needed, most of it from sources outside the state. Hayes found this report profoundly discouraging, as he confided to his diary: "The use of money I have little faith in, and I am confident no such large sums can be raised." [6] The Republicans consequently had to rely on an intensive speaking campaign, led by Morton and Congressman William D. Kelley of Pennsylvania, both of whom were known to be sympathetic toward demands for inflating the currency. Indiana Republicans were fully aware that the greatest obstacle to their success was "the paralyzed condition of business and industries, the multitude of people out of employment & the consequent dissatisfaction and desire to see some change of policy, with the hope of revival of business. These people thoughtlessly say that any change of administration [in Washington] will be better than the present &c." [7] Party leaders were not certain how this notion could be countered.

A traditional appeal to the passions of the Civil War seemed best. It was no coincidence that the annual encampment of the Grand Army of the Republic was scheduled to be held in Indian-

5. Howard R. Burnett, "The Last Pioneer Governor of Indiana—'Blue Jeans' Williams," *Indiana Magazine of History*, XXII (June, 1926), 110–23.

6. Entry for August 13, 1876, in T. Harry Williams (ed.), *Hayes: The Diary of a President, 1875–1881, Covering the Disputed Election, the End of Reconstruction, and the Beginning of Civil Service* (New York: David McKay Company, Inc., 1964), 28–29.

7. John W. Foster to Ben. Harrison, August 15, 1876, Benjamin Harrison Papers, Manuscript Division, Library of Congress.

apolis three weeks before the state election. On September 20 and 21 thousands of veterans from all across the North pitched their tents, watched a parade three miles long, and listened to countless hours of speeches designed to rekindle their old hatred of the South. Robert G. Ingersoll was there to deliver his stock political address. Harrison, a brevet brigadier general during the war, joined James A. Garfield in touring the three large campgrounds.[8]

Even that did not seem to help much. So Hayes asked William E. Chandler to visit Indiana and find out what was wrong. This Chandler, McCormick's predecessor as secretary of the national committee, was widely regarded as one of the party's best organizers. He had already spent time in Maine as a special trouble shooter.[9] Chandler stayed a week in the Hoosier State and found the outlook difficult to judge: "Our speakers, many of them [,] are confident we shall elect Harrison, but they believe he will run ahead of the rest of the ticket; and they are more or less influenced in their judgments, by the effect upon them of the enthusiasm of their own meetings." He himself was not as optimistic: "All I learn here confirms our view of the importance of a decided majority in Ohio."[10] The state committee reported that Indiana had been very thoroughly canvassed, but the members were at a loss to judge the impact of the Greenback ticket. They thought that the Democrats were about 1,500 votes ahead.[11] Chandler was also surprised to learn that Tilden had not spent more money in Indiana: "Will he not open the barrel of money at last? This is his last opportunity; if he does not embrace it he is gone."[12]

But the Democrats were not taking Indiana for granted. They

8. Sievers, *Benjamin Harrison, Hoosier Statesman,* 117–19.
9. R. C. McCormick to Wm. E. Chandler, August 21, 1876, and W. S. Dodge to W. E. Chandler, August 21, 1876, both in William E. Chandler Papers, Manuscript Division, Library of Congress.
10. Wm. E. Chandler to Hayes, September 27, 1876, in Rutherford B. Hayes Papers, Rutherford B. Hayes Library, Fremont, Ohio.
11. W. R. Holloway to E. D. Morgan, September 28, 1876, in Edwin D. Morgan Papers, New York State Library.
12. Wm. E. Chandler to Hayes, September 28, 1876, in Hayes Papers.

staged over five hundred rallies throughout the state during July, August, and September.[13] One of the easterners sent to address these meetings was concerned that such efforts were not enough. He spent much of his time "trying to show the imperative need of a close canvass of the counties. . . . Speeches are good, but *work* is wanted and those who know how to work worse wanted." [14] Tilden persuaded Samuel J. Randall to go to Indiana to work on organizational matters in late September.[15] Randall devoted a week to this assignment and as soon as he returned east was promptly called back by a series of frantic telegrams from state leaders.[16] Senator William H. Barnum of Connecticut joined Randall's effort. By the time they were through, one Hoosier Democrat commented in awe, "Indiana has never been so canvassed and shaken up." [17]

The need to counter the "bloody shirt" tactics of their opponents was a source of great anxiety to the Democrats; so they imitated part of the Republican campaign, staging a reunion of Democratic veterans in Indianapolis on October 5, just five days before the election. The turnout was much smaller than at the G.A.R. affair.[18] But the very idea of such a gathering alarmed Republicans. Panicky leaders in Washington and elsewhere exchanged rumors of fantastic Democratic schemes for flooding Indiana with toughs and illegal voters.[19] William E. Chandler saw less cause for concern, however, assuring McCormick that state party officials "have made ample preparation for it in Indianapolis and with the precautionary measures which you

13. Burnett, " 'Blue Jeans' Williams," 122.
14. [R. Vaux] to Randall, September 16, 1876, in Samuel J. Randall Papers, University of Pennsylvania Library.
15. Randall to C. F. Black, September 21, 1876, in Jeremiah S. Black Papers, Manuscript Division, Library of Congress; Pelton to Randall, September 23, 1876, in Randall Papers.
16. Telegram, W. Henderson to Randall, October 4, 1876, telegram, Wm. McCandless to Randall, October 4, 1876, and telegram, W. H. Barnum to Randall, October 5, 1876, all in Randall Papers.
17. W. E. Niblack to Hewitt, October 7, 1876, in Samuel J. Tilden Papers, New York Public Library.
18. Chicago *Daily News*, October 4, 5, 1876.
19. See, for example, W. Dennison to Comly, September 27, 1876, in James M. Comly Papers, Ohio Historical Society Library.

have adopted in New Yk, Phila & Balto. they will prevent injury. The Indianapolis boys are prepared with an organized force to resist rioting, and repeating [;] all they want is the detectives." [20]

Then an unexpected development on October 4 materially altered the course of the gubernatorial race. Anson Wolcott, the Greenback candidate, conceding that he could not win, and foreseeing no prospect for inflation if either Hayes or Tilden were elected, withdrew and in a public letter announced his personal support of Harrison. The Democrats immediately denounced Wolcott's move as part of a corrupt bargain. A sizable number of Greenbackers angrily substituted Henry W. Harrington at the top of their ticket. And the leaders of the two major parties saw their carefully prepared estimates of the probable outcome of the election rendered instantly obsolete. [21]

The real possibility that Indiana would vote Democratic caused Hayes misgivings about the inordinate significance his party attached to the state: "It is common to say 'if Indiana and Ohio go right in October', 'If Indiana is for us' &c &c, thus hinging all on Indiana. Now Indiana is a Democratic State. Emigration of Republicans west and the greenback heresy have made it so.... The true pivot is New York. Let us therefore prepare our friends and the public not to be disheartened if Indiana is wrong. Especially our friends in the East. *October will not decide the election unless both Ohio and Indiana go the same way.*" [22]

Hayes's analysis actually made Ohio rather than New York the crucial state; if it, too, were lost, there would be no deliverance from disaster. The governor's nomination had always been urged by his friends on the ground that the Buckeye State would then be safe for the Republicans. [23] Small wonder, therefore, that when Ohio was discovered to be extremely close, party leaders

20. W. [E. Chandler] to R. C. McCormick, October 4, 1876, in Zachariah Chandler Papers, Manuscript Division, Library of Congress.
21. Sievers, *Benjamin Harrison, Hoosier Statesman*, 119–21.
22. Hayes to Wm. H. Smith, September 9, 1876, in Hayes Papers.
23. Entry for October 15, 1876, in Williams (ed.), *Hayes: The Diary of a President*, 42.

everywhere lost their composure. John Sherman, shortly after his return from the long session of Congress, expressed "much solicitude" about the situation: "I do not see the signs of activity on our own part shown by the Dem. Party." He questioned the ability of State Chairman A. T. Wikoff, a hard worker who had held the same position during Hayes's triumphant gubernatorial campaign of the previous year.[24] James M. Comly of the *Ohio State Journal* admitted that "it was the Pope's big toe that saved us last fall," and he wished he had it again. Comly was especially alarmed that "about 300 negroes in the Columbus district attended the Democratic primaries and have decided they will vote for Tom Ewing [for Congress]."[25] William Henry Smith reassured Comly, "There is one thing that we have always, and I have found out west that it is always efficient in stirring up Republicans where all things else fail, viz: 'The bloody shirt.'" Smith, giving what seemed to be the inevitable solution, advised Comly to "telegraph for Col. Robt. Ingersoll at once & turn him loose."[26] The national committee also responded according to formula, sending William E. Chandler to check the Ohio canvass. This time Chandler found that his services were unnecessary: "Everything possible is being done that men can do."[27] The Republican majority was expected to be so slender that Smith decided to cover the election himself for the Western Associated Press to "see that there is no mistake about the tone of the despatches going east especially."[28] Manning F. Force, who ran for Congress unsuccessfully in a Cincinnati district, thought the campaign had been unusually well organized on both sides: "The republican committees, and most of their local executive committees did admirable work. I have never known more complete preparation in this county. But the

24. Sherman to Hayes, August 23, 1876, in Hayes Papers.
25. ———Thomson to Medill, August 21 [1876], in William Henry Smith Collection, Indiana Historical Society Library.
26. Wm. Henry Smith to Comly, August 26, 1876, in Comly Papers.
27. R. C. McCormick to Hayes, September 24, 1876, and Wm. E. Chandler to Hayes, October 6, 1876, both in Hayes Papers.
28. Wm. Henry Smith to Hayes, October 4, 1876, *ibid.*

democrats were still more thorough. They made a complete poll of their vote before the election." [29]

On October 10 the nation's politicians held their collective breath, and the voters of Indiana and Ohio went to the polls. It took two days to count the ballots and add up all the returns. In Indiana the Republicans, with the help of advantageous district boundaries, won control of the legislature and gained five congressional seats, but "Blue Jeans" Williams was elected governor by five thousand votes. Democrats were the victors in every statewide contest. The highest office at stake in Ohio was secretary of state, and a Republican won that post by 6,600 votes. In two other elections held the same day, Nebraska was overwhelmingly Republican, whereas West Virginia was just as predictably Democratic.[30] The battle in the October states, as Hayes had foreseen, ended inconclusively. The final month of the campaign was going to be very hard fought indeed.

2

The Republican leaders were fully agreed as to the strategy they would have to follow. After meeting at length with members of the national committee, William E. Chandler told Hayes that there were fourteen states, with 144 electoral votes, in which the party was certain to prevail: Maine, New Hampshire, Vermont, Massachusetts, Rhode Island, Pennsylvania, Ohio, Michigan, Illinois, Iowa, Minnesota, Kansas, Nebraska, and Colorado. Of these only New Hampshire, Pennsylvania, and Illinois could even be considered contested. Success in New York, with 35 electoral votes, and Wisconsin, with 10, would give the Republican ticket a total of 189, 4 more than needed. Should the Empire State be lost, defeat could still be averted: "If we can carry Cal. 6 which McCormick says is sure," along with New Jersey, Indiana, and Nevada, "all possible to be carried," those states would produce thirty-three electoral votes among them, so "we

29. M. F. Force to Hayes, October 14, 1876, *ibid.*
30. *The Tribune Almanac and Political Register for 1877*, 74–76, 90–91, 111–13, 124–25.

can win without New Yk [.] " ³¹ At the same time, Chandler was not at all optimistic about Dixie. He thought the Carolinas "the only Southern states we can hope to carry." ³² Chandler's analysis received Hayes's prompt endorsement: "The contest is now with the East. The inflation States have done better for the hard-money candidates than you had a right to expect. Now let the hard-money States do as well, and we are safe." ³³ Wheeler concurred: "New York is to decide the contest. *I* have no hopes of Indiana in Nov'r. Nor of *any* Southern State." ³⁴ McCormick, too, admitted that "we should be prepared for a solid South for Tilden." ³⁵

New York, then, was the indispensable state. It was also the home of the imperious Roscoe Conkling, who as yet had not lifted a finger in behalf of the Republican cause. Senator Phineas W. Hitchcock, on his way home to Nebraska after the adjournment of Congress, stopped at Saratoga Springs, where he encountered Conkling sulking in seclusion. Hitchcock warned Hayes of the New Yorker's mood:

Senator Conkling . . . *seemed* to *feel* exactly like the brother of the *prodigal Son*, viz, *that all glory* was now being given to the *few* who had *"erred* and strayed" while those *who* had *never* faltered & who constituted the *great* body of the party get nothing but rebuffs. He is very bitter about the course of The *Times*, in this respect, says The Times sets up to be your *special* organ and that it is doing nothing but abuse the regular life long hard working Republicans. That there is a few *hundred* "liberals ["] and 450000 *regulars*, and the proposition is to hand every [thing] over to the *disorganizers*.³⁶

Conkling was angry because his defeat for the presidency at Cincinnati was followed in his own state by another attack: reformers challenged his prerogative of naming the Republican state ticket. Conkling's choice for governor was Alonzo B. Cor-

31. [W. E.] C[handler] to Hayes, October 13, 1876, in Hayes Papers.
32. W. E. Chandler to Hayes, October 12, 1876, *ibid.*
33. Typescript copy, Hayes to R. C. McCormick, October 14, 1876, *ibid.*
34. W. A. Wheeler to Hayes, October 16, 1876, *ibid.*
35. R. C. McCormick to Hayes, October 16, 1876, *ibid.*
36. P. W. Hitchcock to Hayes, August 20, 1876, *ibid.*

nell, the naval officer in the New York customhouse. In opposition to Cornell, the New York *Tribune* supported William M. Evarts, who as attorney general had been counsel for the defense in the impeachment trial of Andrew Johnson. The *Times* proposed E. D. Morgan. William A. Wheeler, stressing that the party needed "a nominee who can draw upon the Dem. vote in the City of New York," privately judged either Morgan or Evarts to be better than Cornell.[37] Thus the battle lines were drawn. For a time it appeared the New York party would wreck itself on this issue. Certainly Conkling would not stand another public disappointment. Tom Platt, undoubtedly speaking for his chief, told Hayes that either "Mr. Cornell will be nominated, or some one whom his friends shall indicate. Any other result will be disastrous no matter what the rose-water politicians may say to the contrary. The men who control the organization & do the work must be satisfied if we are to win, in our State." [38]

On the eve of the state convention Conkling's lieutenants caucused all night. They found that the nominations the next day could be controlled by the machine, but not in the interest of Cornell. Too many city delegates were afraid that alienation of the reform element would be tantamount to defeat at the polls. Cornell would have to be dropped and someone else taken up in his place.[39] Evarts, also, was prepared to compromise, recognizing that "a nomination over the heads of Conkling & Co., instead of at their request would only widen breaches instead of healing them." [40] Evarts allowed his name to be used in the convention principally to keep pressure on the stalwarts.[41] On August 23 the party regulars flocked to Morgan and nominated him easily on the first ballot. With the liberals concentrating on Evarts, Morgan was acceptable to Conkling because his

37. Wheeler to Hayes, July 25, 1876, *ibid.*
38. T. C. Platt to Hayes, August 7, 1876, *ibid.*
39. New York *World*, August 24, 1876.
40. Whitelaw Reid to E. A. Merritt, August 21, 1876, quoted in Royal Cortissoz, *The Life of Whitelaw Reid* (2 vols.; New York: Charles Scribner's Sons, 1921), I, 348–49.
41. Chester L. Barrows, *William M. Evarts: Lawyer, Diplomat, Statesman* (Chapel Hill: University of North Carolina Press, 1941), 297–98.

selection could be made to appear a victory over the "soreheads." The elderly Morgan was also less likely to challenge Conkling's seat in the Senate two years hence.[42] To emphasize the lesson to be drawn from the convention, that the machine was still in control of things, Conkling's adherents forced Cornell's reappointment as chairman of the state committee. Cornell would thus conduct the gubernatorial campaign of the man who thwarted his own nomination.[43]

The outcome of this discomforting contest appeared, on the surface at least, to be acceptable to all. The leader of the reformers, George William Curtis, boasted to Hayes: "If you read between the lines you cannot have mistaken the meaning of the action of the New York Convention. It was an insurrection against the machine expressed in the way natural to a strict party convention, but none the less significant. Mr. Morgan's name had been universally associated with that of Mr. Evarts as the representative of reform, and his candidacy is accepted in the same spirit." [44] A short while later, Tom Platt gave the stalwarts' view:

The nomination of Gov. Morgan was probably the best that could have been made, under the circumstances. Altho' not the first choice of Mr Conkling's friends ... they cheerfully acquiesced in it and are giving him a general & hearty support. The Governor, while really as much a "machine" man as Mr Cornell, having done as much in times past to build, oil & run the machine as any politician in the State and enjoyed its benefits, had not at this present time been advertised by the metropolitan press as a machinist and thus rendered so obnoxious. No man perhaps was so well calculated to combine all the elements of the Party.[45]

It is difficult to escape the conclusion that the battle between the reformers and the regulars was, after all, only a struggle for power.

Morgan entered hopefully into his campaign for the governor-

---

42. W. K. Rogers to Hayes, August 19, 1876, in Hayes Papers.
43. New York *World*, August 24, 1876.
44. Curtis to Hayes, August 31, 1876, in Hayes Papers.
45. Platt to Hayes, September 23, 1876, *ibid.*

ship and preserved his cheerful spirit for a long while. He remarked in September: "The canvass in this State has not looked better at any time since I have been active in political affairs than it does now at the corresponding seasons of the year. Govr Tildens efforts for his own success are marvellous, and nothing will be left undone that he deems important to be done, or that will in any way aid the Election. On the other hand *our* friends all over the State are active, and promise good results in all parts of it." [46] The day before the October elections he still supposed "the indications are as good in the State of N York, as I have ever known them." [47]

Following the loss in Indiana, Zachariah Chandler was roused to a new pitch of activity, but he was determined to leave the New York contest entirely in the hands of the state committee.[48] Stories had begun to circulate of grave inadequacies in the conduct of the New York campaign. Conkling spoke in public only once—in his home town of Utica—and Cornell was reported to be "sour & disappointed & to say the least lukewarm [.] " A correspondent of William Henry Smith complained of "a strange lack of judgment in the selection of speakers in many instances. Take this case. In a community not far from here [New York City] quite a number of Irish Catholics had about made up their minds to support Hayes. [T]he Ex Com sent a speaker who without inquiry as to state of feeling there, spoke two hours making his chief point against the Catholics & losing votes for the Rep's." [49] Working one of the strongest Republican counties in the central part of the state, John Cochrane was pleased with the size and enthusiasm of the meetings he addressed. But he found "here, as elsewhere that 'the weightier matters of the law' are neglected. The details of committee work are not attended to thoroughly." His explanation was significant: "I find

46. E. D. Morgan to Hayes, September 23, 1876, *ibid.*
47. Letterpress copy, Morgan to Andrew D. White, October 9, 1876, in Morgan Papers.
48. Edward F. Noyes to Hayes, October 19, 1876, in Hayes Papers.
49. C. A. Boynton to [Wm. Henry] Smith, October 22, 1876, in William Henry Smith Papers, Ohio Historical Society Library.

that most of our people are *cowed* by the conviction that Tilden's canvass is perfect. They seem to be torpid under the impression that 'it is of no use', that they cannot prevail against the perfect system of Tilden." There was something even more disturbing than inactivity on the part of local leaders. Cochrane discovered "everywhere an impression that the State Com[mitt]ee is not doing its duty. The County Come of this County has heard nothing from them, they say, and dont know that they have any knowledge of the County."[50] When one reform Republican called at party headquarters to scold officials there about deficiencies in the campaign, he was denied access to Cornell, and the national committee "declined to interfere as 'it was not their business.' "[51]

Morgan became alert to the situation only during the last ten days of October. Checking quickly into the grumbling about Cornell's performance, he decided that the chairman was not at fault: "I believe that most of the state committee have been hard working, pains taking, and faithful men." Morgan observed that a hundred speakers were stumping the state at a total cost of at least $25,000 and that "documents have been sent in far greater numbers than before." He added, "Money will be in proper hands in each election dist to get voters to the Polls who might not otherwise come, and also at the expense of the state committee." The canvass of the electorate had not always been carried out properly, but Morgan placed the blame on "the want of proper party interest felt in the election, in some places in the State."[52] The Republican candidate chose not to take any chances, however. When the state committee failed to tend to an important detail, Morgan brought it to Cornell's attention none too gently: "There is a great demand for one good forceful speaker in each of the strongest Republican Counties in the State such as Chataqua [*sic*], Cattaraugus, St. Lawrence, Cayuga, and some local speakers are not enough. . . . Govr.

50. John Cochrane to Morgan, October 13, 1876, in Morgan Papers.
51. John Binney to Morgan, October 24, 1876, *ibid.*
52. Letterpress copy, Morgan to B. F. Hall, October 22, 1876, *ibid.*

Hayes wrote me that they found in Ohio their greatest gains and old time majorities in the best known Republican counties. A word to the wise is sufficient." [53] Morgan also sent special agents "into every County in the state to look especially after the canvassing and doubtful voters, to get out all the vote." [54] And he corresponded vigorously with county chairmen, urging that nothing "be left undone that can be done to ensure every vote for Hayes & Wheeler." [55] Fund raising, too, was the candidate's own responsibility, for the more respectable Republicans in New York disdained machine politicians like Cornell. Morgan, who had made a fortune as a highly resourceful merchant, prospered in this endeavor as well, collecting $47,750 in contributions of a thousand dollars or more.[56]

The New York Republicans were not alone in having serious divisions within their midst. Two shifting alliances had been brawling with each other for control of the Democratic party in New York City ever since the overthrow of "Boss" Tweed. Perceiving enormous potential benefits from Democratic control of the federal government, these factions were willing to put aside their dispute for the duration of the presidential campaign if they could do so on acceptable terms. On August 18, therefore, a joint committee of twelve men, composed in equal parts of representatives of Tammany Hall and the coalition of anti-Tammany forces, was created to apportion between the two groups the city's delegates at the forthcoming state convention.[57] This conference committee held daily meetings but at first made little progress.[58] Finally, the night before the Democratic convention opened in Saratoga Springs, a temporary truce was arranged. John Kelly had previously offered the anti-

53. Letterpress copy, Morgan to A. B. Cornell, October 23, 1876, *ibid.* See also letterpress copy, Morgan to Cornell, October 11, 1876, *ibid.*
54. Letterpress copy, Morgan to E. H. Roberts, October 25, 1876, *ibid.*
55. Letterpress copy, Morgan to J. B. Murray, October 25, 1876, and letterpress copy, Morgan to H. Richardson. October 24, 1876, both *ibid.*
56. James A. Rawley, *Edwin D. Morgan, 1811–1883: Merchant in Politics* (New York: Columbia University Press, 1955), 256–57.
57. New York *World*, August 19, 1876.
58. *Ibid.*, August 22, 1876.

Tammany faction the right to select one third of the city's delegates. John Morrissey had demanded that the opposition receive one half. Settlement was reached by granting the anti-Tammany men slightly less than two fifths of the delegates, and by supplementing this concession with three places out of seven on the state committee and two presidential electors as well.[59] For a brief moment it appeared that the New York Democratic party had afforded itself an unwontedly peaceful September. That the condition did not last was owing chiefly to the party's presidential candidate and his most ardent supporters.

To enhance his credibility as the nation's leading exponent of reform, Tilden wanted a gubernatorial ticket of unimpeachable credentials in his own state. The obvious choice to head that ticket was Horatio Seymour, Civil War governor and himself an ex-presidential candidate. Seymour, however, was in failing health and responded to numerous inquiries by stating that he would not run.[60] Manton Marble, until May, 1876, the editor of the New York *World*, would have liked the nomination and had the support of the New York *Herald*; but Samuel Barlow reminded him that he could not "escape harsh criticism . . . for Copperheadism during the war."[61] Barlow thought Hewitt would make an excellent governor, but cautioned Tilden that his selection would be "like your running, his name adds little to your own strength." Barlow suggested that Congressman Clarkson N. Potter would be the nominee who could reinforce the national ticket the most, precisely because he was popular with the New York Democrats least friendly toward Tilden.[62] Potter's liability, in Tilden's view, was that he could not be

59. *Ibid.*, August 30, 1876.
60. Stewart Mitchell, *Horatio Seymour of New York* (Cambridge: Harvard University Press, 1938), 521–22.
61. New York *Herald*, July 26, 1876, quoted in New York *World*, July 27, 1876; M[anton] M[arble] to Barlow, August 8, 1876, and letterpress copy, Barlow to Marble, August 10, 1876, both in Samuel Latham Mitchell Barlow Papers, Henry E. Huntington Library, San Marino, California.
62. Letterpress copy, Barlow to Tilden, August 28, 1876, in Barlow Papers. See also letterpress copy, Barlow to Marble, August 23, 1876, and letterpress copy, Barlow to Tilden, August 24, 1876, both *ibid.*

dramatically portrayed as the embodiment of reform. So Tilden decided that William Dorsheimer, the hero of the currency debate at St. Louis and the incumbent lieutenant governor, would be the best choice.

It was at this point that he made a serious misjudgment. Tilden could not properly attend the convention and did not want to appear as though he were dictating the choice of his successor. As a result, he indicated publicly that he had no preference, at the same time telling his advisers privately to work for Dorsheimer's nomination.[63] The convention had been in session only a few hours on August 30 when Tilden's friends realized that Dorsheimer would probably be defeated by Congressman Potter. Since this might look like a rebuke to the party's presidential candidate, they stampeded the convention into nominating Seymour by acclamation. Two respected delegates, S. T. Fairchild and J. Thomas Spriggs, hurried from Saratoga to Utica as a committee to urge Seymour to accept the honor. He should stand for election and help make Tilden president, they were supposed to explain, and then he could resign the governorship in favor of his running mate. But before they reached their destination, the former governor telegraphed his declination. Fairchild and Spriggs talked to Seymour at length on August 31 and sent word back to make up the rest of the state ticket. Since it appeared that Seymour had agreed to cooperate, the convention performed the rest of its duties, renominating Dorsheimer for lieutenant governor and eventually adjourning. Seymour, however, had not changed his mind. Fairchild and Spriggs had either overestimated their powers of persuasion or mistakenly believed they could accomplish their purpose by presenting the stubborn Seymour with a *fait accompli*.

After two weeks of demoralizing confusion, the convention had to be reassembled. With Dorsheimer already on the ticket, the Tildenites turned to their third choice for governor, Lucius

63. W. W. McFarland to Marble, September 7, 1876, in Manton Malone Marble Papers, Manuscript Division, Library of Congress; letterpress copy, Barlow to M. M[arble], September 4, 1876, in Barlow Papers.

Robinson, the stodgy and colorless state controller. He was triumphant over Potter on the first ballot—with one and a half votes to spare.[64] An embarrassing episode, which should never have been permitted to occur, was thereby brought to an end. Even Manton Marble, who practically worshipped Tilden, agreed that his idol's course at Saratoga had been as foolish as John Kelly's: "As to [the] Governorship it was Tilden's to indicate at either convention; Kelly's to indicate at the second convention provided he had limited himself to the friends of Tilden. At the first convention, Tilden indicated Dorsheimer who was the only man in the party except John Bigelow whom he couldn't nominate. At the second convention Kelly tried Potter, who was always impossible as any other opponent of Tilden was, when put forward by Kelly." [65]

The Democratic canvass in New York was conducted in the meticulous manner that Tilden had pioneered during his eight years as state chairman. Every available speaker was employed, campaign literature was distributed in enormous quantities, and the political leaning of each voter in the state was ascertained. A Republican living in the central part of the state told Morgan in bewilderment: "From all the back towns, in this and adjoining counties, the information comes that they are flooded with lying democratic bills and pamphlets. They are received by voters directed to them individually by name. It is believed that the democratic bureaux, in your City and at Albany, have procured the names of all the voters in the State, and are sending these mischievously lying missives directed to their addresses through the mail." [66] The Democrats were alert to every group of voters they could hope to attract. Wheeler, from his home near the Canadian border north of the Adirondack mountains, noted that the "most persistent effort" was being made to convert the traditionally Republican French population "upon the plea that the Dem. party is the friend of their Church." [67] As on the na-

64. Mitchell, *Horatio Seymour of New York*, 522–26.
65. M. M[arble] to Barlow, October 3, 1876, in Barlow Papers.
66. F. E. Spinner to Morgan, October 22, 1876, in Morgan Papers.
67. Wheeler to Hayes, October 16, 1876, in Hayes Papers.

tional level, this large, industrious undertaking was very costly; but the party seems to have raised most of the funds that were needed. Fifteen members of the electoral ticket, for example, gave $7,200 together.[68] Seymour underwrote the campaign in his upstate county alone to the sum of $1,500.[69] Probably the most peculiar feature of the Democratic canvass was the attitude of Lucius Robinson. When Senator Kernan asked him to make a series of speeches along the state's southern tier of counties, he declined:

Before my nomination I stated repeatedly in opposition to making me the candidate that unless I resigned the comptrollership I could not take any active part in the canvass. I find it so now. I am invited & urged to speak in all directions. If I begin there will be no stopping place. Besides I can get no time to begin. The fiscal year closed on Saturday. An immense amount of payments must be made & accounts examined at once & materials gathered up for the annual report. . . . I am therefore obliged to remain here every hour. . . . I would gladly resign, but no man can now take my place until the annual report is completed, & to abandon it would look like fleeing from the post of public duty.[70]

Robinson did not care much for public speaking anyway. It hardly mattered. New York was the one place where Tilden and Hewitt could safely rely on their "perfect system." Morgan, hearing that Tilden was predicting a Democratic majority of thirty thousand in the Empire State, was understandably uneasy.[71]

Belatedly recognizing that they were in trouble, the Republicans bestirred themselves for a last desperate drive for victory, all their bickering elements laboring, if not together, at least toward the same end. From Cincinnati, Murat Halstead volunteered to make a speech in New York on the "Southern Claims," in which he would charge that, given the chance, the Democrats

68. S. T. Fairchild to D. S. Lamont, November 25, 1876, in Daniel Scott Lamont Papers, Manuscript Division, Library of Congress.
69. Mitchell, *Horatio Seymour of New York*, 555–56.
70. L. Robinson to Kernan, October 3, 1876, in Francis Kernan Correspondence, John M. Olin Research Library, Cornell University.
71. Morgan to Hayes, October 21, 1876, in Hayes Papers.

would pass legislation to have the national government pay southerners untold millions of dollars in compensation for wartime damages. Hayes liked the idea and referred Halstead to Morgan. The Cincinnati editor was soon invited east to deliver his blast at a Cooper Union meeting on October 25.[72] Morgan, meanwhile, prepared a circular letter on the subject.[73] Then the reformers in the party had their turn. They staged a massive rally at Cooper Union on November 1 and another, attended by twelve thousand people, on Wall Street three days later. At the former, William M. Evarts dealt with the "Southern Claims." [74] About the same time, the National Reform League took it upon itself to do some of the house-to-house canvassing the regular committees were said to have omitted.[75]

Simultaneously, the regulars were preparing to play what they earnestly believed would be their trump cards: John I. Davenport and the federal elections law. Davenport was a fanatic. During the Civil War he had been in charge of military intelligence for the Army of the James: "It was part of my business to obtain a complete roster of Lee's army, with the regiments, regimental commanders, brigades, divisions, and corps. I was expected to know where these regiments and brigades were throughout the day and night, and was brought in constant communication with the General commanding." With the coming of peace, Davenport had difficulty finding a civilian position that suited his acquired taste for intrigue. He returned to New York, was admitted to the bar at the age of twenty-

72. M. Halstead to Hayes, October 14, 1876, *ibid.*; Hayes to Halstead, October 14, 1876, in Murat Halstead Collection; Historical and Philosophical Society of Ohio, Cincinnati; Hayes to Morgan, October 16, 1876, in Morgan Papers; Halstead to Wykoff [*sic*], October 19, 1876, in Hayes Papers.

73. Lithographed circular, Morgan to [the voters of New York State], October 14, 1876, in Murat Halstead Collection, Historical and Philosophical—

74. A. G. Browne, Jr., to Comly, November 2, 1876, in Comly Papers; Francis A. Stout and Ellwood E. Thorne to Hayes, December 4, 1876, in Hayes Papers; Barrows, *William M. Evarts*, 298–99.

75. Printed circular, Henry Randall Waite and A. N. Cole to [members of New York Auxiliary, National Reform League], November, 1876, in Hayes Papers.

one, journeyed west with Carl Schurz to help found the Detroit *Post*, then wandered back to New York for a brief stint with Horace Greeley's *Tribune*. Finally he resigned himself to the mundane life of a practicing attorney. Davenport was fortunate that the nature of his military service and the intensity of his Republicanism had meantime become known to the right people. When the Union League Club needed an experienced lawyer to investigate the mass naturalizations which preceded the election of 1868, he was selected. Davenport was then twenty-four and about to begin a remarkable career. Following the adoption in Congress of a series of amendments to the naturalization laws in 1870, a federal judge appointed him United States commissioner to enforce those statutes in the second judicial circuit. Upon enactment of the comprehensive elections law a year later, he also became chief supervisor for the city of New York, a post he held for twenty-three years.[76]

Davenport set to work at once devising his own "perfect system" for eliminating fraudulent voting. He began by compiling a set of large-scale maps designed to indicate every structure in the city: "These maps are corrected for me regularly (under contract) every thirty days, so that if you put a wing on your house I know it within a month. The number of a house is given, the number of stories, the number of rooms; and if it is used for other than a dwelling house the fact is mentioned, as in the case of a stoneyard or a manufactory, or something of that kind." Davenport, who compared the information listed in the city's register of voters against his own data concerning buildings, explained his procedure: "If I find ten men registered today from a house where there were only two registered last year, I go right to the map and see whether a six story tenement has been put up in place of a two story house." Davenport's next step was the preparation of four thousand registration books, one for each block in the city. In these he gave the name of every

76. Albie Burke, "Federal Regulation of Congressional Elections in Northern Cities, 1871–1894" (Ph.D. dissertation, University of Chicago, 1968), 71, 180.

voter, a description of his appearance, his exact address, his election district, and, if foreign born, the details of his naturalization. The information in the block books was then gathered together into a single alphabetical index, which in 1876 filled forty-two large volumes. During the week-long fall registration period, in years when congressional elections were held, two federal supervisors armed with notebooks were present in each election district. These supervisors were "required . . . to make lists of persons registering, and in so doing obtain from the applicants the names and other particulars of registration, and enter the same in the book. Merely copying the entries from the [city] Inspector's books will not be sufficient." Each night the notebooks were brought to Davenport's home and checked against the maps, block books, and index: "Between 1 and 2 o'clock on the night of each day of registration I am in possession of the entire registry of that day." Discrepancies were verified through the mail. When notices came back marked "addressee unknown," Davenport assumed the voters involved were fraudulently registered. He placed public notices in Republican newspapers warning them by name not to come to the polls and swore out warrants for their arrest if they should try to cast ballots. Since federal supervisors were superior in authority to city inspectors, elections in New York were actually conducted under Davenport's registration. The city register was allowed to stand only in off-year contests.

Davenport's system was as expensive to operate as Tilden's. The difference was that most of the money came from the federal government. In 1876 the Grant administration spent $31,780 on the salaries of 1,144 supervisors in New York City and $48,535 for a force of 2,300 deputy marshals to assist and protect them. Davenport had to pay the many clerks required to work on his books and maps out of his own pocket. He drew three separate government salaries in 1876—$19,383 as chief supervisor, $3,000 plus various fees as United States commissioner, and $3,500 as clerk of the Second United States Circuit Court; and still he could not meet his expenses. He told a congressional committee after the election that he was then $25,000 in debt. Indeed there had not been a time since 1870 when he was not embarrassed to the extent of at least $10,000; yet he appeared not to mind. He converted his entire house into a registration headquarters, while his family was forced to seek refuge at a nearby hotel. When the federal elections law was repealed in 1894, the purpose went out of Davenport's life. Before his death he was verging on insanity.[77]

In the centennial campaign, however, he was at the height of his fame. Zach Chandler thought his register was worth fifty thousand votes.[78] Morgan marveled at the eight hundred men Davenport employed "in various ways verifying the registry— sleeping in houses where doubtful voters register from &c., &c." [79] Davenport himself stated that "there will not be 100 fraudulent votes polled in the city." [80] Although registration throughout the states of New Jersey and New York was unexpectedly heavy, William E. Chandler remained calm. "The facilities for preventing frauds," he told Hayes, "are almost perfect and Davenport and the Brooklyn & Jersey City supervisors express their complete confidence in their ability to secure an honest vote or nearly so." [81] On the eve of the election, Cornell telegraphed Hayes: "With an experience of ten years in this Committee I have never seen a canvass of the State of New York close with such flattering promise of success & I have the most abiding confidence that our electoral vote will be cast for you [.] " [82]

3

New York was the center of attraction between October 10 and November 7, but this political circus had more than one ring. In Massachusetts, a state he never expected to win, Tilden never-

77. *Ibid.*, 180–89, 202.
78. L. C. Wier to Hayes, July 7, 1876, in Hayes Papers.
79. Letterpress copy, Morgan to Roberts, October 25, 1876, in Morgan Papers.
80. Rogers to Hayes, November 2, 1876, in Hayes Papers.
81. W. E. Chandler to Hayes, October 30, 1876, *ibid.*
82. Telegram, Cornell to Hayes, November 6, 1876, *ibid.*

theless saw an opportunity to promote the reform reputation of his party in a way that would be helpful elsewhere. On August 7, Edward Avery, chairman of the state committee, approached Charles Francis Adams, the Liberal Republicans' original choice for the presidency, and asked him whether he would accept a Democratic nomination for governor. Adams said he would, but only if the vote of the state convention was "unequivocally" in his favor, a condition he did not believe could be met. Avery replied that it surely would be. Frederick O. Prince, secretary of the national committee, then joined Avery and other Massachusetts leaders in speaking to William Gaston, who as part of the "Tidal Wave" had achieved an astonishing upset in the gubernatorial race of 1874, only to be defeated for reelection the next year. Gaston agreed to relinquish his claims to the nomination in favor of Adams. In Boston, however, Irish leaders were unhappy with these developments. Adams had incurred their wrath in 1866, while serving as minister to Great Britain, when he had officially conveyed the apology of the United States for the Fenian raids against Canada. Gaston, consequently, changed his mind and allowed his name to be used in preconvention maneuvering. Yet he lacked the support outside of Boston necessary to win and in the end was forced, even before the balloting began, to move the nomination of Adams by acclamation. Adams was sure he saw the hand of the Democratic party's presidential candidate at work in securing Gaston's withdrawal: "I conjecture that Mr Tilden had sent an intimation through the Committee that it would be for his ultimate benefit, in case of the party success, to make the present sacrifice." [83] Whether his analysis was right or wrong, Adams' terms for taking the honor had been met. For the next two months he quietly remained at his summer home in Quincy, working on his father's memoirs

83. Charles Francis Adams Diary, August 7, September 2, 6, 1876, in The Adams Papers, Massachusetts Historical Society; F. O. Prince to Tilden, August 28, 1876, and Charles Francis Adams [Jr.] to Bigelow, January 10, 1906, both in John Bigelow (ed.), *Letters and Literary Memorials of Samuel J. Tilden* (2 vols.; New York: Harper and Brothers, 1908), II, 451–53.

and occasionally receiving visitors. His sole contribution to the Democratic campaign, beyond lending it respectability, consisted of writing two letters advocating the election of Tilden, intended for publication in New York and Ohio.[84] Ten days before the election, rumors, possibly inspired by the Democratic headquarters in New York, began to circulate that Adams was Tilden's choice for secretary of state. The austere Bostonian was inundated with letters on the subject, yet displayed no outward reaction.[85]

The best indication of the enthusiasm and determination exhibited by Democratic state leaders is to be found in Wisconsin. The Democrats were defeated in that state in every election from the founding of the Republican party until the onset of the postwar depression. Then, in the wake of the Panic of 1873, William R. Taylor became the first Democratic governor in nearly a generation. Taylor lost his bid for a second term in 1875 by less than nine hundred votes, but Democrats carried all the other statewide offices. Almost immediately Wisconsin Chairman Wendell A. Anderson began laying plans for the presidential campaign. He wrote his county chairmen asking them to preserve their committees intact so that the 1876 effort could begin where the previous year's work left off. Anderson's goal was "to have an organization that will be very effective when the campaign opens," a condition normally achieved, if ever, only shortly before election day.[86] At the end of January, 1876, Anderson circulated a proposal he had drawn up for establishing local committees in each township that would be available for circulating documents in English, German, and Norwegian. To avoid resentment over centralization in the party, he suggested that care should be taken so that it would "appear that

84. Letterbook copy, C. F. Adams to Daniel Magone, September 25, 1876, letterbook copy, C. F. Adams to R. Brinkerhoff, September 27, 1876, and Charles Francis Adams Diary, September 30, October 2, 1876, all in Adams Papers.
85. Charles Francis Adams Diary, October 28, 1876, *ibid.*
86. Printed circular, Wendell A. Anderson to [chairmen of the Central County Organizations], December 9, 1875, in Wendell A. Anderson Papers, State Historical Society of Wisconsin.

this request is made by your county committee, with a view to effective work in the campaign, rather than by suggestion of [the] Central Committee." [87] Anderson knew what he was doing. When the state committee in Illinois tried to bypass the county organizations in the distribution of canvassing materials, it was greeted with a stern lecture.

> We fear that the independent action which you propose will result in no practicable good, nor effect any objects that you could not as easily accomplish through our agency while on the other hand, the Centralizing Action proposed by you, divesting local organizations of legitimate action, will we all assume in our case, result in harm, by creating confusion in our plans, and discord and want of harmony between our committees—where the County Committees are inefficient this Centralizing paternal action may be beneficial but with us it is not needed.[88]

The response to Anderson's attempt at early preparation was not very encouraging. He noted in March: "I was in hope to have received reports from all counties before this time. I know the difficulties presented in many counties, and am not disposed to be critical, still trusting the blanks [with the names of town committee members] will be filled and returned as early as practicable." Anderson then disclosed a plan to hand out sixteen-page pamphlets to each voter at the largely nonpartisan local elections on April 4, explaining that "we can secure a more thorough distribution at that time . . . than at any other time this year." [89] Such activities required money, and Anderson turned to all the party's potential donors with the advice that $10,000 expended judiciously in the spring would have an effect equal to $25,000 spent later.[90] Anderson repeatedly urged the appointment of resident executive committees at each county seat, since such

87. Printed circular, Anderson to [chairmen of the Central County Organizations], January 31, 1876, *ibid.*
88. R. M. Atkinson to B. F. Bergen, September 5, 1876, in Cyrus Hall McCormick Papers, State Historical Society of Wisconsin.
89. Printed circular, Anderson to [chairmen of the Central County Organizations], March 14, 1876, in Anderson Papers.
90. Printed circular, [Anderson to "prominent members of our party throughout the state"], March 16, 1876, *ibid.*

bodies could be assembled more quickly than the full committees and handled the work of a campaign more efficiently.[91] He also wanted local candidates to be chosen early so that the usual acrimonious struggles over nominations could be shortened.[92]

The frequency with which these suggestions had to be reiterated indicated once more the difficulty of effecting changes in party organization even when the initiative came from within a state and was tempered by a willingness to settle for much less than a "perfect system." The Democratic campaign was well conducted in Wisconsin but was not free from problems. So erratic were the county committees in notifying the national committee in New York of their requirements for canvass books that the entire state's supply only reached Madison on October 17. They were distributed by state officials.[93] After the election a member of the state committee complained, "If the Central Committee of the Nation had opened their eyes to the necessity of carrying Wisconsin in July, and had given us the talent, time & money wasted on Illinois & Michigan, we would have carried the State." [94] Colonel Pelton's traveling trouble shooter, H. H. Finley, thought otherwise. Even before the election he believed that a poorly conducted campaign in populous Milwaukee County would cost the party its normal majority there and that the outcome in the county would spell the difference between an upset victory and defeat.[95]

Although accomplishing only mixed results, Democrats everywhere seem to have placed great emphasis on their local canvassing. The chairman of the party in Michigan even wanted to compare plans of organization with Anderson; his own, he said, was being pushed "with great success," but there was

91. Printed circulars, Anderson to [chairmen of the Central County Organizations], April 27, June 21, 1876, *ibid.*

92. Printed circular, Anderson to [chairmen of the Central County Organizations], August 8, 1776 [*sic*], *ibid.*

93. Printed circular, Anderson to [chairmen of the Central County Organizations], October 18, 1876, *ibid.*

94. Andrew Proudfit to Anderson, November 14. 1876, *ibid.*

95. H. H. Finley to Cyrus H. McCormick, November 6, 10, 1876, in McCormick Papers.

always something new to be learned.[96] And the county chairman who scolded the Illinois state committee for undermining his own authority explained the machinery that had already been established in his locale:

> Our Central Committee is in clear & immediate communication with the township committees so that matter for distribution can be placed in their hands within 24 hours after its receipt by us. The township committees have appointed sub-committees of three active working men in the several school districts of their respective townships and, matters sent by us to the town coms will be in the hands of the sub district men within a few hours after its receipt by the town coms, thus ensuring its immediate and certain distribution to the individual voters.

The subcommittees in the townships, he continued, would also be responsible for ascertaining the political preferences of each voter and for seeing to it that every Democrat appeared at the polls on election day.[97] Here was exactly what Hewitt had in mind all along.

The Republicans, by contrast, gave substantially less attention to these matters. William Henry Smith was chagrined to find that Illinois was in no better shape than New York in this respect. Appealing to Senator John A. Logan to "cancel his speaking engagements & devote the remainder of his time to the work of organization & preparation for the polls," he was told that Logan's appointments had already been announced and could not be withdrawn.[98] Smith then began pressuring the state committee to reorder its priorities. A week before the election a committee member was sent to New York to "learn the details" of Davenport's system,[99] but this last-ditch endeavor would be of little help. Davenport's techniques, like Tilden's, had taken years to develop.

96. Don M. Dickinson to Anderson, August 7, 1876, in Anderson Papers.
97. Atkinson to Bergen, September 5, 1876, in McCormick Papers.
98. Wm. Henry Smith to Hayes, October 22 [1876], in Hayes Papers; Mrs. John A. Logan to Wm. Henry Smith, October 23, 1876, in Smith Papers.
99. Wm. Henry Smith to Hayes, October 30, 1876, in Hayes Papers.

The Republicans were concerned about Illinois because there, also, they were faced with an unexpected challenge. Their gubernatorial candidate, Shelby M. Cullom, had been linked to one of the scandals arising out of the exposure of the Whiskey Ring. Cullom, unlike Orth in Indiana, repeatedly denied any involvement, but of course the Democrats made the accusation a central issue in their campaign.[100] The Democrats also adopted a strategy on the money question that proved to be very effective in Illinois. After ratifying the essentially hard-money platform approved at the St. Louis convention, they endorsed Lewis Steward, the Independent Greenback candidate for governor. Hard-money Democrats were dissatisfied, yet Steward was able to mollify most of them simply by refusing to discuss his controversial views in a gubernatorial contest. The acting chairman of the Illinois Democratic party defended the legitimacy of Steward's course: "He is the nominee of two Conventions and cannot very well do so without giving offense to the one side or the other. (The Gov. of a state has nothing to do with the financial question). He is in his principles a Democrat with all that that implies." [101]

4

In contrast to the intense interest shown in a dozen or more northern states, there was one region concerning which both national committees would have preferred to feign total ignorance—the eleven states of the late Confederacy. There campaigns for office possessed an urgent desperation unknown to the rest of the land. A native Georgia Republican who had served

100. James W. Neilson, *Shelby M. Cullom: Prairie State Republican* (Urbana: University of Illinois Press, 1962), 39–40; William C. Searles, "Governor Cullom and the Pekin Whiskey Ring Scandal," *Journal of the Illinois State Historical Society,* LI (Spring, 1958), 28–41; fragment, [Horace White] to Schurz, August 4, 1876, in Hayes Papers.
101. Ernest Ludlow Bogart and Charles Manfred Thompson, *The Industrial State, 1870–1893,* The Centennial History of Illinois, IV (Springfield: Illinois Centennial Commission, 1920), 109–13; G. Koerner to J. F. Snyder, August 5, 1876, and Daniel Cameron to Snyder, September 6, 1876, both in John Francis Snyder Papers, Illinois State Historical Library.

briefly as attorney general in Grant's first administration explained: "In the Southern States, few men, if any, have taken their side in present politics from any opinions concerning currency, taxation, expenditure, civil service, foreign policy or Indian policy. Such matters are altogether secondary here. Men are Republican or Democrat according as they are or are not attached to the last three amendments of the Constitution." [102] Political alignments, in short, took shape principally along racial lines.

For more than a dozen years Republicans had been searching for a way to relieve the increasing antagonism based on color, at least to the extent of attracting a substantial body of white adherents without having to soften their own commitment to the achievements of the Civil War. Throughout they were tragically unsuccessful either in bolstering the position of the former slaves or in overcoming the suspicions of most southern whites. Unable to mitigate the racial fears and hatreds which had grown up over two and a half centuries, and unwilling to countenance the massive land reform that George W. Julian and Wendell Phillips assured them would give blacks a secure place in southern society, the Republican party fell back on a negative program of protecting the political and civil rights of the freedmen. Southern Republicans gained thereby the allegiance of a huge, poverty-stricken, and largely uneducated black electorate; but at the same time they became dependent on the federal government for protection against the violent excesses of implacably hostile whites. Despite the occasional hopeful signs, southern race relations, rather than improving, deteriorated still further.

Where whites outnumbered blacks—Virginia, Tennessee, Arkansas, Texas, Georgia, Alabama—Republican governments lasted only a short time and then were swept away, seemingly forever. In states where black voters were numerically equal or even in the majority, the process took a little longer; but the

102. Letterpress copy, Amos T. Akerman to George W. Friedley, August 22, 1876, in Amos T. Akerman Letterbooks, University of Virginia Library.

reversion to white dominance inevitably occurred and in a manner which starkly revealed the grievous failure of Reconstruction. For a time the enactment of federal laws to control the terrorist activities of the Ku Klux Klan and similar groups and the deployment of regular army units in areas where disturbances were reported buttressed the southern Republicans and reinforced the restraining influence of the more respectable and conservative Democrats. Then the economy faltered, and in 1874 the Republicans lost their majority in the national House of Representatives. Correctly interpreting these developments as indications that the attention of the northern public had been distracted from the frustrating problems of Reconstruction, determined whites set out to "redeem" the last five southern states from the hands of the Republicans.

In Mississippi their actions would become known as the "Revolution of 1875." Whatever was required for success was justified. In the name of ridding the state government of irresponsible black and carpetbag officeholders, the least responsible elements in white society were given *carte blanche*. A small town journal proclaimed from its masthead: "A white man in a white man's place. A black man in a black man's place. Each according to the 'eternal fitness of things.' " Another was yet more frank in an editorial: "*Mississippi is a white man's country, and by the Eternal God we'll rule it.*" Democratic newspapers published the names of white Republicans who were to be socially ostracized. Black farm workers were told not to vote Republican if they expected to find employment on local plantations. Republican meetings were forcibly broken up, Republican leaders were threatened with violence, and in a series of "riots" in Republican counties several score of black men were shot to death while scarcely a white was injured. When a more scrupulous Democrat such as L. Q. C. Lamar sought an end to this reign of terror, his objections were trampled under foot along with the rights of black Mississippians. Governor Adelbert Ames appealed despondently to the Grant administration for help, only to be met by the attorney general's reply, "The whole public are tired of these annual autumnal outbreaks in the South." The state of Ohio was just then in the midst of a crucial gubernatorial contest. If troops were sent to Mississippi once more, William Allen might defeat Rutherford B. Hayes. No troops were sent. As a result, predominantly black Mississippi went Democratic by thirty thousand votes. Overwhelmingly black counties cast fewer than a dozen Republican ballots.[103] It was the most degrading election in the history of the American republic.

The reestablishment of white supremacy in Mississippi was like a specter hanging over the presidential and gubernatorial contests of 1876 in North and South Carolina, Florida, and Louisiana. The national leaders of both major parties were deeply concerned about the prospects for a fair election in those states. If there were new outbreaks of violence, the Republicans would find themselves faced with the delicate task of sailing between Scylla and Charybdis. On the one hand was their need for southern electoral votes, whereas on the other was a vocal northern opposition to the continued use of soldiers to guard the polls. The Democrats, for their part, were afraid that even if they won legitimately, Grant might use the army to perpetuate Republican rule.

Events in Louisiana during the preceding four years had already demonstrated how potent presidential intervention could be. The Republican party in that state was shattered in 1872 by a savage struggle for power between the incumbent governor, Henry Clay Warmoth, an adventurer from Illinois, and United States Marshal Stephen B. Packard, head of the so-called "customhouse" wing. When Packard's friends obtained the upper hand in the party, Warmoth joined the Democrats in the formation of a fusion ticket. In an arrangement which superficially resembled that in national politics, Packard's regulars supported Grant for president and William Pitt Kellogg for governor, while the Warmoth dissidents and the Democrats

103. Vernon Lane Wharton, *The Negro in Mississippi, 1865–1890* (Chapel Hill: University of North Carolina Press, 1947), 181–98; James Wilford Garner, *Reconstruction in Mississippi* (New York: Macmillan Company, 1901), 375–401.

campaigned for Horace Greeley and John McEnery. The fusion candidates seemed to have an excellent chance for victory, since Warmoth as governor had had many black followers and would undoubtedly carry some of them across party lines; indeed, the fusion nominee for secretary of state, Samuel Armstead, was himself black. The election, observers agreed, was uncommonly peaceful for reconstruction Louisiana, but it was marred by a number of fraudulent acts on both sides which vitiated the results. On the face of the parish returns, the Greeley-McEnery ticket was triumphant with nearly ten thousand votes to spare. Seizing on some dubious legal technicalities, the Republicans refused to recognize the returning board headed by Governor Warmoth, created a contesting board of their own, altered or rejected the returns from several parishes, and declared Grant and Kellogg to be the winners. A long and dangerous deadlock ensued. The two houses of Congress concurred in refusing to count the state's electoral votes, but that decision was not hard to reach. On the day when the rival sets of electors met to cast their ballots, not a single parish return had yet been canvassed by either returning board. Congress failed to act, however, on the more difficult question of the competing state governments. Grant, therefore, recognized Kellogg as Louisiana's *de facto* governor. The Democrats, sincerely thinking McEnery had won, were, of course, incensed. In September, 1874, after a pitched battle on the streets of New Orleans in which fifty-six people died, Kellogg was forcibly overthrown and took refuge in the customhouse. Instantly, Grant ordered the military authorities in Louisiana to sustain the legal governor of the state. McEnery's supporters offered no resistance, and within five days Kellogg was back in his office. It was in the wake of these extraordinary events that Congressman William A. Wheeler arranged his famous compromise: the Democrats agreed not to depose Kellogg, and in return the Republicans permitted Wheeler's congressional committee to arbitrate the nineteen disputed seats in the lower house of the state legislature, most of which went ultimately to Democrats. All the while it was apparent that

Kellogg, deprived of federal backing, could not retain the governorship for a week.[104]

When the campaign of 1876 opened, the same explosive prospect remained. Louisiana Republicans nominated Marshal Packard for the governorship, with Warmoth, who had returned to the fold, settling for a seat in Congress. The Democrats united behind Francis T. Nicholls, a successful lawyer of socially prominent family background. That Nicholls was popular with white Louisianans went without saying—in Confederate service he had lost his left arm at the battle of Winchester in 1862 and his left leg at Chancellorsville.[105] The Democrats, accordingly, concentrated on gaining black votes. There had been scattered outbreaks of racial violence in late 1875 and early 1876, and white Democrats organized a number of mounted rifle clubs during the spring and summer. Yet once the campaign began, the state was surprisingly free of disorders.[106] Democratic leaders understood all too well the eagerness with which the Republican returning board would seize on any available pretext to throw out a Democratic majority at the polls. The "Mississippi plan" would not work in Louisiana.

In deciding to appeal to their former bondsmen, the Democrats had received encouragement from some of the most powerful black politicians in the South. During the first years of Reconstruction the great mass of recently freed slaves had been lacking in political experience and had found it necessary to follow white Republican counsel rather blindly. By 1876, however, they had developed their own leaders, a few of whom regarded the bland Republican assumption that blacks would always vote the same way as a subtle, but nonetheless irritating, form of racism. Blanche K. Bruce of Mississippi, the only black member of the United States Senate, complained to that body in February that too many Republicans understood the "bloody shirt" better than they did the situation in the South. P. B. S.

104. Ella Lonn, *Reconstruction in Louisiana after 1868* (New York: G. P. Putnam's Sons, 1918), 138–379.
105. *Ibid.*, 406–12.
106. *Ibid.*, 412–14.

Pinchback of Louisiana told a National Negro Convention in April that blacks "would never again vote the Republican ticket in a solid column." C. S. Smith of Alabama, speaking to the same audience, openly advised his brothers to look to their southern white friends, especially those who before the Civil War had been members of the Whig party.[107]

Louisiana Democrats soon found they had a variety of grounds on which they could appeal to black voters. In some parishes there were black politicians, disgusted at the incessant fighting in the Republican party, disappointed over their own lack of recognition, or convinced the Democrats were going to win, who were willing to cooperate. Everywhere there were black men who, like many white Louisianans, thought that their taxes were too high or that the school term provided their children was too short. Agricultural wages had dropped from eighteen dollars a month to about ten dollars in the aftermath of the Panic of 1873, and all during that time the Republicans were in power; so some black farm workers decided to "vote for the Democrats and see what would happen." General Nicholls assured a group of anxious blacks in New Orleans that the Democratic party fully accepted the consequences of the Civil War, as their platform clearly had stated: "The laws should be general in their operation and any law directed against a class or race in the community would meet my most determined opposition. No such attempt, however, will be made, for independently of the constitutional barriers which would stand in the way, the Democratic and Conservative sentiment of the whole State is united against such action. To disregard and go back upon the pledges which I have given on this subject would be to disgrace me before the country." Occasional departures from the peaceful policy decreed by the Democratic leadership did occur, but they were minor and confined largely to East Feliciana Parish.[108]

107. Dee Brown, *The Year of the Century: 1876* (New York: Charles Scribner's Sons, 1966), 199–200.

108. T. B. Tunnell, Jr., "The Negro, the Republican Party, and the Election of 1876 in Louisiana," *Louisiana History*, VII (Spring, 1966), 101–16; Lonn, *Reconstruction in Louisiana after 1868*, 419–25.

While the Democrats made a coordinated effort to win the confidence of black Louisianans, their opponents waged a desultory campaign at best. Warmoth admitted to Hayes that there would not even be a local Republican ticket in some parishes, which would cost the party several thousand votes. Both he and Kellogg pleaded for the stationing of a cavalry regiment, composed of black troops, at strategic points in the predominantly black counties: "It would so encourage the people that they would not be killed for voting the Rep. ticket, they would turn out en-masse. Now they are depressed & very many have joined Democratic clubs."[109] In the acknowledged absence of proper exertion on their own part, the Republican chiefs would rely on the presence of the army.

They were also making provision to utilize once more the returning-board strategy which had saved them four years before. Their state committee carefully instructed parish chairmen on the procedures for filing sworn protests with the local returns, alleging Democratic interference with the right to register and vote:

In every case named in your statement, please give date, place and nature of the offense, by whom committed if known, if the perpetrators of any offense were *disguised* please state the fact, state name, residence, occupation and color of person upon or against whom the offense was committed, names and residences of witnesses, what effect the offense had upon the person or persons against whom it was committed or upon his or their neighborhood, and every circumstance within your knowledge which will serve to fix and exhibit the *political* animus of the offense.[110]

Should sufficient evidence of overt coercion be lacking, the Republicans were ready to fall back on a set of abstract statistics to prove that a Democratic victory in Louisiana was all but legally impossible and must be due, therefore, to more artful

---

109. Typescript copy, H. C. Warmoth to Hayes, October 18, 1876, and Wm. P. Kellogg to R. C. McCormick, October 16, 1876, both in Hayes Papers.
110. Lithographed circulars, D. J. M. A. Jewett to [Republican parish committee chairmen], October 15, 17, 1876, *ibid.*

forms of intimidation. The registration lists showed a substantial black voting majority and the Republicans would claim that blacks rarely voted Democratic voluntarily. The accuracy of those registration lists, however, was a subject of heated controversy. The federal decennial census in 1870 had shown the two races in the state to be almost equal in population, whereas a Republican state census in 1875 had revealed the existence of twenty thousand more adult blacks than whites. Democrats claimed the census of 1875 was designed solely to justify the registration figures of 1876. They may have been right. At any rate, the state census was supervised by the same man who was later placed in charge of gathering affidavits regarding Democratic "outrages." [111] Two days before the election, Kellogg cleared the way for throwing out the votes of disputed parishes by notifying Zach Chandler of the reports he had received concerning willful obstruction of the electoral process:

> Under the State law voters are entitled to vote at any poll in the parish in which they reside. The colored people generally are attempting to reach the parish seats of these parishes in order to vote under the protection of the authorities. Numbers of them have been intercepted by the White League pickets and their registration-papers destroyed. In some instances they have been terribly beaten. Some six hundred colored men who have managed to avoid these pickets and reach the town of Monroe, Ouchita [*sic*] Parish, have been ordered by the Democratic mayor to leave town immediately.
> In West Feliciana several colored men have come in in like manner to Bayou Sara, the parish seat. The White League of that parish, aided by armed bodies from the adjoining counties in Mississippi, have picketed the approaches to the town to prevent others coming in.[112]

The Republicans in Florida were beset with much the same kind of factionalism that had sapped the strength of the party in Louisiana. Their state convention renominated the incumbent governor, Marcellus L. Stearns, a product of Maine who had

111. Lonn, *Reconstruction in Louisiana after 1868*, 425–26.
112. Quoted in Harry Barnard, *Rutherford B. Hayes and His America* (Indianapolis: Bobbs-Merrill Company, Inc., 1954), 321–22.

arrived in Florida in 1866 as an official of the Freedmen's Bureau. Thereupon the friends of United States Senator Simon B. Conover, a bitter enemy of Stearns, walked out. From June to September Conover ran for the governorship as an independent. There were even separate Stearns and Conover electoral slates in the field, and although both were pledged to Hayes and Wheeler, the votes they received would be counted in opposition to each other, to the detriment of the party's national ticket. Not until the campaign was three months old did the national leadership succeed in convincing Conover that stern retribution would be exacted if he did not withdraw from the race and take his electoral candidates with him.[113] The Democratic nominee for governor was George F. Drew, a native of New Hampshire who had moved south twenty years before the Civil War and had made a fortune in the lumber business. As a former Whig, an opponent of secession, and at best a lukewarm supporter of the Confederacy, Drew was expected to lure moderate votes away from the Republicans.[114] Thus, in Florida also, the party in power was in trouble.

Florida had more white voters than black, but a significant number of whites were northern men by birth and had hitherto been Republicans. The Democratic party campaigned for their votes by emphasizing the conservative economic interests that they shared. However, when it came to dealing with the black population, the Democrats were not so restrained. There was little violence, although threats were sometimes made. Elections had become so corrupt in this sparsely settled state that violence was seldom considered necessary. Economic intimidation was far more effective and difficult to detect. For example, the Democratic Club of Monticello publicly resolved "to give the first preference in all things to those men who vote for reform; and

113. William Watson Davis, *The Civil War and Reconstruction in Florida*, Columbia University Studies in History, Economics and Public Law, LIII (New York: Columbia University, 1913), 689–91; John F. Rollins to Wm. E. Chandler, August 9, 1876, in William E. Chandler Papers.
114. Davis, *Civil War and Reconstruction in Florida*, 691–92.

to give second preference in all things to those who do not vote at all; that in employing or hiring, or renting land to any such persons [Republicans] a distinction of 25% will be made against such persons; that merchants, lawyers and doctors, in extending credit to such persons, make the same distinction." Some large employers gave each of their black laborers a numbered Democratic ticket along with the straightforward instruction, "I want to see it come out of the ballot-box to-morrow night." Republican leaders in a few sharply contested counties planned to counter Democratic force with fraud. Since they controlled the election machinery, they would simply throw in the number of extra ballots required to salvage the victory to which they were sure they were entitled. Each party excused its own activities by pointing to what the other was doing.[115]

The most exciting battle in Dixie was fought in South Carolina between two of the most fascinating men of the Reconstruction era. Daniel H. Chamberlain was a native of Massachusetts, a graduate of Yale University who attended Harvard Law School for a year and then joined the Union army. In 1866, convinced of the inherent superiority of free labor to slave, he settled in South Carolina to become a cotton planter. He failed and only afterwards turned to politics. During four years as attorney general he associated freely with some of the least-reputable figures in the Republican party. Elected governor in 1874 as an orthodox Radical, Chamberlain astonished everybody, transforming himself overnight into a crusading reformer. He stopped the sale of pardons, raised the level of judicial appointments, reduced state spending (the *sine qua non* of reform in the nineteenth century), and repeatedly vetoed legislation he felt was not in the public interest.[116] So favorable an image did Chamberlain make for himself that Carl Schurz wanted to draw him into the movement that was planning the Fifth Avenue Hotel Conference. Chamberlain declined to participate, but only

115. *Ibid.*, 694–700.
116. Hampton M. Jarrell, *Wade Hampton and the Negro: The Road Not Taken* (Columbia: University of South Carolina Press, 1950), 41–46.

on the ground that his standing with the Grant administration had already become dangerously low.[117]

The majority of the white people in South Carolina were impressed and said so. In fact, the Democratic party, which had not organized a campaign under its own banner since 1868, appeared willing to endorse Chamberlain for reelection if he were again nominated by the Republicans. South Carolina had thirty thousand more black voters than white, a ratio of nearly three to two. All things considered, it seemed wiser to many Democrats to support a respectable carpetbagger than to go their own way and court almost certain defeat.

Then, at the peak of his popularity, Chamberlain's world fell apart. On July 8 the rifle clubs of Aiken and Edgefield counties invaded the black community of Hamburg and demanded that its militia company surrender its arms. The militiamen, all of whom were black, refused; so that evening several hundred whites attacked the armory with rifles and a cannon. After several hours of skirmishing they overran the large brick building, sacked the town, and captured about thirty blacks, not all of whom were militiamen. Only two men died during the fighting, one white and one black. However, a short time later the rifle clubs shot and killed five of their prisoners.[118] Most leading Democrats were shocked by the episode, which they deemed senseless and unjustified, but they were even angrier at Governor Chamberlain's reaction. Perhaps under pressure to prove his devotion to the Republican party, rather than ordering an impartial inquiry Chamberlain denounced the "Hamburg Massacre" as political in nature, designed expressly to discourage blacks from voting. He also asked Grant for more troops. White South Carolinians quickly lost sight of the original atrocity in their fury at what seemed a return to "bayonet rule." Within

117. Schurz to Bowles, January 16, 1876, and D. H. Chamberlain to Bowles, February 2, 1876, both in Samuel Bowles Papers, Yale University Library.
118. Joel Williamson, *After Slavery: The Negro in South Carolina During Reconstruction, 1861–1877* (Chapel Hill: University of North Carolina Press, 1965), 266–70.

four days the Democratic state committee called a convention to consider the advisability of independent nominations.

This decision represented a triumph for two Edgefield residents, M. C. Butler and Martin W. Gary, the earliest advocates of a "straight-out" Democratic ticket. Butler was the leader of the assault on Hamburg, although he had nothing directly to do with the murder of the prisoners. Gary secured the agreement of Wade Hampton III to seek the governorship.[119] Hampton was the ideal candidate. Once one of the wealthiest men in South Carolina, the owner of more than a thousand slaves, he was the commanding officer of the cavalry attached to General Robert E. Lee's Army of Northern Virginia. Though in much reduced circumstances following the Confederate defeat, Hampton remained the embodiment of the finest ideals of the old Charleston aristocracy. He was one of the first white men in the South to advocate limited extension of the suffrage to the freedmen—specifically, he suggested that all voters, regardless of color, be subject to the same literacy and property qualifications. The Radical formula for reconstruction having been imposed by Congress, however, Hampton turned away from politics in revulsion. He was prepared to give blacks the privilege of selecting their governors from among men like himself, but he would not consent to be ruled by them.[120] When the Democratic convention met, Hampton was chosen by acclamation. The Republicans, despite some grumbling in their midst, renominated Chamberlain—there was nothing else they could do.[121]

No sooner was Hampton in the race than he parted company with the men who had first asked him to run. Gary and Butler, motivated by an intense race hatred and obsessed with the forceful "redemption" of Mississippi the previous fall, proposed the same tactics for South Carolina. Hampton vigorously disagreed.

119. Jarrell, *Wade Hampton and the Negro*, 46–52; Williamson, *After Slavery*, 407–408.
120. Williamson, *After Slavery*, 406–407.
121. Manly Wade Wellman, *Giant in Grey: A Biography of Wade Hampton of South Carolina* (New York: Charles Scribner's Sons, 1949), 240–49, 256.

Instinctively a conservative in the best sense of the term, he intended to accept the Civil War amendments and build from there, appealing to black Carolinians for their votes on the pledge that he would serve them better than his opponent could:

The only way to bring about prosperity in this state is to bring the two races in friendly relation together. The democratic party in South Carolina, of whom I am the exponent, has promised that every citizen of this state is to be the equal of all; he is to have every right given him by the Constitution of the United States and of this state.... And I pledge my faith, and I pledge it for those gentlemen who are on the ticket with me, that if we are elected, as far as in us lies, we will observe, protect, and defend the rights of the colored man as quickly as [of] any man in South Carolina.... If there is a white man in this assembly, [who] because he is a democrat, or because he is a white man, believes that when I am elected governor, if I should be, that I will stand between him and the law, or grant him any privilege or immunity that shall not be granted to the colored man, he is mistaken.

Thus Hampton addressed a white audience, in a speech which was later printed in pamphlet form for circulation among black voters. Indication that his philosophy would prevail in the campaign over that of his sponsor came when A. C. Haskell, a proponent of the peace policy, was selected state chairman, while Gary was left off the executive committee altogether.[122]

Through the summer and fall blacks were inducted into Democratic clubs, especially in the towns and cities, invited to Democratic rallies, and promised a more efficient distribution of school funds and other benefits. Speaking to biracial meetings, Hampton invariably directed most of his remarks to his black auditors. The Democratic state convention had been a lily-white affair, and the ticket it produced consisted only of white men. There were, however, black Democratic candidates for local office in some counties and at least one prominent black leader, Martin R. Dulaney, took the stump for Tilden and Hampton.[123]

122. Jarrell, *Wade Hampton and the Negro*, 53–54, 56–60, 73–74.
123. Williamson, *After Slavery*, 408–409; Francis Butler Simkins and Robert Hilliard Woody, *South Carolina During Reconstruction* (Chapel Hill: University of North Carolina Press, 1932), 509–12.

After the election Hampton publicly attributed his strong showing to the votes of former slaves, of which he estimated he had received seventeen thousand, although that figure may have been too high.[124] The Democratic performance held such promise for the future that some Republicans who planned to vote for Hayes and Wheeler, most notably Judge Thomas J. Mackey, decided to mark their ballots for Hampton instead of Chamberlain. When they became aware of this circumstance, Democratic officials discussed the possibility of withdrawing their party's presidential ticket in an effort to encourage more Republicans to "cross over Jordan"; but the idea received little support and was quickly abandoned.[125]

The majority of Democrats earnestly endeavored to avoid the excesses employed in Mississippi; yet it should not be assumed that politicking in South Carolina was the same as in Indiana or New York. The campaign of 1876 in the Palmetto State at times became very rough. Though Hampton effectively ruled out the use of force, he said nothing about its display. To emphasize their strength, white Democrats in rural counties, and occasionally blacks as well, donned red flannel shirts as a gesture of defiance to the Republicans' "bloody shirt" and marched or rode to political meetings in military formation, their tightly drawn lines sometimes stretching a half-mile or more.[126] In predominantly black Barnwell, Aiken, and Edgefield counties, the region

---

124. Jarrell, *Wade Hampton and the Negro*, 61. Chamberlain claimed that only 3,000 blacks voted for Hampton, but he made his statement during the electoral dispute while trying to demonstrate the widespread use of intimidation by the Democrats. A black attorney who worked in the campaign placed the figure at 10,000. A. C. Haskell estimated 15,000. Newspaper stories in 1877 and 1878 spoke of 16,000. See *ibid.*, 99. Historians who have studied the campaign do not agree either. Hampton M. Jarrell, after a careful comparison of voting and population statistics, preferred Haskell's estimate—15,000—whereas Joel Williamson is skeptical that the number was much more than 2,000. See *ibid.*, 101, and Williamson, *After Slavery*, 409–11.

125. Jarrell, *Wade Hampton and the Negro*, 67, 74, 115–16; D. D. Wallace, "The Question of the Withdrawal of the Democratic Presidential Electors in South Carolina in 1876," *Journal of Southern History*, VIII (August, 1942), 376–85.

126. Jarrell, *Wade Hampton and the Negro*, 70.

where Gary and Butler's influence was greatest, even sharper practices were adopted. Democrats demanded "equal time" at their opponents' rallies, as Republican L. Cass Carpenter breathlessly explained upon his return to Charleston:

I have just reached here from a meeting called by the republicans, of one of the most thoroughgoing republican counties in the state, the county of Barnwell, which two years ago gave 1500 majority for the republican ticket, whither I went with His Excellency Governor Chamberlain to make a public speech upon the political situation. We were met there with the usual democratic demonstration, consisting of about 600 mounted, armed men from various parts of the county, who rode on to the ground and took up their position near the stand. You must bear in mind the fact, that this was a republican meeting, called under republican auspices, and at which it was supposed none but republicans would take part. Gov. Chamberlain was the first speaker, and every man who knows him knows that he is too much of a gentleman to do, or say anything to insult, or irritate any man. He spoke for about an hour in a calm dignified manner, and in any other, but a South Carolina democratic crowd would have secured the approval of his audience. Here, however, it was different. He was interrupted several times with impertinent questions, and finally sat down. He was followed by W Gilmore Sims [*sic*], a son of the poet Sims, in a violent and abusive tirade against "Carpet Baggers" in General, but Chamberlain in particular. He indulged in such "manly and chivalric" expressions as "he is a Carrion Crow, a Buzzard who has come down here to prey upon *our* people and steal from them their substance." "He is a seedy adventurer, who had no constituency at home, and has come to rob people who have no interest in common with him." In this way he went on for about half an hour, being constantly applauded by the rebel followers who accompanied him. The old "rebel yell" was heard every minute or two.

After Sims, I spoke for a half an hour or more, but was constantly interrupted with insulting questions. I succeeded in closing, however, with the audience in good humor, although every means possible were resorted to by the democrats to exasperate me.

Now came the turning point in the meeting. Mr. Geo. D. Tillman [brother of "Pitchfork Ben" Tillman] of Edgefield, a rabid rebel fire-eater who has just been nominated upon the Wade Hampton ticket as Congressman from the fifth district, now represented by Congressman Smalls, followed me. Never, since I have had a recollection, did I hear such inflamatory [*sic*] and seditious language as was uttered by him. He boldly and openly advocated assassination, and used the following expressions. Turning to his white-line followers several hundreds in numbers, armed to the teeth he said: "Why don't you hang em," (pointing to Governor Chamberlain and myself.) "Hang em now," ["] begin at once, and if you men of Barnwell are too cowardly to do it, send a telegram to Edgefield and I will guarantee enough trusty men to come here and do it for you."

At this there went up that unearthly "yell" so often heard by union soldiers when fighting for the supremacy of the old flag. At times it seemed almost impossible to prevent a conflict, which, if it had once started, every republican speaker, or leading man there would have been murdered in cold blood.

Congressman [S. L.] Hoge followed Tillman, and had hardly got fairly begun before half a dozen pistols were drawn upon him, for some fancied insult given by him in reply to an insulting question from the rebel crew around him. The danger at this time was imminent, but was happily averted. Insult upon insult was offered us all, but the democratic crowd seemed to take special delight in applying their epithets to the Governor, and to Mr. Hoge. The[y] called the Governor a "G—d d—n Son of a b—tch." Hoge they called, the "Ohio Hog.," and in fact did everything possible to provoke us to retort. Happily for all, the meeting broke up quietly, and both parties retired to their respective homes.

Carpenter added that he had previously attended four other meetings of the same type.[127] Hampton seems to have wanted an end to such confrontations, but had to settle for urging restraint upon the white men of Gary's section of the state.[128] Economic coercion, bribery, and threats of bodily harm were also used in various places and not just in Gary's bailiwick.[129]

Nevertheless, the campaign was reasonably free of violence, given the state of almost unbearable tension in which it was waged. There were only two disturbances of a distinctly political nature, and both were started by blacks still enraged at the killings in Hamburg. On September 6 a black mob attacked the leaders of a black Democratic club in Charleston, and a night

127. L. Cass Carpenter to Wm. E. Chandler, August 26, 1876, in William E. Chandler Papers.
128. Jarrell, *Wade Hampton and the Negro*, 67–68.
129. *Ibid.*, 70–71.

of rioting and looting followed. Several people were injured, with one white man later dying. A month later a group of blacks fired into what was supposed to be a peaceful "joint discussion" at Cainhoy in a rural part of the same county; five whites lost their lives. The bloodiest outbreak of the fall occurred in September at Ellenton in Aiken County. There two black men robbed and beat a white woman, and in the days of sniping that followed fifteen blacks and two whites were killed. The Ellenton incidents were a spontaneous product of mutual racial antagonism, unorganized, and without political overtones. Moreover, order was restored as soon as federal troops approached.

The Republicans, however, were becoming desperate. Their canvass was disintegrating. Chamberlain, severely shaken by his early experiences when Democrats had demanded "equal time," had retired timidly to his office. Depressed at the prospect of defeat, he seized on the Ellenton clashes and the elaborate maneuvers publicly staged by the Democratic rifle clubs as a basis for again asking for more soldiers. Grant was visiting the West Coast and was unable to comply immediately, but he returned to Washington just in time for the Republican defeat in Indiana, a loss which instantly enhanced the importance of South Carolina in the presidential election. General William T. Sherman telegraphed General Thomas H. Ruger in Columbia: "We are all back from California. If you want anything say so. I want all measures to originate with you. Get along with the minimum force necessary, but you shall have all we can give if you need them." Ruger replied: "Think I have troops sufficient unless circumstances change. . . . No special disorder has occurred since Ellenton riot last month. If I need more troops I will ask for them." The next day Grant nevertheless stripped every army post in the Department of the South of its extra personnel in order to beef up the forces in South Carolina. The rifle clubs promptly disappeared, though they did not disband. The outward calm, which had characterized most of the state anyway, was preserved, and the campaign continued much as before.[130] The presence of the soldiers was necessarily of little more than symbolic importance. In this summer of Custer's Last Stand, there were only 2,800 officers and men in all the states of the old Confederacy.[131] The reaction to Grant's order was mixed, as could have been predicted. Senator John J. Patterson of South Carolina told Hayes it would give the Republicans a victory in that state by twenty thousand votes.[132] On the other hand, Charles Nordhoff furiously announced his intention of voting for Tilden, and Horace White quietly did the same.[133]

North Carolina was the fourth southern state in which a Republican occupied the governor's chair. The situation differed from that in the other three, however, because the Democrats already held massive majorities in both houses of the legislature, and there was little suspense about the outcome of the centennial campaign. For their gubernatorial candidate the Democrats chose Zebulon B. Vance, the man who had governed the Old North State when it was part of the Confederacy. To oppose him the Republicans headed their ticket with Judge Thomas Settle, a secessionist as a member of the legislature in the 1850s, who had later reversed himself and played a leading role in the organization of the Republican party in North Carolina. These two men had faced each other under dramatic circumstances once before. Settle was the victorious prosecutor and Vance the unsuccessful defense attorney in the 1866 murder trial of Tom Dula, the "Tom Dooley" of folk-song fame. Coming from similar backgrounds and being on friendly terms with one another, Settle and Vance agreed to stump the state together, staging a series of Lincoln-Douglas style debates on issues of local and

130. Simkins and Woody, *South Carolina During Reconstruction*, 502–509; Jarrell, *Wade Hampton and the Negro*, 65–67, 77–80.
131. Clarence C. Clendenen, "President Hayes' 'Withdrawal' of the Troops—An Enduring Myth," *South Carolina Historical Magazine*, LXX (October, 1969), 243–46.
132. Jno. J. Patterson to Hayes, October 22, 1876, in Hayes Papers.
133. Nordhoff to Bowles, October 15, 1876, in Bowles Papers; Nordhoff to Hayes, October 15, 1876, and Comly to Hayes, January 8, 1877, both in Hayes Papers.

national significance. They began at Rutherfordton in late July, and during the next three months appeared in sixty-five counties in verbal matches lasting four hours or more. Only in the last ten days of the canvass did they separate to address a few strictly partisan meetings. Here was American politics at its finest.[134]

In general, however, electioneering in the South differed so drastically from that in the rest of the country that the national leaders of both parties felt uncomfortable when they had to deal with states below the Potomac and Ohio rivers. Democratic officials received repeated warnings about the peculiarities in the voting machinery in some parts of Dixie. A Louisianan wrote Tilden on September 1:

> As one deeply interested in the result of the approaching National Election, I deem it my duty to direct your attention to the means by which the Radicals intend to carry the State of Louisiana [.] The one is their Board of Registration & the other their Returning Board. . . . It is in their power to throw out every parish in the State where the Democrats have a majority & their award is final. The Supreme Court has decided that the judgment of the Returning Board is not subject to revision. Now these two Boards and this Registration & Election law are created & enacted for the sole purpose of enabling the Radical Party to carry the Elections of Louisiana by fraud.[135]

Such reports just served to make New Yorkers more uneasy. An emissary of the Florida Democratic party called on Tilden in late August to caution him that although the state ticket was safe, the national ticket was in peril. He wanted help. According to Bigelow, "the Govr. told him he looked to him to carry Florida & presented him with his photograph." [136] The Floridian tried to

134. Glenn Tucker, *Zeb Vance: Champion of Personal Freedom* (Indianapolis: Bobbs-Merrill Company, Inc., 1965), 456–59; J. G. de Roulhac Hamilton, *Reconstruction in North Carolina*, Columbia University Studies in History, Economics and Public Law, LVIII (New York: Columbia University Press, 1914), 591, 593, 603–604, 649–52.

135. R. W. Knickerbocker to Tilden, September 1, 1876, in Tilden Papers.

136. John Bigelow Diary, August 24, 26, 1876, in John Bigelow Papers, New York Public Library.

impress upon Hewitt the need for carrying his state by a majority so large that the Republicans would be discouraged from any attempt at fraud: "I told him with 10 thousand dollars I could insure the state, and that I would give 1 thousand dollars towards the fund . . . but he said he could not do anything more for Florida than was being done." [137] The national committee was too preoccupied with Indiana and New York. Wade Hampton complained to Marble that his state committee could not even get advice from party headquarters in New York: "Of course we are most anxious to aid in the general election, but you can understand our solicitude to find out how we can best do this. The Com. say they can get no suggestions from the Nat. Com. & even no replies to communications. This has discouraged them & they are at a loss what to do. . . . The vote of the state can be secured for Tilden, & I think that we can have a quiet election if we can raise funds to preserve the peace." [138] When one of the national leaders did offer a suggestion, it was usually either innocuous or fatuous. Hewitt, for example, counseled L. Q. C. Lamar, "I trust there will be no outbreaks in the South no matter how great the provocation may be, which will tend to impede the steady gain which we are making upon the enemy." [139]

On the Republican side the story was similar. The agency most concerned with the South was not the national committee but the Justice Department. Attorney General Alphonso Taft spent much of his time meeting with politicians from that section, investigating allegations of Democratic intimidation, and making preparations for guarding the polling places.[140] On election day 166 deputy marshals were on duty in North Carolina, 338 in

137. Jn. Stokes Boyd to Bigelow, November 14, 1876, in John Bigelow, *Retrospections of an Active Life* (5 vols.; Garden City, N.Y.: Doubleday, Page and Company, 1909–13), V, 286–87.
138. Wade Hampton to Marble, September 19, 1876, in Marble Papers.
139. Hewitt to L. Q. C. Lamar, October 20, 1876, in L. Q. C. Lamar and Edward Mayes Papers, Mississippi Department of Archives and History.
140. A. Taft to Hayes, August 23, September 12, 1876, in Hayes Papers.

South Carolina, 745 in Florida, and 840 in Louisiana. Two hundred and seventy supervisors served in New Orleans at a cost of $8,578.[141] On the other hand, when Zach Chandler asked William E. Chandler to visit North and South Carolina and Florida, the latter refused. He had already been to Maine, Ohio, Indiana, and New York, and that was enough. He went home to New Hampshire instead.[142]

5

When Indianans chose "Blue Jeans" Williams as their governor in October, the Democrats, inured to disappointment, were scarcely able to believe it. "Tilden is really to be elected," gasped Samuel J. Randall; "I can see it all around me." [143] A member of the Illinois state committee exulted, "After sixteen long years of *darkness*, daylight is at last breaking [.] "[144] And August Belmont, whose checkbook had carried the party through the darkest of those years, told a Manhattan Club rally, with Tilden himself in attendance: "Victory is in the air! That mighty orb of our political system—Democracy—is passing out of its long eclipse." [145]

Not unnaturally, as the enthusiasm of their opponents increased, the Republicans were enveloped in gloom. Hayes admitted to his diary, "The contest is close and yet doubtful with the chances, as I see them, rather against us." Unable to bring himself to believe that the American people would knowingly place in office a party as ineffectual and wrongheaded as the Democrats, Hayes attributed his impending defeat to bribery and repeating in the North and to coercion in the South.[146]

There was one other conceivable outcome to the election which

141. Burke, "Federal Regulation of Congressional Elections," 112–13, 125–29, 172.
142. J. M. Forbes to Zach. Chandler, January 2, 1877, in William E. Chandler Papers.
143. Randall to C. F. Black, October 13, 1876, in Black Papers.
144. J. A. Mallory to Snyder, October 14, 1876, in Snyder Papers.
145. Quoted in Irving Katz, *August Belmont: A Political Biography* (New York: Columbia University Press, 1968), 224.
146. Entry for November 1, 1876, in Williams (ed.), *Hayes: The Diary of a President*, 45–46.

farsighted men thought about—a disputed result. Hayes and Charles Francis Adams considered that possibility in their diaries.[147] The New York *World* and Louisville *Courier-Journal* speculated about it in print.[148] Murat Halstead used it in his Cooper Union address as an argument for voting against Tilden: "A disputed presidential election would Mexicanize us. There is incalculable ruin in it. If the New York electoral vote is given the Democratic candidate, we are imminently threatened with this degradation. If New York is Republican, the danger is over." [149]

Congress, of course, had the ultimate authority for declaring the winners of the presidential and vice-presidential races. Under the Twenty-second Joint Rule, adopted in 1865, no state's electoral vote could be counted unless both houses consented. Then, the Democrats gained control of the House of Representatives in 1874, and the Republicans suddenly discovered that the rule was inadequate. The Senate receded from it with the organization of the Forty-fourth Congress in December, 1875. No agreement was reached on a replacement, however; so in 1876 there was no established procedure for dealing with a contested state.[150] And Louisiana, just four years before, had submitted two contradictory sets of electoral votes. Still, suggesting that their opponents would provoke a crisis which could lead to a second civil war was something politicos did in campaign speeches; it was not something they really believed in their hearts.

6

On November 7, eight and a half million Americans went to the polls, exceeding the 1872 mark by fully two million. Both candidates received more ballots than any previous president,

147. Entry for October 22, 1876, *ibid.*, 44–45; Charles Francis Adams Diary, October 12, 19, 1876, in Adams Papers.
148. New York *World*, October 31, 1876; Joseph Frazier Wall, *Henry Watterson: Reconstructed Rebel* (New York: Oxford University Press, 1956), 137.
149. Quoted in Barnard, *Rutherford B. Hayes and His America*, 314.
150. Selig Adler, "The Senatorial Career of George Franklin Edmunds, 1866–1891" (Ph.D. dissertation, University of Illinois, 1934), 139–41.

with Tilden pulling away to a quarter-million vote lead. Building a plurality of 70,000 in New York City and Brooklyn, he carried his home state by 32,000. Then Connecticut, New Jersey, and Indiana went Democratic and it appeared that most of the South would also.[151] The nation's press, in its editions the next morning, was all but unanimous in sharing the view of the Chicago *Daily News* that Tilden had won "by a very considerable majority of the electoral vote." [152]

151. W. Dean Burnham, *Presidential Ballots, 1836–1892* (Baltimore: Johns Hopkins Press, 1955), 246–57, 632–47.
152. Chicago *Daily News*, November 8, 1876.

Chapter VI □ Stalemate

ON ELECTION night General Daniel E. Sickles, resigning himself to the Tilden victory he believed was inevitable, went to the theater instead of joining his Republican friends in following the returns. Not until he was on his way home at nearly midnight did he stop by the national committee headquarters in the Fifth Avenue Hotel "to hear the news." Sickles, whose devotion to the Union and the Republican party was unquestioned—he had lost a leg at Gettysburg and served more recently as minister to Spain—was startled to find the place all but deserted. Only the chief clerk, M. A. Clancy, was there, and he was "packing up the records and papers of the Committee." Zach Chandler had given up an hour before, taking a friendly bottle of whiskey to his room "for company and consolation." The result was just what Sickles had expected, yet the reality of a Democratic triumph was so hard to accept that the ex-soldier had to see for himself the dispatches from the various states. Clancy directed him to Chandler's vacant desk. Sickles shuffled through the telegrams and agreed that the outlook was bleak. Giving the matter careful consideration, however, he decided that the election, both nationally and in a number of individual states, was too close to abandon as hopeless. If enough of the doubtful states went Republican, Hayes still might emerge successful. Sickles accordingly drafted a telegram to be sent to Governor Chamberlain of South Carolina, Governor

Kellogg of Louisiana, former senator Thomas W. Osborn of Florida, and the chairman of the Republican committee in Oregon: "With your state sure for Hayes, he is elected. Hold your state." Sickles wanted his message transmitted over Zach Chandler's signature, but Clancy wondered whether that would be proper. Just then Chester A. Arthur, the collector of the Port of New York and one of Conkling's close associates, entered. He assured Clancy he would share responsibility for the telegrams. Because his wife was ill, Arthur could not await the responses, but Sickles remained. Favorable replies arrived from South Carolina at three in the morning and from Oregon shortly before six; no word at all was received from the other two states. Sickles then fired off a second round of telegrams, warning of the dangers of Democratic intrigue. Finally, satisfied that nothing else could be done, he resumed his journey home. In the east the sky was already growing bright.[1]

Half an hour later William E. Chandler appeared. He had voted at his home in New Hampshire, boarded a train for Boston, and caught the night express to New York. By the time he reached the Fifth Avenue Hotel, it was daylight. Clancy was informing Chandler of the discouraging details of the previous evening when another breathless figure rushed in. He was John C. Reid, managing editor of the New York *Times*. A survivor of the horrors of the Confederate army's Libby Prison in Richmond during the war, Reid's hatred of all Democrats, northerners and southerners alike, was both fanatical and comprehensible. When the rest of the Republican press declared that Tilden was victorious, Reid prevailed upon his associates to concede nothing. The last edition of the *Times* on November 8 proclaimed: "The Results Still Uncertain." Reid was emboldened in his course by a telegraphic inquiry from New York State Democratic Chairman Daniel E. Magone: "Please give your estimate of electoral votes secured for Tilden. Answer at once."

1. Jerome L. Sternstein (ed.), "The Sickles Memorandum: Another Look at the Hayes-Tilden Election-Night Conspiracy," *Journal of Southern History*, XXXII (August, 1966), 346–49, 354–56.

Perhaps the Democrats, too, were still in doubt. As soon as his work at the paper was finished, Reid grabbed a couple of 6 A.M. dispatches announcing that Florida and Oregon had gone Republican and hurried to the rooms of the national committee.[2] There he met the dejected Chandler. He displayed the late reports he had brought with him and explained the refusal of the *Times* to admit defeat. The younger Chandler then went to Zach Chandler's desk and found copies of the telegrams Sickles had sent using the elder Chandler's name. There were also answers from two states which seemed to confirm Reid's calculations. The two men ran upstairs to the room where the national chairman was sleeping. After pounding on his door for several minutes they succeeded in rousing him, but of course could get no information about the telegrams on the desk. The weary and bewildered Zach Chandler told William Chandler to do whatever he thought best. Back in the offices of the committee, Chandler drafted his own telegrams to be sent to Louisiana, Florida, South Carolina, Nevada, and Oregon. His communication to Chamberlain was typical: "Hayes is elected if we have carried South Carolina, Florida, and Louisiana. Can you hold your State? Answer immediately." Chandler and Reid were clearly contemplating use of the returning boards in three of the Republican states of the South to nullify Democratic majorities which might appear on the face of the returns. In a brilliant flash of insight the next day, Chandler even recognized the possibility that the Democratic governor of Oregon might retaliate by withholding his certificate from the Republican electors. To counter this threat Chandler suggested that the Republican governor of North Carolina refuse to certify his state's Democratic electors. By midmorning, when Zach Chandler had recovered sufficiently to come downstairs, the Democrats had definitely carried sixteen states with 184 electoral votes, while

2. Reid first narrated his own role in these events in the New York *Times*, June 15, 1887. See also Paul Leland Haworth, *The Hayes-Tilden Disputed Presidential Election of 1876* (Cleveland: Burrows Brothers Company, 1906), 46–47; Dee Brown, *The Year of the Century: 1876* (New York: Charles Scribner's Sons, 1966), 316.

the Republicans were sure of nineteen states with 166. The three southern states alone were undecided. "Old Zach" conferred with the rest of the Republican leaders in New York and issued the terse statement, "Hayes has 185 votes and is elected." William Chandler consoled the Republican candidate, "One majority is as good as twenty if we hold it but we are more liable to be cheated out of it." [3]

1

The audacious acts of Sickles, Reid, and the two Chandlers threw the entire country into confusion. Even Hayes was caught unawares. On election night a small party of close friends assembled at his home in Fremont hoping to celebrate the returns as they came in by telegraph. But the discovery that the party had again carried Ohio by only a narrow margin quickly placed a damper on the rest of the evening. When a scattering of reports indicated that the majority for Tilden in New York City would substantially exceed the Republican advantage upstate, Hayes and his wife took leave of their guests and retired, satisfied that the issue had been decided: "Both of us felt more anxiety about the South—about the colored people especially than about anything else sinister in the result. My hope of a sound currency will somehow be realized. Civil Service reform will be delayed, but the great injury is in the South. There the amendments will be nullified, disorder will continue, prosperity to both whites and colored people, will be pushed off for years." [4] Coming downstairs the next morning, Hayes was greeted by a telegram

3. [W. E.] C[handler] to Hayes, November 9, 1876, in Rutherford B. Hayes Papers, Rutherford B. Hayes Library, Fremont, Ohio; memorandum by W. E. Chandler, "The Hayes-Tilden canvass in 1876," in William E. Chandler Papers, Manuscript Division, Library of Congress. This memorandum was written in 1903 or later. See Sternstein (ed.), "The Sickles Memorandum," 345*n*. See also Harry Barnard, *Rutherford B. Hayes and His America* (Indianapolis: Bobbs-Merrill Company, Inc., 1954), 319; Leon Burr Richardson, *William E. Chandler, Republican* (New York: Dodd, Mead and Company, 1940), 184–86.

4. Entry for November 11, 1876, in T. Harry Williams (ed.), *Hayes: The Diary of a President, 1875–1881, Covering the Disputed Election, the End of Reconstruction, and the Beginning of Civil Service* (New York: David McKay Company, Inc., 1964), 47–50.

from the manager of the New York office of the Western Associated Press: "Despatches indicate New Jersey gone Democratic Leaving no further doubt of Tildens election [.] "[5] That afternoon, following Zach Chandler's claim of victory, Hayes told a group of reporters: "I think we are defeated, spite of recent good news. I am of opinion that the Democrats have carried the country and elected Tilden, as it now seems necessary for the Republicans to carry all the States now set down as doubtful to secure even a majority of one. I don't think encouraging despatches ought to be given to the public now, because they might mislead enthusiastic friends to bet on the election and lose their money. I do heartily deprecate such despatches." [6] Bringing his diary up to date on Saturday, November 11, Hayes still believed "the election has resulted in the defeat of the Republicans after a very close contest." [7] Indeed, as late as Sunday morning he thought "the figures indicate that Florida has been carried by the Democrats. No doubt both fraud and violence intervened to produce the result. But the same is true in many Southern States. We shall—the fair minded men of the country will—history will hold that the Republicans were by fraud and violence and intimidation, by a nullification of the 15*th* amendment, deprived of the victory which they fairly won. But we must, I now think, prepare ourselves to accept the inevitable. I do it with composure and cheerfulness." [8] Hayes was not alone among Republicans in conceding that he had lost. Congressman James A. Garfield concluded bitterly on Thursday, "It now appears that we were defeated by the combined power of rebellion, catholicism and whiskey a trinity very hard to conquer." [9] (Garfield thus foreshadowed the disastrous

5. Telegram, Geo. Jones to W. K. Rogers, November 8 [1876], in Hayes Papers.

6. New York *Sun*, November 9, 1876.

7. Entry for November 11, 1876, in Williams (ed.), *Hayes: The Diary of a President*, 47.

8. Entry for November 12, 1876, *ibid.*, 50–51.

9. Quoted in Theodore Clarke Smith, *The Life and Letters of James Abram Garfield* (2 vols.; New Haven: Yale University Press, 1925), I, 613.

"Rum, Romanism, and Rebellion" remark of the Reverend Samuel D. Burchard in the Blaine canvass of 1884.)

If the Republican candidate himself required several days to credit seriously the statements that he had won, the amazement and utter disbelief of the Democrats can readily be imagined. After the jubilant festivity of election night they were reduced to flooding the telegraph wires with frantic pleas for more information.[10] The one man who seems not to have been surprised was Tilden. It is entirely possible, though it cannot be fully substantiated, that the scholarly and reserved Tilden *never* expected to be inaugurated. At any rate, he resigned himself at once to the likelihood of being counted out. On the Thursday following the election, John Bigelow went riding with Tilden. They "agreed that whether he had been elected or not, there was nothing to reproach him with in his defeat. The result shows that nothing but the Reform issue he had made, saved the ticket and that Bayard or any one else could have made no head at all against the cry of the bloody shirt which has been after all the piece de resistance of the Reps. in this canvass." Bigelow was not so calm. He reflected angrily that the nation's destiny might well hinge on the returning board of Louisiana, so completely lacking in public confidence: "Another civil war may be the consequence of this state of things and we may enter upon the next century under a difft. form of govt. from that of which for nearly a century we have been boasting."[11]

There were some Democrats who urged the necessity of claiming the presidency by force on the ground that the office was rightfully Tilden's. However, a profound desire for peace was much more prevalent. Two weeks after the election, Tilden, Bigelow, and Hewitt conferred in Albany on the advisability of naming General George B. McClellan as Tilden's "adjutant."

10. The Cyrus Hall McCormick Papers, State Historical Society of Wisconsin, alone contain hundreds of such telegrams from Illinois county chairmen and leaders of adjacent states, dated November 8 through 10, 1876.
11. John Bigelow Diary, November 11, 1876, in John Bigelow Papers, New York Public Library.

Bigelow opposed the suggestion as a "red rag" in the eyes of the Republicans and the idea was soon dropped.[12] The Chicago *Daily News*, meanwhile, thought the uninterrupted flow of contradictory reports from the disputed states had given the more ardent spirits on both sides time to cool off. The paper continued to stress the need for "wise, exalted statesmanship," and the "well settled determination of the American people" that any solution to the impasse be pacific.[13] Tilden and Hendricks both tried to assure the public that there would be no violence. On the day following his ride with Bigelow, Tilden told a reporter: "Be satisfied with the reflection that the people are too patriotic, too intelligent, too self-poised to allow anything perilous to be done—anything that may disturb or destroy our peculiar form of government. Don't be alarmed." [14] Shortly thereafter Hendricks cautioned another journalist, "I think that it is of great importance that all Democrats and good citizens generally should keep perfectly cool and preserve their temper till the crisis is over." [15] The New York *Sun*, which under the editorship of Charles A. Dana was the paper most likely to express the views of Tilden, went so far as to hint that the Republican scheme to steal the three southern states' votes, "if accomplished with the forms of law, will be submitted to by all parties." [16]

The problem confronting the Democratic party was how legally to block such a scheme. On November 9, as soon as he discerned the nature of the electoral dispute, Henry Watterson, the youthful editor of the Louisville *Courier-Journal*, telegraphed Tilden, "Our friends in Louisiana need moral support and personal advisement [.] " He informed Tilden that he was leaving

12. *Ibid.*, November 22, 1876.
13. Chicago *Daily News*, November 13, 25, December 20, 1876.
14. New York *Herald*, November 11, 1876.
15. New York *World*, November 25, 1876.
16. New York *Sun*, November 13, 1876. Some historians have exaggerated the danger of civil war for dramatic purposes. See Allan Nevins, *Abram S. Hewitt: With Some Account of Peter Cooper* (New York: Harper and Brothers, 1935), 336; Barnard, *Rutherford B. Hayes and His America*, 341–45; and C. Vann Woodward, *Reunion and Reaction: The Compromise of 1877 and the End of Reconstruction* (Boston: Little, Brown and Company, 1951), 110–13.

for New Orleans at once and asked that the most respected men in the party be sent to join him: "A strong Demonstration will defeat [the] Designs of [the] Returning Board [.] " [17] Tilden and Hewitt followed this advice. Within a couple of days, John M. Palmer, Lyman Trumbull, William R. Morrison, Samuel J. Randall, James R. Doolittle, George W. Julian, John W. Stevenson, Oswald Ottendorfer, Professor William Graham Sumner of Yale, and other noted Democrats were on their way to the Crescent City at the request of the national committee.[18] Hewitt very nearly accomplished a major coup when he asked Charles Francis Adams to "witness" the count of presidential votes in Louisiana. Adams consented to escort his wife on a trip to New York the next day in order to confer further on the subject. On the train, however, he met some of the other gentlemen headed for the South, men "of the deeper died democracy"; and so he decided not to accompany them on the rest of their journey.[19]

The Republican decision to dispatch "visiting statesmen" of their own was reached almost simultaneously. At the Wednesday morning conference that resulted in Zach Chandler's victory statement, William E. Chandler agreed to go to Florida to keep an eye on things in the state that then seemed most critical. He set off to Washington at once and, after passing the night there, departed for Tallahassee on Thursday morning.[20] The first Republican to learn of the Democratic "visiting statesmen" was William Henry Smith, with his many telegraph company contacts. Smith immediately warned Governor Kellogg in Louisiana. Then he wired Republican leaders in Cincinnati, Indianapolis, and Des Moines to send observers to New Orleans to

17. Telegram, Watterson to Tilden, November 9, 1876, in Samuel J. Tilden Papers, New York Public Library.
18. Abram S. Hewitt, "Secret History of the Disputed Election, 1876–77," in Allan Nevins (ed.), *Selected Writings of Abram S. Hewitt* (New York: Columbia University Press, 1937), 162; two telegrams, Hewitt to Bayard, November 10, 1876, in Thomas F. Bayard Papers, Manuscript Division, Library of Congress.
19. Charles Francis Adams Diary, November 10, 11, 1876, in The Adams Papers, Massachusetts Historical Society.
20. Richardson, *William E. Chandler*, 186.

counter the presence of the Democrats.[21] Kellogg appealed to Grant, Zach Chandler, and the leaders of several northern state organizations for support.[22] On November 10 the president began telegraphing party dignitaries all across the country to spend time in Lousiana.[23] Oliver P. Morton, still in San Francisco after finishing the campaign on the West Coast, recommended additional names.[24] Before long the Republican witnesses, led by John Sherman and James A. Garfield, rivaled their opponents in both number and prestige.[25] A somewhat less famous cast, including General Lew Wallace for the Republicans and Manton Marble for the Democrats, joined the younger Chandler in Florida.[26]

Carl Schurz, equally anxious that Hayes should be inaugurated and that the result "should not be tainted by any suspicion of unfair dealing," took heart from the fact that "men of high character" would watch the proceedings of the returning boards. He suggested that Benjamin H. Bristow be added to the list. "The verdict of such gentlemen would command universal credit." [27] At the request of Hayes, William Dennison invited Bristow to New Orleans. When Grant dispatched his own ob-

21. Letterpress copy of telegram [in cipher], Wm. Henry Smith to "Back," November 9, 1876, and letterpress copy of draft of telegram, Wm. Henry Smith to Ric'd Smith and others [November 9, 1876?], both in William Henry Smith Papers, Ohio Historical Society Library; Wm. Henry Smith to Hayes, November 10, 1876, in Hayes Papers.

22. Handwritten copy of telegram, [Gen. Forsythe to Wm. Henry Smith, November 10, 1876], in Smith Papers; James P. Root to Comley [sic], November 10, 1876, in James M. Comly Papers, Ohio Historical Society Library; telegram, Friedley to Pratt, [November] 12, 1876, in Daniel D. Pratt Papers, Indiana State Library; Lew Wallace, *An Autobiography* (2 vols.; New York: Harper and Brothers, 1906), II, 900–901.

23. The Ulysses S. Grant Papers, Manuscript Division, Library of Congress, contain a score or more of telegraphic replies to Grant's requests.

24. Telegram, O. P. Morton and A. A. Sargent to Grant, November 12, 1876, *ibid.*

25. John Sherman, *Recollections of Forty Years in the House, Senate and Cabinet: An Autobiography* (2 vols.; Chicago: Werner Company, 1895), I, 553–55.

26. Jerrell H. Shofner, "Florida in the Balance: The Electoral Count of 1876," *Florida Historical Quarterly*, XLVII (October, 1968), 124–25.

27. Schurz to Hayes, November 10, 1876, in Hayes Papers.

servers, however, Bristow's mission was cancelled, having been personally vetoed by the president. Hayes chose not to intervene further.[28] Schurz's confidence in the judgment of the "visiting statesmen" would probably not have been sustained anyway.

2

Election day in Louisiana had passed quietly on the whole, with most places of business in New Orleans closed and shuttered for the occasion. Minor incidents of intimidation were reported at first from only two rural parishes. As in most other states the turnout was extremely heavy. More than a week elapsed before it was clear that on the face of the returns Democrat Francis T. Nicholls had been chosen to succeed Kellogg as governor, while the Tilden electors had all received majorities of at least 6,300 votes.[29] Both by law and by practice, however, the ballots as initially counted did not determine the final result.

When they reached New Orleans, the Democratic "visiting statesmen," basing their opinions on the votes actually cast, announced that their party had swept the state. They selected John M. Palmer as their spokesman and had him interview Governor Kellogg and each of the four Republicans on the returning board. These meetings were all that were needed to convince the Democrats of the eventual outcome of the Louisiana dispute. Among the members of the board, Palmer respected only G. Casenave, the black undertaker, as "an honest man from his standpoint, but he thought the interests of the colored race demanded the election of Hayes to the presidency, and blinded by prejudice he was incapable of doing justice to the subject or of a decision according to law." [30]

The Republican witnesses, of course, were just as sure as the

28. Ross A. Webb, *Benjamin Helm Bristow: Border State Politician* (Lexington: University Press of Kentucky, 1969), 261.
29. Ella Lonn, *Reconstruction in Louisiana after 1868* (New York: G. P. Putnam's Sons, 1918), 430–38, 459–60.
30. Ralph J. Roske, " 'Visiting Statesmen' in Louisiana, 1876," *Mid-America*, XXXIII (April, 1951), 92–93; John M. Palmer, *Personal Recollections of John M. Palmer: The Story of an Earnest Life* (Cincinnati: Robert Clarke Company, 1901), 397–99.

Democrats that their side had won. Since half the state's voters were black and some of the whites were Republican, there was by definition, they felt, no legitimate way the party could be defeated. Black men simply did not vote Democratic by choice. Northern Republicans were therefore prepared in advance to hear that the brutal coercive tactics of their opponents had caused the adverse result. Not surprisingly, their southern brethren were more than adequately supplied with hair-raising tales. C. B. Farwell wrote William Henry Smith: "From what I can hear, 'the north' will never know the real condition of things here. The half has not been told—assassination for political opinions is so common that little seems to [be] thought of it— so I am informed." [31] After less than twenty-four hours in New Orleans, Congressman Garfield was satisfied that "the lawful vote" would give the state to Hayes.[32]

The Republican leaders of Louisiana were about to embark on the same course they would have followed had no questions of national importance been involved. The fact that the presidency depended on their actions merely served to give them confidence that they would be sustained in Washington. Hayes could not well be made chief executive of the nation unless Packard, who had received more ballots than three of the Republican electors, was made governor of the state. Many northern Republicans who otherwise might not have justified use of the returning board were willing to defend its operations if it saved Hayes. But they had to have a strong case to bring back to their own constituencies—the sheer brazenness that had served the Louisiana authorities in 1872 and 1874 would not suffice. The Republican "visiting statesmen," therefore, divided the contested parishes among themselves, "with the view of a careful examination of every paper and detail." [33] Garfield, who was responsible for West Feliciana, noted: "The papers are very volu-

31. C. B. F[arwell] to [W. H.] Smith, November 19, 1876, in William Henry Smith Collection, Indiana Historical Society Library.
32. Robert Granville Caldwell, *James A. Garfield, Party Chieftain* (New York: Dodd, Mead and Company, 1931), 253.
33. Sherman to Hayes, November 23, 1876, quoted in Sherman, *Recollections of Forty Years*, I, 558–59.

minous and many of them are made out by men who were not familiar with legal forms. But I will be able to draft a paper on the state of affairs in that parish which will show our Northern people how justly the vote can be thrown out." [34]

In a desperate effort to obtain a fair count, the visiting Democrats suggested to their Republican counterparts that the two groups cooperate in urging the returning board to canvass the vote in a strictly nonpartisan manner. John Sherman, acting as spokesman for the Republicans, refused, stating somewhat irrelevantly that his associates were present as individuals and had no authority either to represent their party or to interfere in Louisiana affairs. [35] The returning board members themselves preferred to conduct their proceedings in secret. Such a decision, Garfield was afraid, would "serve to inflame the public mind with suspicion that the Board were determined to count a Republican majority right or wrong." So Garfield and his friends devoted an entire day to hammering out a compromise arrangement under which five Democrats and five Republicans would be invited to attend the meetings of the board while the rest of the public was excluded. The ten witnesses would not have to work together, however, for they were to be admitted only as passive spectators. [36]

The returning board formally organized on November 16. As presiding officer the other three members chose J. Madison Wells, whom Sherman had described nine years earlier as "a political trickster and dishonest man. . . . His conduct has been as sinuous as the mark left in the dust by a snake." Now, it seemed, Sherman had changed his mind: "Wells was a Union man from the time the war broke out, and although he suffered greatly by it in the loss of property, he never faltered in his devotion to the Union cause. His experience in public life has been great and varied, and his capacity to discharge the duties assumed cannot

34. Quoted in Smith, *Life and Letters of James Abram Garfield*, I, 618.
35. Roske, " 'Visting Statesmen' in Louisiana," 93–94.
36. Smith, *Life and Letters of James Abram Garfield*, I, 617; James A. Garfield Diary, November 17, 1876, in James A. Garfield Papers, Manuscript Division, Library of Congress.

be questioned." Under Louisiana law the returning board should
have consisted of five men, at least one of whom was required to
be a representative of the minority party. The only Democratic
member had resigned in 1874; yet the Republican majority consistently refused to fill the vacancy. The Democrats raised this
question at eight different sessions of the board but could get no
satisfaction.[37] When the individual returns were taken up, the
areas about which there was no dispute were disposed of first.
Then the board listened to extensive testimony from the officials
and attorneys of both parties concerning alleged fraud and intimidation in East and West Feliciana, Ouachita, Grant, More-
house, and several other parishes. On December 1 the hearings
were abruptly terminated, and the board retired for a series of
secret discussions to make its decisions. The visiting Republicans
were so optimistic that they packed up their bags and went
home.[38] As early as November 22 one of them had written
William Henry Smith: "The vote cast, illegal & legal combined
as you are aware, is against us, but I have no reason to-day to
fear the result. I am in constant communication with those who
know, and they assure me that all will be well." [39]

Almost as soon as the board began meeting privately, reports
started to circulate that the loyalty of one or more members was
for sale. The rumors were well-founded. A New Orleans Democrat, following several interviews with Wells, told Henry Watterson the board would certify the Tilden electors in return for a
consideration of $100,000 apiece for the two white members and
$25,000 each for the two blacks. Watterson, who was skeptical,
displayed no interest. Wells then sought compensation from the
national leaders of his own party, only to be rebuffed once more.
Next he sent an emissary to New York to offer the state's electoral votes to Tilden for $1,000,000; Tilden and Hewitt both
refused. At last, without Tilden's knowledge, Colonel Pelton

37. Lonn, *Reconstruction in Louisiana after 1868*, 443–48.
38. Roske, " 'Visiting Statesmen' in Louisiana," 95–100; Lonn, *Reconstruction in Louisiana after 1868*, 451–56.
39. C. B. [Farwell] to [W. H.] Smith, November 22, 1876, in Smith
Collection.

entered into negotiations involving the sum of $200,000, but time ran out before an agreement could be reached.[40]

On December 5 the returning board announced that it had thrown out the entire vote from Grant and East Feliciana parishes and rejected individual polls from twenty-two others. In all, the board refused to count about fifteen thousand of the ballots cast; of these more than thirteen thousand were Democratic. In the face of majorities of more than six thousand for Tilden and eight thousand for Nicholls, the board declared Hayes and Packard the winners by margins of three to four thousand votes.[41]

Events in Florida conformed to much the same pattern, except that the election was closer and the fraud and intimidation real. Under state law a voter could cast his ballot at any poll in the county where he lived. This practice was common in the South, being designed to permit blacks to vote at the county seats under the protection of state and federal authorities. But it also made the detection of repeating all but impossible. In Levy County more than a hundred Democrats were accused of voting on the mainland in the morning and then boarding the ferry to Cedar Key where they voted again in the afternoon. The Democrats thereupon seized the Cedar Key ballot box and held it until the county canvassing board met on November 13. They explained that they wanted to prevent the Republicans from tampering with it. In Leon County the Republican inspector at one poll stuffed seventy-three miniature Republican ballots—he called them "jokers"—into the box and then added to the poll lists the names of seventy-three people who voted elsewhere in the county. Ballot boxes in Jackson and Columbia counties were found to contain a number of Democratic tickets bearing Republican symbols on their face. Illiterate black voters had obviously been tricked with these tickets: unable to read the names on one

40. Lonn, *Reconstruction in Louisiana after 1868*, 457–59; Henry Watterson, "The Hayes-Tilden Contest for the Presidency: Inside Story of a Great Political Crisis," *Century Magazine*, LXXXVI (May, 1913), 14; Roske, " 'Visiting Statesmen' in Louisiana," 98–99.
41. Lonn, *Reconstruction in Louisiana after 1868*, 459–61.

side, they had trusted the symbols on the other.[42] Because of these and other departures from legitimate electoral procedures, the true wishes of Florida's voters in 1876 can never be known. When reports were finally received from every county—and in this frontier state returns from the more remote sections did not reach Tallahassee until several weeks after the election—it appeared that one party or the other would win by less than a hundred votes out of more than forty-eight thousand.

The "visiting statesmen," accordingly, had their hands full. As soon as they arrived, the dignitaries of both parties divided up the important counties and began assembling affidavits to defend the results at the polls they had carried and to challenge the totals at those they had lost. The position of the Republicans was especially difficult, as most of the white population was aroused against them. The state party leaders could provide little help. William E. Chandler found that there were only two practicing Republican attorneys in all of Florida. One was elderly and in poor health, and the other, a candidate for Congress, had his own future to look after.[43] Three members of Grant's cabinet, Secretary of the Treasury Morrill, Attorney General Taft, and Postmaster General Tyner, aided Chandler by sending a dozen capable inspectors and detectives.[44] Relations between the visitors of the two parties were less civil than in Louisiana. When he decided that the returns from some of the counties in southern Florida were suspiciously slow in reaching the state capital, Chandler dispatched couriers to investigate. The two agents sent to Manatee County were stopped by a group of armed men halfway to their destination and were told they could proceed no farther without a pass from the Democratic state committee. In retaliation the Republican governor and secretary of state refused to disclose the official returns as they

42. Jerrell H. Shofner, "Fraud and Intimidation in the Florida Election of 1876," *Florida Historical Quarterly*, XLII (April, 1964), 321–30; Shofner, "Florida in the Balance," 141–42.

43. Shofner, "Florida in the Balance," 125–29; Richardson, *William E. Chandler*, 187.

44. Jas. N. Tyner to Comly, November 14, 1876, in Hayes Papers.

came in. To do so, they maintained, would have the effect of telling their opponents how much to alter the figures in the counties controlled by Democratic officials whose reports, they added, were being withheld for that purpose.[45]

At least two of the Republicans sent to Florida were deeply affected by the demoralization they saw around them. Lew Wallace, soon to be the author of *Ben-Hur*, confessed to his wife:

It is terrible to see the extent to which all classes go in their determination to win. Conscience offers no restraint. Nothing is so common as the resort to perjury, unless it is violence—in short, I do not know whom to believe. . . . Money and intimidation can obtain the oath of white men as well as black to any required statement. A ton of affidavits could be carted into the state-house to-morrow, and not a word of truth in them, except the names of the parties swearing, and their ages and places of residence. Now what can come from such a state of things? If we win, our methods are subject to impeachment for possible fraud. If the enemy win, it is the same thing exactly—doubt, suspicion, irritation go with the consequence, whatever it may be.[46]

Francis C. Barlow went further, abandoning his party's cause completely. As New York attorney general, Barlow had been instrumental, along with Tilden, in taking successful legal action against the Tweed Ring. In Florida, Chandler assigned him to predominantly black Alachua County, plainly expecting him to gather evidence to strengthen the Republican defense of that county's reported vote. Instead, Barlow checked into rumors that several hundred fraudulent ballots had been cast by members of his own party in Archer Precinct. When he announced that the Democratic claims were well-founded, the incredulous Chandler angrily called him back to Tallahassee and replaced him in Alachua with former governor Edward F. Noyes of Ohio. Barlow persisted in openly discussing his contention that the Democratic party was entitled to the vote of Florida, leading another Republican "statesman" to comment, "Think of a

45. Shofner, "Florida in the Balance," 127. 130.
46. Wallace, *An Autobiography*, II, 901–903.

lawyer confessing he had no case in the presence of the jury." [47] Barlow later offered "to draw up a statement of the questions involved, & the issues of fact & law, & it will thereby appear that there were questions before the B. [Board] as to which men might fairly differ, & people will see that there was not the wholesale fraud which the Democrats pretend." [48] Nevertheless, his candid remarks were extremely embarrassing to the Republican party at a time when popular sentiment about the Florida dispute was still being formed.

The Florida canvassing board consisted of two Republicans and a Democrat, all of whom were white men, natives of the South, and former Whigs. Secretary of State Samuel B. McLin, born in east Tennessee, was a lawyer and journalist. Comptroller of Public Accounts Clayton A. Cowgill was a Delaware physician who served as a surgeon in the Union army and then settled in Florida to grow oranges. William Archer Cocke, the Democrat, "was a Virginian by birth, a graduate of William and Mary, and author of several works on law and constitutional history." His decision to bolt the Democratic party and support Grant over Greeley in 1872 eventuated in his appointment as state attorney general and thus qualified him to sit as one of the official canvassers. He never actually gave his allegiance to the Republican party, however. In general, the Florida board enjoyed much wider respect than did the Louisiana panel. [49]

State law required the canvassing board to begin its work within thirty-five days of the election or as soon as all the returns were received. With the Dade County return still missing, the board was in a position to delay its count until December 6, the very day set by federal law for the meeting of the electoral colleges. On November 17 the Democratic state committee demanded that the board commence at once; the board, dividing two to one, refused. The Democrats then turned to the courts,

47. Shofner, "Florida in the Balance," 126–27, 140.
48. Francis C. Barlow to Wm. E. Chandler, December 11, 1876, in William E. Chandler Papers.
49. Shofner, "Florida in the Balance," 132–33.

seeking a writ of mandamus ordering the canvassers to proceed with their duties. The impasse was finally broken when Cowgill, impressed by Barlow's announcement that the Democrats had won the state, decided that their case deserved to be heard and reversed his previous position. In another two-to-one ruling, the board agreed to start the count on November 27.[50]

On the face of the returns it was found that Hayes had a majority over Tilden of forty-three votes. The Democrats bitterly protested the return from Baker County. There an irregularly constituted local canvassing board had exceeded its authority by throwing out the entire vote from two Democratic precincts on the basis of rumor; in the first case, it was said, one qualified voter had been turned away from the polling place, and in the second seven illegal ballots had been accepted. The state board agreed to restore the vote of both precincts. That action gave Tilden a majority of ninety-four, but it also established a precedent for going behind other returns. McLin and Cowgill soon endorsed Republican challenges to several Democratic counties involving much larger majorities, the pattern of their decisions clearly revealing their partisanship. In the course of the huge mass of conflicting testimony taken in reference to Republican Alachua County, Edward F. Noyes, Barlow's replacement as watchdog for that return, asked Republican county chairman L. G. Dennis to take the stand. Dennis said he would not, unless Noyes were prepared to lose the county. Yet the board accepted the Alachua return by the customary margin of two to one. On December 6 the Hayes electors were declared legally chosen by more than nine hundred votes. A smaller majority could more easily have been defended before the public. However, the state ticket had run several hundred votes behind Hayes, and unless they were included in the party's victory, Governor Stearns and his friends might be expected to abandon the presidential contest. A few days later Democrat Cocke encountered Republican McLin on the streets of Tallahassee and

50. *Ibid.*, 130–33.

beat him on the head with his cane. The attack was reminiscent of Preston Brooks and Charles Sumner, but the consequences, of course, were far less momentous.[51]

The situation in South Carolina differed from that in the other disputed states in several respects. After a short period of uncertainty, it became clear that the Republican presidential electors had all been victorious by six hundred to a thousand votes, even on the face of the county returns. The struggle following the election centered principally on control of the legislature, the governorship, and the rest of the state-wide offices. There were, consequently, few "visiting statesmen." Wade Hampton, running ahead of his party, announced, on the basis of the ballots actually cast, that he had defeated Governor Chamberlain by 1,100 votes. The other contests were extremely close, a Republican leading for attorney general by seven votes out of more than 182,000. Hayes was undoubtedly entitled to the electors from the Palmetto State, but the merits of the rival party claims otherwise are impossible to judge: more votes appear to have been cast in South Carolina than there were eligible voters. In defiance of an explicit requirement of the state constitution and despite repeated Democratic complaints, the Republican legislature had consistently refused to enact a registration law. It was a comparatively simple matter, accordingly, for a resident of South Carolina to vote more than once or for a citizen of North Carolina or Georgia to vote in the wrong state. The conspicuous calm of election day was misleading as an indicator of honest adherence to democratic procedures.

The South Carolina canvassing board, composed of five Republican officeholders, three of them candidates who would pass on their own bids for reelection, organized for business on November 10. Recognizing that this board would probably revise selected returns in an effort to save Chamberlain along with the presidential ticket, the Democratic leaders appealed to the state supreme court for writs of prohibition barring any but a

51. *Ibid.*, 134–39.

purely ministerial count. The justices, all Republican, responded by ordering the board to confine itself to the mere aggregation of the officially reported county totals when treating the contests for electors, members of the legislature, and congressmen. The board possessed the power to review judicially the vote for six state offices, but only the legislature could canvass the returns for governor and lieutenant governor. On November 22, the day it was compelled by law to complete its work, the board declared that because of wholesale fraud and intimidation, no valid election had taken place in Edgefield and Laurens counties. That decision assured continued Republican ascendancy in both houses of the legislature. The board then canvassed ministerially the legislative races held in the remainder of the state, altered the vote to elect the Republican candidates for comptroller and superintendent of education, and adjourned. The legislative session opened four days later. When the Republicans in the house of representatives refused to admit the eight Democrats who claimed to have been chosen from Edgefield and Laurens on the ground that they lacked certificates of election, the rest of the Democratic members walked out and organized their own house. South Carolina was about to acquire rival governments.[52]

3

Confronted with the grim determination of the last southern Republican regimes to maintain their control by manipulating the tabulation of votes, the Democratic "visiting statesmen" soon discovered they had little power. George W. Julian, writing from New Orleans, explained to his wife: "It is believed here the Board will turn us all out in a day or so, go into secret session, & declare the result in favor of Hays [*sic*]. If so we can only make an appeal to the country & go home." [53] Quickly perceiving the hopelessness of a struggle before any of the

52. Hampton M. Jarrell, *Wade Hampton and the Negro: The Road Not Taken* (Columbia: University of South Carolina Press, 1950), 87–99; Francis Butler Simkins and Robert Hilliard Woody, *South Carolina During Reconstruction* (Chapel Hill: University of North Carolina Press, 1932), 514–23.
53. Geo. W. Julian to Laura G. Julian, November 24, 1876, in George

returning boards, Henry Watterson recommended on November 13 that Tilden make a direct proposal to Hayes regarding joint measures to secure a fair count. Samuel J. Randall, L. Q. C. Lamar, and Oswald Ottendorfer joined Watterson in reiterating this suggestion the next day.[54] The reception that would have greeted such a proposition is strictly a matter for speculation. The Democratic leaders had read Hayes's skeptical remarks two days after the election, but the Republican candidate had already overcome his earlier doubts. In any event, Tilden chose to ignore Watterson's advice.

Tilden also received innumerable requests that he speak out and arouse popular opinion. Close advisers and obscure party workers alike urged the use of peaceful public meetings to mobilize extensive support.[55] A New Orleans Democrat counseled that any action would have to originate in the North, because only the North could restrain the desperate carpetbag governments of the disputed states.[56] Zebulon Vance, the governor-elect of North Carolina, was pessimistic for that very reason: "Only the most prompt and determined resistance can avert the utter destruction of Constitutional government. The South *cant* make this resistance, for obvious reasons, and the North *will* not. They are too busy making money." [57] Another southerner, after serving as a "visiting statesman" in both Lou-

---

W. Julian Papers, Indiana State Library. James R. Doolittle came to the same conclusion. See Doolittle to Wm. F. Coolbaugh, November 14, 1876, in James Rood Doolittle Papers, State Historical Society of Wisconsin.

54. Telegram, Watterson to Tilden, November 13, 1876, and telegram, Randall, Lamar, Watterson, and Oswald Ottendorfer to Tilden, November 14, 1876, both in Tilden Papers.

55. Benjamin Rush to Tilden, November 18, 1876, in John Bigelow (ed.), *Letters and Literary Memorials of Samuel J. Tilden* (2 vols.; New York: Harper and Brothers, 1908), II, 488–89; Chas. B. Mann to Tilden, November 16, 1876, and August Belmont to Tilden, November 9, 1876, both in Tilden Papers; Irving Katz, *August Belmont: A Political Biography* (New York: Columbia University Press, 1968), 228–29; William C. Hudson, *Random Recollections of an Old Political Reporter* (New York: Cupples and Leon Company, 1911), 70–71.

56. John B. Lafitte to S. B. French, November 11, 1876, in Tilden Papers.

57. Z. B. Vance to Mrs. Cornelia Phillips Spencer, November 27, 1876, in Cornelia Phillips Spencer Papers, North Carolina Department of Archives and History.

isiana and Florida, warned Tilden at the end of November, "The entire democracy of the south feel more than ever that they are leaning on a bag of mush when they look for aid & comfort from the north." [58]

Yet nothing was done. Although both Tilden and Hendricks spoke freely of the importance of popular opinion,[59] the deeply conservative Tilden was somewhat afraid of the multitude. In early December Hewitt prepared a speech containing a call for a series of pacific assemblies, "to protest," as he said later, "against the frauds which had been committed." He submitted the speech for Tilden's approval, and Tilden in turn made some changes, then "struck out the passage inviting public meetings on the ground that in the excited state of public feeling there would be violence," and finally canceled the oration altogether.[60] A month later Watterson, with Tilden's knowledge, delivered an address, which was also published as an editorial in the Louisville *Courier-Journal*, summoning a hundred thousand Democrats to Washington to exercise the right of peaceful petition before the Republican Senate.[61] Some years afterwards Watterson recalled, "The Democrats at once set about denying the sinister and violent purpose ascribed to it by the Republicans." [62]

The inability of the party leadership to develop a decisive and consistent course of action was the most crucial shortcoming of the Democratic party in the electoral crisis. No appeal was made to Hayes, no encouragement was given to the embattled southerners, no attempt was undertaken to dramatize the Democratic position before the public. This inactivity had two fateful consequences. It permitted, perhaps even encouraged, the Re-

58. C. Gibson to Tilden, November 28, 1876, in Tilden Papers.
59. New York *Herald*, November 11, 1876; New York *World*, November 25, 1876.
60. Hewitt, "Secret History of the Disputed Election, 1876–77," in Nevins (ed.), *Selected Writings of Abram S. Hewitt*, 162–63.
61. Henry Watterson, *"Marse Henry": An Autobiography* (2 vols.; New York: George H. Doran Company, 1919), I, 302–303. The speech, as it appeared in the Louisville *Courier-Journal*, is reprinted in Arthur Krock (ed.), *The Editorials of Henry Watterson* (New York: George H. Doran Company, 1923), 54–55.
62. Watterson, *"Marse Henry,"* I, 303.

publicans to carry out their plans boldly and confidently. At the same time, Tilden's (and Hewitt's) failure to assert vigorous, perceptible control was the first step in creating a power vacuum that allowed the party's centrifugal forces to pull it asunder. The Democratic party never fully recovered the initiative in the dispute.

Tilden's biographer has described the candidate's policy at this time as "watchful waiting." According to this view, Tilden's highest concern was "for forms of law, the Constitution, and the sanctity of precedent," rather than public opinion as an end in itself.[63] Presumably, the presentation of an airtight legal case could be relied on to touch the conscience of the nation, and an indignant populace would eventually bring overwhelming pressure on the Republican schemers to surrender.

The formal procedure for obtaining legal redress was less than clear, however. The electoral votes of Louisiana, Florida, and South Carolina were certainly going to be cast for Hayes, regardless of any Democratic claims to those states. The beleaguered Democrats could try to force Congress to deal with their grievance only by having their own electors meet and forward contesting votes to Washington. What would happen then was anybody's guess.

The language of the Constitution specified only that the electors of each state should compile a list of their votes, "which List they shall sign and certify, and transmit sealed to the Seat of the Government of the United States, directed to the President of the Senate. The President of the Senate shall, in the Presence of the Senate and the House of Representatives, open all the Certificates, and the Votes shall then be counted." The Twelfth Amendment, ratified in 1804, repeated the same instructions. The Founding Fathers obviously had not foreseen the situation which arose in Louisiana in 1872 and in several states in 1876. The Constitution they had constructed so carefully offered no guidance as to which body or individual should

63. Alexander Clarence Flick, *Samuel Jones Tilden: A Study in Political Sagacity* (New York: Dodd, Mead and Company, 1939), 353–54.

choose between conflicting sets of votes. In the early years of the Republic the president of the Senate (normally the vice-president of the United States) had not only opened, but counted the electoral votes, with the two houses of Congress present as witnesses. His role was purely ministerial, however, for there were no disputed certificates. By the time of the Civil War, when significant questions did arise concerning the right of the seceded states to participate in a national election, the two houses had themselves assumed the power to resolve such matters. The president of the Senate was relegated to the role of presiding officer at a joint session, performing the mere clerical duty of tallying the votes Congress decided to accept.[64] Under the Twenty-second Joint Rule, for example, either house could object to the legitimacy of a state's electors. Thus, in February, 1873, the two houses of Congress concurred in rejecting the vote of Louisiana, while the Senate alone barred that of Arkansas.[65] But the Senate receded from this rule as soon as the Democrats gained a majority in the House, and when the Democratic speaker suggested that it was still in effect, the Senate, with near unanimity, reiterated that it was not.

Oliver P. Morton sought to replace the Twenty-second Joint Rule with a measure requiring the concurrence of the two houses either to reject the vote of a state submitting only one certificate or to accept the vote of a state from which there were two or more. The Senate passed the Morton bill twice prior to the election, but the angry and suspicious Democrats voted against it, and in the House they refused even to discuss it.[66] Morton's proposal, oddly enough, would probably have made Tilden president. As it was, there was only the frustrating language of the

64. J. Hampton Dougherty, *The Electoral System of the United States: Its History, together with a Study of the Perils That Have Attended Its Operations, an Analysis of the Several Efforts by Legislation to Avert These Perils, and a Proposed Remedy by Amendment of the Constitution* (New York: G. P. Putnam's Sons, 1906), 13–91.

65. James Ford Rhodes, *History of the United States from the Compromise of 1850 to the Final Restoration of Home Rule at the South in 1877* (7 vols.; New York: Macmillan Company, 1893–1906), VII, 241.

66. Dougherty, *The Electoral System*, 91–103.

Constitution to fall back on. The Republicans argued that under the circumstances the president of the Senate would have to count. Vice-President Henry Wilson having died, the individual in question was Senator Thomas W. Ferry of Michigan, a pronounced partisan. The Democrats countered that the authors of the Constitution never intended to give to one man, who might himself be an aspirant for the presidency, the power to act in cases involving conflicting certificates. Either the two houses together must investigate the disputed returns or all such votes must be thrown out. Then no candidate would have a majority in the electoral college and the House and Senate respectively would choose the next president and vice-president —undoubtedly Tilden and Wheeler.

4

The Democratic party's hope of compelling Congress to go back of the certificates from the contested states and examine the merits of the rival claims was strengthened suddenly in mid-November by a series of wholly unexpected events in Oregon. That Hayes had carried Oregon by more than a thousand votes the Democrats freely admitted. But the Constitution stated that "no Senator or Representative, or Person holding an Office of Trust or Profit under the United States, shall be appointed an Elector"; and John W. Watts, one of the Republican electors, was postmaster at Lafayette, Oregon, at an annual salary of $280. He was clearly ineligible. William E. Chandler had anticipated that the Democrats might cause trouble in Oregon; however, not even he ever dreamed that they would be given such a serviceable pretext.

Watts and other Oregon Republicans had known of this problem all summer, yet remained unconcerned, blandly assuming that the legal technicality involved could be easily removed by having Watts relinquish his post office if he were elected in November.[67] They were evidently unaware that the Constitu-

67. Phillip W. Kennedy, "Oregon and the Disputed Election of 1876," *Pacific Northwest Quarterly*, LX (July, 1969), 135–38.

tional Convention had discussed this matter at length and had inserted the clause in question for a specific purpose. It was designed to safeguard electors against pressure from either the president or Congress. Such protection would help insure the separation of the executive and legislative branches of the government and at the same time would prevent a president from gaining a second term by threatening officeholding electors with the loss of their jobs.[68] The development of strong political parties whose electors were bound by oath to vote in accordance with the nominations at their national conventions had rendered this stipulation substantially obsolete. Nevertheless, a Senate committee composed of Henry Clay, Felix Grundy, and Silas Wright reported in 1837 that the clause "ought to be carried in its whole spirit into rigid execution . . . . This provision of the Constitution, it is believed, excludes and disqualifies deputy postmasters from the appointment of electors; and the disqualification relates to the time of the appointments, and that a resignation of the office of deputy postmaster after his appointment as elector would not entitle him to vote as elector under the Constitution." [69]

A week after the election Postmaster General Tyner accepted the resignation of Watts and of another postmaster who had been chosen as elector in Vermont: "How any people could commit such an act of folly as to elect such men to positions of such responsibility, is beyond my comprehension; but then you know there have been fools in all the past, and there will be fools for at least thirty years yet." [70] The next day Abram S. Hewitt telegraphed Lafayette F. Grover, the Democratic governor of Oregon: "Upon careful investigation, the legal opinion is that the votes cast for a Federal office-holder are void, and that the person receiving the next highest number of votes should receive the certificate of appointment. . . . This will force Congress

68. Max Farrand (ed.), *The Records of the Federal Convention of 1787* (rev. ed., 4 vols.; New Haven: Yale University Press, 1966), II, 69, 517–21.

69. *Senate Documents*, 24th Cong., 2nd Sess., No. 144, pp. 1–2.

70. Tyner to Comly, November 14, 1876, in Hayes Papers.

to go behind the certificate, and open the way to get into merits of all cases, which is not only just, but which will relieve the embarrassment of the situation." [71] The Democrats contended that since Watts was ineligible on election day, it was as if his name had never appeared on the ballot. In accordance with federal law, Governor Grover on December 4 issued certificates testifying that W. H. Odell and John C. Cartwright, Republicans, and E. A. Cronin, Democrat, were the legally appointed electors of Oregon. Unfortunately for the Democratic party, the effectiveness of this maneuver had already been somewhat weakened because the official responsible for canvassing the vote, Secretary of State S. F. Chadwick, although a Democrat, had departed from Hewitt's instructions and issued his own certificate, bearing the state seal and declaring that Odell, Cartwright, and Watts had received the most ballots.

When the electors met in Salem two days later to perform their duties, Cronin made a halfhearted attempt to vote with Odell and Cartwright, but they objected. The electors of both parties thereupon acted under a federal law that authorized each state to provide its own manner for filling vacancies in its electoral college and under an Oregon statute that placed this responsibility on the electors themselves. Cronin declared that both Odell and Cartwright had abdicated their positions and designated two Democrats, J. N. T. Miller and John Parker, to serve in their stead. Parker and Miller voted for Hayes and Wheeler, whereas Cronin cast his ballot for Tilden and Hendricks. Backed by Governor Grover's signature, Cronin then forwarded the Democratic return to Washington. Meanwhile, Odell and Cartwright acknowledged that Watts was ineligible, but they maintained that a vacancy within the meaning of the law was thereby created. The people of Oregon, after all, had undeniably preferred a Republican president. Watts having resigned both as postmaster and as elector, Odell and Cartwright therefore appointed him to fill his own vacancy. Three

71. Telegram, Hewitt to L. F. Grover, November 15, 1876, quoted in Kennedy, "Oregon and the Disputed Election of 1876," 137.

electoral votes for Hayes and Wheeler, accompanied by the certificate of the secretary of state, were soon on their way to the president of the Senate.[72]

The Democrats attached enormous importance to the Oregon strategem. Unless unprincipled partisanship ruled in Congress, the Republican scheme, they felt, had been checked. The New York *Sun* exulted:

This certificate from Oregon gives Mr. Tilden 185 votes, and if allowed to stand unquestioned, it elects him. We presume, however, that it will be questioned by the Republican majority in the Senate; but this will render it impossible for the Republicans to carry through and consummate with a high hand, as they had intended, their scheme of counting out Mr. Tilden and counting in Mr. Hayes by the Electoral votes of the three fraudulent States. When the validity of the certificate from Oregon is questioned in the Senate, the right of the House of Representatives to object to and to exclude the fraudulent votes cast by the great Republican conspiracy in South Carolina, Louisiana, and Florida, will have to be recognized and admitted. The prospect of a settlement of this controversy in accordance with common sense and justice is immensely improved.[73]

The national committees of both parties promptly asked their state chairmen to check the qualifications of all opposing electors. The Democrats, of course, were looking for more federal officeholders, the Republicans for ex-Confederates whose political disabilities under the third section of the Fourteenth Amendment had not yet been removed by Congress.[74] Missouri Republicans thought they had found just the case the party needed, but Zach Chandler frankly discounted the importance of the whole eligibility question. Missouri, he said, "voted for Tilden and will undoubtedly be so counted, while Oregon as clearly voted for Hayes and her three electoral votes will no doubt be so counted."[75]

72. *Ibid.*, 138–39.
73. New York *Sun*, December 8, 1876.
74. Daniel Cameron to George Edmunds, Jr., December 14, 1876, in McCormick Papers; circular letter, R. C. McCormick to [Republican state chairmen], December 9, 1876, in Hayes Papers.
75. Telegram, J. B. McCullough to Zachariah Chandler, November 27, 1876, and letterpress copy, Z. Chandler to George H. Shields, Decem-

5

The Constitution required that all electors cast their votes on the same day, designated by Congress as the first Wednesday in December. On the sixth day of that month, therefore, thirty-seven state capitals besides Salem hosted meetings of electoral colleges. In twenty-two previous presidential elections this occasion had been so routine as to be practically devoid of interest; but the centennial year was different.

In Columbia, South Carolina, where there were by that time two opposing bodies claiming to be the lower house of the legislature, it was only appropriate that there should be rival electoral colleges. Each college voted for president and vice-president and forwarded returns to the national capital, the Republican papers being accompanied by the certificate of Governor Chamberlain, while the Democratic documents bore no gubernatorial signature at all. Within eight days the Republican house of representatives would declare Chamberlain to have been reelected, the Democratic house would make a comparable assertion for Wade Hampton, and the state would be able to boast two governors as well.[76]

The credentials of the contesting electoral colleges in Louisiana were certified respectively by Governor Kellogg and John McEnery, the fusion candidate who had been counted out in 1872. The Republican electors had to overcome several predicaments they created for themselves. Two of their number were federal bureaucrats. Following the Watts example, these men had to resign both as officeholders and as electors and then accept reappointment to their own vacancies before they could vote for Hayes and Wheeler. After the Republican certificate reached Washington, Senator Ferry discovered from the improper endorsements on the envelope that the leaders of his party in Louisiana were ignorant of the constitutional instruc-

---

ber 13 [1876], both in Zachariah Chandler Papers, Manuscript Division, Library of Congress.

76. Simkins and Woody, *South Carolina during Reconstruction*, 522–31; Jarrell, *Wade Hampton and the Negro*, 106–12.

tion that presidential and vice-presidential votes be cast and certified separately; so the Hayes electors had to reconvene in New Orleans on December 29 and fill out another certificate which they antedated December 6. Two electors were absent at this meeting, so their signatures were simply forged to the new return. There were, therefore, three sets of votes from Louisiana.[77]

Florida also produced multiple returns. Once more, only the Republican certificate was regular in form, having been authorized both by the canvassing board and by Governor Stearns. In opposition, the Democratic electors voted for Tilden and Hendricks, sent their certificates to Washington without the governor's required signature, and turned to the state courts for an adjudication of their claims. They filed an action of *quo warranto*, challenging the right of the Hayes electors to cast the vote of Florida in the presidential contest. Shortly thereafter, when the board of canvassers prepared to count the ballots in the election of state officers, the Democrats again went to court, applying for a writ of mandamus. The Democrats wanted the board restricted to the mere addition of the figures reported in the county returns. On December 14 the state supreme court issued the writ of mandamus, a decision that had the effect of making George F. Drew, the Democratic candidate, the next governor. The *quo warranto* action, on the other hand, was lost, partly because it was initiated subsequent to the meeting of the electors.

On New Year's day, Drew was quietly inaugurated and the Reconstruction era in Florida came to an end. During January the Democratic legislature adopted a measure providing for a second canvass of the presidential votes and, after the new tally was declared to be in favor of Tilden and Hendricks, a law directing the governor to certify the Democratic electors. Drew did so on January 26, and a third set of votes was dispatched to Senator Ferry. This final return was in many respects a symbolic gesture. Florida Democrats were overjoyed at terminating

77. Lonn, *Reconstruction in Louisiana after 1868*, 462–65.

Republican control of their state government. They still wished ardently to see Tilden seated as president, but they knew they would have to leave his destiny in the hands of the party's national leaders, almost all of whom were northerners. They were also prepared to deal with a Republican as president if Tilden were defeated, and they made the fact known to Republican contacts in the North who in turn conveyed the information to Hayes at his home in Fremont.[78] These private assurances represented a prudent exercise in self-preservation, and beyond that Florida Democrats did not go.

Local Republicans, too, generally lost interest in the presidential question after Drew became governor. They thought they had carried Florida for their state ticket as well as for Hayes, and they were baffled when the two were treated separately in the count. Their role in the electoral dispute was concluded on December 6, however, and the national leaders of their party could safely disregard them from then on.

Thus, when all the presidential electors had finished their single day of official service, there were 184 votes for Tilden, 165 for Hayes, and 20 claimed for both candidates. The stalemate was complete.

78. Jerrell H. Shofner, "Florida Courts and the Disputed Election of 1876," *Florida Historical Quarterly*, XLVIII (July, 1969), 26–41; Sargent to Morton, December 22, 1876, in William E. Chandler Papers.

Chapter VII □ The Compromises of 1877

THE DEADLOCK over the counting of contested electoral votes was potentially as grave as the crisis that ensued on the election of Lincoln in 1860. Yet the sense of foreboding which characterized the terrible secession winter was never present in the months following the indecisive Hayes-Tilden election. The leaders of both parties were anxious but they were not alarmed, and the apprehension they expressed concerned more often the possibility of defeat than the danger of violence. Republicans and Democrats alike seemed to agree that in the end a peaceful solution to the nation's political complications would be found. Either a mutually acceptable compromise would be worked out or one party would accept a temporary defeat and take its case to the electorate in 1878 and 1880.

President Grant and his cabinet devoted most of their first meeting after the election to a careful review of the steps that could be taken by the federal government to guard against the outbreak of widespread rioting or even an assassination attempt.[1] When a train carrying Republican messengers from Tallahassee to West Florida was derailed under suspicious circumstances the morning after the polls closed, Governor Stearns asked for the protection of additional soldiers. Grant responded

1. Allan Nevins, *Hamilton Fish: The Inner History of the Grant Administration* (rev. ed., 2 vols.; New York: Frederick Ungar Publishing Company, 1957), II, 844.

by ordering twelve companies moved from South Carolina to Florida. But no further disorders were reported; the troops were free to spend their time hunting, fishing, and enjoying the warmth of Florida's winter sun.[2] These measures were all strictly precautionary. Attorney General Taft told Hayes, "The President is receiving every day, threatening letters, or letters declaring that there is a plot to resist your inauguration, and to kill him." Yet no one in the administration took this mail seriously, not even Zach Chandler. Plausible stories were investigated only because, as Taft noted, "it will not be amiss to be observant of what is going on." [3]

James A. Garfield, confined to his bed by a persistent cold, devoted himself in mid-December to an examination of previous controversies involving electoral votes. After completing his study of the famous tie between Jefferson and Burr in 1800, he expostulated in his diary: "I have long been indignant at the fact that in nearly every period of our history American statesmen have been croaking of the downfall of the Republic. When a party or politician is disappointed it seems to be the habit to fall back and prophesy the failure of the Republic. The same thing is reappearing in the present entanglement. I take no stock in this theory of ruin." [4] On Christmas day Garfield wrote an Ohio friend, "The political sky does not get brighter very fast and there are some troublous signs, but I still hope that we may [be] able to find our way through without a tempest." [5] Garfield thus typified the attitude of most thoughtful Americans in the midst of the electoral dispute.

For either party to have carried its strategy for victory

2. Jerrell H. Shofner, "Florida in the Balance: The Electoral Count of 1876," *Florida Historical Quarterly*, XLVII (October, 1968), 123–24.
3. Taft to Hayes, December 6, 1876, in Rutherford B. Hayes Papers, Rutherford B. Hayes Library, Fremont, Ohio; letterpress copy, Z. Chandler to J. G. Hatchett, December 21 [1876], in Zachariah Chandler Papers, Manuscript Division, Library of Congress.
4. Garfield Diary, December 15, 1876, in James A. Garfield Papers, Manuscript Division, Library of Congress.
5. Garfield to Chas. E. Henry, December 25, 1876, in Charles E. Henry Papers, Hiram College Library.

through to completion would have required a degree of reckless-ness, courage, and devotion that many members of both organi-zations could not summon. The Republican leaders wanted the president of the Senate to insist on his own exclusive right to judge which electoral certificates were valid, even though no previous president of the Senate had exercised that power in a comparable situation. For their part the Democrats expected the House of Representatives to refuse to participate in a joint ses-sion with the Senate unless the privilege of counting contested votes was claimed in advance by the two houses. In truth neither party possessed enough internal cohesion to maintain these positions indefinitely. Neither, therefore, could win the presi-dency solely on its own terms.

1

How did Tilden and his associates handle their case as the stalemate developed? Above all, they kept their wits about them. Although Charles Francis Adams thought Tilden "a good deal oppressed by his responsibility" at a time when the electoral dispute was only a week old, the former minister to Great Britain was plainly impressed with the way the New York governor conducted himself.[6] Samuel Barlow, who saw the Democratic candidate frequently, described Tilden as "calm, firm and confident" at Thanksgiving, "calm, cool and very well" in December, and "very strong and hopeful" early in January. His frail health was holding up beautifully.[7]

Having resolved at the outset on a purely legal solution to the crisis, Tilden spent most of November and December personally supervising John Bigelow and others in the preparation of *The Presidential Counts*, a lengthy compilation of the precedents bearing on the counting of electoral votes. In the "Analytical Introduction" that Bigelow helped him write, Tilden brought

6. Charles Francis Adams Diary, November 11, 13, 14, 1876, in The Adams Papers, Massachusetts Historical Society.
7. Letterpress copy, Barlow to C. A. Dana, November 23, 1876, letter-press copy, Barlow to Richd. Taylor, December 12, 1876, and letterpress copy, Barlow to Bayard, January 11, 1877, all in Samuel Latham Mitchell Barlow Papers, Henry E. Huntington Library, San Marino, California.

together an impressive array of evidence to support his view that the two houses acting concurrently must determine which votes should be accepted as legitimate. He also argued that Congress could establish any procedures the members elected to follow in implementing Article II, Section 1, of the Constitution. But what if the majority of senators and representatives could not agree on procedures? Tilden did not say.[8]

The Presidential Counts was published by D. Appleton and Company on January 2. According to Manton Marble, Tilden's foremost objective was to show that in previous Senate debates, especially in regard to the Twenty-second Joint Rule and Morton's proposed substitute, various prominent Republicans, as recently as 1875, had advocated a position essentially the same as that now held by the Democrats, namely that the president of the Senate acting alone could not count the electoral votes. This fact having been distinctly demonstrated, Tilden thought, the Republicans would be forced to retreat from the untenable legal position they had taken and must either concede the election outright or permit the House to select the next president. All the Democrats had to do was to deny the Republican claims and to wait, or, as Marble put it, "delay and debate." [9] Hewitt, too, endorsed this simple plan.[10]

The successful execution of this or any strategy, of course,

8. *The Presidential Counts: A Complete Official Record of the Proceedings of Congress at the Counting of the Electoral Votes in All the Elections of President and Vice-President of the United States; together with All Congressional Debates Incident thereto, or to Proposed Legislation upon That Subject. With an Analytical Introduction* (New York: D. Appleton and Company, 1877). The "Analytical Introduction" also appears in John Bigelow (ed.), *The Writings and Speeches of Samuel J. Tilden* (2 vols.; New York: Harper and Brothers, 1885), II, 386–450. On the preparation of this volume, see John Bigelow Diary, November 22, December 25, 1876, in John Bigelow Papers, New York Public Library.
9. Manton Marble, "A Secret Chapter of Political History," pamphlet (N.p., [1878]), 8–12. A copy is in the Manton Malone Marble Papers, Manuscript Division, Library of Congress. Tilden dictated his own statement on this matter to George W. Smith, his private secretary, in 1878, specifically to sustain Marble's explanation. See John Bigelow (ed.), *Letters and Literary Memorials of Samuel J. Tilden* (2 vols.; New York: Harper and Brothers, 1908), II, 528–30.
10. Hewitt to William E. Dodge, December 20, 1876, in Allan Nevins Collection, Columbia University Library.

was dependent on careful coordination of the actions and statements of all prominent Democrats. Republican politicians who had long dreaded their own image of Tilden, deeming him the nation's premier wirepuller, were incapable of believing that their opponents might prove deficient in this respect. James M. Comly, in Washington as the personal emissary of Hayes, met with Attorney General Taft on January 2, and the two men "went over the ground of the future, as its necessities seemed to be forecast by the present policy of Tilden—(for the whole Democratic policy is begotten, generated, delivered, nourished and 'brought up' by this one man—all other Democrats are only his implements in the nibbling and tricking and scheming to get one more vote)." [11] In fact, the other leaders of the Democratic party were never completely sure of Tilden's intentions and often had to shift for themselves.

The identity of Tilden's principal spokesman in the House of Representatives, for example, was something of a mystery, although the candidate was certainly not lacking for personal and political friends there. National Chairman Abram S. Hewitt was a member and might be presumed to speak with authority. Samuel J. Randall was chosen to succeed the late Michael Kerr as speaker largely because he was known to be Tilden's personal choice for that post.[12] Henry Watterson of Kentucky had just been elected to fill an unexpired term. And when Smith Ely resigned his seat to become mayor of New York, Tilden quickly arranged for David Dudley Field to be nominated and elected in his place. Field had voted for Hayes, but was convinced that the Democrats had won; he was expected to serve as the Democratic party's chief legal authority on Capitol Hill.[13] Yet Tilden seems to have taken none of these men fully into his confidence.[14]

11. Comly to Hayes, January 8, 1877, in Hayes Papers.
12. Frank B. Evans, *Pennsylvania Politics, 1872–1877: A Study in Political Leadership* (Harrisburg: Pennsylvania Historical and Museum Commission, 1966), 289.
13. Henry M. Field, *The Life of David Dudley Field* (New York: Charles Scribner's Sons, 1898), 270; Stanley Matthews to Hayes, December 15, 1876, in Hayes Papers.
14. Joseph M. Rogers, "How Hayes Became President," *McClure's*

Watching from the other side of the aisle, Garfield was soon aware that "the Democrats are without a policy or a leader. They are full of passion and want to do something desperate but hardly know how to get at it. They adjourned the House before two o'clock and went into caucus." [15]

House Democrats held a number of caucuses in December. At one of these meetings a demand was made for the impeachment of President Grant. The idea was deliberated at length and received substantial support. Hewitt, Watterson, Lamar, and other responsible leaders counseled moderation, however, and finally moved to refer the question to a special committee that Randall packed with the most cautious and restrained members of the party. The special committee in turn advised that no action be taken "for or against" impeachment until a later date.[16] The caucus also created an "advisory committee," composed of the most able Democrats of both houses, to serve for the duration of the crisis; but beyond providing a forum for discussion, this committee does not seem to have accomplished much either.[17]

On the weekend of December 9, Randall, Watterson, and Hewitt led a delegation of congressmen to New York City to consult with Tilden and to learn from him the role that they were to play in the dispute. The candidate asked only that they be patient. He noted that both houses of Congress had recently appointed investigating committees to visit each of the contested southern states. The predominantly Democratic House committees would certainly produce abundant testimony illustrating the fraudulence of the Republican claims. Until then, Tilden suggested, nothing needed to be done. Randall explained

Magazine, XXIII (May, 1904), 80. Rogers was an acquaintance of Watterson and Hewitt.

15. Garfield Diary, December 8, 1876, in Garfield Papers. See also his entry for December 11, 1876.

16. New York *World*, December 7, 8, 1876.

17. Allan Nevins, *Abram S. Hewitt: With Some Account of Peter Cooper* (New York: Harper and Brothers, 1935), 351; Henry Watterson, "The Hayes-Tilden Contest for the Presidency: Inside Story of a Great Political Crisis," *Century Magazine*, LXXXVI (May, 1913), 9, 11.

238 □ *The Politics of Inertia*

Tilden's position to the rest of his House colleagues at yet another caucus on December 11.[18]

Tilden talked again with a group of prominent congressional Democrats at a dinner given by August Belmont on December 23. Even Belmont's son thought this occasion "very disappointing, and without much result in the way of arriving at any understanding." [19] The next day Senator Bayard of Delaware and Representative Lamar of Mississippi saw Tilden for four hours at the candidate's Gramercy Park home. They went, as Bayard later phrased it, especially "to sit at his feet and gather his instruction." Nevertheless, beyond being shown the compilation of precedents, they went away "uninformed and uninstructed." [20] Governor Hendricks, too, deeply resented the fact that after one meeting in New York in November, Tilden "never said Turkey to him." [21]

Actually, the highest councils of the Democratic party encountered two separate impediments in their efforts to reach an agreement on a common course. The first was that Tilden, knowing he was considered the president-elect by the other leaders of the party, saw little reason to consult them. He assumed that his fellow Democrats would never question his prerogative of deciding what strategy would be most likely to eventuate in his own inauguration, nor did he doubt that they would gladly leave the conduct of that plan in his hands. As a result, when asked, he would summarize his legalistic conception of the electoral dispute and outline briefly the lawyerly preparations he was making to defend his case, but he seldom volunteered any information and never asked other party officials to join in the formulation of policy. Such a lack of communication had to produce confusion and did, even over *The Presiden-*

18. Albert Virgil House, Jr., "The Political Career of Samuel Jackson Randall" (Ph.D. dissertation, University of Wisconsin, 1934), 92–93.
19. Perry Belmont to Bayard, December 31, 1876, in Thomas F. Bayard Papers, Manuscript Division, Library of Congress.
20. Edward Spencer, *An Outline of the Public Life and Services of Thomas F. Bayard, Senator of the United States from the State of Delaware, 1869–1880* (New York: D. Appleton and Company, 1880), 261.
21. Watterson to Tilden, July 2, 1878, in Marble Papers.

tial Counts. A Democratic congressman spent several weeks in December on a duplicate collection of precedents for the House Judiciary Committee, wholly unaware of Tilden's endeavor.[22] State leaders, too, often worked at cross-purposes because of their ignorance of Tilden's wishes. In Illinois many Democrats wanted to hold a state convention to dramatize the party's demand for justice.[23] State Chairman Cyrus Hall McCormick refused to assemble the state central committee to issue a formal call for a convention and his decision was heartily endorsed by one of Tilden's aides: "When the time comes for a public popular demonstration the signal will be given from here and the whole country will act together coherently and effectively. Until such signal is given all should remain quiet and trust in the wisdom of our leader." [24] McCormick was soon faced with an uprising in his state organization. Some members were determined to have a convention regardless of party approval,[25] others were equally opposed,[26] whereas a third faction was anxious that the central committee meet, if only to avert further dissension on the eve of a senatorial election in the legislature.[27] In the end a majority of the state committee arranged an emergency session without their chairman's consent. McCormick reluctantly attended but was unable to prevent the summoning of a mass convention for January 8, Andrew Jackson Day. Colonel Pelton, almost certainly acting at Tilden's behest, wrote McCormick on January 5 that the convention "should take positive ground

22. Abram S. Hewitt, "Secret History of the Disputed Election, 1876–77," in Allan Nevins (ed.), *Selected Writings of Abram S. Hewitt* (New York: Columbia University Press, 1937), 166.
23. B. F. Bergen to C. H. McCormick, November 21, 1876, in Cyrus Hall McCormick Papers, State Historical Society of Wisconsin.
24. H. H. Finley to Cyrus H. McCormick, November 29, 1876, *ibid.*
25. Telegram, Bergen to C. H. McCormick, November 20, 1876, H. P. Shumway to McCormick, December 16, 1876, and G. Edmunds, Jr., to McCormick, December 18, 1876, all *ibid.*
26. Telegram, Jno. W. Smith to McCormick, December 19, 1876, and telegram, W. T. Davidson to McCormick, December 20, 1876, both *ibid.*
27. Telegram, Lewis B. Parsons to McCormick, December 19, 1876, telegram, J. M. Bush to McCormick, December 19, 1876, and telegram, B. F. Bergen, John A. McClernand, and C. A. Keys to McCormick, December 20, 1876, all *ibid.*

without being allowed to go off into the promulgation of extreme ideas." Pelton hoped any resolutions or petitions to Congress that might be adopted would stress the power of the two houses, rather than the president of the Senate, to count the electoral votes.[28] Other state and city leaders had to grope their way through the same fog of uncertainty.[29] On January 8 conventions were held in Indiana, Ohio, Virginia, and the District of Columbia, as well as in Illinois, but there was little for them to do besides listen to speeches.[30]

The second source of division within the party leadership stemmed from the belief of many Democrats that Tilden's approach, to the extent that they understood it at all, was too conservative, too hesitant, too passive to succeed. Sidney Webster of New York, following a series of "very free and full conferences" with Tilden, was thoroughly dissatisfied with the candidate's view of the dispute. He appealed to his friend Senator Bayard, beseeching him, "Something must be done *immediately* to prevent *drifting*, which may be fatal."[31] The possibility that Tilden might let the presidency slip through his fingers was even more disturbing for southern Democrats. The dignified and courteous governor "made a very good impression" on Representative Lamar and Senator John B. Gordon of Georgia at Belmont's dinner party.[32] But Senator Gordon was acutely distressed at the prospect of eventual defeat and returned to New York a week later expressly to say to Tilden:

I thought we were being robbed of our victory by our own supineness. . . . If these Revolutionists knew that it was not safe to con-

28. Pelton to C. H. McCormick, January 5, 1877, *ibid.*
29. Wm. McClelland to Randall, December 13, 1876, in Samuel J. Randall Papers, University of Pennsylvania Library; printed circular, H. L. Palmer *et al.* to Geo. B. Smith, December 19, 1876, in George B. Smith Papers, State Historical Society of Wisconsin; Edward Campbell, Jr., to Cyrus H. McCormick, December 21, 1876, in McCormick Papers; printed circular, Wendell A. Anderson to [chairmen of the County Central Committees], January 1, 1877, in Wendell A. Anderson Papers, State Historical Society of Wisconsin.
30. Chicago *Times*, January 9, 1877.
31. Sidney Webster to Bayard, December 14, 1876, in Bayard Papers.
32. Perry Belmont to Bayard, December 31, 1876, *ibid.*

summate their wicked purposes they would turn from them. I am a Southern Rebel & therefore can only say what our people in [the] South feel. There is but one sentiment & that is that Tilden & Hendricks are fairly, Constitutionally elected & ought to be inaugurated. If the Democrats w'd through Speeches, resolutions, the press & mass meetings let the Country know that it was their purpose to inaugurate the men whom the people had elected [,] we should at once see these desperate leaders of the Republican party forsaken by the masses behind them. If we announce by our silence beforehand that we intend to acquiesce in any outrage they may perpetrate, we only invite aggression from them & prepare our own friends for a degrading submission. Such are my opinions & they have the strength of convictions.[33]

Congressman Eppa Hunton of Virginia also thought Tilden should have taken a firmer stand.[34]

The Democrats of the South had attached so much importance to winning the election of 1876 that the prospect of defeat was intolerable. Were the loss of the presidency to appear likely, the southerners could be expected to salvage as much as they were able from the wreckage of their original hopes. R. B. Bradford, a congressman from Ohio, warned Tilden about this danger in the middle of December:

I am in intimate relations with many southern members, and I am convinced if we fail to secure them the victory they have assisted us in obtaining they will make conditions with Hayes, who has already assured them of his intention to admit them into his confidence and provide for them in the highest places of his administration. Many of the Southern States were originally whig states, as you are aware, and always presented a great opposing power to the democracy, and have recently been with us as a consequence of the war and republican outrage. The purpose of Mr. Hayes is to capture for his party that once great force in the South, and the machinery has already to my certain knowledge been set in motion for that object. . . .

I was at a gathering of forty or fifty southern members this week, and as I am a native Virginian, they unrestrainedly expressed

33. J. B. Gordon to Barlow, January 2, 1877, in Barlow Papers.
34. Eppa Hunton, *Autobiography of Eppa Hunton* (Richmond, Va.: William Byrd Press, Inc., 1933), 164, 193.

their views in my presence, and the sentiment of all who spoke freely was to abandon the democracy if there was a failure to maintain every right in the present contest.[35]

Obviously, any accommodation with Hayes would begin with a Democratic offer to guarantee a peaceful inauguration on March 4 in return for Republican renunciation of the pretensions of Chamberlain and Packard to be the governors-elect of South Carolina and Louisiana.

2

Once Rutherford B. Hayes had made up his mind that his party had legitimately carried the disputed southern states, he assumed as unyielding a position as any Republican on the proper means to settle the controversy. Carefully scrutinizing every report received from Louisiana, Hayes approved the conduct of the many Ohioans serving as "visiting statesmen." To John Sherman he wrote: "A fair election would have given us about forty electoral votes at the south—at least that many. But we are not to allow our friends to defeat one outrage and fraud by another. There must be nothing crooked on our part. Let Mr. Tilden have the place by violence, intimidation and fraud, rather than undertake to prevent it by means that will not bear the severest scrutiny." [36] Six of the Republican witnesses, including Sherman, Garfield, and Eugene Hale of Maine, stopped at Columbus on December 5 on their way back to Washington. They assured Hayes, his son Webb, and newspaper publisher James M. Comly:

It was the opinion of all the Republicans who went down to N[ew] O[rleans] that the Republican ticket was lawfully and honestly entitled to be declared elected. That largely more Parishes and Polls ought to be thrown out for violence and intimidation, than was necessary to elect the whole Rep ticket State and National; that

35. R. B. Bradford to Tilden, December 18, 1876, in Samuel J. Tilden Papers, New York Public Library.
36. Hayes to Sherman, November 27, 1876, quoted in John Sherman, *Recollections of Forty Years in the House, Senate and Cabinet: An Autobiography* (2 vols.; Chicago: Werner Company, 1895), I, 559.

a fair election would have given the Republicans not less than thirteen to fifteen thousand majority; that the intimidation was deliberately planned, and systematically executed by means of rifle clubs organized in the Parishes selected for the process of intimidation known as "bull dozing". I asked each of the gentlemen for his individual views. All concurred in saying in the strongest terms that the evidence and law entitled the Republican ticket to the certificate of election, and that the result would in their opinion be accordingly.[37]

Hayes esteemed these men highly and their answers to his questions were just those he wanted to hear. He was fully satisfied.

Thereafter Hayes heartily endorsed his party's official view of the way to resolve the dispute. He told Sherman: "I believe the Vice President alone has the constitutional power to count the votes and declare the result. Everything in the nature of a contest as to electoral votes is an affair of the states. The rest is a mere ministerial duty. Therefore it is not right, in my judgment, for Congress to interfere"; [38] and attorney Samuel Shellabarger: "My judgement is that neither House of Congress, nor both combined, have any right to interfere in the count. It is for the Vice President to do it all. His action is final" [39] and William K. Rogers: "The true thing is, a firm adherence to the Constitution. The V. P. ought to be able to finish the work at one sitting." [40]

Hayes calmly accepted the fact that such a course would be apt to produce two presidents and requested Shellabarger to consider the legal questions that "may arise after the count is declared in favor of the Republican candidates, between them and the Democrats who are also sworn into office. Such as quo

---

37. Entry for December 5, 1876, in T. Harry Williams (ed.), *Hayes: The Diary of a President, 1875–1881, Covering the Disputed Election, the End of Reconstruction, and the Beginning of Civil Service* (New York: David McKay Company, Inc., 1964), 54–55.
38. Hayes to Sherman, January 5, 1877, quoted in Sherman, *Recollections of Forty Years*, I, 561.
39. Typescript copy, Hayes to S. Shellabarger, December 29, 1876, in Hayes Papers.
40. Hayes to W. K. Rogers, December 31, 1876, *ibid.*

warrantos, etc., etc.; efforts to get or keep possession of the Gov't office and property, and the like. In short the questions Tilden can make claiming to be *de jure* Pres't, and the Republican *de facto*." [41] The Republican candidate, it would appear, was prepared to have the political crisis become even more serious than it already was. The responsibility, he felt, would lie with his adversary.

3

Yet perhaps a confrontation over the powers of the president of the Senate could be avoided—not, to be sure, by a Republican surrender but, quite the contrary, through the cooperation of certain Democrats. Some Republicans thought they saw such an opportunity, and there were solid reasons why they should have. On December 1, at the suggestion of Murat Halstead of the Cincinnati *Commercial*, Colonel William H. Roberts, managing editor of the New Orleans *Times*, interviewed Hayes privately in Columbus. Roberts professed to represent the views of L. Q. C. Lamar, Wade Hampton, John B. Gordon, and other respected southerners, though he did not pretend to speak for them. The editor wanted to know what Hayes would do, if he became president, in reference to the rival governments emerging in New Orleans and Charleston. As he later recalled the conversation, he told the Republican candidate, "If we felt that you were friendly to us, we would not make that desperate personal fight to keep you out that we certainly will make if you are not friendly." [42] Here was the first concrete indication that some southern Democratic leaders were getting ready to fend for themselves in case Tilden were defeated.

The significance of this incident should not be exaggerated, although the jubilant Republicans promptly blew it up out of all

41. Typescript copy, Hayes to Shellabarger, January 2, 1877, *ibid.*
42. Harry Barnard, *Rutherford B. Hayes and His America* (Indianapolis: Bobbs-Merrill Company, Inc., 1954), 357–58; C. Vann Woodward, *Reunion and Reaction: The Compromise of 1877 and the End of Reconstruction* (Boston: Little, Brown and Company, 1951), 25–26.

proportion. The politicians to whom Roberts referred were not proposing a "deal" as such, but merely seeking to keep all their options open. Gordon ardently desired the inauguration of Tilden, while Lamar was chairman of the advisory committee appointed by the Democratic House caucus. Hampton's position was slightly different simply because Tilden's claim to South Carolina was weak at best, whereas his own strength there was daily increasing. Hampton, accordingly, soon wrote identical letters to each presidential candidate, declaring that "profound peace prevails throughout this State; that the course of judicial proceeding is obstructed by no combination of citizens thereof"; that no cause would be given for federal intervention; and that the people intended to thwart the usurpation of Chamberlain through strictly legal means.[43] Halstead interpreted Hampton's message as "an overture... from the Peace Party of the South," primarily because that was what he wanted it to be. He was especially impressed that the courier chosen to carry the note was Judge Thomas J. Mackey, who had campaigned for "Hayes *and* Hampton."[44] Nevertheless, it is likely that Hampton was only concerned with the removal of the remaining soldiers from the statehouse, which would enable him to consolidate his own power at home.

At any rate, in his response to Roberts, Hayes was typically evasive, taking refuge behind his letter of acceptance of the previous July, insisting that it "covered the whole ground" and that "it meant all it said and all that it implied." Both men seemed pleased with their talk. Hayes noted, "In case of my election there will be further conference, and I hope for good results."[45] Shortly thereafter Roberts promised Comly, "You will find the South ready to meet any overtures of peace half way."[46]

43. Wade Hampton to Hayes, December 23, 1876, in Hayes Papers.
44. M. Halstead to Hayes, December 27, 1876, *ibid.*
45. Entry for December 1, 1876, in Williams (ed.), *Hayes: The Diary of a President*, 52–53.
46. W. H. Roberts to Comly, December 14, 1876, in James M. Comly Papers, Ohio Historical Society Library.

Similar signs of a readiness to make terms with Hayes—under special circumstances and for a price—were soon apparent in Washington. Democratic Representative Casey Young of Memphis approached Republican Representative William B. Williams of Michigan, using language similar to that employed by Roberts. He indicated it would be helpful if Congressman Garfield, who was a recognized friend of Hayes in addition to being Blaine's successor as Republican leader in the House, would deliver a speech spelling out the policy he expected the governor of Ohio to adopt toward the South as president. If Garfield's address were encouraging, Young thought, fifty Democrats would help block a separate count by the House.[47] Young's fifty Democrats undoubtedly referred to the caucus of southerners that Representative Bradford had warned Tilden about, in which case the Tennessean was mistaking the intentions of many of his colleagues. Garfield advised Hayes of this development, adding that it was not an isolated occurrence: "Several Southern men have said, within a week, that in the matters of internal improvements, they had been much better treated by Republicans than they were likely to be by the Democrats—and they talk a good deal about the old Whigs having been forced, unwillingly, into the Democratic party."[48]

In their enthusiasm, both the friends of Hayes and some of the southerners they talked with quickly fell into the habit of throwing around rather loosely a variety of figures concerning the number of "ex-Whigs" and "old Henry Clay Whigs" in the Democratic party. They also spoke freely of the "persistence of Whiggery" in the South.[49] But in fact, many of the most promi-

47. W. B. Williams to Garfield, December 11, 1876, in Hayes Papers.
48. Garfield to Hayes, December 12, 1876, *ibid.*
49. Professor C. Vann Woodward, in his discussion of "The Rejuvenation of Whiggery," essentially adopted this terminology as his own, apparently unaware that he was thereby confusing a political party (the Whigs) with an economic doctrine (whiggery) and both of these with the political factionalism characteristic of the Democrats and Republicans alike in the nineteenth century. See Woodward, *Reunion and Reaction,* 22–50. For a valuable corrective, see John Vollmer Mering, "Persistent Whiggery in the Confederate South: A Reconsideration," *South Atlantic Quarterly,* LXIX (Winter, 1970), 126–28, 141–42.

nent southern figures, including Hampton, Lamar, Gordon, Joseph E. Brown of Georgia, and David M. Key of Tennessee, who participated in the talks across party and sectional lines had never been anything but Democrats; and there was no compelling reason why Democrats should take a consistent stand on the use of federal revenues to finance internal improvement projects or any other economic issues, when Republicans were unable to do so either.

Perhaps for this reason Garfield doubted Young's figure of fifty southerners disposed toward cooperation, "but if a third of that number, would come out for peace, and acquiescence in your election, it would do much to prevent immediate trouble, & to make your future work easier." Something else bothered Garfield: "Just what sort of assurances the South wants, is not quite so clear; for they are a little vague in their expressions." [50] Although the Ohio congressman inclined to make the requested speech, he remained skeptical. "The movement of the Southern Members against the violent policy of Northern Democrats is more marked than ever," he observed on December 13, "but I doubt if it will amount to anything in the long run." [51] The "violent policy of Northern Democrats," of course, was sheer partisan rhetoric, signifying nothing more than the Tildenites' argument that the president of the Senate lacked the authority to count disputed returns.

Such meetings as that between Young and Williams could not long take place in the narrow confines of the nation's capital without the press corps becoming aware of them. Appropriately, one of the first reporters to grasp the full implications of the situation was Henry Van Ness Boynton, who possessed a well-trained eye for intrigue and, indeed, had earlier taken a prominent part in the journalistic campaign against Blaine's presidential candidacy. Boynton informed his employer, Richard Smith of the Cincinnati *Daily Gazette*, and the latter communicated the story to William Henry Smith of the Western Asso-

---

50. Garfield to Hayes, December 12, 1876, in Hayes Papers.
51. Garfield Diary, December 13, 1876, in Garfield Papers.

ciated Press. William Henry Smith was already thinking along the same lines. He had developed a warm friendship with Colonel Andrew J. Kellar, publisher of the Memphis *Avalanche* and intimate acquaintance of Casey Young. Kellar had been a Whig before the Civil War, a Union man in 1860 who served in the Confederate army out of loyalty to his state. Kellar hated the Reconstruction policy of the Republicans, but as a spokesman for Tennessee's growing railroad and industrial interests he never felt entirely at home in the Democratic party either. Since the national conventions six months before, he and William Henry Smith had been discussing the prospects for a major realignment in American politics. Smith told Hayes, "It is his [Kellar's] earnest desire to aid in building up a conservative Republican party in the South, that shall effectively destroy the color line & save the poor colored people." [52] Actually, the version Smith gave Hayes was not exactly what Kellar had said in June; then the colonel had remarked, "We must eliminate the negro & have two parties there again." [53] Sentiments so blunt would have been disturbing to the conscientious Hayes. But that was beside the point. Smith now arranged for Kellar to spend four days in Washington setting up additional contacts with representatives of the white South.[54]

When the four days were over, Boynton hailed Kellar's mission as a great success: "He was able to do that part of the work which was the most difficult for us, namely sounding certain southern men. He has their confidence & he easily got near them." Boynton then detailed exactly what was being attempted in Washington:

To a number [of southern Democrats] who have said that they thought it very important, if not absolutely necessary, that Gov.

52. Wm. Henry Smith to Hayes, December 7, 1876, in Hayes Papers. See also letterpress copy, Wm. Henry Smith to Whitelaw Reid, December 18 [1876], in William Henry Smith Papers, Ohio Historical Society Library.
53. Letterpress copy of memorandum, "Notes on the St. Louis Convention," n.d. [1876], in Smith Papers.
54. Wm. Henry Smith to Hayes, December 14, 1876, in Hayes Papers.

Hayes should publicly avow his views, I have said that it would be nothing more than a repetition of his letter of acceptance; but that those not satisfied with that, might be fully convinced, perhaps, by private assurances which they could not but deem as satisfactory. I tell them further that it would excite less opposition on both sides if the whole thing should be quietly done. That the *practical* question was to secure thirty-six democrats, who, when the votes connected with the presidential question are taken will vote "no" upon every proposition in the least revolutionary in its tendency [that is, opposing Senator Ferry's right to count]. Without the passage of resolutions which are essentially revolutionary the hands of the House are tied, & the great army of blusterers throughout the land would vanish instantly, & Northern extreme democrats, & Southern secession adherents would be laid aside together. Thirty six votes is the maximum number required. [The House contained 181 Democrats, 107 Republicans, and 3 Independents.] In the probable contingencies of absence, and a slight lack of cooperation in extreme measures by some Democrats of the North doubtless thirty votes will be more than enough. These obtained, a peaceful inauguration would of course follow—& then the policy could be openly declared & at once carried into effect.

It looks to me now as if enough Southern men could be induced to so declare themselves on the floor upon the general policy, as to give us the balance of power in the House at the time of the Joint Convention. It is not necessary that all who vote "no" should place themselves where they would be even apparently acting with republicans. They could place their whole action upon the statement that by no act of theirs should the party with which they were connected adopt revolutionary measures.[55]

It is evident that Boynton, Smith, Garfield, and even Hayes were thinking about a second, long-range objective in addition to smoothing the way for a Republican succession. This extended purpose, implicit in Hayes's often-mentioned letter of acceptance, probably originated even before the electoral dispute began. It centered around the creation of a new Republican party in the South, largely free of the influences of the Reconstruction era. By this time nearly all Republicans recognized that the Radical program of Reconstruction was no longer politi-

---

55. H. V. Boynton to Wm. Henry Smith, December 20, 1876, *ibid.*

cally viable, even though they were not necessarily sure what should replace it. Garfield wrote a trusted friend:

The future of the negro is a gloomy one unless some new method can be introduced to adjust him to his surroundings. His labor is indispensable to the prosperity of the South. His power to vote is a mortal offense to his late masters. If they control it, it will be not only a wrong to him but a dangerous increase of their power. If he votes against them, as he almost universally inclines to do, he will perpetuate the antagonism which now bears such baneful fruit. I am tangled in the meshes of this strange problem.[56]

The success of the plan to revitalize the southern Republican party depended on the affiliation of a substantial number of business-minded Democrats with the new organization. Few southern politicians or journalists were ready to make a commitment of that kind, although three who were—Young, Kellar, and Roberts—happened to have the ear of Hayes's friends. Most southern Democrats had no particular objection to the idea of a reformed Republicanism gaining currency, especially if it aided them in obtaining their own essential goal—assurance that Reconstruction would be over regardless of who became president—but they were otherwise uninterested. The eager Republicans were unable to distinguish among the differing motives of the Democrats they talked to, despite the fact that Kellar himself was angered when Lamar, one of the conservatives he counted on, pressured Representative Benjamin H. Hill of Georgia not to deliver "a great peace speech" he had written.[57] Smith vaguely understood that "our strong position is in the certainty that Hayes will be declared elected and will be inaugurated"; but he did not discern why.[58] Similarly, Roberts commented that the severest criticism of his conciliatory meet-

56. Garfield to Burke A. Hinsdale, December 4, 1876, in Mary L. Hinsdale (ed.), *Garfield-Hinsdale Letters: Correspondence between James Abram Garfield and Burke Aaron Hinsdale* (Ann Arbor: University of Michigan Press, 1949), 345.
57. Halstead to Hayes, December 21, 1876, in Hayes Papers. See also D. D. Cone to Alfred E. Lee, December 25, 1876, *ibid.*
58. Letterpress copy, Wm. Henry Smith to Boynton, December 15, 1876, in Smith Papers.

ing with Hayes came from the Democrats of the Northwest, notably those from Indiana and Illinois. By contrast, he failed to detect the eminently restrained course of Tilden's closest allies, and so never recognized the true source of concern to southern Democratic leaders.[59]

Excited as they were at the prospect of dividing the Democrats in the House, Boynton and Kellar nevertheless did not trust enough southerners to respond favorably to the seating of Hayes from purely political considerations. While Kellar was in Washington, they devised a supplementary scheme for securing some of the votes they estimated the Republicans would need. Their plan was to exploit one of the fondest dreams of southern commercial interests, a railroad through Texas and the New Mexico Territory to California. As long ago as 1853 the Gadsden Purchase had been negotiated with Mexico principally to facilitate construction of a transcontinental line along this "32nd parallel route." At that time Stephen A. Douglas had countered with his Kansas-Nebraska bill, designed to encourage settlement westward from Iowa and thus enhance the economic feasibility of a Pacific road that would follow the central or "Platte River route." It was primarily a question of whether New Orleans or Chicago would be the eastern terminus. The alacrity with which most southern politicians had rushed to support the Douglas proposal, thereby admitting that the extension of slavery was more important to them than a southern Pacific railway, had provided a vivid indication of the extent to which planter interests prevailed over commercial in the antebellum South. Now slavery was dead; the Union Pacific-Central Pacific Railroad—built with lavish federal assistance when southern senators and representatives were absent from Congress—was an awe-inspiring reality; and, as Kellar and Boynton well knew, the ambition for a competing line through Texas was very much alive.

In 1871 and 1872 Thomas A. Scott, vice-president of the sprawling Pennsylvania Railroad, secured from Congress a

59. W. H. Roberts to Comly, December 14, 1876, in Comly Papers.

land grant amounting potentially to almost sixteen million acres as a subsidy for the Texas and Pacific Railway, to run from Marshall, Texas, through El Paso to San Diego. Construction began quickly in October, 1872. Eleven months later a panic swept Wall Street, the entire economy declined sharply, and Scott found himself desperately overextended. The laying of track had to be halted at Fort Worth, less than two hundred miles from the start. Scott concluded that work could only be resumed with some form of direct cash assistance from the federal government, comparable to the loan Congress had provided the builders of the first transcontinental road. The difficulty was that in the wake of the Crédit Mobilier scandal, neither Republicans nor Democrats on Capitol Hill had much taste for propositions of that sort. Fully aware that the alternative was financial ruin, the backers of the Texas and Pacific mounted an elaborate campaign among the merchants, bankers, manufacturers, and newspapermen of the lower Mississippi and Ohio Valley states in an effort to save their project. Over the months they agreed to add parallel branch lines connecting their road to St. Louis, Memphis, Vicksburg, Baton Rouge, and New Orleans, all calculated to make the Texas and Pacific irresistible to the congressional representatives of that region. At the end of 1876, however, Scott and his associates still had not obtained the resources necessary to continue construction.[60]

It may be safely assumed that Kellar was the man who initially perceived a relationship between Scott's plight and that of Hayes, for he was himself a director of the company founded to build the Memphis branch. On his return home from Washington, Kellar stopped in Cincinnati to discuss the matter with Richard Smith, while Boynton broached the subject to William Henry Smith:

> What we want for *practical* success is thirty or thirty-six votes.
> West Tennessee, Arkansas [,] a large Kentucky element, Louisiana, Texas, Mississippi *and Tom Scott* want help for the Texas & Pacific Road.

60. Woodward, *Reunion and Reaction*, 68–100.

These are strong arguments for making that project an exception to the republican policy of opposition to subsidies—provided the aid is within proper bounds, & properly secured.

These arguments may be briefly stated in some such form as this.

1. It is fair that the South should have a road at the hands of the government, as the North has received aid for one.

2. The country needs a competing line.

3. The Texas line is below the snow line, has much better grades than the upper route, & has a better country for a larger distance from its eastern terminii [*sic*].

4. The government needs it to supply its southwestern posts, & to help solve the Indian question.

5. It has important international bearings running along the border of, & tapping the richest mineral regions of Mexico.

If such arguments & views commend themselves to Gov. Hayes, & Tom Scott, & the prominent representatives of the States I have named could *know* this, Scott with his whole force would come here, & get those votes in spite of all human forces, & all the howlings which blusterers North & South could put up. I have never had the least relations with the Texas Pacific Lobby. But I know its power here, & see or think I see a way of using it to accomplish a great good—with no sacrifice whatever of the best national interests of the country.

If Gov. H. feels disposed toward this enterprise, as many of the best & most honest men in the republican party do—there could certainly be no impropriety for some recognized friend of his, giving Scott to understand it. He would go to work without any suggestions whatever.[61]

The Kellar-Boynton plan for harnessing Scott's lobby in behalf of a pacific and Republican settlement of the electoral dispute was promising at first glance, but its apparent simplicity was deceptive. For one thing, Collis P. Huntington, one of the principal figures in the syndicate which had built the Central Pacific Railroad, had organized a second company called the Southern Pacific and offered to build a line from Los Angeles to Fort Worth entirely without government funds. Huntington was anxious to preserve the Central Pacific's West Coast freight monopoly and asked merely that his new enterprise be rewarded

61. Boynton to Wm. Henry Smith, December 20, 1876, in William Henry Smith Collection, Indiana Historical Society Library.

with the Texas and Pacific land grant. Huntington's lobbyists battled Scott's to a standstill during the first session of the Forty-fourth Congress and bade fair to do so again in the second. Although most southerners of both parties preferred Scott's grandiose system, few northern congressmen on either side of the aisle felt they could vote for it while Huntington's more sensible arrangement was available. Scott and Huntington tentatively reconciled their differences during the second week in January, but the terms they assented to would have constituted such a gigantic raid on the Treasury that their compromise bill never had a chance of passage.[62] The accord, moreover, would expire if not enacted into law by March 4. Scott agreed to terminate the Texas and Pacific at a point one hundred miles west of El Paso; the Southern Pacific would build from there to the coast. In return Huntington joined in the demand that Congress guarantee both principal and interest on the railroads' bonds up to $40,000 a mile for the main road, $30,000 a mile for the four eastern branches, and $35,000 a mile for the San Diego branch, thus making the bonds salable even in the depression. With 1,187 miles of trunk line and 1,378 miles of branches, the potential government liability would be over $223 million, more than twice the entire previous federal expenditure for railroads, canals, and roads combined![63] Boynton had qualified his original endorsement of the Texas and Pacific with the specification that the aid be "within proper bounds, & properly secured," and in fairness to him it must be noted that his letter to Smith was written before these extravagant provisions were made public.

Under the circumstances it is hardly surprising that many northern Republicans could no more see their way clear to support the Texas and Pacific-Southern Pacific bill than could most northern Democrats. Joseph Medill, an outspoken foe of rail-

62. Grenville M. Dodge, the engineer in charge of building the Texas and Pacific (and the head of Scott's lobby as well), and Representative Lamar, the floor manager of the compromise bill in the House, both recognized that the many branches were actually a serious obstacle to success outside the Southwest. See Woodward, *Reunion and Reaction*, 131; R. T[aylor] to Barlow, January 7, 1877, in Barlow Papers.
63. Woodward, *Reunion and Reaction*, 113–16, 128–32.

road subsidies, when informed of the Kellar-Boynton strategy by William Henry Smith, remarked pointedly that Smith could tell Hayes, "I do not consider the price too high for so great a good." [64] That was before he knew the full price. Then, the Chicago *Tribune* sided with the New York *Times* in violently denouncing the Scott-Huntington compact. The *Times* called it "the most outrageous job now before the country." [65] Similarly, Congressmen James A. Garfield and Charles Foster of Ohio "thought a large following might be gained for the Republican party in the South by favoring this road, and both asserted that Texas might be made a Republican State by advocating the road. . . . Both said they had no doubt of being able to build up a strong Southern following for a Republican Administration by advocating such Southern public improvements as had been granted to the North during the war." They frankly regretted, therefore, that "the Republican party was so squarely committed against further subsidies as to prevent them from advocating the building of the Texas Pacific R. R. by the help of Congress." [66] Garfield opposed the Scott bill when it was taken up in the House Committee on Pacific Railroads, of which he was a member.[67] Southern Democratic advocates of the Texas and Pacific surely recognized that the enemies of the railroad were not exclusively of their own party. On the other hand, although Tilden himself almost certainly objected to the subsidy, two of his warmest adherents, Samuel Barlow and Richard Taylor, favored the project. Taylor wrote Barlow: "Had your friend Scott, at an early period of the Session, come to you frankly about the bill, I could have so modified it, and into working shape, as to have secured its adoption. Now, you may take your account that it will not pass." [68] The Texas and Pacific Railroad, in

64. Letterpress copy, Wm. Henry Smith to Boynton, December 22, 1876, in Smith Papers.
65. Woodward, *Reunion and Reaction*, 134–35.
66. Comly to Hayes, January 8, 1877, in Hayes Papers.
67. Garfield Diary, January 11, 1877, in Garfield Papers.
68. Letterpress copy, Barlow to W. L. Grant, July 14, 1876, letterpress copy, Barlow to Taylor, January 19, 1877, and R. T[aylor] to Barlow, January 23, 1877, all in Barlow Papers.

other words, was not a very clear-cut issue around which to engineer the political realignment of the South.

Boynton and Kellar probably overestimated the influence the railroad men had in Congress, anyway. Boynton fell into the habit of describing Scott and his lobby in language as reverent as it was vague: "He knows *how* to work. I do not know him, & have no relations—even indirect—with his lobby. But I know its *power*." If Boynton knew Scott's power, he supplied no specific examples of its successful use.[69] In fact, the boosters of the Texas and Pacific had achieved their only legislative triumphs in 1871 and 1872, prior to the discovery of the manipulations of the Crédit Mobilier and before the Union Pacific defaulted on its obligations to the federal government. From that time forward Scott was consistently unable to get what he wanted, though not for lack of trying.

Hayes, fully informed by Garfield, William Henry Smith, and others after each round of conversations with leading men of the South, kept the whole situation in far better perspective than his friends. Republican leaders in Washington wished him to designate "some confidential friend" who "could be here during the remainder of this winter." Congressman John A. Kasson explained: "Some friend of yours disconnected from congressional life, & not provoking democratic prejudice, could ascertain whether any reliance can be placed on the sentiment I have mentioned, & whether that, added to the more conservative democracy of the Senate, is likely to be able to save the country from the shame of a Mexican contest over the presidency. He would be able, also, to indicate the probable spirit of your administration, if not its policy, touching questions which most concern the South."[70] Edward F. Noyes seconded Kasson's advice: "Pardon the suggestion that the Southern matter must be handled with great caution, very delicately. It will not do to

---

69. Boynton to Wm. Henry Smith, December 26 [1876], in Smith Collection.
70. John A. Kasson to Hayes, December 17, 1876, in Hayes Papers.

make one new friend and lose ten old ones." [71] Hayes, instinctively cautious, scarcely required such admonition:

Something like your views as to a friend, or friends, at W. has been mentioned by a good many. There are two sides to it. It seems to me that Comly and Shellabarger and Dennison can give such facts about my general ways of thinking and action as will accomplish all that is right and practicable. I am in the habit of saying that we can better afford defeat by the knavery of the adversary or the crotchets or treachery of friends, than success by intrigues. Of course, I understand you to mean that we must have men at W. prepared to defeat the corrupt practices of our adversaries. For this purpose the gentlemen I name can be useful, and other of our friends who may be in W. can lend a helping hand. This must be left to volunteers. For me to select and send to W. a *representative* would, in my judgment, be a mistake. Think of it.[72]

In short, the governor was keenly interested in what was being done in his name; but he preferred to remain "quietly" at home, uninvolved, "committing myself to no person or policy beyond that which the public may fairly infer from my letter and other published and authorized utterances." [73] After being shown Boynton's plan for involving the Texas and Pacific in the search for southern votes, Hayes was sufficiently impressed that even his normal hesitancy could not hide his enthusiasm:

I do not wish to be committed to details. It is so desirable to restore peace and prosperity to the South that I have given a good deal of thought to it. The two things I would be exceptionally liberal about are education and internal improvements of a national character. Nothing I can think of would do more to promote business prosperity, immigration and a change in the sentiments of the Southern people on the unfortunate topic. Too much politics, too little attention to business is the bane of that part of our country.[74]

On second thought, however, he told Smith: "I am not a believer in the trustworthiness of the forces you hope to rally. After we

71. Edward F. Noyes to Hayes, December 20, 1876, *ibid.*
72. Typescript copy, Hayes to Noyes, December 31, 1876, *ibid.*
73. Typescript copy, Hayes to Wm. Dennison, December 17, 1876, *ibid.*
74. Hayes to Wm. Henry Smith, December 24, 1876, *ibid.*

are in, I believe a wise and liberal policy can accomplish a great deal. But we must rely on our own strength to secure our rights. With firmness it can be done." [75] Regardless of how potent the Texas and Pacific influence might otherwise have proved, Boynton was unable to make contact with Tom Scott until January 14. Then the journalist assured Richard Smith:

[Scott] will go to work in the matter *personally*, & with the skill & discreetness for which he is justly celebrated. The talk we had was a long one, covering all the ground, & I am [sure] you would have been much pleased & encouraged by it. From today there will be no lack of help; for Scott's whole powerful machinery will be set in motion at once, & I am sure you will be able to detect the influence of it in *votes* within ten days. Scott is for Ferry's declaring the result without flinching, & I believe it must come to that in the end. If we can commit the South, (a part of it), against revolutionary resolutions it is the short way out of the muddle—perhaps the shortest in any event.[76]

Boynton was wrong. By January 14 there was no chance at all that the president of the Senate would count the votes. Tilden's "watchful waiting" had begun to produce results of its own.

4

The Republican politicians and journalists who were watching the South so closely believed that they could break down their opponents' majority in the House of Representatives by widen-

75. Hayes to William Henry Smith, January 3, 1877, in Charles Richard Williams (ed.), *Diary and Letters of Rutherford Birchard Hayes* (5 vols.; Columbus: Ohio State Archaeological and Historical Society, 1922–26), III, 399.
76. Boynton to [Richard] Smith, January 14, 1877, in Smith Collection. See also Boynton to [W. H.] Smith, January 14, 1877, *ibid.* C. Vann Woodward confessed that he was surprised to find two letters from Boynton to "Smith," both containing essentially the same information and bearing the same date. See Woodward, *Reunion and Reaction*, 119*n*. There is, of course, an explanation. Boynton wrote to both Richard and William Henry, addressing each correspondent "My dear Smith." Richard, not knowing whether his Washington reporter was feeding the same details to his namesake in Chicago, forwarded the letters he received to William Henry. Thus, both sets were preserved in the same collection.

ing a substantial crack they discovered in the Democratic organization. The Democratic party, however, was not unique in embracing an array of interests held together in less than perfect harmony with each other. Quite the contrary, such factionalism was characteristic of American political parties throughout the nineteenth century. The Republicans themselves were not immune.

Indications that Senator Conkling was standing somewhat aloof from the rest of his party were communicated to Tilden within two weeks of the election. J. Thomas Spriggs, an official of the New York Democratic party, talked with Conkling for an hour on November 19 and reported: "He says of course he is desirous his party should succeed, but if it is expected he will consent to succeed by fraud they are mistaken. . . . He asked me what position our people meant to assume, and whether they meant to act upon the *good-boy* principle of submission, or whether we mean to have it understood that Tilden has been elected and by the Eternal he shall be inaugurated? Thinks the latter course advisable; the submission policy he don't much believe in." Like the Republicans who exaggerated the significance of Roberts' visit to Hayes, Spriggs read too much into Conkling's words, telling Tilden, "You may rely entirely upon his *hearty cooperation*." [77] It is unlikely that the astute Tilden attached undue importance to this development, but it was surely an encouraging sign. There is no evidence that the Democrats sought to influence the sensitive Conkling directly, although the New York *Sun* showered him suddenly with unwonted compliments: "Senator Roscoe Conkling, though he is a strong partisan, has never been mixed up with the corruptions of his party. He is a proud man, incapable of meanness or evasion or the sacrifice of personal dignity to gain ambitious ends. . . . He is fearless and indomitable." The paper then hinted broadly that the political muddle "is his great opportunity, and he has

77. J. Thomas Spriggs to Tilden, November 19, 1876, in Bigelow (ed.), *Letters and Literary Memorials of Samuel J. Tilden*, II, 491–92.

the ability and resources to meet it in such a way as to make his name as a public man foremost in the estimation of the people." [78]

The Republicans learned shortly thereafter that the reports of Conkling's disaffection were not unfounded. Secretary of War J. D. Cameron and Congressman Tom Platt of New York button-holed Senator Sherman and demanded his assistance in obtaining certain clarifications from Hayes. Albert D. Shaw, consul general at Toronto and an "intimate personal Friend" of Conkling, desired a letter of introduction to the candidate, which Sherman promptly supplied. Sherman also rushed off a note to Hayes, reminding him of "the importance of assuring Col Shaw that you will come into the Presidential office with a determination to do exact Justice to all without fear favor or predujice [*sic*] and this alleged hostility to Conckling [*sic*] has no foundation whatever. He is undoubtedly a man of great ability and influence and we do not want either his opposition or cold reserve[.] " [79] When they met in Columbus on December 17, Conkling's envoy began by expressing his concern that the "apprehension" of some Republicans—that Hayes was "in the hands of the Reform element"—might cost the party "the friendship and support of enough Senators on the approaching struggle in the Senate to change the result of the Presidential election, and bring in Mr Tilden." Shaw avoided the mention of any names in this connection, but in discussing Conkling's enemies he was not so restrained, accusing Schurz, Bristow, George William Curtis, and even Morton of "bad faith" and disparaging William E. Chandler and Blaine as well. Shaw declared that New York's senior senator ought to be "offered" the post of secretary of state, presumably so he could gracefully decline it and in that way enhance his stature in the Senate.[80] As for Hayes, his reply was in character: "I told him I was in no way

78. New York *Sun*, November 28, 1876.
79. Sherman to Hayes, December 12, 1876, in Hayes Papers.
80. Entry for December 17, 1876, in Williams (ed.), *Hayes: The Diary of a President*, 58–59.

committed to persons or as to policies except as the public knew—that I would try to deal fairly and justly by all elements of the party—and talked as I always do about the South." The governor thought Shaw "seemed pleased with his interview." [81] Hayes and Shaw may have been satisfied, but Conkling, it appears, was not. Only five days passed before Shaw wrote from Washington to counsel Hayes:

For your sake and the vast interests you represent, the time has come when more than a general outline of your policy should be unfolded to two or three discreet and leading men here, who have responsibilities in common with you in this momentous crisis.

As I so freely and frankly advised you a few days ago, I believe you have it in your power to transform present doubting into courageous hope and confidence by a confidential assurance of such a nature as to be entirely consistent with your dignity and duty—and also, perfectly proper at the same time.

I see evidences of unrest here—and *rumor*—like the fabled vision of old, runs riot in the absence of assured facts. [82]

The verbal fencing ended there, for Hayes refused to elucidate his intentions further. By Christmas the opinion among Republicans in the nation's capital was "pretty general" that Conkling would support "the doctrine that the House has an equal voice in the Count." [83] The senator, in fact, adhered to that position for the remainder of the electoral dispute. [84]

The impending break between Conkling and Hayes was not the sole complication the Republicans had to worry about. Fissures were appearing simultaneously at several points in the party structure. Even the attitude of President Grant was a source of anxiety. On December 3 Abram S. Hewitt had a long private interview with Grant, in the course of which the president expressed the belief that Tilden had carried Louisiana by a

81. Typescript copy, Hayes to Sherman, December 17, 1876, in Hayes Papers.
82. Albert D. Shaw to Hayes, December 22, 1876, *ibid.*
83. J. N. T[yner] to [Comly], December 23, 1876, *ibid.*
84. Dennison to Comly, January 11, 1877, in Comly Papers; Conkling to Edwards Pierrepont, February 8, 1877, in Edwards Pierrepont Papers, Yale University Library.

decisive majority and added that "it would not be unreasonable" for the state's electoral vote to be rejected entirely, "on account of irregularities," as in 1872. The election would then be thrown into the House and Tilden presumably would be chosen the nation's next chief executive. If that occurred, the Democratic candidate "would be inaugurated as quietly as he, General Grant, had been." [85] The next day the president analyzed the electoral dispute in essentially the same terms at a special meeting of the cabinet. He regretted that Hayes could only be seated on the basis of decisions rendered by the Louisiana returning board, "whose past character has deprived it of any claims to confidence." [86]

The Republicans were horrified. Someone, they concluded, perhaps Conkling, was poisoning the president's mind. Garfield was dismayed to learn that Francis A. Stout and Ellwood E. Thorne of New York, members of the Republican Reform Club who had spoken to Hayes in Columbus, were now in Washington energetically circulating their own description of their conversation with the candidate: "I am informed that one of them has reported that they said to you. 'You are probably aware that Senator Conkling did nothing to aid your Election,' & that you answered 'I received no help either from him or his friends,' and that they express their satisfaction with the prospect that the senator, & such as he, will be ignored during your term." [87] Stout and Thorne had indeed accused Conkling and his friends of treachery, but Hayes would never have replied so imprudently. In the privacy of his diary he noted carefully, "Their facts were not very conclusive, but tended to show a lack of hearty support." [88] Garfield suspected that the president had heard Stout and Thorne's version.

Any resentment on Grant's part obviously had to be removed.

---

85. Nevins, *Abram S. Hewitt*, 337–40.
86. Nevins, *Hamilton Fish*, II, 849–50.
87. Garfield to Hayes, December 9, 1876, in Hayes Papers.
88. Entry for December 5, 1876, in Williams (ed.), *Hayes: The Diary of a President*, 54; Francis A. Stout and Ellwood E. Thorne to Hayes, December 4, 1876, in Hayes Papers.

After nearly two weeks of hesitation concerning how to proceed, Sherman and Morton arranged for Attorney General Taft to see Hayes in Columbus about the problem.[89] The governor in turn authorized Sherman to reassure the president or anyone else in the party who doubted his good will. Then he gave Taft a personal letter to deliver to Grant.[90] The moody and often bewildered man in the White House, possessed of a peculiar facility for reducing complex political questions to matters of personal loyalty, was highly gratified. Instantly he voiced a desire to meet with Hayes and suggested as an appropriate occasion the regular Saturday night gathering of a gentlemen's club he belonged to in Philadelphia.[91] Hayes, of course, declined.

Grant had previously indicated that it would be in the interest of the party for James M. Comly to come to Washington, and the editor had already decided to heed the advice.[92] One of his first stops was at the executive mansion for a two-hour discussion with the president on January 4. Comly pointed out that he was "not in any sense the agent or personal representative of Governor Hayes." There was but one topic on which he was "authorized to speak . . . confidentially, by authority," and that was the "staunch friendship" the governor had felt for Grant "from the time of Fort Donelson down to this day." He reaffirmed Hayes's desire to avoid anything that could seem to be a reflection upon the President or a censure of his Administration." Comly was very specific:

I assured the President that there was not one chance in a million that you [Hayes] would appoint Bristow to a Cabinet position in view of the fact that he had made himself so personally obnoxious to the President and to so large a section of the Republican party. The President was much gratified at this assurance, and showed strong

89. Sherman and Morton to Hayes, December 21, 1876, and Sherman to Hayes, December 22, 1876, both in Hayes Papers.
90. Hayes to Sherman, December 25, 1876, in Sherman, *Recollections of Forty Years*, I, 561; Taft to Hayes, December 27, 1876, in Hayes Papers.
91. Taft to Hayes, December 31, 1876, and Geo. W. Childs to Hayes, January 2, 1877, both in Hayes Papers.
92. J. N. T[yner] to [Comly], December 23, 1876, *ibid.*

emotion. It was plain that he had not been without the need of this assurance, and that the doubt in his mind had been skillfully manipulated by somebody. *At this point in the conversation he drew the friendly cigars from his pocket* and tendered one to me as he settled down to a quiet smoke and a confidential talk. This is the best symptom any one can have.[93]

While Comly and Hayes were immensely relieved, the interesting thing is that Grant long retained his quiet conviction that Tilden, having been victorious in Louisiana, would be his successor.[94]

Of more immediate consequence, a number of senators were said to be ready to cooperate with Conkling in abandoning the argument that Senator Ferry alone could count the electoral votes. Southern Republicans, for example, were not at all pleased with the meetings they read about between friends of Hayes and their own bitterest enemies, the southern Democrats. William E. Chandler accepted their attitude as perfectly natural: "They have no future in their states; all they can (selfishly) hope for is what consideration & patronage the administration may give them." [95] One of these southern senators spelled out his misgivings to Postmaster General Tyner "freely and ferociously." Tyner inferred, "The spirit of mischief is at work among them, with the evident purpose of driving them from us." [96] The southern Republicans were especially angry about speculation that Hayes would "fill his cabinet" with "halfway Republicans," men who opposed President Grant's "vigorous Republican measures" to protect voters and maintain order at the polls.[97] These men had potentially the same incentive to make terms with the Democrats of their own states that Hamp-

93. Comly to Hayes, January 8, 1877, *ibid.*
94. George W. Childs, *Recollections of General Grant: With an Account of the Presentation of the Portraits of Generals Grant, Sherman, and Sheridan at the U. S. Military Academy West Point* (Philadelphia: Collins Printing House, 1890), 15; A. K. McClure, *Our Presidents and How We Make Them* (New York: Harper and Brothers, 1909), 223.
95. Wm. E. Chandler to Hayes, January 13, 1877, in Hayes Papers.
96. J. N. T[yner] to Comly, January 11, 1877, in Comly Papers.
97. R. C. McCormick to Rogers, December 21, 1876, in Hayes Papers.

ton and Nicholls had to reach an agreement with Hayes: a need to safeguard their political and social futures. Senator Thomas J. Robertson of South Carolina was widely believed to have lined up with the Democrats already.

Other senators, too, were uncomfortable with their party's official position. In the course of previous debates on the subject, several prominent Republicans had declared unequivocally that the president of the Senate lacked the authority to count disputed votes. A little inconsistency now and then in behalf of a cause so vital might not bother an intense partisan like Morton, but it was unthinkable to the conscientious and deliberate George F. Edmunds of Vermont, one of the most respected legal minds in the government. On December 11 Edmunds rather optimistically introduced a constitutional amendment giving to the Supreme Court the power to receive, open, and count all of the electoral certificates. The purely ministerial functions of the president of the Senate would be performed by the chief justice.[98] Edmunds was wise enough to realize after a few days that there would probably not be sufficient time to complete the cumbersome process of ratification. Yet he was not perturbed, telling Carl Schurz:

I do not think it is the purpose of the republicans to maintain, or that they believe that the President of the Senate has power to do the counting of the votes and to decide the doubtful cases of himself. If no provision should be made by law, I incline myself to think it would be his duty to open all the certificates and display in an arithmetical sense the footing of the votes, good, bad and indifferent, so as in the presence of the two Houses—the great witnesses of the occasion—to display the precise condition of the papers—nothing more....

My own opinion is, as I have again and again contended, that as the law stands, the Supreme Court of the District of Columbia and on appeal from it, the Supreme Court of the United States would be

98. Selig Adler, "The Senatorial Career of George Franklin Edmunds, 1866–1891" (Ph.D. dissertation, University of Illinois, 1934), 141–42; Norbert Kuntz, "Edmunds' Contrivance: Senator George Edmunds of Vermont and the Electoral Compromise of 1877," *Vermont History*, XXXVIII (Autumn, 1970), 308–309.

obliged to decide upon the contending claims of the two persons to the great office in question, as well as to the smallest one known to the laws. And there at last, if we can do nothing else, is the anchor of our safety.[99]

Senator Jerome B. Chaffee of Colorado was tormented by thoughts of the political consequences that might attend his party's policy. He complained to Tyner, "We shall be bothered with public opinion if we inaugurate Hayes, and we can't afford to do it if the testimony before the investigating committees don't completely justify us; and if we inaugurate him at all, it will send us to h———." [100] Chaffee's concern about public opinion was warranted. A significant proportion of the nation's conservative Republican and independent electorate was impatient with the prolonged deadlock in Congress. John Murray Forbes described the growing insistence within the economically depressed business community for some kind of compromise and urged Zach Chandler to consider cordially Edmunds' proposed appeal to the Supreme Court. He added, "We can afford to abide by their judgement, far better than to insist on having our own way by force." [101] Charles Francis Adams, Jr., recommended that Schurz join his father in bringing Hayes and Tilden together in an appeal for a new election.[102] The Chicago *Tribune* unearthed an obscure law adopted by Congress many years before, under which it suggested a new election could be held in Louisiana.[103] Jacob D. Cox, a devoted Republican and a personal friend of Hayes, confessed to Schurz, "I am unhappy in the involuntary belief that we cannot sustain the action of the Louisiana Board, & that we are in danger of what seems to me almost fatal, the inauguration of Hayes by fraudulent returns." [104]

99. Geo. F. Edmunds to Schurz, December 23, 1876, in Carl Schurz Papers, Manuscript Division, Library of Congress.
100. J. N. T[yner] to [Comly], December 23, 1876, in Hayes Papers.
101. J. M. Forbes to Zach. Chandler, January 2, 1877, in William E. Chandler Papers, Manuscript Division, Library of Congress.
102. C. F. Adams, Jr., to Schurz, December 18, 1876, in Schurz Papers.
103. Clipping from Chicago *Tribune*, n.d., in Schurz to Edmunds, January 5, 1877, *ibid*.
104. J. D. Cox to Schurz, December 25, 1876, *ibid*.

Schurz went directly to the candidate. "We must look the undeniable fact in the face," he told Hayes, "that the Republican party is to-day morally very much weaker than it was on the day of election, and it will grow weaker still in the same measure as it countenances arbitrary acts of power." He asked Hayes to endorse publicly a referral of the dispute to the Supreme Court: "If the Supreme Court counts the electoral votes and declares the result, that result will be accepted as legal, just and legitimate by every American citizen." [105] Hayes admired Schurz too much to dismiss his idea out of hand. "Its general tone and purpose strike me favorably," he volunteered.[106] The governor, however, preferred to "drift," as Schurz put it, allowing the German leader's next letters to remain unanswered. So Schurz approached his friends in Congress instead, "entreating them to devise and urge some method, formal or informal, to submit at least the question of the relative power of the President of the Senate and of the two Houses in counting the Electoral votes either to the members of the Supreme Court or some other impartial tribunal invented for the occasion." [107]

Two days after Christmas, E. B. Wight, the Washington correspondent for both the Boston *Journal* and the Chicago *Tribune*, counted heads in the Senate and decided there were not enough votes to instruct Ferry to settle the presidential question unilaterally: "And it is scarcely probable, it is altogether improbable, that Ferry would assume such a tremendous responsibility without a specific resolution directing him so to do, and in the face of a refusal of the Senate to pass such a resolution." The Senate contained forty-six Republicans and twenty-nine Democrats. The Republicans, therefore, could afford to lose only nine of their members. If Conkling and Edmunds were committed to oppose a count by the president of the Senate—and Wight was certain they were—it was reasonable to expect seven Republicans to follow them "from Constitutional convictions,

---

105. Schurz to Hayes, December 4, 1876, in Hayes Papers.
106. Hayes to Shurz [*sic*], December 6, 1876, in Schurz Papers.
107. Schurz to Cox, December 28, 1876, in Jacob D. Cox Papers, Oberlin College Archives.

from their own record, through the influence of stronger minds, through fears as to the future of the country, through spite." The New Yorker was known to be influential with the carpet-baggers, and the Vermonter's legal opinions were usually accepted by several of the more "judicial" northerners.[108] On January 14 William E. Chandler confirmed Wight's analysis.[109]

Disheartened and perplexed, the managers of the Republican campaign struggled to hold their party together. William E. Chandler revived earlier proposals that Hayes send a personal representative to Washington, someone empowered to speak with authority to the various wavering elements and then report back to Columbus. Hayes absolutely refused: "There are several Ohio men in *W.* who know my methods of thinking and acting in public affairs. They can, of their own motion, speak confidently. Such men as Shellabarger, Comly, Noyes, Little, etc., etc., not in official position at W., and various Senators and Representatives can perhaps do and say all that can properly be said and done. All this must, I am confident, be left to volunteers such as the men I name or allude to." [110] The leaders in Washington were on their own. On January 5, five Ohioans met "to organize and unitize the Hayes strength"—Attorney General Taft, Sherman, Garfield, William Dennison, and James M. Comly, fresh from his interview with Grant. They reviewed the entire political situation and determined "to resist all defection." Dennison offered to speak to some of the southern Republicans and suggested that each man present do his part. Sherman snapped in response: "I will do any thing I can, but I'll be damned if I do that. I can't talk with those fellows—don't know how to get at them. Somebody else must do it." Taft winked and pointed out that since becoming head of the Department of Justice, he "had occasionally found it in his power to be serviceable to the Republicans of the South"; he thought he

108. E. B. Wight to W. W. Clapp, December 27, 1876, in William Warland Clapp Papers, Manuscript Division, Library of Congress.
109. [W. E.] C[handler] to Hayes, January 14, 1877, in Hayes Papers.
110. Wm. E. Chandler to Hayes, December 29, 1876, and Hayes to Wm. E. Chandler, December 31, 1876, both *ibid.*

might have some influence with them. As for Conkling, who was all but given up as lost, "it was thought best to combine a delicate appreciation of his commanding character, with a somewhat robust intimation how easily such talents might be lost to the Republican party and sent into retirement by too much deliberation over the difficulties of counting the vote." [111] Three days later a score of Republicans gathered at Sherman's house. They were supposed to draft a common strategy for the party to follow until the count, but being unable to agree on what the Democrats were going to do, they made little progress.[112] Before a week was over, the two Chandlers were seeking to bring together still another conference, and Garfield was "appointed as one of six of Hayes' friends to confer with doubtful Senators, and confirm their courage." [113] The Republicans were plainly wandering in circles of confusion. They resolved on courses of action they lacked the means to carry into effect. But it probably did not matter. A solution to the electoral dispute was already being improvised by the moderates of both parties in Congress.

5

The concept of an electoral commission, "a tribunal to whom may be referred at once, *without debate* or excitement, all disputed points," [114] was discussed as soon as it was clear the outcome of the election would be contested. On December 7, three days after the new session of Congress convened, Republican Representative George W. McCrary of Iowa introduced a resolution providing for the appointment of a special committee of the House to prepare "such a measure, either legislative or constitutional, as may in their judgment be best calculated" to

111. Comly to Hayes, January 8, 1877, *ibid.*; Garfield Diary, January 5, 1877, in Garfield Papers.
112. Dennison to Comly, January 9, 11, 1877, in Comly Papers.
113. Wm. E. Chandler to Hayes, January 13, 1877, in Hayes Papers; Garfield Diary, January 14, 1877, in Garfield Papers.
114. William P. Craighill to George W. Morgan, November 24, 1876, in Bigelow (ed.), *Letters and Literary Memorials of Samuel J. Tilden,* II, 495–96.

settle the crisis. McCrary's resolution frankly recognized the existence of grave "differences of opinion as to the proper mode of counting the electoral votes for President and Vice-President, and as to the manner of determining questions that may arise as to the legality and validity of returns made of such votes by the several States." It specifically suggested "a tribunal whose authority none can question and whose decision all will accept as final." The Judiciary Committee reported favorably on the idea a week later and the resolution was adopted by the full House without debate. Speaker Randall named Henry B. Payne of Ohio chairman of the committee. Eppa Hunton, Abram S. Hewitt, and William M. Springer of Illinois were the other Democrats chosen; McCrary, George F. Hoar of Massachusetts, and George Willard of Michigan were the Republicans.

Senator Edmunds on December 15 proposed the creation of a similar committee by the upper chamber to act in cooperation with its House counterpart. His resolution also passed without visible opposition. Senator Ferry appointed Edmunds chairman and designated Republicans Oliver P. Morton, Frederick T. Frelinghuysen of New Jersey, and John A. Logan of Illinois, and Democrats Allen G. Thurman, Thomas F. Bayard, and Matthew W. Ransom of North Carolina as the other members.[115] Logan was fighting an uphill battle for reelection in his state's legislature at the time and asked to be excused from service "on condition that a reliable Republican shd. be put in his place." Morton and Ferry approved, Logan resigned from the committee, and "after consulting many Senators" Ferry selected Conkling for the vacant position. Sherman protested this action, but when Ferry offered to appoint him instead, the Ohioan refused on the ground that it would be "impolitic." Comly wondered "whether C. might not resent being second choice, after Logan declined— and the general opinion was that he would." But Ferry thought

115. Milton Harlow Northrup, "A Grave Crisis in American History: The Inner History of the Origin and Formation of the Electoral Commission of 1877," *Century Magazine*, LXII (October, 1901), 924.

"it would have a good effect to put C. on, and give him a recognition, as well as interest him in the inquiry." [116]

The special committees were completed just before Congress took its regular two-week holiday recess, and they did not assemble until January 3. In the interim most of their members occupied themselves with an intensive study of the precedents for counting the electoral votes. When the committees at last began meeting separately on a daily basis, they continued to make little headway, devoting most of their time to a rehash of the very procedural questions which had already deadlocked Congress itself. The only noteworthy development was Conkling's unqualified statement that Ferry could not count the votes on his own.[117] Finally, on January 10, McCrary and Edmunds once more seized the initiative, simultaneously presenting to their respective panels slightly different plans for referring the whole range of controverted issues to a commission independent of Congress. This tribunal's judgments would be binding unless both houses concurred in overruling them—an entirely unlikely possibility. McCrary proposed that the commission consist of Chief Justice Morrison R. Waite and an unspecified number of associate justices, and Edmunds advised the inclusion of senators and representatives as well. The Democratic majority on the House committee insisted on two changes in the McCrary formula. They wanted the concurrence of the Senate and House to be required for the acceptance of a decision of the commission, rather than for its rejection, thus making that body's rulings merely advisory; and they stipulated that Waite, whose pronounced Republican sympathies were notorious, must be excluded from the tribunal. The Democrats preferred the neat political balance provided by taking the five senior associate justices: Republicans Noah H. Swayne and Samuel F. Miller, Democrats Nathan Clifford and Stephen J. Field, and David

116. Wm. Henry Smith to Hayes, December 30, 1876, Sherman to Hayes, January 3, 1876 [1877], and Comly to Hayes, January 8, 1877, all in Hayes Papers.
117. Sherman to Hayes, January 3, 1876 [1877], *ibid.*

Davis, the former ally of Abraham Lincoln who was now studiously independent. By January 12 the special committees were ready to meet with each other.[118]

Payne, as chairman of the House group, moved that the revised McCrary plan be substituted for that of Edmunds, but his motion lost on a tie vote, seven to seven. The Democrats of both committees then turned to the task of altering the scheme developed by the Republican senators.[119] That design called for a thirteen-member tribunal composed of the four senior associate justices—Clifford, Swayne, Davis, and Miller—and nine members of Congress, obtained by allowing each house to nominate five men, with one to be dropped by lot. The Democrats objected to the application of chance in the selection of the congressional contingent. An impasse was avoided by expanding the commission to fifteen men, keeping all ten from the legislative branch, and making the judicial allotment five. With the congressional membership expected to be evenly divided politically, the composition of the Supreme Court delegation assumed the same importance it had had under the House draft. On Saturday, January 13, agreement was almost reached on a proposal to take the six senior associate justices—three Republicans, two Democrats, and Davis—and eliminate one by lot. Representative Springer, however, was not sure he liked that arrangement and requested two days to think it over. The other committeemen tried to persuade him but Springer was adamant; so a final decision was postponed until Monday. During the weekend, word of the emerging compromise was leaked to the press.[120]

That weekend, too, Hewitt hurried to New York to consult Tilden. Manton Marble later claimed that he was present at this Sunday conference. Hewitt explicitly denied his statement, yet Tilden just as explicitly supported it. John Bigelow was also there at least part of the time. At any rate, it was on this

---

118. Northrup, "A Grave Crisis in American History," 924–26.
119. Hunton, *Autobiography*, 165.
120. Northrup, "A Grave Crisis in American History," 926–27.

occasion that Tilden, who had received a copy of the McCrary plan only the previous day, first learned of the more elaborate Edmunds proposal. The candidate was unhappy, even angry. He realized that some form of arbitration might become necessary, but the work of the House and Senate committees was "too precipitate." The count would not begin until the second Wednesday in February, which in 1877 was the fourteenth, still a month away. "The fears of collision are exaggerated. And why surrender now? You can always surrender. That is all you have to do after being beaten. Why surrender before the battle, for fear of having to surrender after the battle is over?" Tilden nevertheless agreed to discuss the details of the bill. He objected most strenuously to the "six judge plan" with its provision for drawing straws: "I may lose the Presidency, but I will not raffle for it." In addition he wanted the commission's power to go behind the disputed returns and examine the merits of each case carefully defined in the law. Tilden was annoyed that congressional consideration of the tribunal had proceeded so far in secret before he was informed. Hewitt assured him that the Democratically controlled House committee would not act on the compromise unless Tilden approved. The Democrats on the Senate committee, on the other hand, had already spoken in favor of the bill and would concur in reporting it regardless of what Tilden or the House panel decided. "Is it not rather late, then, to consult me?" asked Tilden. "They do not consult you," Hewitt replied. "They are public men and have their own duties and responsibilities. I consult you." [121]

Hewitt was back in Washington on Monday, January 15, when the joint committee resumed its discussion. Payne announced that the Democrats could no longer accept the "six judge plan" and suggested instead the final "five judge plan" of the House

121. Hewitt, "Secret History of the Disputed Election, 1876–77," in Nevins (ed.), *Selected Writings of Abram S. Hewitt*, 167–68; memorandum dictated by Tilden to George W. Smith [1878?], in Bigelow (ed.), *Letters and Literary Memorials of Samuel J. Tilden*, II, 528–32; Marble, "A Secret Chapter of Political History," 15–20; John Bigelow Diary, January 18, 1877, in Bigelow Papers.

committee and its meticulous political balance. The Republicans stood firm. The next day Payne offered a concession in exchange for the "five judge plan": the Democrats would reverse themselves and consent to language which would make the decisions of the tribunal binding. McCrary, who had helped write it, now had reservations about the "five judge plan," however: "I have a high opinion of the Supreme Court. The proposition to have five judges alone, as originally contained in the House bill, is very different from having them mixed up with a committee of partisans from the House and Senate." Hewitt agreed: "I should be very glad, for my part, to have the Senate and House left out altogether, and to submit the whole question to the five judges, and make their decision final, unless overruled by the concurrent vote of both houses." McCrary said he regretted that such a proposition probably could not be passed. In the afternoon, Conkling advanced a "four judge plan"—he would appoint the four senior associate justices and let them choose the fifth. Conkling thus omitted Field, fifth in seniority, and counted Davis as a Democrat. The majority on the House committee was unimpressed. After all, Payne pointed out, Davis was the candidate of the Greenbackers against the Democrats in the senatorial election being conducted that very day in the Illinois legislature.

Then, on Wednesday, Edmunds pieced together an arrangement satisfactory to both committees. He proposed to designate Justices Clifford, Field, Miller, and William Strong, two Democrats and two Republicans, by their circuits and empower them to select the fifth judge and fifteenth member of the commission, whom everybody assumed would be Davis. This was the "five judge plan" in disguise. In return the Democrats acceded to a wording which permitted the commission itself to determine whether it could go behind the disputed returns. This version of the bill, Thurman noted, "creates no new power, but submits all disputes to this tribunal with the same powers, no more, no less, that belong to Congress jointly or severally. It is as near a non-committal bill, as to disputed questions, as could be made." The concurrence of the House and Senate would be necessary to reverse a decision. To give the electoral commission sufficient time to consider each contested state, the date for commencing the count was moved forward to February 1.[122]

Tilden was kept abreast of these negotiations by telegraph. He made several recommendations for improving the judicial composition of the tribunal and repeatedly urged "more opportunity for deliberation and consultation." He remained opposed to what he believed to be a premature resort to compromise. Yet he did not make his views in this regard distinctly clear to Hewitt or to the other Democrats on the House committee. His most astute comment was transmitted only after the Edmunds formula had been agreed to: "Nothing but great and certain public danger not to be escaped in any other way could excuse such a measure. We are overpressed by exaggerated fears and forget that the other side will have greater troubles than we unless relieved by some agreement. They have no way out but by usurpation; are bullying us with what they dare not do or will break down in attempting." [123] Eppa Hunton delayed the signing of the joint committee's report in an effort to learn Tilden's wishes. But the only information he could get from Colonel Pelton, who was in Washington, was the comment, "His uncle wanted a better bill." [124] Tilden apparently felt that his leadership role had been largely taken from him. After talking to the candidate, Samuel Barlow agreed that he was "in the hands of this Committee & whatever is done, must be assented to as well done." [125] That was the price that

122. Northrup, "A Grave Crisis in American History," 927–32.
123. Hewitt, "Secret History of the Disputed Election, 1876–77," in Nevins (ed.), *Selected Writings of Abram S. Hewitt,* 168–69; memorandum dictated by Tilden to George W. Smith [1878?], in Bigelow (ed.), *Letters and Literary Memorials of Samuel J. Tilden,* II, 532–35; Marble, "A Secret Chapter of Political History," 21–22.
124. Hunton, *Autobiography,* 169; typescript copy, Hewitt to Eppa Hunton, February 18, 1888, in Abram Stevens Hewitt Papers, Cooper Union Library.
125. Letterpress copy, Barlow to W. H. Taylor, January 18, 1877, in Barlow Papers. W. H. Taylor was Barlow's law clerk. Barlow probably meant to address this letter to Richard Taylor, who had been writing him frequently. This interpretation is supported by the fact that Barlow saluted his correspondent as "General."

had to be paid for too readily discounting the possibility that the Democratic leaders in Congress might seek their own solution to the crisis. In the end everyone but Morton signed the report. As soon as the details of the electoral compromise were revealed, Democrats and Republicans alike found themselves badly divided by the proposal. On the Democratic side, the New York *Sun* hesitantly endorsed the idea on the theory that if Morton was against it, it must be all right. Only after the bill had been adopted did the paper do a full about-face in its editorial stance.[126] The *World* was constant in its emphatic expressions of support.[127] By contrast, Montgomery Blair's Washington *Union*, established specifically to defend Tilden's cause, was consistently hostile.[128] August Belmont and Samuel Barlow noted that the New York financial community was grateful for any speedy, peaceful resolution of the long and unsettling impasse which was distracting people from normal business pursuits.[129] Among Tilden's advisers, Bigelow and Watterson opposed the plan.[130] Hewitt was one of its authors. In Indianapolis, Thomas A. Hendricks told the press of his hearty approval.[131] Richard Taylor and Montgomery Blair thought Senators Thurman and Bayard had worked for the commission because they "have never been reconciled to Tilden's nomination —deeming themselves much better entitled to the confidence and leadership of the Party." Taylor, a Louisianan, warned that if the Democrats in Congress voted for the arbitration "juggle" and the tribunal then decided in favor of Hayes, "the entire south will instantly make terms with the Republicans [.]

126. New York *Sun*, January 23, 24, 25, 26, 27, 29, 31, February 1, 1877.
127. New York *World*, January 18, 24, 25, 1877.
128. William Ernest Smith, *The Francis Preston Blair Family in Politics* (2 vols.; New York: Macmillan Company, 1933), II, 482–84.
129. [August] B[elmont] to Marble [January 14, 1877], in Marble Papers; letterpress copy, Barlow to Richd. Taylor, January 19, 1877, in Barlow Papers.
130. John Bigelow Diary, January 18, 1877, in Bigelow Papers; Watterson, *"Marse Henry": An Autobiography* (2 vols.; New York: George H. Doran Company, 1919), I, 307.
131. New York *World*, January 21, 1877.

T'would be their only hope and I should earnestly advise that course." [132]

Taylor's only consolation was that the Republicans were also split by the issue: "The more moderate part of the Rad. [Radical] Party is hopelessly sundered from the extremists." [133] Taylor was right, although the schism did not occur along traditional radical-conservative lines as he implied. Sherman, Garfield, William Dennison, and Edward F. Noyes all fought the enactment of the compromise. Dennison was indignant because the measure "amounts to the giving a certainty for an uncertainty." [134] William Henry Smith asked Sherman whether the friends of Justices Miller and Strong could prevail on those gentlemen to refuse service on the commission.[135] On the other hand, President Grant, backed by the eloquence of Secretary of State Hamilton Fish, resolutely defended the tribunal and helped obtain Republican votes for it.[136] The Indianapolis Board of Trade rebuked Morton for his opposition.[137] William E. Chandler concluded realistically: "We shall have to take the Grand National Canvassing Board with whatever result comes from it. The pressure for some measure of relief is great, and above all is the practical difficulty if we do not pass it, that a majority of Senators do not hold that the President of the Senate can count the votes. What then should we do? Ferry could not count without the support of a majority of either House." Chandler added that he was already engaged in prepar-

132. R. T[aylor] to Barlow, January 14, 16, 1877, in Barlow Papers; John White Stevenson Diary, January 15, 1877, in John White Stevenson Papers, University of Kentucky Library.
133. R. T[aylor] to Barlow, January 23, 1877, in Barlow Papers.
134. Dennison to Hayes, January 20, 1877, Sherman to Hayes, January 18, 1877, and Garfield to Hayes, January 19, 1877, all in Hayes Papers; Noyes to [W. E.] Chandler, January 24, 1877, in William E. Chandler Papers.
135. Letterpress copy, Wm. Henry Smith to Sherman, January 20, 1877, in Smith Papers.
136. Nevins, *Hamilton Fish*, II, 855–56; Hamilton Fish to John A. Dix, January 23, 1877, and Fish to Hamilton Fish, Jr., January 29, 1877, both in Hamilton Fish Papers, Manuscript Division, Library of Congress.
137. R. S. Foster and H. A. Milton to Morton, January 23, 1877, in Oliver P. Morton Papers, Indiana State Library.

ing the legal arguments the Republicans would employ before the "Grand National Canvassing Board." [138] Carl Schurz pleaded in a series of long, impassioned letters that Hayes must not resist the compromise:

Whatever their views and wishes may have been before,—now that a measure like this, agreed upon by the foremost men of the Senate and the House, is before Congress and the country, with that popular support which springs from a general demand for a just and impartial decision, your friends ought to understand, that you cannot afford, even by implication, to appear hostile to this settlement,— just as, by the way, they ought to have understood, when at New Orleans, that, as your friends, it was their imperative duty to insist, with all the influence at their disposal, upon the appointment of a democratic member of the Returning Board, according to the statute of the State, so as to take away from the proceedings of that Board their exclusive and therefore so suspicious partisan character. If the Conference bill should fail by Republican opposition, and you then be declared elected by the President of the Senate, the sentiment of the country will be so overwhelmingly against you, that, if the House sets up Tilden as a Counter-President, as it then will certainly do, it will be no mere puppet-show.[139]

Congressman Charles Foster, who represented Hayes's district, essentially agreed with the reasoning used by Schurz and supported the compromise.[140] But Hayes did not. The governor's explanation, given the gravity of the situation, provided a telling indication of the smallness of his mind: "The leading constitutional objection to it, perhaps, is that the appointment of the Commission by Act of Congress violates that part of the Constitution which gives the appointment of all other officers 'to the President. ['] " [141]

No one regretted the report of the joint committee more than

138. Wm. E. Chandler to [A. E. Lee(?), January 24, 1877], in Hayes Papers.
139. Schurz to Hayes, January 12, 21, 1877, *ibid.*
140. C. Foster to Hayes, January 21, 1877, *ibid.*
141. Entry for January 21, 1877, in Williams (ed.), *Hayes: The Diary of a President*, 69–70. See also typescript copy, Hayes to Sherman, January 21, 1877, in Hayes Papers; and Hayes to Shurz [*sic*], January 23, 1877, in Schurz Papers.

did the self-appointed intermediaries who had been energetically scurrying between certain southern Democrats, various friends of Hayes, and the associates of Tom Scott. The pressure for a settlement which had given their intricate diplomacy an air of importance, of urgency even, was at once relaxed and the incentive for reaching an agreement across party lines significantly lessened. Scott's legislative program was dealt another setback. After investing so much effort in it, Boynton may be excused for believing that his own plan for inaugurating Hayes was the best. He told Comly: "If the knowledge which a few of us possessed could have been imparted to all republicans, I think we could still have held them up to a count by Ferry, & could have put it through without violence from the democrats [.] But the matters to which I refer & of which you know were not such as could be trusted outside of a narrow circle." [142]

The extent to which the electoral commission bill became a Democratic measure was apparent on January 26 as the members of Congress filed past the tellers on the issue of final passage. Still in session from the previous day, the Senate acted in the early hours of the morning, adopting the bill 47 to 17. Republicans favored the proposal 24 to 16, Democrats 23 to 1. In the afternoon the margin of approval in the House was 191 to 86. A majority of the Republicans, 68 to 33, voted against arbitration, but they were overwhelmed by the Democrats who supported the compromise 158 to 18.[143] In the two Houses together, 57 Republicans voted for the commission and 84 against, 181 Democrats for and 19 against.

6

It was during the closing hours of debate on the commission in the Senate that word of one of the strangest events of the

142. Boynton to Comly, January 25, 1877, in Hayes Papers.
143. *Congressional Record*, 44th Cong., 2nd Sess., Vol. V, Pt. 2, pp. 913, 1050. The *Record* does not give party affiliations. This information was obtained from the biographical section of Ben: Perley Poore, *Congressional Directory, Compiled for the Use of Congress* (Washington: Government Printing Office, 1877), 44th Cong., 2nd Sess., 5–72.

electoral crisis reached Washington. Agreement on a compromise bill had been possible only because David Davis of Illinois, reputedly independent, was available as the fifth justice on the tribunal. The legislation had been so written as virtually to compel his selection. The matter was especially crucial to the Democrats. Beyond Davis and the two Democratic justices already designated in the bill, there was no other member of the Supreme Court whose political complexion suited them; yet on January 25 Davis was elected to the United States Senate by the Illinois legislature, with most of his backing coming from Democrats. The prospect was suddenly raised that he would not serve on the commission. At the very moment when many Democrats thought their chances were brightest, their optimism was rudely shattered.

How could such a disastrous breakdown in party strategy occur? In his "Secret History" of the election dispute, Hewitt offered no explanation other than the comment that Davis was chosen by the Democrats "reinforced by 7 Republican votes." [144] A check of the *Journals* of the Illinois legislature reveals that even this intriguing hint was inaccurate. On the decisive fortieth ballot every Democrat save two who were absent voted for Davis. They were joined by eight Greenbackers to provide the simple majority required. While the Republicans were divided, none cast his vote for Davis.[145] The justice himself did not seek the Senate seat,[146] although he was the first choice of

144. Hewitt, "Secret History of the Disputed Election, 1876–77," in Nevins (ed.), *Selected Writings of Abram S. Hewitt*, 171.

145. *Journal of the House of Representatives of the Thirtieth General Assembly of the State of Illinois, Begun and Held at Springfield, January 3, 1877* (Springfield: D. W. Lusk, 1877), 8–10, 149–50; *Journal of the Senate of the Thirtieth General Assembly of the State of Illinois, Begun and Held at Springfield, January 3, 1877* (Springfield: D. W. Lusk, 1877), 1, 7–8, 83–84, 217. Party affiliations are not given in these journals and no such listing is readily available. However, by examining the votes to organize each house at the start of the session, votes which are on a strict party line basis, such affiliations can be rather easily determined.

146. Photostat, James E. Harvey to Mrs. David Davis, March 17, 1887, in David Davis Papers, Chicago Historical Society Library. Harvey was a close friend of Davis and was his personal secretary during his term in the Senate. He wrote this letter in an effort to clear up the justice's

the few Greenbackers. The question is why the Democrats threw their support to him on January 24 and 25, following nearly two weeks of indecisive balloting.

The same day the Democrats began swinging their votes to Davis, William Henry Smith wrote an irate letter to Hayes: "The hand of Mr. Tilden has been seen in Illinois politics for two weeks past, in urging Democratic members of the Legislature to take up Judge David Davis for Senator. The plan [came] near being successful today and may be entirely so tomorrow. This is a part of the scheme to capture the Presidency through the Commission of Arbitration. Davis elected to the Senate by Democratic votes wd. feel under obligation, as the fifth judge, to give the Presidency to Tilden." [147] It is inconceivable that Tilden himself would have condoned such a scheme. A transparent attempt to prejudice the commission would have completely destroyed the image of moral righteousness he had worked so hard to create. But could one of his lieutenants have been behind the maneuver? It seems so.

Cyrus Hall McCormick was told in November that should he seek the Illinois Senate seat, he would have Tilden's encouragement. In December, Colonel Pelton volunteered the services of Henry H. Finley to help organize McCormick's campaign.[148] Although the wealthy industrialist decided not to run, he did send for Finley on January 3 when the Senate race began heating up.[149] Finley's activities during the next three weeks are not clear, but neither are they difficult to imagine. As soon as the senatorial contest was settled, he telegraphed Pelton, "Judge

---

position in regard to the electoral commission. Frank D. Orme, another friend and secretary of Davis, read the letter and signed his initials to it after adding these words: "I know this to be a true history of the case."

147. Wm. Henry Smith to Hayes, January 24, 1877, in Hayes Papers. See also letterpress copy, Wm. Henry Smith to Sherman, January 24, 1877, in Smith Papers.

148. Henry H. Finley to Cyrus H. McCormick, November 28, 1876, and Pelton to McCormick, December 13, 1876, both in McCormick Papers.

149. Draft, C. H. McCormick to Finley, December 15, 1876, telegram, Pelton to McCormick, January 3, 1877, and telegram, Finley to McCormick, January 4, 1877, all *ibid.*

Davis Elected Senator by McCormick's friends." [150] Finley later wrote McCormick, complaining about the "duplicity of Judge Davis, now well known and understood. . . . Davis could have saved us. He promised to do so and to allow his appointment on the commission and then connived to have himself rejected. . . . No blame attaches to us for his election as Senator [.] He would have been false to us if he had not been elected [.] " [151] Pelton and Finley obviously believed they had some kind of understanding with Davis. Pelton was certainly irresponsible enough, having already made attempts to buy that vital one-hundred-eighty-fifth electoral vote in each of the disputed states, entirely without Tilden's knowledge, justifying his activity as "ransoming stolen goods." [152]

The election of Davis is most remarkable for the lack of communication and coordination it reveals within the Democratic party. Tilden and Hewitt seem to have made no effort to guard against the danger that Davis might be unavailable; yet speculation that the justice would be the successful candidate for the Senate appeared in the Chicago *Times* as early as January 11.[153] Tilden was aware of this possibility three days later when he first learned of the electoral commission bill, but he said nothing to Hewitt.[154] The use of Davis' name by the Greenbackers on the early ballots was mentioned by Representative Payne at a meeting of the joint committee, though he, also, saw no great significance in the matter. The caucus at which the Democratic legislators agreed to switch to Davis was held the morning of January 24 and was prominently reported in the

150. Telegram, Finley to Pelton, January 25, 1877, in Tilden Papers.
151. Finley to McCormick, February 11, 1877, in McCormick Papers.
152. Paul Leland Haworth, *The Hayes-Tilden Disputed Presidential Election of 1876* (Cleveland: Burrows Brothers Company, 1906), 315–27; Shofner, "Florida in the Balance," 138–39; Harold C. Dippre, "Corruption and the Disputed Election Vote of Oregon in the 1876 Election," *Oregon Historical Quarterly*, LXVII (September, 1966), 263–65; Philip W. Kennedy, "Oregon and the Disputed Election of 1876," *Pacific Northwest Quarterly*, LX (July, 1969), 137, 141–42.
153. Chicago *Times*, January 11, 1877.
154. Alexander Clarence Flick, *Samuel Jones Tilden: A Study in Political Sagacity* (New York: Dodd, Mead and Company, 1939), 383.

Chicago *Times* the next day. The *Times*, the foremost Democratic paper in the West, welcomed the development in its editorial.[155] And still the national party leaders were apparently uninterested in what was happening in Illinois. Moreover, Tilden was unable to control the movements of an aide who was a close relative and who lived in his home on Gramercy Park. When Hewitt was informed of Davis' election, the news left him speechless.[156] The Republicans, of course, were correspondingly elated.[157]

The decisive position on the commission was offered to Davis, and just as the Democrats had feared, he turned it down. There is some evidence that Davis was opposed to the tribunal and would have declined to serve under any circumstances.[158] He had for a long time been courting a presidential nomination from either party; any opinion he expressed as a member of the commission would surely have antagonized at least one. Since he did not resign from the Supreme Court until March 5, he technically could have served had he wanted to.[159] The Senate seat was a convenient excuse, one the Democrats should never have presented him.

With Davis unavailable, the fifteenth seat on the electoral commission was given to Joseph P. Bradley. To most Democrats he was the least distasteful choice that remained. Even after the dispute was settled, Hewitt referred to Bradley as a man "whom I had personally known for many years in New Jersey as a very able lawyer and a man of the highest integrity." [160] An example of that ability and integrity had been given in 1870 when Bradley, sitting in Newark, New Jersey, as a judge of the United

155. Chicago *Times*, January 25, 1877.
156. Northrup, "A Grave Crisis in American History," 933–34.
157. Dennison to Comly, January 26, 1877, in Comly Papers; Garfield to Comley [*sic*], January 24, 1877, in Hayes Papers.
158. Photostat, James E. Harvey to Mrs. David Davis, March 17, 1887, in Davis Papers. See also Wm. Henry Smith to Hayes, February 17, 1877, in Hayes Papers.
159. Willard L. King, *Lincoln's Manager: David Davis* (Cambridge: Harvard University Press, 1960), 294.
160. Hewitt, "Secret History of the Disputed Election, 1876–77," in Nevins (ed.), *Selected Writings of Abram S. Hewitt*, 171.

States Circuit Court for the Western District of Texas, bent and twisted judicial procedure to turn the valuable property of the defunct Memphis, El Paso, and Pacific Railroad over to the Texas and Pacific.[161] If Hewitt recognized this circumstantial link between Bradley and the southern railroad negotiations periodically hinted at in the press, it did not strike him at the time as especially consequential. For their part, the Republicans were delighted with Bradley. R. C. McCormick called his party loyalty *"unflinching,"* and H. V. Boynton considered him more reliable than either Ward Hunt or Noah H. Swayne.[162] In fairness to Bradley it must be observed that he was being placed in an extremely difficult position: "he was expected to sink all political bias and be an impartial arbiter while his brothers on the bench had been chosen because of their political predilections." [163]

Ten commissioners were to be members of Congress, five chosen by each house. It was understood when the bill was written that in accordance with normal congressional practice, three of the five in each case would be representatives of the majority party, thus assuring the desired political balance. A bipartisan meeting of legislative leaders further agreed that each party could nominate its own candidates for the tribunal who would then be routinely confirmed. In that way needless wrangling over the organization of the commission could be avoided.[164] The Democrats speedily designated Senators Bayard and Thurman, and Representatives Payne, Hunton, and Josiah G. Abbott of Massachusetts.[165] In their caucuses the Republicans, on the other hand, had to overcome their customary dissension. In the Senate, Sherman, who had personally declined to

161. Woodward, *Reunion and Reaction*, 157–58.
162. Postscript, dated January 23, 1877, in R. C. McCormick to Hayes, January 19, 1877; and Boynton to Comly, January 25, 1877, both in Hayes Papers.
163. James Ford Rhodes, *History of the United States from the Compromise of 1850 to the Final Restoration of Home Rule at the South in 1877* (7 vols.; New York: Macmillan Company, 1893–1906), VII, 264.
164. Stevenson Diary, January 27, 1877, in Stevenson Papers.
165. *Ibid.*, January 29, 1877.

serve, moved the appointment of Edmunds, Morton, and Samuel
J. R. McMillan of Minnesota. Edmunds objected, saying that all
three Republican senators should come from the joint committee or none. A tense pause followed before Conkling, declaring that "the duties would be inconvenient if not distasteful to
him," expressed a willingness to be passed over. No one could be
sure he was sincere. Ultimately, Edmunds, Morton, and Frelinghuysen, all veterans of the joint committee, were selected.[166] The
Republicans of the House nominated Garfield and Hoar, although the latter was almost defeated by a speech made in his
favor by Julius H. Seelye of Massachusetts, who managed to
sound very much like a Democrat.[167] There was never any question that the congressional members of the commission would
be strictly partisan in their judgments. That certainty was
confirmed by the choice of Morton and Garfield—men who had
from the beginning strenuously opposed arbitration.[168]

Since the proceedings of the electoral commission would be
judicial in nature and highly technical, the various issues involved could best be presented by trained counsel. The two
parties accordingly set about employing the finest legal talent
in the land. Tilden and Hewitt retained Charles O'Conor,
Jeremiah S. Black, David Dudley Field, and others. The Republican National Committee engaged William M. Evarts, Edwin
W. Stoughton, Stanley Matthews, and Samuel Shellabarger.
"Visiting Statesmen" Edward F. Noyes, Lew Wallace, William
E. Chandler, and George H. Williams would assist the Republican attorneys with the appropriate cases.[169] During the last
days of January these learned counselors could be found buried
midst mountains of volumes in the law library of the Justice
Department in preparation for what Hayes called "the law case
of all history." [170]

166. Wm. E. Chandler to [Hayes?], Monday night [January 29, 1877],
in Hayes Papers.
167. Garfield Diary, January 27, 1877, in Garfield Papers.
168. See *ibid.*, January 29, 1877.
169. R. C. McCormick to Hayes, February 2, 1877, in Hayes Papers.
170. Hayes to B. A. Hayes, February 1, 1877, *ibid.*

7

On the first of February, as provided in the electoral commission act, the two houses of Congress assembled in joint session to begin the count of electoral votes. All went smoothly until Florida, the first disputed state, was reached; its three certificates were submitted to the commission and the Congress recessed to await the decision.

For the next four days the Old Senate Chamber, regular home of the Supreme Court, was jammed far beyond its limited capacity, as the fifteen commissioners heard the pleas of the Democratic and Republican attorneys. The Democrats offered to prove that Tilden and Hendricks had received a majority of the popular votes cast, that the legitimate result of the election had been reversed by a partisan returning board which had exceeded its authority, and that all three branches of the state government had subsequently endorsed the claims of the Democratic electors. The Republicans replied with two arguments. They insisted that the signature of the duly recognized governor, as specified in the Constitution, must be accepted as conclusive evidence that a certificate was legal, so long as that certificate did not falsify the official record on which it was based; and they maintained that the commission could not go behind the returns of a state unless it were prepared to go behind the county returns as well and investigate every facet of the election in that state. Since such an investigation obviously could not be completed before March 4, the commission had no alternative to counting the certificate that, on its face, met all the legal requirements.[171] The first issue posed, therefore, was the very one Congress had evaded—whether the tribunal possessed the authority to examine evidence beyond that contained in the certificates themselves.

On February 6 the commissioners met in executive session to

---

171. Jerrell H. Shofner, "Florida Courts and the Disputed Election of 1876," *Florida Historical Quarterly*, XLVIII (July, 1969), 43; Chester L. Barrows, *William M. Evarts: Lawyer, Diplomat, Statesman* (Chapel Hill: University of North Carolina Press, 1941), 302–305.

start their deliberations; not even a stenographer was present.[172] One by one, each of the congressional members except Payne explained his views. This procedure consumed the entire seven-hour meeting. The next day the executive session continued, as Payne and Justices Field, Strong, and Miller delivered speeches of varying length. Finally, at 2:13 P.M. Bradley rose to read his opinion. Garfield described the occasion in his diary: "All were intent, because B. held the casting vote. It was a curious study to watch the faces as he read. All were making a manifest effort to appear unconcerned. It was ten minutes before it became evident that he was against the authority to hear extrinsic evidence." Justice Clifford summarized the Democratic position and Thurman and Edmunds closed the debate. The commission, dividing along strict party lines, then voted eight to seven not to receive additional evidence "except such as relates to the eligibility of F. C. Humphreys, one of the electors," whom the Democrats said was a federal officeholder at the time of his election. At four o'clock the doors were thrown open. The commission formally announced its preliminary decision and adjourned for the day. The Democrats tried to display a brave front, but they recognized the implications of the partisan alignment revealed on the tribunal.[173]

After listening to another day of argument from the opposing counsel, both on the validity of the rival electoral certificates and

172. A transcript was kept of the legal arguments presented before the commission. It appears as Part 4 of the *Congressional Record,* 44th Cong., 2nd Sess. No record was made, however, of the actual deliberations of the commission. See Garfield to Hinsdale, February 12, 1877, in Hinsdale (ed.), *Garfield-Hinsdale Letters,* 358. At least three members of the tribunal kept diaries, but Bradley's and Garfield's are largely uninformative, whereas Payne destroyed his. See Rhodes, *History of the United States,* VII, 269. Edmunds destroyed all of his papers. See Adler, "The Senatorial Career of George Franklin Edmunds," 159. Representative Abbott prepared a "Minority Report" for the Democrats, but it is little more than a reiteration of his party's views. See Charles Cowley, "The Minority Report of the Electoral Commission," *Magazine of American History,* XXVII (February, 1892), 81–92.

173. Garfield Diary, February 6, 7, 1877, in Garfield Papers; Joseph P. Bradley Diary, February 5, 6, 7, 1877, in Joseph P. Bradley Papers, New Jersey Historical Society; New York *World,* February 8, 1877.

on the eligibility of Humphreys, the commissioners returned to executive session on the ninth. Early in the afternoon, Bradley again indicated he supported the Republican position. When the Democrats realized that they had been unable to demonstrate convincingly that Humphreys was a shipping commissioner on November 7, Thurman offered a resolution stating that the man had resigned before the election and hence was not ineligible. Morton responded that Humphreys' vote was valid regardless of his status as an officeholder. Garfield preferred to dodge that question with a resolution proclaiming simply that the Republican electoral votes were the ones provided for in the Constitution. In time the Garfield motion was approved, eight to seven. By the same margin the commission then adopted a brief report giving the basis of its judgment and adjourned.[174]

The Democrats were thunderstruck. At once they denounced Bradley for his partisanship and accused him of betraying the trust the nation had placed in him. The New York *Sun* rediscovered his connection with the Texas and Pacific Railway. It was not until six months afterwards, however, that the *Sun* published a very serious charge concerning the justice's conduct on the eve of the Florida decision: "During the whole of that night, Judge Bradley's house in Washington was surrounded by the carriages of visitors who came to see him apparently about the decision of the Electoral Commission. . . . These visitors included leading Republicans as well as persons deeply interested in the Texas Pacific Railroad scheme." [175] Years later Hewitt, in his "Secret History," disclosed that John G. Stevens, a mutual friend of Bradley and himself, had visited the justice on the evening in question and at midnight returned to Hewitt's home, where he was staying as a guest. Stevens did not mention any carriages outside Bradley's house, but did say he had read the justice's "opinion in favor of counting the vote of the Democratic electors." Hewitt continued: "Such a

174. Garfield Diary, February 9, 1877, in Garfield Papers; Barnard, *Rutherford B. Hayes and His America*, 373.
175. Woodward, *Reunion and Reaction*, 156–60.

judgment insured the election of Tilden. . . . I attended the delivery of the judgment the next day without the slightest intimation from any quarter that Judge Bradley had changed his mind. In fact, the reading of the opinion, until the few concluding paragraphs were reached, was strictly in accordance with the report of Mr. Stevens. The change was made between midnight and sunrise." [176] Other versions of this tale were circulating as early as the spring of 1877.

Bradley absolutely denied the Democratic imputations: "The whole thing is a falsehood. Not one visitor called at my house that evening, and during the whole sitting of the commission I had no private discussion whatever of the subjects at issue with any person interested on the Republican side, and but few words with any persons. Indeed, I zealously sought to avoid all discussion outside the commission itself." [177] For the most part the historical record sustains Bradley. The accusations against him originated only after the dispute was over, and they were manifestly inaccurate in several respects. The justice did, of course, read a statement the gist of which was unclear at the outset. However, that opinion concerned the question of evidence rather than the electoral votes as such, and it was delivered, like all of Bradley's individual remarks, in secret session, when Hewitt could not possibly have been in attendance. The Democratic chairman must have obtained that information later from a member of the commission. Moreover, Hewitt identified the date of the decision as February 8, when no verdicts of any kind were rendered. He probably meant the dramatic preliminary decision of February 7. Yet the night preceding the vote on the admission of evidence, Bradley entertained no midnight visitors of either party. The justice's son remarked at the time that his father, suffering through a series of sleepless nights, "went to bed at eleven and got up at

---

176. Hewitt, "Secret History of the Disputed Election, 1876–77," in Nevins (ed.), *Selected Writings of Abram S. Hewitt*, 172–73.
177. Bradley to the Newark *Daily Advertiser* and the Electoral Commission, September 6 [1877], in Bigelow (ed.), *Letters and Literary Memorials of Samuel J. Tilden*, II, 568–69.

three." [178] In short, the Democratic account of Bradley's activities was at the least badly garbled and conceivably fabricated out of sheer rage and whole cloth.

The immediate effect of the Florida decisions was to dissolve the Democratic party into a leaderless mass. Tilden, who had faded into the background when the electoral commission bill became public, privately gave up. On the evening the commission voted not to investigate the Florida returns, he went for a long stroll with John Bigelow around Gramercy Park and "discussed the pleasant places in Europe for him to visit next summer. He inclined to spend most of his time in England." [179] A few days later August Belmont met the candidate and was "astonished and gratified to see how well he keeps up his courage. Though he looks upon his case as well nigh desperate, he is firm and wants to fight to the last." [180] Tilden might battle to the end, but his "courage" was composed of three quarters resignation and only one quarter perseverance, for he fully understood that the end was coming. He just did not believe there was any reason to make things easier for his lifelong opponents. Jeremiah S. Black colorfully expressed the same sentiment: "God damn them, they will beat us and elect Hayes, but we shall give them all the trouble we can." [181]

The rest of the party was thrown into confusion, unsure of what course to follow. On the one hand, Senators William H. Barnum of Connecticut and Francis Kernan of New York, both strong supporters of Tilden's nomination, quickly went to work after the preliminary judgment in an effort to prevent trouble among the Democrats in Congress if Florida were awarded to Hayes. They were joined in their labors by Senator John W. Stevenson of Kentucky.[182] Yet Belmont, conservative banker

178. Perry Belmont to August Belmont, February 8, 1877, in Perry Belmont, *An American Democrat: The Recollections of Perry Belmont* (New York: Columbia University Press, 1940), 197–98.
179. John Bigelow Diary, February 9, 1877, in Bigelow Papers.
180. August Belmont to Perry Belmont, February 12, 1877, in Belmont, *An American Democrat*, 201.
181. Quoted in Barnard, *Rutherford B. Hayes and His America*, 373.
182. Stevenson Diary, February 9, 1877, in Stevenson Papers.

that he was, nevertheless wanted the Democratic minority to resign from the commission: "It is good, sound reasoning for a judge or arbitrator to withdraw from a case which he is to judge upon evidence when that evidence is withheld. If all our members withdraw, the President of the Senate holds over, and we have a new election next autumn. This may be considered revolutionary, but it is better to fight now than to lie down and have our liberties trampled upon." [183] In Washington, Belmont's son discovered that neither Bayard nor Payne would consider such a step, while Kernan still approved of the commission, deeming it better than "a deadlock and two claimants for the Presidency." [184]

The Florida decision was formally delivered to a joint session of Congress on the afternoon of Saturday, February 10. The Democrats filed a written notice of their objection. Under the provisions of the electoral commission act, the Senate returned to its own chamber to allow each house to debate the judgment for a maximum of two hours before voting to accept or reject it. In a sense this was a futile gesture, for the Senate would certainly express its approval, and the verdict of the tribunal would thereby be made final. Slowly, the House returned to order. Representative William Pitt Lynde of Wisconsin held a "not wholly harmonious conference" with Speaker Randall at the chair. Returning to his seat, Lynde was recognized by Randall and promptly moved a recess until Monday morning. A shiver of intense excitement swept the House. The Republicans protested that the motion violated the terms of the arbitration law. William M. Springer of Illinois answered that it did not. As the debate continued, the atmosphere gradually relaxed. According to the congressional correspondent of the New York *World*: "An indefinable feeling that the House was on the edge of a breach of the great compromise vanished. . . . The idea was gradually filtering out that this recess was not part

183. August Belmont to Perry Belmont, February 12, 1877, in Belmont, *An American Democrat*, 200–201.
184. Perry Belmont to August Belmont, February 12, 1877, *ibid.*, 199–200.

of a plan to delay the count indefinitely, and the interest fell away from its earlier tension." Finally, Randall ruled that the motion was in order and the recess was carried by an almost strictly party vote, 163 to 108.[185]

The Democrats of the House were casting about wildly for a policy. Some of them were so incensed at the failure of the commission to decide the Florida case on what they believed to be its merits that they spoke of a filibuster—continuing the recess from day to day until March 4 to compel a new election. Others wanted the Democrats on the commission to refuse to participate in any further mockery of the principles of arbitration. Cooler heads, however, pointed out that the party had agreed in advance to abide by the tribunal's pronouncements. Given this obvious irresolution, the *World's* reporter needed no special ability as a clairvoyant to predict that the House would duly consider the Florida decision on the morning of the twelfth.[186] And indeed, immediately after the opening prayer David Dudley Field, one of Tilden's "representatives," moved that the verdict of the commission be rejected and that the state be counted for Tilden and Hendricks. Proctor Knott of Kentucky offered a substitute referring the Florida case back to the commission on the ground that the original judgment was not based on all the available evidence. Randall ruled that Knott's resolution was out of order. Following the allotted two hours of desultory debate, Field's motion was adopted, 168 to 103.[187] Of course, it accomplished nothing.

8

The Republicans, meanwhile, experienced a very nervous Saturday night and Monday morning. They could not be certain that the House Democrats would not resort to a filibuster. After all, only two years earlier Randall had conducted one very

185. New York *World*, February 11, 1877.
186. *Ibid.*, February 12, 1877. See also Dennison to Hayes, Saturday PM [February 10, 1877], in Hayes Papers.
187. New York *World*, February 13, 1877; *Congressional Record*, 44th Cong., 2nd Sess., Vol. V, Pt. 2, pp. 1502–1503.

successfully, delaying to death the so-called "Force Bill." [188] This threat led a few of Hayes's more conspiratorial supporters to resume their conversations with the Democratic South. On Sunday Boynton cheerfully told William Henry Smith: "At the most opportune time the good seed we planted brings pleasant fruit. Enough Southern men stand in the way of filibustering to make it certain in my mind that the democrats can not beat Gov. Hayes by delay, even if they attempt it. As a republican I hope they will make the effort, for it will surely fail, & with failure through lack of votes in their own party must come great good to us." Boynton neglected a chance at this point to explain why the southerners had voted for the recess the previous day. Instead, he continued:

Col. Kellar feels confident that his friends can & will control the situation now. For them it is much simplified. They have only to say that good faith, honor, & respect for law all bind them not to impede the execution of the new law for the counting. If our purely political part of the plan does not defeat democratic success through filibustering, I am sure the Scott help will. I shall expect to see hard & effective work there. If filibustering begins you may have the strongest possible confidence that it will have a brief life, & a disgraceful death.[189]

Though he did not realize it, Boynton, deceived by his own image of a diabolical Tilden and by an irresistable temptation to pull a fast one on his political adversaries, was seriously misinterpreting the intention of a majority of the Democrats in the House. He and his friends especially underestimated the determination of the southern Democrats to obtain some consolation for their party's latest defeat. Boynton and company thus magnified their own importance in the events that were to follow. In the process, they laid the foundation for a popular but misleading version of the negotiations which preceded the peaceful resolution of the electoral crisis; for recent historians,

188. Evans, *Pennsylvania Politics, 1872–1877*, 147.
189. Boynton to Wm. Henry Smith, February 11 [1877], in Smith Collection. See also Boynton to [Richard] Smith, February 11 [1877], *ibid.*

especially C. Vann Woodward, have drawn heavily on their correspondence in fashioning their own accounts of the "Compromise of 1877." [190]

Some form of accommodation would have been offered the South even without Boynton's interference, even had there been no threat of a filibuster. A small cluster of Ohio Republicans closely associated with Hayes believed that the moment had arrived to initiate a new policy of conciliation toward the former Confederate states. As Jacob D. Cox analyzed the situation:

The lapse of time has so far consolidated and established the political rights of the Negroes that their separate organization as a party is no longer essential to their safety. On the contrary, it is now the cause of their greatest danger. The whites of the South will recognize the political equality of the blacks if this does not threaten to continue the rule of a class distinguished by *race*; but if the "color-line" is continued, nothing can prevent all the remaining Southern states from following the example of Mississippi, and the political rights of the blacks will exist only in name, and for the purpose of conferring upon the real governing class the additional representation in Congress.

Since a restoration of some form of white rule was all but inevitable, Cox reasoned, Hayes should accept that fact and address himself to the challenge of securing governments composed of the natural leaders of the section:

Upon the basis of a hearty & earnest avowal on the part of Southern white men that they will in honorable good faith accept & defend the present Constitutional rights of the freedman, we ought not to have great difficulty in finding means to rally to the support of a Republican administration a strong body of the best men representing the capital, the intelligence, the virtue & revived patriotism of the old population of the South, willing to cooperate in the good work of bringing in an era of real peace, prosperity & good brotherhood.[191]

190. Woodward, *Reunion and Reaction*, 166–203.
191. Cox to Hayes, January 31, 1877, in Hayes Papers.

Hayes told Cox, "On the Southern question your views and mine are so precisely the same that if called on to write down a policy I could adopt your language." [192]

On February 10, the day the Florida decision was read to Congress, Representative Charles Foster, noting that the Republicans in Washington were now heavily engaged in cabinet-making, gave Hayes some advice on the subject: "I think it is certain that you can secure a large and respectable following in the South, without bargaining of any sort (I hate bargains) [.] Many of them are anxious to identify themselves with the Rpn. party, believing it best for them to do so." Foster suggested the appointment of two cabinet members from the South, one of Republican background such as Senator James L. Alcorn of Mississippi and "the other a conservative democrat of Old Whig or Douglass [sic] antecedents." [193] Three days later, with Florida officially counted and Louisiana before the commission, Stanley Matthews informed Hayes that he had been approached by a southern Democrat he described as "well posted and in communication with the leaders," but whom he did not identify. This anonymous individual "came to discuss with me *the question of your Cabinet* and for the purpose of suggesting the names of suitable gentlemen from the South to go in, upon the basis of a policy directed to the disintegration of the Democratic party." [194] Matthews' unnamed southerner was probably Andrew J. Kellar, who had recently returned to Washington and who may have influenced Foster, too. What immediate benefit did the Republicans hope to gain from this new departure? Joseph Medill unnecessarily summarized that consideration for Richard Smith, who already understood perfectly: "The next House of Reps. is Dem. by 5 to 8 maj. and which they will increase to 15 or 20 by turning out our fellows in the close and contested districts. It is all important to the

192. Hayes to Cox, February 2, 1877, in Cox Papers.
193. Foster to Hayes, February 10, 1877, in Hayes Papers.
194. Stanley Matthews to Hayes, February 13, 1877, *ibid.*

success of President Hayes Administration that there shall be a Republican working majority in both Houses. How shall it be secured? Obviously it can only be done by attaching to the Administration a number of Southern Conservatives who feel friendly towards Mr. Hayes." [195]

The man who supplied the driving force behind the effort to have a southern Democrat appointed to the cabinet was Kellar. He did not know Hayes personally and had little direct contact with the Republican leaders in Congress, so he worked through the Republican candidate's journalist friends. "The first acts of Gov. Hayes as President that will be looked to by the South with intense solicitude," he reminded William Henry Smith, "will be his cabinet appointments. However noble & patriotic his inaugural [address] may be ... [it] will not remove the feeling of distrust in the hearts of the people of the South in their apprehension that his administration will be a 'third term of Grant.' ... The first acts, not the first words, of President Hayes will be potent for great good." Kellar had a specific appointment in mind—Senator David M. Key of Tennessee.[196] Key had been designated to fill on an interim basis the vacancy created by the death of Senator and former president Andrew Johnson. He had received an unusual degree of favorable recognition throughout the North and widespread notoriety in his own state in March, 1876, as the only Democrat to vote in favor of a Republican resolution ordering an investigation of the violent election of 1875 in Mississippi. Although he felt the charges leveled by Senators Morton and Boutwell were unjust, Key explained in his maiden speech that a negative vote would be interpreted as an indication that the Democrats had something to hide. One of the first Tennesseans to congratulate him for his sagacity was Andrew J. Kellar. In January, 1877, despite Kellar's personal assistance in trying to organize the legislature in his favor and despite the last minute support of the state's Republicans,

195. Medill to Richard Smith, February 17, 1877, *ibid.*
196. Andrew J. Kellar to Wm. H. Smith, February 16, 1877, in Smith Collection.

Key was narrowly defeated in his bid for election to the remaining four years of Johnson's term. His vote for the Mississippi inquiry and his moderation in the electoral dispute were part of his undoing.[197] These developments all served to underscore the fitness of including Key in the cabinet. On February 13 Kellar asked Key for permission to propose his name in conversations with some friends of Hayes. Key consented: "If, without requiring of me the sacrifice of any personal or political independence, you find that my name can be used for the good of the South, in your best judgment, you are at liberty to use it." [198] A few days later, again probably at Kellar's instigation, a small caucus of southern conservatives of both parties, meeting at the home of Senator Alcorn, endorsed the appointment of Key.[199] Kellar meanwhile sent Key's encouraging letter to William Henry Smith, and Smith forwarded it to Hayes. By February 27 Kellar was able to assure Key that he was "quite confident a position in the Cabinet will be tendered to you." [200]

All of these arrangements were brought up for discussion without the threat of a filibuster. They were designed not to secure Hayes's inauguration, but to strengthen his administration after he had been inducted into office.

Charles Nordhoff, who had begun talking about a realignment of American politics months before the election, thought the choice of one or two southerners for the cabinet would have great effect, but he warned Foster that the Republicans could not hope to succeed with such a plan unless they were ready to

197. David M. Abshire, *The South Rejects a Prophet: The Life of Senator D. M. Key, 1824–1900* (New York: Frederick A. Praeger, 1967), 82–87, 125–39; pamphlet, "The Mississippi Election: Speech of Hon. D. M. Key, of Tennessee, in the United States Senate, March 31, 1876" (Washington: n.p., 1876), copy in David M. Key Papers, Chattanooga Public Library; Rees B. Edmondson to Key, May 9, 1876, in Key Papers.

198. Kellar to Key, February 13, 1877, and draft of telegram, [Key to Kellar, February 1877], both in Key Papers; Key to [Kellar], February 16, 1877, in New York *Times*, March 8, 1877. This letter first appeared in Kellar's paper, the Memphis *Avalanche*, March 8, 1877.

199. Wm. Henry Smith to Hayes, February 17, 1877, in Hayes Papers.

200. Kellar to Wm. Henry Smith, February 20, 1877, in Smith Papers; Kellar to Key, February 27, 1877, in Key Papers.

abandon Governor Chamberlain of South Carolina and Governor Packard of Louisiana "as soon as possible." [201] Medill agreed:

If President Hayes undertakes to keep Packard in the Gov's Chair there will be "organized h——l" all the time. He will go around lik[e] a man with a thorn in his foot, without peace or freedom from pain until it is extracted. He will have to hold Packard up by bayonets and gunboats, and put down insurrections about once in 90 days; and we shall be expected to defend and justify such Federal interference in behalf of an odious carpet-bag desperado as the South regards him. To maintain Packard in place will make it impossible to secure Southern conservative support for Haye's [*sic*] Administration; it will spoil every thing; lose us the Speaker (Garfield) of the next House, and the political control of it. There is only one thing to do in the premises viz: to drop Packard. . . . So of Chamberlain, he should be retired from the gubernatorial chair which he can not hold a minute if the troops are removed.[202]

Here was a stumbling block of no mean size obstructing the road to a new southern policy. Some Republicans thought it a strange thing indeed to begin the revitalization of their party in the South by turning their backs on the last two Republican governors of that section. William Henry Smith could not quite comprehend the wisdom of such an approach: "You cannot dismiss those gentlemen with a waive of the hand." [203] Neither could John Sherman: "I see no way but the recognition of the Packard Government followed by the utmost liberality to the South." [204]

Nordhoff and Medill were right—Louisiana and South Carolina were the key to the situation. Kellar, Boynton, Smith, and Sherman were hopeful that a cabinet post, along with the wealth of patronage jobs such a position invariably controlled at the start of a new administration, and the promise of sympathetic consideration of reasonable requests for financial aid

201. Nordhoff to Foster, February 15 [1877], in Hayes Papers.
202. Medill to Richard Smith, February 17, 1877, *ibid.*
203. Wm. Henry Smith to Richard Smith, February 19, 1877, *ibid.*
204. Sherman to Hayes, February 18, 1877, *ibid.*

to internal improvements would attract the support of enough southerners to give the Republicans control of the next House of Representatives; yet there was never more than a handful of Democrats interested in such a proposition. What the white South wanted most was "home rule," the assurance that even if Tilden were counted out, Nicholls and Hampton would not be. As a result, the vast majority of southern Democrats sought an entirely different kind of "deal" from that which preoccupied Boynton and Kellar.

By the middle of February the conditions existing in South Carolina and Louisiana were essentially the same. Each state had two governors and two legislatures. In each case the white population had succeeded in isolating the Republican claimants to the degree that the latter controlled the statehouses and little else. Taxes were voluntarily being paid to the Hampton and Nicholls "governments" at the same time that the collectors appointed by Chamberlain and Packard could raise virtually no revenue. Local officials increasingly honored the decisions of the Democratic governors, while state agencies were forced, even if reluctantly, to apply to the Democratic legislatures to obtain funds needed to maintain their operations. In Louisiana members of the Republican house and senate had drifted over to the Democrats and given them a quorum of lawmakers whose election had been acknowledged by both sides. In short, the Republican governments were evaporating.[205] Although federal troops were present in both New Orleans and Columbia, they were under strict orders to preserve the peace and to remain otherwise uninvolved. The soldiers accordingly prevented the Democrats from forcibly ejecting the Republican officials in the statehouses, but they did nothing to halt the erosion of Republican strength. Grant, weary after eight years of recur-

205. Francis Butler Simkins and Robert Hilliard Woody, *South Carolina During Reconstruction* (Chapel Hill: University of North Carolina Press, 1932), 534–36; Hampton M. Jarrell, *Wade Hampton and the Negro: The Road Not Taken* (Columbia: University of South Carolina Press, 1950), 113; Ella Lonn, *Reconstruction in Louisiana after 1868* (New York: G. P. Putnam's Sons, 1918), 478–94.

rent crises in the South and perhaps chastened by the criticism leveled even by some members of his own party when he reinstated Kellogg in office two years before, scrupulously refused to interfere in either state. In the cabinet debates between Secretary of War Cameron, Secretary of the Interior Chandler, and Attorney General Taft, on the one hand, and Secretary of State Fish on the other, the president repeatedly sided with the conservative Fish.[206] The prospects for toppling the last decaying relics of the Reconstruction era were undoubtedly bright therefore. Still, the Democrats could not forget what had happened in Louisiana in 1874. They wanted more positive indications of the intentions of Grant and especially Hayes, and the insistency with which they sought clarification on this point increased as Tilden's fate became certain.

The four votes of Florida were officially recorded for Hayes at a joint session on February 12. The Republicans expected the Democrats to challenge the eligibility of an Illinois elector and were surprised when the count proceeded without interruption until Louisiana was reached.[207] The three returns from that state were referred to the electoral commission. Arguments by opposing counsel consumed three days. On the sixteenth the tribunal met behind closed doors for eleven hours. To Garfield it was "a day of the most nervous strain and anxiety I have . . . ever passed since Chickamauga." Not till late in the afternoon was a decision in favor of Hayes foreshadowed: "We had no hint of the conclusion to be reached until Bradley was twenty minutes into his speech. The suspense was painful, and the efforts of members to appear unconcerned, gave strong proof of the intensity of the feeling. I could hear or fancied I could hear the watches of the members ticking in their pockets. When Bradley reached a proposition that made his result evident, there was a long breath of relief—up or down—but actual

206. Nevins, *Hamilton Fish*, II, 845–49, 851–53; Taft to Hayes, February 14, 1877, in Hayes Papers.
207. Shellabarger to Hayes, February 10, 1877, in Hayes Papers; Garfield Diary, February 12, 1877, in Garfield Papers.

relief to all, from the long suspense." [208] A messenger from Justice Clifford notified the two houses of Congress at noon, Saturday the seventeenth, that the judgment of the commission was ready for delivery. Acting by arrangement with the Democratic leadership, Representative Lamar of Mississippi immediately moved that the clerk of the House inform the members of the Senate that they would be received back in joint session at 11 A.M. on Monday. As had happened a week earlier, this postponement was carried by an almost strictly party vote, 152 to 111, only eight Democrats opposing it—Erastus Wells of Missouri and seven northerners.[209] Garfield thought the Democrats showed "every disposition to prevent the completion of the count by delay, though some of the better men among them say that they wish to gain time to cool down the fiery spirits of their extreme men." [210]

The southern Democrats now redoubled their efforts to obtain a commitment from the Republicans about the South. On Friday evening E. A. Burke, a personal representative of "Governor" Nicholls, confronted Stanley Matthews as the two men were leaving the Supreme Court Room in the Capitol where they had just heard the preliminary reading of the Louisiana decision. Burke described the volatile state of affairs in New Orleans and said the people of his state would never willingly submit to the installation of Packard as governor. Matthews replied that although he was not in any sense authorized to negotiate, he was positive, based on his long friendship with Hayes, dating back to their college days, that the Ohio governor did not desire the continuation of carpetbag rule.[211] It is doubtful that Hayes would have sanctioned so categorical a statement. Only the day before he had taken refuge once more behind his letter of acceptance in a short note to Sherman: "I prefer to make no new

208. Garfield Diary, February 16, 1877, in Garfield Papers; Bradley Diary, February 12, 13, 14, 15, 16, 1877, in Bradley Papers.
209. *Congressional Record*, 44th Cong., 2nd Sess., Vol. V, Pt. 2, pp. 1664–65; New York *World*, February 18, 1877.
210. Garfield Diary, February 17, 1877, in Garfield Papers.
211. Lonn, *Reconstruction in Louisiana after 1868*, 495–502.

declarations. But you may say if you deem it advisable that you *know* that I will stand by the friendly and encouraging words of that letter and by all that they imply. You cannot express that too strongly." [212] Sherman thought the governor's circumspection altogether wise and proper. In conversations "with many Southern men," he told Hayes, he confined himself to the general observation "that you undoubtedly would stand by the words of your letter of acceptance in spirit and in substance; and that you would make the Southern question a specialty in your Administration; but I have not quoted you directly and did not think it wise to do so." [213]

Matthews and Burke spoke again on Sunday. Burke said he was personally disposed to believe the assurances he had received regarding Hayes's attitude. He questioned the good will of such men as Sherman, Garfield, Morton, and Blaine, however, and doubted that Hayes could implement any change in policy against their united opposition. The assurances the South wanted most, Burke continued, could come only from these "strong" leaders of the Republican party. Matthews explained that he could not speak for them. In that case, Burke retorted, the congressmen from Louisiana would lead a filibuster to prevent the inauguration of Hayes. [214]

Burke was bluffing. Just the night before, the Democratic caucus had debated the matter and decided, sixty-nine to forty, that "the count of the electoral vote shall proceed without dilatory opposition" until its completion. Support for the filibuster came primarily from western Democrats. The entire New York delegation and most of the southerners who were present disapproved of any further delay. [215] Burke knew all about this caucus resolution. In fact, on his way to see Matthews he called on Hewitt for the specific purpose of protesting the abandon-

212. Hayes to Sherman, February 15, 1877, in Sherman, *Recollections of Forty Years*, I, 561–62.
213. Sherman to Hayes, February 17, 1877, in Hayes Papers.
214. Lonn, *Reconstruction in Louisiana after 1868*, 503–504.
215. New York *World*, February 18, 1877.

ment of Louisiana by his own party.[216] Never was the lack of coordination and purpose in the Democratic party more in evidence.

On Monday the Louisiana decision was formally presented to a joint session of Congress, and the two houses separated to consider it. In the Senate the Democrats' last lingering hopes were quickly extinguished. For several days some of them had been telling each other that Conkling, leading perhaps a dozen Republican senators, would object to the commission's verdict and thus pave the way for a Democratic president. The imperious New Yorker was himself the source of these rumors. The Republican party, of course, had long been more deeply rent by internal feuding than even the Democratic party. The southern Republicans, few of whom had at any time evinced much enthusiasm for Hayes, were now further agitated by the talk of a new policy looking toward the conciliation of men they considered their mortal enemies. They responded by demanding the selection of one of their own number for the cabinet, preferring Senator J. R. West of Louisiana. They were opposed to the choice of a southern Democrat "under any circumstances." [217] Matthews took the danger of their disaffection seriously, warning Hayes of the need for "the most absolute silence on your part in respect to your Cabinet appointments until after the official declaration of your election is made." [218] When Conkling hinted broadly that he was contemplating revolt, it was probably his heavy-handed way of informing Hayes that he and his southern friends wanted to be consulted about the composition of the coming administration. If so, he was rebuffed anew. Yet to carry out his threat would be suicidal. As a result, although the Senate debated the Louisiana judgment for two hours amid heightening excitement, Conkling

216. Lonn, *Reconstruction in Louisiana after 1868*, 504–505.
217. S. W. Dorsey to Hayes, February 17, 1877, in Hayes Papers; Dorsey to Comly, February 17, 1877, and Dennison to Comly [February 23, 1877], both in Comly Papers.
218. Matthews to Hayes, February 23, 1877, in Hayes Papers.

never appeared. Deprived of his guidance his followers meekly toed the party mark. The next day, Conkling said he had been out of town and professed never to have heard the stories of his dissatisfaction.[219]

Meanwhile, a majority of the Democrats in the House resorted once more to obstruction, carrying Fernando Wood's motion for a recess, 140 to 130. Only twenty-four Democrats voted against the delay, seventeen of them from the North and West.[220] Burke and other southerners trying to extract concessions from the Republicans had worked feverishly among the congressmen of their own party to produce this result. Burke later described the revived filibuster to Nicholls as a "spasmodic movement organized to save Louisiana and South Carolina and largely composed of members who allow us to use them for [the] purpose [of] securing substantial assurance for our State, but who cannot be held together for any other purpose. The movement was organized by ourselves independent of the original opponents of the count and after the party was helplessly demoralized." [221]

On Monday night the Democrats held another caucus and appeared thoroughly bewildered. Several southern members opened the discussion by cautioning against any "unnecessary" prolongation of the count. Yet one of them, Charles E. Hooker of Mississippi, then proposed that the Louisiana judgment be remanded to the commission for reconsideration. There was general agreement that such a procedure was impossible under the law. Milton I. Southard of Ohio, an "irreconcilable," perplexed by the death and sudden resurrection of the filibuster, moved simply that the House recess each day until March 4. Seeking perhaps to ascertain the ultimate purpose of the body, Speaker Randall suggested that "in an emergency the House might amend the act of 1792, so that the Secretary of State could be made Acting President of the United States until a

219. Stevenson Diary, February 19, 20, 1877, in Stevenson Papers.
220. *Congressional Record*, 44th Cong., 2nd Sess., Vol. V, Pt. 2, p. 1684.
221. Typescript copy of telegram, E. A. Burke to F. T. Nicholls, February 27, 1877, in William E. Chandler Papers.

new election [could] be held, and that the House in the meantime should take a recess from day to day till that amendment
was accepted by the Senate, which he thought might be the
case." Randall supposed that if the 1792 statute was left unchanged, the completion of the count could still be blocked and
a second election arranged under existing laws. Proctor Knott
and Thomas L. Jones of Kentucky and each of the Ohio men
present signified their approval of Randall's scheme "or any
other legitimate course" which would forestall the seating of
Hayes. John Young Brown, a party to Kellar's negotiations,
offered a substitute declaring that the count should continue
without additional interruption. Randall pointed out that in the
absence of action to the contrary, Brown's motion was already
party policy, having been agreed on at the previous caucus.
Another resolution, providing that Hampton and Nicholls be
recognized as the lawful governors of their respective states
in all future appropriation bills, was introduced but not discussed. In the end the caucus adjourned without reaching a
positive decision.[222]

If this meeting accomplished nothing directly, it was nevertheless utilized to good effect by the southerners, for immediately afterwards several of them called on Charles Foster to
describe Randall's "violent speech." They wanted to know what
assurances Foster could give that Hayes's rule would not be
"that of the bayonet towards the South." After consulting
Matthews, Garfield, and Evarts about the matter, Foster agreed
to make a conciliatory speech in Congress the next day.[223] At
once the threat of a filibuster receded. On Tuesday morning the
House debated on Louisiana and went through the formality
of rejecting the commission's decision.[224] When the joint session
resumed, the votes of Louisiana, Maine, Maryland, and Massachusetts were counted before a group of Democrats objected

222. New York *World*, February 20, 1877.
223. Foster to Hayes, February 21, 1877, in Hayes Papers.
224. *Congressional Record*, 44th Cong., 2nd Sess., Vol. V, Pt. 2, pp.
1702–1703.

to the eligibility of a Michigan elector. There being but one return from that state, the case did not need to go before the commission. Instead, the houses parted to consider the question for the customary two hours. Since their concurrence was necessary to exclude the disputed Michigan vote, the issue was probably raised strictly as a means of delay. Indeed, as soon as the senators had filed from the room, Southard of Ohio moved a recess. His proposal was crushed, 192 to 57; even the Democrats generally voted against it.[225] In this auspicious atmosphere Foster obtained the floor to deliver his remarks about Hayes's southern policy: "I feel certain that I shall be sustained by his acts when I say that his highest ambition will be to administer the Government so patriotically and wisely as to wipe away any and all necessity or excuse for the formation of parties on a sectional basis and all traces of party color lines; that thereafter and forever we shall hear no more of a solid South or a united North. The flag shall float over States, not provinces, over freemen, and not subjects." [226] Foster's speech pointed in the right direction, but it was very general and did not commit the "strong" leaders of the Republican party. Later that afternoon, when Congress returned to joint session and counted the votes of Michigan, the Democrats objected to an elector from Nevada. That action broke up the joint session, and the Democratic majority in the House at once forced another recess, ninety-seven to eighty-eight.[227] This latest slowdown was in the nature of a warning. On Wednesday the joint session commenced again, long enough for Nevada to be counted and for Oregon to be referred to the commission.

At this point the friends of Hayes were themselves baffled by the dizzying zig-zag course of their adversaries. More than one southern Democrat was devoting half his time to organization of the filibuster and half to conversations with Republicans in which he explained that only the responsible Union men of the

225. *Ibid.*, Pt. 3, p. 1705.
226. Quoted in Lonn, *Reconstruction in Louisiana after 1868*, 506–507.
227. *Congressional Record*, 44th Cong., 2nd Sess., Vol. V, Pt. 3, p. 1723.

South could counter the obstructionism of Tilden's northern Democratic allies. All the while the count was permitted to proceed fast enough to make certain it could be completed by March 4, yet slowly enough to lend credence to intimations that it might not be. No gambler ever presented a more inscrutable poker face than did these leaders of the white South.[228]

What must the Republicans do to regain control of the situation? Kellar was satisfied they had only to avow openly the program he had been urging upon them: "The chief embarrassment in the way of victory over Tammany Hall, is the silence of Gov. Hayes as to his policy towards the South." Could the governor not publicly announce his intention of appointing Key to the cabinet?[229] William Henry Smith answered that if Hayes did so, his statement would produce "a hundred difficulties." Smith was more familiar than Kellar with the factionalism which was tearing the Republican party apart: "The only thing he [Hayes] can do is to preserve silence and patiently wait for the legal forms to be concluded."[230] It should be noted that Kellar's efforts to stop the filibuster ran directly counter to the endeavors of most southerners and that the objective he sought was one they did not share.[231]

In contrast to Kellar's fits of depression, Boynton was convinced that victory was virtually in hand: "Gen Dodge has the whole of Scotts force at work, & that with the purely political part will I feel *confident* defeat the desperate men."[232] Boynton wholly misunderstood who "the desperate men" were. Moreover, he partially misjudged the reason the Texas and Pacific lobby was laboring so diligently. Oppressed by the

228. The Republicans were completely fooled. See the discussion between Republican Congressman John A. Kasson of Iowa and Hamilton Fish on February 18, described in Nevins, *Hamilton Fish*, II, 856.
229. Kellar to Wm. Henry Smith, February 20, 1877, in Smith Papers. See also Kellar to Wm. Henry Smith, February 17, 1877, in Smith Collection.
230. Letterpress copy, Wm. Henry Smith to Kellar, February 20, 1877, in Smith Papers.
231. See Woodward, *Reunion and Reaction*, 199.
232. Boynton to Wm. Henry Smith, February 18, 22, 1877, in Smith Collection.

knowledge that Scott's treaty with Huntington and the Southern Pacific would expire on March 4, Dodge was concerned not that Hayes would be defeated but that the count would drag on so long that the subsidy bill could not be enacted in the current session of Congress; and the repeated votes in favor of a recess demonstrated that his lobbyists were having little success in speeding things up. Since he could not really expect to avoid another showdown with Huntington under the circumstances, Dodge sought to strengthen his own forces. Toward this end he organized a campaign to get George W. McCrary, one of the authors of the electoral commission bill and a friend of the Texas and Pacific, into the cabinet.[233]

Evidently, few Republicans besides Matthews, Foster, and William Dennison fully recognized the immediate importance of an agreement concerning the future government of Louisiana and South Carolina. However, on February 22, a seemingly minor indiscretion attested the accuracy of their perception. While editor James M. Comly was confined to his bed by illness, a reporter for the *Ohio State Journal* foolishly printed a long article defending the Republican officials in Louisiana and urging Grant to use the military to protect Packard. The next day copies of the story were placed on the desk of every Democrat in the House.[234] Comly being an intimate associate of Hayes, the offending editorial could reasonably be construed as representing the Ohio governor's true feelings. Here was the ideal pretext for demanding more concrete assurance from the Republicans. To emphasize the point a recess was proposed in midafternoon and carried, 131 to 108. Only eighteen Democrats, fifteen of them from the North, voted against it.[235]

233. Stanley P. Hirshson, *Grenville M. Dodge: Soldier, Politician, Railroad Pioneer* (Bloomington: Indiana University Press, 1967), 203; G. M. Dodge to Hayes, February 15, 1877, in Hayes Papers.
234. Barnard, *Rutherford B. Hayes and His America*, 383; telegram, Boynton to Comly, February 23, 1877, telegram, Matthews, Foster, and Dennison to Comly, February 23, 1877, and draft of letter or telegram, A. W. Francisco to [Matthews, February 1877], all in Hayes Papers. Most of the draft is in Hayes's handwriting.
235. *Congressional Record*, 44th Cong., 2nd Sess., Vol. V, Pt. 3, p. 1884.

On Saturday, the twenty-fourth, the Democratic leaders once more engineered a series of rapid shifts in direction, resembling the maneuvers of a sailboat tacking against the wind. It began with the reading of the commission decision awarding Oregon to Hayes. After the Senate had departed, the inevitable proposal for a recess of the House was defeated, 158 to 112, fifty-one Democrats—thirty-one of them from the North—voting with the Republicans to thwart it. When a motion was made to reconsider, Randall ruled it out of order on the ground that it was dilatory. A short while later Hewitt delivered an emotional speech castigating the electoral commission for its partisanship but pointing out, also, that the Democrats had freely supported the bill that created it. He called for an end to the filibuster, thus revealing to the Republicans that Tilden's warmest adherents were prepared to acquiesce in the seating of Hayes.[236] Hewitt's performance was designed primarily to impress upon the intransigents of his own party the fact that the count would eventually be completed. Again the joint session resumed. Oregon was counted, and immediately the Democrats questioned the eligibility of an elector from Pennsylvania. This time, with Hewitt scurrying about the floor of the House to change the requisite number of votes, the motion for a recess passed, 133 to 122. The reversal was clearly intended for the thoughtful consideration of the Republicans.[237]

At last, on Monday the twenty-sixth, meaningful negotiations took place. They began in the morning when Burke had "a long and satisfactory interview with the President." Burke could scarcely conceal the elation he felt as he telegraphed Nicholls immediately afterwards with the news:

[Grant] says unequivocally that he is satisfied that the Nicholls government is the government which should stand in Louisiana, and that he believes it will stand, because it is sustained by the most influential elements of the State, and that the Packard govern-

236. *Ibid.*, Pt. 3, pp. 1905–1907, 1914–15.
237. *Ibid.*, Pt. 3, p. 1919; Walker Blaine to Mrs. James G. Blaine, February 24, 1877, in James G. Blaine Papers, Manuscript Division, Library of Congress.

ment cannot exist without the support of troops; that the sentiment of the country is clearly opposed to the further use of troops in upholding a State government ... that in his opinion there would be no interference with the Nicholls government unless, carried away by possession of power, violent excesses were committed. The President said he had avoided action because he did not wish to inaugurate a policy that might embarrass his successor. You may use this, as the President said he desired his views to be known.[238]

Shortly thereafter Matthews and Dennison informed Burke that Senator Sherman wanted to see him. A meeting was hastily arranged in a locked committee room at the Capitol. Sherman asked what was necessary to stop the filibuster. Burke shrugged off the implication that he could control the actions of the House, but suggested that an order from the president removing the troops from the statehouse in New Orleans might help. Preferring not to make a commitment of that kind, Sherman declared that the president would surely refuse to cooperate. Burke then dramatically withdrew from his pocket a copy of the dispatch he had sent to Nicholls with Grant's consent. That gesture entirely broke down Sherman's resistance. He submissively joined Matthews and Dennison in assuring Burke that Hayes would pursue the identical plan initiated by Grant.

That night, in Matthews' room at Wormley's Hotel, a ratification meeting of sorts quietly assembled. Five Ohioans— Matthews, Dennison, Foster, Sherman, and Garfield—acted in behalf of Hayes; Burke and Congressmen E. John Ellis and William M. Levy represented the Democrats of Louisiana. Henry Watterson was there, too. He had been invited by Matthews (his uncle) to serve as referee and was subsequently requested by M. C. Butler to be the spokesman for South Carolina.[239] Each of the Republicans except Garfield repeated his earlier promises concerning Hayes's southern policy. Garfield, who had not been a party to the earlier discussions, was uncomfortable, "stating that nobody had any authority to speak

238. Quoted in Barnard, *Rutherford B. Hayes and His America*, 386.
239. Joseph Frazier Wall, *Henry Watterson: Reconstructed Rebel* (New York: Oxford University Press, 1956), 165.

for Gov Hayes, beyond his party platform & letter of acceptance, & it would be neither honorable nor wise to do so, if any one had such authority." For himself he "had no doubt that the new administration would deal justly and generously by the south, and the whole nation would honor those southern men who are resisting anarchy, and thus are preventing civil war; but neither they nor we could afford to do anything that would be or appear to be a political bargain." Garfield thought "Matthews did not like my remarks"; and so he left.[240] The conference, however, continued. The Louisianans pledged that the Nicholls government would protect the equal civil and political rights of all men and would promote equal educational opportunities for both white and black children. The laws of the state would be enforced impartially and there would be no persecution for past political activity. Agreement was also reached on the ticklish matter of Louisiana's Senate seats. The term of J. R. West was about to expire. To succeed him the Republican legislature had already elected William Pitt Kellogg. The other seat had been vacant since the disputed election of 1872, the Senate having repeatedly denied P. B. S. Pinchback, the Republican claimant, the right to assume the office. The Democratic legislature had recently chosen James B. Eustis to fill the remaining two years of this "short term." Aware that the Republican control of the next Senate would be precarious at best, Matthews was determined at least to save Kellogg. Burke, Ellis, and Levy finally vowed that the Nicholls legislature would postpone the election of a rival for Kellogg's seat until after March 10. By that time Kellogg and perhaps Eustis would probably have been sworn in by the Senate. Such were the "Wormley agreements."

During the next two days a caucus of Democratic legislators in New Orleans consented to the delay in choosing a "long term" senator; Matthews and Foster gave Senator John B. Gordon of Georgia and Representative John Young Brown of Kentucky a written statement of their expectations regarding Hayes's

240. Garfield Diary, February 26, 1877, in Garfield Papers.

treatment of the South; Hayes indicated that Matthews and Foster correctly represented his views; and Grant agreed to issue orders for the withdrawal of the soldiers as soon as Hayes was officially declared elected.[241] Meanwhile the Democratic leaders in the House allowed the count to progress just far enough to insure its ultimate conclusion. On Monday, referral of the South Carolina certificates to the electoral commission halted the proceedings. On Tuesday, a recess by the narrow margin of 121 to 120 did the job. After the counting of South Carolina on Wednesday, Hewitt created an uproar in the joint session by introducing a package he said contained a second set of electoral votes from Vermont. The houses were obliged to part and the count was thereby extended for an additional day. Hewitt ventured upon this daring maneuver at the request of the southern negotiators: "In this transaction I had the full approval and co-operation of Speaker Randall, who had agreed with me that in the last event filibustering should be suppressed and the count completed even though no understanding was reached in regard to the Louisiana case." [242]

Finally, on Thursday, March 1, Levy made a short speech in which he announced that his state and South Carolina had received the assurances they had sought. Speaker Randall then forced the completion of the count by the early hours of Friday morning. Some three score Democratic "die-hards" fought him every inch of the way, but their struggle was hopeless.[243] On every motion for a recess, beginning the day of the Florida decision, the strongest backing for the filibuster had come from the West and South, whereas the core of Democratic opposition had been found in the conservative Northeast, among Tilden's original partisans. When the equally conservative Democrats

241. Lonn, *Reconstruction in Louisiana after 1868*, 507–16; Woodward, *Reunion and Reaction*, 195–98; E. Jno. Ellis to Bayard, February 27, 1877, in Bayard Papers; typescript copies of telegrams, E. A. Burke, E. John Ellis, and William M. Levy to F. T. Nicholls, February 27, 28, 1877, in William E. Chandler Papers.
242. Hewitt, "Secret History of the Disputed Election, 1876–77," in Nevins (ed.), *Selected Writings of Abram S. Hewitt*, 175–77.
243. Woodward, *Reunion and Reaction*, 201.

cooperating with Burke, Levy, and Ellis changed their votes, the contest was over. Burke had been bluffing all along, but the Republicans did not care to call his hand.

Hayes was privately sworn in as president on Saturday, March 3, after a quiet dinner with the Grants in the White House. Public inaugural ceremonies were staged without incident two days later.

9

In the final analysis, the electoral dispute ended as it did because Hayes worked harder to hold the jealous factions of his party together in the crisis than did his Democratic adversary and because Tilden, after being outgeneraled, had the courage and grace to accept defeat. The leaders of both parties had to contend with a number of embarrassingly visible fault lines which weakened the structure of their organizations. The Republicans were especially vulnerable. They faced the particularly formidable challenge of trying to combine in one party spokesmen of northern business interests and representatives of landless and illiterate black laborers. The fact that they had half a dozen "strong" leaders and the Democrats only one also proved a handicap—as Hayes, who was not one of the "strong" leaders, well understood. Compared to the divisions which threatened to wreck the Republican cause, the task of keeping the Democratic party united should have been easy. Yet it was a task for which the cold and secretive Tilden was peculiarly unfitted.

As it happened, Tilden and Hayes both lost command of their troops at almost precisely the same moment. The result was the electoral commission—the real "compromise of 1877." The Republican leadership feared this contrivance most, but the Democrats promptly helped them gain an eight-to-seven majority on it. The commission then determined the outcome of the election. Three more weeks of almost unbearable tension followed in what can only now be seen to have been a spectacular bluff game. The Democrats acquiesced in the seating of Hayes, for there was nothing else they could do; in return, Hayes promised to remove the troops supporting Packard and Chamberlain, a policy to which he was all but publicly committed beforehand. With that the crisis ended. It would have ended on exactly the same terms if no understanding had been reached.[244]

244. Woodward, in his study of the electoral dispute, concentrated on the maneuvers of Kellar, Boynton, and William Henry Smith because he was unaware that the factionalism within the Republican party was so serious or that Tilden conceded defeat so readily. The intersectional contacts Kellar established in Washington provided a valuable and accurate insight into the changing aspirations of the southern establishment—just what Woodward was looking for. He was frankly unconcerned with those Democrats and Republicans who did not participate in the "compromise" negotiations. As a result, he obtained only a partial view of the complex pattern of events leading to the inauguration of Hayes. When that pattern is seen in its entirety, however, it is clear that the diffusion of power in both major parties, and not the machinations of a handful of journalists, was instrumental in preserving the peace in 1877.

Chapter VIII □ The Persistence of Inertia

THE MOST remarkable feature of the presidential election of 1876 is how little it altered the course of American political history. The democratic system the people were so proud of could easily have broken down in the electoral dispute, but it did not; and the nation's political wars continued much as before.

After their defeat at the hands of the Louisiana returning board and the electoral commission, the Democrats composed themselves quickly and began preparing for the next election. The New York *World* stressed that Hayes would exercise the powers of his office only through Democratic sufferance, and the *Sun* appeared on March 3 with heavy black lines of mourning between its columns.[1] That same day the House of Representatives struck the first blow in the campaign of 1880 by passing a resolution reviewing the gross frauds perpetrated by the Republicans and declaring that Tilden and Hendricks had been duly elected.[2] Democrats debated among themselves whether they should condescend to participate in events that recognized Hayes as president. Most of them, including Justices Clifford and Field, boycotted the inauguration.[3] Manton Marble

1. New York *World*, March 3, 1877; New York *Sun*, March 3, 1877.
2. *Congressional Record*, 44th Cong., 2nd Sess., Vol. V, Pt. 3, pp. 2225–27.
3. Harry Barnard, *Rutherford B. Hayes and His America* (Indianapolis: Bobbs-Merrill Company, Inc., 1954), 401.

refused to hand over the five hundred cigars he had bet on the outcome of the election: "That Mr Hayes is to-day acting as President nobody denies: that he came to the place & office by election I could not consent to admit, not even by so trivial an act as knocking the ash off a cigar." [4]

Charles Francis Adams, deeply affected by the long decline in political morals, of which he considered the seating of Hayes to be merely the culmination, wrote Tilden, "On this day when you *ought* to have been the President of these United States I seize the opportunity to bear my testimony to the calm and dignified manner in which you have passed through this great trial." [5] Tilden was indeed calm. He accepted the counting in of Hayes on March 2 without "any change in his manner except perhaps that he was less absorbed than usual and more interested in current affairs." [6] Tilden's icy reaction may well have been a reflection of his physical weakness. He had never fully recovered from his stroke in 1875. His condition was sometimes precarious and required constant attention. Bigelow privately admitted that it was enough of a handicap during the dispute "to qualify very much the dignity of his position as the unquestionable choice of the nation." [7] A few weeks later Tilden and Bigelow sailed for Europe.

Hewitt meanwhile was enduring much criticism for the loss of the presidency. Tilden, Marble, Bigelow, and Watterson all held him responsible, along with Thurman and Bayard, for the electoral commission, which they said had been the salvation of the Republican party.[8] Similarly, the irreconcilables in Congress condemned Hewitt for selling out the Democratic party during the struggle over the filibuster. Tired, disappointed after the investment of so much labor and money, and resentful

4. Draft, M. M[arble] to Chas. A. Whittier, November 10, 1877, in Manton Malone Marble Papers, Manuscript Division, Library of Congress.
5. Charles Francis Adams to Tilden, March 5, 1877, in Samuel J. Tilden Papers, New York Public Library.
6. John Bigelow Diary, March 17, 1877, in John Bigelow Papers, New York Public Library.
7. *Ibid.*, April 1, 1877.
8. *Ibid.*, March 17, 1877.

of the carping of his own friends, Hewitt dashed off an angry letter to the national committee, defending his actions throughout the crisis and announcing his resignation as chairman.[9] Otherwise, the Democratic party was unchanged.

On the Republican side, also, the picture retained all its familiar elements. Hayes got his administration off to a stormy beginning just by announcing his cabinet selections. He chose David M. Key as postmaster general (the richest patronage-dispensing position), Carl Schurz as secretary of the interior, and William M. Evarts as secretary of state—a southern Democrat, a Liberal Republican, and the attorney for the defense in the impeachment trial of Andrew Johnson. The party's Old Guard—Blaine, Conkling, Cameron, and the Chandlers—greeted this news with a shriek of outrage; yet the president's choices were genuinely popular and the Old Guard had to accept them.[10] Relations between Hayes and his rivals for the nomination remained tempestuous throughout the rest of his term. Had such prima donnas as Conkling and Blaine been capable of working with each other, they might have seriously jeopardized the president's entire program. Hayes, however, had little to worry about on that score.

Following what southerners considered an unconscionable delay, the troops were finally withdrawn from the statehouses in Columbia and New Orleans. Grant told Burke on March 2 that he had issued orders for their removal. Evidently, in the chaos accompanying the last-minute completion of the count, those instructions were misplaced or misunderstood.[11] When Hayes entered the presidency, he hesitated to act, as was his custom,

9. Hewitt to the National Democratic Committee, March 3, 1877, in John Bigelow (ed.), *Letters and Literary Memorials of Samuel J. Tilden* (2 vols.; New York: Harper and Brothers, 1908), II, 549–53.
10. Entry for March 14, 1877, in T. Harry Williams (ed.), *Hayes: The Diary of a President, 1875–1881, Covering the Disputed Election, the End of Reconstruction, and the Beginning of Civil Service* (New York: David McKay Company, Inc., 1964), 80–81.
11. C. Vann Woodward, *Reunion and Reaction: The Compromise of 1877 and the End of Reconstruction* (Boston: Little, Brown and Company, 1951), 202.

until he had discovered the most judicious way to proceed. At last, he called Chamberlain and Hampton to the White House, obtained the Democratic governor's personal adherence to the principles expressed in the now famous letter of acceptance, and told the Republican governor that he could no longer have the protection of the army. Chamberlain went home, denounced the president's actions, and surrendered his office. To dispose of the Louisiana wrangle, Hayes appointed a special commission that traveled to New Orleans and by a variety of means secured the abandonment of the Republican legislature by most of its own members. The Packard regime collapsed and the troops returned to their regular barracks outside the city.[12]

With the exception of Key's appointment to the cabinet and the confirmation of Hampton and Nicholls as governors of their states, the several negotiations which took place during the electoral dispute bore no fruit. The southern Democrats failed to support Garfield for speaker. The Republicans did not gain control of the House. Hayes did not come to the rescue of the Texas and Pacific Railway. On this last point the strictures of Carl Schurz proved more congenial to the new president than the promptings of Dodge, Boynton, and William Henry Smith. In his inaugural address Hayes would not commit himself beyond the general comment that the "material development" of the South deserved "the considerate care of the National Government, within the just limits prescribed by the Constitution and wise public economy." Thereafter, Scott's project received no encouragement whatever from the White House.[13] Dodge complained that even some of his erstwhile southern supporters

12. Francis Butler Simkins and Robert Hilliard Woody, *South Carolina During Reconstruction* (Chapel Hill: University of North Carolina Press, 1932), 539–41; Ella Lonn, *Reconstruction in Louisiana after 1868* (New York: G. P. Putnam's Sons, 1918), 519–25; Clarence C. Clendenen, "President Hayes' 'Withdrawal' of the Troops—An Enduring Myth," *South Carolina Historical Magazine,* LXX (October, 1969), 242, 246–50.

13. Hayes to Schurz, January 29, 1877, in Carl Schurz Papers, Manuscript Division, Library of Congress; Schurz to Hayes, February 2, 1877, in Rutherford B. Hayes Papers, Rutherford B. Hayes Library, Fremont, Ohio; Hayes to Shurz [*sic*], February 4, 1877, in Schurz Papers; Barnard, *Rutherford B. Hayes and His America,* 409–10.

seemed more interested in the affairs of Louisiana and South Carolina than in the proposed railroad.[14] Perhaps the explanation was that Huntington had resumed his own construction without waiting for the subsidy, bridging the Colorado River in Arizona. In the end Scott had to give up. In 1880 he sold his interest in the Texas and Pacific to Jay Gould. When the Southern Pacific linked up with Gould's line a year later, the juncture occurred a hundred miles east of El Paso. Huntington went right on laying track, passing Galveston and reaching New Orleans itself in 1883. The Texas and Pacific was thereby relegated to the status of a feeder line.[15]

Meanwhile, the dream of building a conservative, business-oriented southern Republican party was shattered as soon as the southern Democrats found there was no longer a need to sustain it. Shortly after the removal of the troops, James M. Comly visited Louisiana in behalf of his friend in the White House. The report he sent back was despairing: "The 'old Whig' sentiment I spoke of petered out before we reached New Orleans. There is nothing to hang an old whig party on. The truth is there does not seem to be anything except the Custom House to hang *anything* on." [16]

In retrospect none of these developments is really surprising, for the conversations between the "friends" of Hayes and "representatives" of the South were largely irrelevant to the settlement of the dispute. The two proposals Hayes carried out— the selection of Key as postmaster general and the ultimate abandonment of Packard and Chamberlain—were wholly in accord with the program he began formulating immediately after his nomination. These steps were perfectly calculated to further Hayes's goal of restructuring the Republican party of

14. Stanley P. Hirshson, *Grenville M. Dodge: Soldier, Politician, Railroad Pioneer* (Bloomington: Indiana University Press, 1967), 204.
15. C. Vann Woodward, *Reunion and Reaction: The Compromise of 1877 and the End of Reconstruction* (Boston: Little, Brown and Company, 1951), 235–37; Oscar Osburn Winther, *The Transportation Frontier: Trans-Mississippi West, 1865–1890* (New York: Holt, Rinehart and Winston, 1964), 101–102.
16. Comly to Hayes, May 11, 1877, in Hayes Papers.

the South. But there were limits to how far a respectable, reform-minded gentleman could go. Scott's raid on the Treasury was too gigantic, too obvious. As a result, with the two exceptions noted, Hayes refused to involve himself in the negotiations across party lines both during and after the electoral crisis.

Even if Hayes had formally agreed to all the terms Woodward associates with the Compromise of 1877, he could not have carried them into effect. The Ohioan's control over the rival factions in his own party was too tenuous. In fact, the quite modest alterations in policy toward the South that he did endorse were nearly enough to produce an open revolt. After all, it was scarcely a year since James G. Blaine had thrilled Republicans in the House with his denunciation of Jefferson Davis as the author of the hideous crimes of Andersonville, and not yet six months since Robert G. Ingersoll had mesmerized Republican audiences with his histrionic waving of the "bloody shirt." It was too soon for any radical departures from the past.

Even the most famous change Hayes assented to—the withdrawal of the troops which had previously protected southern Republicans at the polls and in the statehouses—was, strictly speaking, not a change at all. That policy can be traced directly back to Grant's refusal to intervene in the disgraceful Mississippi campaign of 1875. Grant's action, like Hayes's in 1877, reflected realistically the state of northern public opinion, which no longer supported the deployment of the military as a mechanism for enforcing Radical Reconstruction. The Radical program had obviously failed, and the southern elections of the 1870s underscored the reasons why. Reconstruction was basically a social and economic problem. The Republicans, unsure how to handle the South's racism and too conservative to deal effectively with the section's poverty, proposed instead a political solution. Manhood suffrage became almost a panacea for them. They soon learned, however, how easily an impoverished and despised minority could be cheated out of political rights. By 1877 there was no choice but to admit that the Fifteenth Amendment had not accomplished its real purpose. That is what Grant and Hayes did. Working out a new policy to replace the old was another matter. Republican politicians still recognized the urgency of preventing the formation of a "solid South"; but, as in 1865, they could not agree on what approach to pursue. The debate on southern policy reflected and consequently reinforced existing factional divisions, and those divisions in turn prevented the party from following a consistent course for the rest of the century.[17] It was the same as if the party had decided to do nothing.

This tremendous inertia was visible everywhere in nineteenth-century politics. Not only was factionalism practically the central characteristic of both parties, but the precise balance existing between the various factions remained remarkably stable; and no wonder: each faction had its own little constituency on which it could always depend. The diffuseness of power in the Republican and Democratic parties was merely a reflection of the remarkable diversity of the American electorate. If there was one thing nineteenth-century parties did well, it was to represent their constituents. In the process rational programs of government action were trampled underfoot. Professional politicians found that certain issues of recent interest to the voters—like the currency or the use of the Bible in the public schools—were dangerous to discuss, for they divided the parties internally. Besides, except for the brief interlude of Reconstruction, the federal government, especially, had never been an instrument for trying to solve social or economic problems. As a result, the politicians felt safer debating such ancient and predictable issues as the tariff, the spoils system, and the merits of local home rule. The resulting irrelevance of much of the political process was actually one of its principal sources of strength. Because the stakes involved were more symbolic than substantial, much like the outcome of the Army-Navy football game a century later, politicking served as a way

17. Stanley P. Hirshson, *Farewell to the Bloody Shirt: Northern Republicans and the Southern Negro, 1877–1893* (Bloomington: Indiana University Press, 1962).

of transcending the dull routine of everyday life, a means of indentifying with the distinctive democratic greatness of the United States while socializing with like-minded men. Eventually, of course, the tremendous social pressures created by rapid industrialization altered somewhat the composition of each party's following and produced a widespread demand for using the federal government in altogether novel ways to soften the features of urban-industrial life. But it is instructive to note that in the Progressive Era, when politics became more issue-oriented, voter participation declined. Perhaps politics also became less satisfying.

In the meantime, the politicians had to adjust to the factionalism which was an everyday part of their lives. The Republicans won in 1876 with a ticket uniting a moderate reformer from Ohio with a political cipher from New York. Four years later they duplicated the same formula, pairing James A. Garfield with Chester A. Arthur. Only when they switched in 1884 did they lose. Then Blaine's nomination for the presidency became the occasion for the "Mugwump" revolt, as a small but articulate group of Liberals followed Carl Schurz across party lines. Evidently, the nomination of a well-known candidate alienated more voters than it attracted. The experience demonstrated anew the soundness of the proven practices of the past. As for the Democrats, they sought to defeat the "bloody shirt" once and for all in 1880 by forming their ranks behind General Winfield Scott Hancock, the hero of Gettysburg. They found they could do so without significantly altering their customary geographical alignment. Hancock, nominally a resident of Pennsylvania, was stationed at Governor's Island in New York Harbor. His running mate was William H. English, a relic of antebellum days who qualified for the vice-presidency by virtue of living in Indiana. When that combination failed, the Democrats returned with astonishing literalism to the formula of 1876. For the aging Tilden they substituted another sound-money, reform governor of New York, Grover Cleveland, and then they chose as his running mate Thomas A. Hendricks himself. Cleveland and Hendricks were triumphant in 1884, carrying the solid South and the same quartet of northern states Tilden had won eight years before—Indiana, New York, New Jersey, and Connecticut. The tried and true seemed to work. In 1888 neither party modified its prescription for victory beyond seeking to capture its opponent's most vital western state. The Republicans coupled Benjamin Harrison of Indiana with Levi P. Morton of New York, while the Democrats joined Cleveland and Allen G. Thurman of Ohio.

The conduct of campaigns also remained primitive. The leaders of both parties were unhappily aware that their organizations seldom achieved the results they had hoped for; yet they could do little more than suggest, as Michael C. Kerr of Indiana had in 1872, "organization, more complete, thorough & compact than we now have." [18] Undoubtedly, no more complete, thorough, and compact plan was submitted than that of George T. Barnes, the Democratic national committeeman from Georgia in 1880:

That the National Committee should be composed of one member from each State, that such member should be the chairman, or at least connected with the State Executive Committee, that the S[t]ate Executive Committee should be composed of one member from each Congressional District, and that such member should be the chairman, or at least connected with the Congressional District Executive Committee, that the Congressional District Executive Committee should be composed of one member from each County, (or other sub-division in large cities) composing the District, that such member should be the chairman or at least connected with the County Executive Committee—and that the County Executive Committee should in like manner be composed of at least one representative for each sub-division of the County. It occurred to me that a net work connection of this kind would in itself inspire an active spirit in the organization of the party, and would enable the National Committee to obtain direct and reliable information for all its

18. M. C. Kerr to Trumbull, September 1, 1872, in Lyman Trumbull Family Papers, Illinois State Historical Library.

purposes from each and every locality in the Country, and that it also might prove very available for raising necessary funds for the proper conduct of the canvass.[19]

The challenge, however, did not lie in drawing up such "net works." The organizations of both parties already resembled Barnes's outline. The trick was to make an established structure work more efficiently. The gradual creation of a sophisticated institutional apparatus, through the assignment of individual responsibilities to experienced and talented men, would have held more promise than the imposition of a precisely engineered and neatly symmetrical organization chart on men unfamiliar with such things. One of the appeals of working in a party organization was the sense of local importance and national belonging such service conveyed. Becoming a small cog in a vast political machine would scarcely enhance anyone's self-image. The sense of easy equality among friends, to which the party faithful were accustomed, would be diminished. Not until the political parties had lost their role as part of the social life of village America would the demand for efficiency be capable of prevailing over such considerations, and even then the triumph would be partial at best.

Henry Adams once told Samuel J. Tilden, "My own conclusion is that history is simply social development along the lines of weakest resistance, and that in most cases the line of weakest resistance is found as unconsciously by society as by water." [20] Adams must have had the politics of his own time in mind.

---

19. George T. Barnes to Tilden, January 28, 1880, in Tilden Papers.
20. Quoted by Ernest Samuels in his introduction to Henry Adams, *History of the United States of America during the Administrations of Jefferson and Madison* (abr. ed.; Chicago: University of Chicago Press, 1967), xiii.

Essay on Sources

IN THE COURSE of researching this book I have naturally found certain sources more helpful than others. Although I have not departed very much from the traditional types of material generally used in writing political history, I have tried to answer a different set of questions from those asked by previous scholars. As a result, some of my sources proved either more or less helpful than I had been led in advance to expect. I have accordingly focused this essay on the general problem of studying political organization in the campaign of 1876. I have dealt with the most important or characteristic materials, but this listing is by no means complete. Readers seeking more detailed information on the sources for specific events are referred to the footnotes which accompany the text.

Manuscript sources. There are, of course, no party archives to which a scholar can retire when seeking material on Republican or Democratic campaign structures and the policies and decisions of individual leaders. Fortunately, the absence of the telephone and the expense and inconvenience of rail travel compelled party leaders to communicate principally in writing, sometimes even though they lived in the same city. The tradition which dictated that a politician not actively seek the presidency forced the candidates for that office to remain at home or at their regular employment, while their supporters kept them abreast of developments by mail or telegraph. Most political figures of importance preserved their correspondence, and by luck or design a number of these priceless materials have survived, especially on the Republican side.

The obvious place to begin any study of the 1876 election and the electoral dispute is the Rutherford B. Hayes Papers, at the Rutherford B. Hayes Library, Fremont, Ohio, an institution as pleasant to work in as it is remote. Hayes was exceedingly circumspect in the letters he wrote; but contrary to the impression of C. Vann Woodward (*Reunion and Reaction*, 247), he seems to have kept virtually all his incoming correspondence, even those letters forwarded to him by friends with instructions that they be returned or destroyed. Moreover, as a neutral figure in the Republican organization, Hayes found himself in contact with a broad spectrum of the party's jealous leaders. The result is a rare opportunity to study the inner workings of a presidential campaign. The Hayes Library also has a sizable collection of photostats, letterpress copies, and original letters written by Hayes. Scholars may read the typed transcripts which have been prepared from them but must use care. Since Hayes's scratchy handwriting is extremely difficult to decipher, the transcripts contain numerous inaccuracies and should be checked against the originals that library personnel guard so carefully.

It is fortunate for the historian that Hayes was triumphant at Cincinnati in that no comparable body of material survives for any of his rivals for the nomination. The Manuscript Division of the Library of Congress possesses small collections of the papers of James G. Blaine, Benjamin H. Bristow, and Roscoe Conkling; and the Indiana State Library has a few papers of Oliver P. Morton, but none are of much importance. The Blaine Papers are the best of the lot, even though Blaine destroyed most of his correspondence before his death. The Bristow movement was largely the creation of the Liberal Republicans. On this subject the Carl Schurz Papers, in the Library of Congress, and the Samuel Bowles Papers, in the Yale University Library, are indispensable; and the Jacob D. Cox Papers in the Oberlin College Archives are also useful.

Several collections of manuscripts of other Republican leaders are valuable in studying all aspects of the campaign, as well as the electoral dispute. The Library of Congress has the extensive papers of William E. Chandler, James A. Garfield, and John Sherman (the Sherman Papers were not used in this study), and a smaller collection for Zachariah Chandler. The papers of Edwin D. Morgan, at the New York State Library, reveal much about the campaign in the Empire State.

The journalists of the day often knew a great deal more than they published about the maneuvers of leading politicians. Two collections of the papers of William Henry Smith stand out in importance: one at the Indiana Historical Society Library, the other at the Ohio Historical Society Library. The former collection is smaller, but it contains the letters of H. V. Boynton and Andrew J. Kellar that formed the most basic source for Woodward's *Reunion and Reaction*. The Ohio Historical Society Library also has the papers of James M. Comly, useful in illuminating Hayes's career from the time of his gubernatorial campaign in 1875 to his inauguration as president. The William Warland Clapp Papers, at the Library of Congress, contain unusually incisive letters from E. B. Wight and Ben: Perley Poore, Washington correspondents for the Boston *Journal*.

Since there is no single source on the Democratic side comparable to the Hayes Papers, the student of political organization must exercise more patience and ingenuity when researching the opposition party. The situation is even more frustrating because the papers of Samuel J. Tilden might have been the ideal source for the study of party management in the nineteenth century. Unfortunately, Tilden provided in his will for the publication of four volumes of his public papers, and then specified that his executors "burn and destroy any of my letters, papers, or other documents, whether printed or in manuscript, which in their judgment will answer no useful purpose to preserve" (Bigelow [ed.], *Letters and Literary Memorials of Samuel J. Tilden*, I, iii). Tilden's executors carried out his orders with a vengeance, rummaging through his papers on four separate occasions and reducing eighteen full trunks to thirteen small manuscript boxes. The basis for eliminating material will always be a mystery. Presumably, any derogatory items were destroyed, although several inferentially damning pieces were overlooked. Much correspondence of great value in regard to Tilden's chairmanship of the New York State Democratic party and his course during the electoral dispute was obviously removed; a large part of what remains is worthless. These remnants are in the New York Public Library. A much smaller collection of Tilden Papers in the Columbia University Library contains an array of unusual items from the 1876 campaign—convention passes, campaign documents, invitations to mass meetings, circular letters, canvass books, organizational instructions, registration lists, and Democratic tickets.

For the study of Tilden's opponents for the nomination, only one substantial collection exists, the excellent Thomas F. Bayard Papers in the Library of Congress. Bayard's biographer, Charles C. Tansill, was instrumental in obtaining these materials for scholarly use. In the course of arranging them, he separated out most of the valuable letters, which are now preserved in boxes of unbound correspondence. The more numerous bound volumes are generally of little value. The Library of Congress also has a small collection of the papers of William Allen, and the Ohio Historical Society Library owns a slightly larger set of papers of Allen's nephew and rival, Allen G. Thurman. There is no known collection of Thomas A. Hendricks papers.

We probably have more materials preserved by Tilden's many lieutenants than by all the candidates combined. The Library of Congress houses the papers of Manton Malone Marble, Montgomery Blair, and David Ames Wells; the valuable John Bigelow Diary is at the New York Public Library; the John M. Olin Research Library at Cornell University has the sizable Francis Kernan Correspondence; the University of Pennsylvania Library has the recently discovered Samuel J. Randall Papers; and the Cooper Union Library owns a few letters of Abram S. Hewitt. Most of Hewitt's papers were lost in a fire which swept the offices of Cooper and Hewitt many years ago.

In the absence of more voluminous materials preserved by the candidates themselves, it is necessary to search diligently for items of importance among the papers of Democrats who, while no longer active as officeholders, still retained an interest in political affairs. The Samuel Latham Mitchell Barlow Papers, at the Henry E. Huntington Library, San Marino, California, proved especially valuable in this respect, for Barlow was a friend of both Tilden and Bayard, and was closely tied to the Texas and Pacific lobby as well. This collection is very large. Sadly, the numerous letterpress books are badly oxidized. The Jeremiah S. Black Papers at the Library of Congress contain some useful letters to and from the judge's son, Chauncey F. Black. The following collections also contain at least a few helpful items: the Horatio Seymour Papers, New York State Library; George W. Julian Papers, Indiana State Library; William H. English Collection, Indiana Historical Society Library; Lyman Trumbull Family Papers, Illinois State Historical Library; and James Rood Doolittle Papers, State Historical Society of Wisconsin.

Nothing can ever replace the Tilden and Hewitt papers that were lost, but there are several collections which provide insight into the formidable challenge of trying to improve campaign organization. Foremost is the huge collection of Cyrus Hall McCormick Papers at the State Historical Society of Wisconsin. McCormick was nominally the chairman of the Democratic party in Illinois; in fact, he spent most of the summer and fall of 1876 vacationing at Richfield Springs, New York. Daniel Cameron, his lieutenant, wrote frequent reports reviewing the Democratic party's plans for bringing out a full party vote in November. Hundreds of other letters and telegrams from state and county leaders have also been preserved. As a bonus, the McCormick Papers were found to contain communiqués from Henry H. Finley that unraveled the mystery of David Davis' election to the Senate. This collection is even larger and more informative for the campaign of 1872. The Wendell A. Anderson Papers, also at the State Historical Society of Wisconsin, is a smaller collection of similar materials. The John Francis Snyder Papers, at the Illinois State Historical Library, shed light on the often thankless tasks of a county chairman. Other collections of interest for the study of Democratic efforts in the campaign and electoral dispute are: the Charles Francis Adams Diary, Adams Papers, Massachusetts Historical Society Library; David M. Key Papers, Chattanooga Public Library; L. Q. C. Lamar and Edward Mayes Papers, Mississippi Department of Archives and History; and John White Stevenson Diary, University of Kentucky Library.

Printed primary sources. It is unlikely that Rutherford B. Hayes would have kept a diary if he had known it would be published. Though it contains little political information that cannot be found elsewhere, it exposes Hayes's real character with devastating effectiveness. The original is in the Hayes Library, Fremont, Ohio. The portions most useful for this study have been meticulously edited by T. Harry Williams in *Hayes: The Diary of a President, 1875–1881, Covering the Disputed Election, the End of Reconstruction, and the Beginning of Civil Service* (New York: David McKay Company, Inc., 1964). The five-volume *Diary and Letters of Rutherford Birchard Hayes* (Columbus: Ohio State Archaeological and Historical Society, 1922–26), edited by Charles Richard Williams (no relative of T. Harry Williams but the nephew of William Henry Smith), must be used with extreme care, for Williams undertook to improve Hayes's literary style. John Bigelow (ed.), *Letters and Literary Memorials of Samuel J. Tilden* (2 vols.; New York: Harper and Brothers, 1908) and *The Writings and Speeches of Samuel J. Tilden* (2 vols.; New York: Harper and Brothers, 1885), are the volumes provided for in Tilden's will. They bring together a number of important letters and documents. Abram S. Hewitt's "Secret History of the Disputed Election, 1876–77," covering both the campaign and the electoral crisis, appears in Allan Nevins (ed.), *Selected Writings of Abram S. Hewitt* (New York: Columbia University Press, 1937). Manton Marble's version, "A Secret Chapter of Political History," was printed privately as a pamphlet in 1878; a copy is in the Marble

Papers at the Library of Congress. Milton Harlow Northrup, secretary of the Special House Committee, describes the creation of the electoral commission in "A Grave Crisis in American History: The Inner History of the Origin and Formation of the Electoral Commission of 1877," *Century Magazine*, LXII (October, 1901), 923–34.

Newspapers, normally one of the standard sources for political history, played a comparatively minor role in the research for this book. Nineteenth-century newspapers provided excellent surface descriptions of political events. On the other hand, their reporting and analysis of maneuvers behind the scenes were fragmentary and generally untrustworthy. I found I could rely on the partisan press to supply surprisingly detailed accounts of state and local nominating conventions and procedures, political platforms, and campaign rallies. I could not use their speculative and often malicious gossip about party finance, campaign management, and factional quarrels. I consulted six newspaper files at great length: the New York *World* (Democratic), New York *Sun* (independent-Democratic), and New York *Times* (Republican); and the Chicago *Times* (Democratic), Chicago *Daily Tribune* (Republican), and Chicago *Daily News* (independent). When I found such work becoming repetitive, I confined myself to seeking information on specific topics in appropriate papers. In connection with the Republican convention, for example, I turned to the Cincinnati *Daily Gazette*. To have examined the entire file of such a journal, however, would not have been a profitable investment of time.

Secondary sources. Secondary accounts were relied on principally in connection with southern politics, a specialized field of research in its own right. Most of these accounts are based in turn on local newspapers (a source generally favorable to the Democrats) and the extensive investigations of committees of Congress (generally favorable to the Republicans). It requires a sensitive and experienced scholar to distinguish fact from fabrication in connection with the southern elections of the 1870s.

For the state of Florida, I depended heavily on a trio of solidly researched and carefully balanced articles by Jerrell H. Shofner: "Fraud and Intimidation in the Florida Election of 1876," *Florida Historical Quarterly*, XLII (April, 1964), 321–30; "Florida in the Balance: The Electoral Count of 1876," *ibid.*, XLVII (October, 1968), 122–50; and "Florida Courts and the Disputed Election of 1876," *ibid.*, XLVIII (July, 1969), 24–46. William Watson Davis, *The Civil War and Reconstruction in Florida* (New York: Columbia

University, 1913), a product of William Archibald Dunning's famous seminar, is outdated in interpretation but contains some useful details about the 1876 campaign.

The most detailed account of Louisiana affairs is still that of another Dunning student, Ella Lonn, *Reconstruction in Louisiana after 1868* (New York: G. P. Putnam's Sons, 1918). Miss Lonn's undisguised contempt for all blacks clouded her judgment, and she was easily bewildered by the intricate details of Reconstruction politics. Nevertheless, on the events of 1876 and 1877, when she bases her work entirely on the pertinent volumes of congressional testimony, her study is still usable. Two articles of more recent vintage which deal more perceptively with specific aspects of the Louisiana story are Ralph J. Roske, " 'Visiting Statesmen' in Louisiana, 1876," *Mid-America*, XXXIII (April, 1951), 89–102; and especially T. B. Tunnell, Jr., "The Negro, the Republican Party, and the Election of 1876 in Louisiana," *Louisiana History*, VII (Spring, 1966), 101–16.

Reconstruction in South Carolina has been the subject of more and better books than perhaps for any other southern state. Francis Butler Simkins and Robert Hilliard Woody established the pattern with their extensively researched revisionist study, *South Carolina During Reconstruction* (Chapel Hill: University of North Carolina Press, 1932); they cover the 1876 election and its disputed result in great detail. Despite Hampton M. Jarrell's inability to comprehend the gathering momentum of the "Second Reconstruction" after World War II, his observations on the moderate course followed by Wade Hampton in the "redemption" of South Carolina are clearly stated and well supported; see *Wade Hampton and the Negro: The Road Not Taken* (Columbia: University of South Carolina Press, 1950). Joel Williamson, *After Slavery: The Negro in South Carolina During Reconstruction, 1861–1877* (Chapel Hill: University of North Carolina Press, 1965), discusses the election of 1876 only briefly, but dissents from some of the views of Jarrell and Simkins. Also pertinent are Manly Wade Wellman, *Giant in Gray: A Biography of Wade Hampton of South Carolina* (New York: Charles Scribner's Sons, 1949); and D. D. Wallace, "The Question of the Withdrawal of the Democratic Presidential Electors in South Carolina in 1876," *Journal of Southern History*, VIII (August, 1942), 374–85.

My discussion of the 1875 campaign in Mississippi is based on James Wilford Garner, *Reconstruction in Mississippi* (New York: Macmillan Company, 1901), the best and most objective product of the Dunning seminar at Columbia; and Vernon Lane Wharton, *The Negro in Mississippi, 1865–1890* (Chapel Hill: University of North Carolina Press, 1947), which also contains a detailed account. For the colorful Vance-Settle contest of 1876 in North Carolina, I relied on J. G. de Roulhac Hamilton, *Reconstruction in North Carolina* (New York: Columbia University Press, 1914), yet another of the dissertations supervised by Dunning; and Glenn Tucker, *Zeb Vance: Champion of Personal Freedom* (Indianapolis: Bobbs-Merrill Company, Inc., 1965), which was disappointingly superficial in its treatment.

The Oregon story has been told in two recent articles: Harold C. Dippre, "Corruption and the Disputed Election Vote of Oregon in the 1876 Election," *Oregon Historical Quarterly*, LXVII (September, 1966), 257–72; and Philip W. Kennedy, "Oregon and the Disputed Election of 1876," *Pacific Northwest Quarterly*, LX (July, 1969), 135–44. Kennedy's account is more balanced and sophisticated than Dippre's, going beyond a mere discussion of the corruption involved and unraveling the frenzied political maneuvering for the crucial Oregon votes.

There have been three previous book-length works on the national election. Paul Leland Haworth, *The Hayes-Tilden Disputed Presidential Election of 1876* (Cleveland: Burrows Brothers Company, 1906), is a strictly political account, based primarily on congressional documents and newspapers and written before any of the major manuscript sources were available. C. Vann Woodward, *Reunion and Reaction: The Compromise of 1877 and the End of Reconstruction* (Boston: Little, Brown and Company, 1951), concentrates on the electoral dispute and largely ignores the campaign itself. Woodward was the first scholar to recognize the significance of many of the letters in the James M. Comly and William Henry Smith Papers, but he accepted at face value the assertions made by Boynton and Kellar about the importance of their negotiations and so proposed a misleading explanation about the peaceful resolution of the crisis. His work is indispensable, of course, as an account of the negotiations. James Joseph Flynn, "The Disputed Election of 1876" (Ph.D. dissertation, Fordham University, 1953), is a surface treatment at best, marked by numerous errors of fact and interpretation.

For biographical information I relied on Harry Barnard, *Rutherford B. Hayes and His America* (Indianapolis: Bobbs-Merrill Company, Inc., 1954). At the time of writing, Kenneth E. Davison, *The Presidency of Rutherford B. Hayes* (Westport, Conn.: Greenwood

Press, 1972), had not yet appeared. Alexander Clarence Flick, *Samuel Jones Tilden: A Study in Political Sagacity* (New York: Dodd, Mead and Company, 1939), is the only scholarly biography of Tilden. Robert Kelley, "The Thought and Character of Samuel J. Tilden: The Democrat as Inheritor," *Historian*, XXVI (February, 1964), 176–205, is an imaginative summary of the limitations of the Democratic candidate's political thought.

Albie Burke, "Federal Regulation of Congressional Elections in Northern Cities, 1871–1894" (Ph.D. dissertation, University of Chicago, 1968), clears up a great deal of misunderstanding about the Federal Elections Law of 1871 by showing that it was not a Reconstruction measure and, while doing so, elucidates the remarkable activities of John I. Davenport as chief supervisor for New York City. Three other works deserve to be singled out as especially helpful on their respective subjects: Jerome L. Sternstein (ed.), "The Sickles Memorandum: Another Look at the Hayes-Tilden Election-Night Conspiracy," *Journal of Southern History*, XXXII (August, 1966), 342–57; Clarence C. Clendenen, "President Hayes' 'Withdrawal' of the Troops—An Enduring Myth," *South Carolina Historical Magazine*, LXX (October, 1969), 240–50; and David M. Abshire, *The South Rejects a Prophet: The Life of Senator D. M. Key, 1824–1900* (New York: Frederick A. Praeger, 1967).

Index